Birth to Psychic Life

Based on rich clinical experience and on theory from numerous psychoanalytical works, this book explores and analyzes the emergence and development of the psychic life.

Birth to Psychic Life explores the genesis of the psychic apparatus, reconstructs the development of subjectivity, with its ups and downs in babies as in all subjects, and studies the relationship between mental states at the dawn of psychic life and those characteristic of psychopathology. The book refers to Freudian, Kleinian and post-Kleinian works, proposing articulations between the different theoretical models. The referenced works' contributions to the understanding of early psychic disorders, as well as to the implications of infantile psychic suffering in adulthood, are essential. The authors identify the three psychic constellations, recognized by many, that accompany the psychic birth and suggest new more adequate names in view of current works on subjectivity: the auto-sensual position, the symbiotic position and the depressive position. Many other new and original proposals are developed by the authors.

Providing tools to think about the processes of psychic growth, this book will be of interest to all psychoanalysts and psychotherapists working with infants and interested in the impact of early psychic development throughout life.

Albert Ciccone is a psychologist, psychoanalyst and professor of psychopathology and clinical psychology at the Université Lumière-Lyon 2, France. He is also founder and president of the Association lyonnaise pour une psychanalyse à partir de la clinique de l'enfant (ALPACE).

Marc Lhopital is a psychoanalyst; member of the Paris Psychoanalytical Society (IPA), France; clinical psychologist and member of the European Society for Child and Adolescent Psychoanalysis (SEPEA).

THE NEW LIBRARY OF PSYCHOANALYSIS
General Editor: Alessandra Lemma

The New Library of Psychoanalysis was launched in 1987 in association with the Institute of Psychoanalysis, London. It took over from the International Psychoanalytical Library which published many of the early translations of the works of Freud and the writings of most of the leading British and Continental psychoanalysts.

The purpose of the New Library of Psychoanalysis is to facilitate a greater and more widespread appreciation of psychoanalysis and to provide a forum for increasing mutual understanding between psychoanalysts and those working in other disciplines such as the social sciences, medicine, philosophy, history, linguistics, literature and the arts. It aims to represent different trends both in British psychoanalysis and in psychoanalysis generally. The New Library of Psychoanalysis is well placed to make available to the English-speaking world psychoanalytic writings from other European countries and to increase the interchange of ideas between British and American psychoanalysts. Through the *Teaching Series*, the New Library of Psychoanalysis now also publishes books that provide comprehensive, yet accessible, overviews of selected subject areas aimed at those studying psychoanalysis and related fields such as the social sciences, philosophy, literature and the arts.

The Institute, together with the British Psychoanalytical Society, runs a low-fee psychoanalytic clinic, organizes lectures and scientific events concerned with psychoanalysis and publishes the *International Journal of Psychoanalysis*. It runs a training course in psychoanalysis which leads to membership of the International Psychoanalytical Association – the body which preserves internationally agreed standards of training, of professional entry, and of professional ethics and practice for psychoanalysis as initiated and developed by Sigmund Freud. Distinguished members of the Institute have included Michael Balint, Wilfred Bion, Ronald Fairbairn, Anna Freud, Ernest Jones, Melanie Klein, John Rickman and Donald Winnicott.

Previous general editors have included David Tuckett, who played a very active role in the establishment of the New Library. He was followed as general editor by Elizabeth Bott Spillius, who was in turn followed by Susan Budd and then by Dana Birksted-Breen.

Current members of the Advisory Board include Giovanna Di Ceglie, Liz Allison, Anne Patterson, Josh Cohen and Daniel Pick.

Previous members of the Advisory Board include Christopher Bollas, Ronald Britton, Catalina Bronstein, Donald Campbell, Rosemary Davies, Sara Flanders, Stephen Grosz, John Keene, Eglé Laufer, Alessandra Lemma, Juliet Mitchell, Michael Parsons, Rosine Jozef Perelberg, Richard Rusbridger, Mary Target and David Taylor.

A full list of all the titles in the New Library of Psychoanalysis main series is available at https://www.routledge.com/The-New-Library-of-Psychoanalysis/book-series/SE0239

For titles in the New Library of Psychoanalysis 'Teaching' and 'Beyond the Couch' subseries, please visit the Routledge website.

Birth to Psychic Life

Albert Ciccone and Marc Lhopital
Translated by Andrew Weller

LONDON AND NEW YORK

Image credit: © Getty Images

First published 2022
by Routledge
2 Park Square, Milton Park, Abingdon, Oxon OX14 4RN

and by Routledge
605 Third Avenue, New York, NY 10158

Routledge is an imprint of the Taylor & Francis Group, an informa business

© 2022 Albert Ciccone and Marc Lhopital, translated by Andrew Weller

Originally published in France as:

Naissance à la vie psychique, by Albert CICCONE and Marc LHOPITAL

© Dunod 2019 for the third edition, Malakoff

The right of Albert Ciccone and Marc Lhopital to be identified as authors of this work has been asserted in accordance with sections 77 and 78 of the Copyright, Designs and Patents Act 1988.

All rights reserved. No part of this book may be reprinted or reproduced or utilised in any form or by any electronic, mechanical, or other means, now known or hereafter invented, including photocopying and recording, or in any information storage or retrieval system, without permission in writing from the publishers.

Trademark notice: Product or corporate names may be trademarks or registered trademarks, and are used only for identification and explanation without intent to infringe.

British Library Cataloguing-in-Publication Data
A catalogue record for this book is available from the British Library

Library of Congress Cataloging-in-Publication Data
A catalog record has been requested for this book

ISBN: 978-1-032-01369-5 (hbk)
ISBN: 978-1-032-01371-8 (pbk)
ISBN: 978-1-003-17834-7 (ebk)

DOI: 10.4324/9781003178347

Typeset in Bembo
by Deanta Global Publishing Services, Chennai, India

Contents

Acknowledgements	ix
French editor's note	x
Presentation of the 3rd edition	xi
Preface to the 1st edition	xv

Introduction   1

PART I
First postulate   19

1 Introjection and its relations to the construction of the psychical apparatus   21

2 The first containing external object: The momentary object   40

PART II
Second postulate   89

3 The optimal containing object   91

4 Psychic space   114

PART III
Third postulate   131

5 On adhesive identification: Genesis of the psychic skin   133

6 On symbiosis: A common skin   **159**

Contents

7 On the skin-ego: A complete psychic envelope — 174

8 Conclusion: Psychic birth and psychopathological deviations — 200

PART IV
Fourth postulate — 217

9 Splitting and idealization: The life drives/death drives duality — 219

10 The genesis and development of thought-activity — 245

PART V
Fifth postulate — 279

11 Projective identification: Definition and description — 281

12 Projective identification: Motives, consequences, phenomenology — 296

PART VI
Sixth postulate — 307

13 The inadequacies of the containing object — 309

14 Phantasied attacks on the object — 350

15 "Second skin" formation — 356

Epilogue — 367
Bibliography — 371

Acknowledgements

Thanks to Florence Guignard (Swiss and French psychoanalyst and member of IPA), reviewer of this book for The New Library of Psychoanalysis, for her support.

Thanks to the CRPPC (Centre de Recherche en Psychopathologie et Psychologie Clinique) of the Université Lumière Lyon 2, for its help in financing the English translation of this book.

We would like to express our warm gratitude to Didier Anzieu, as well as Dunod Editeur, and in particular Virginie Catoni and Jean Henriet, thanks to whom this book has enjoyed, and continues to enjoy, an extraordinary adventure.

French editor's note

The first version of *Naissance de la vie psychique* (1991) received the "Prix psychologie 1992" awarded by the *Journal des psychologues*.

Presentation of the 3rd edition

The first version of *Naissance de la vie psychique* appeared in 1991. A second reorganized and enlarged edition was published in 2001. As for the second edition, we have once again opted, while fully measuring the scale of the task, for a new revised, expanded and updated edition.

A few words, to begin with, about the history of the birth of this book, whose audience and success have constantly been confirmed; a few words that are worth writing because this history is quite astonishing. This book originated as a *"maîtrise"* (master's degree) in psychology that Marc Lhopital and I did in the context of a unique system of training in France, which still exists at the University Lumière Lyon 2, set up by Alain-Noël Henri, which allows students who have an established professional activity and experience (particularly in the field of healthcare, but also in other social practices) to train in psychology and to acquire knowledge from research work (or several renewed studies) on their practice, the issues at stake in it, and its purposes. Once the *"maîtrise"* has been validated, the students, said to be "in a professional situation", begin the traditional course of professional training for psychologists leading to diplomas that were called DESS (*Diplômes d'état supérieurs specialisées* ... now called "Master's"). The research topic of this *"maîtrise"* concerned the genesis of psychic life and its early disturbances, and came to the attention of the organizers of a colloquium on the work of Didier Anzieu at Arles, in which Didier Anzieu was taking part himself, who asked us to discuss briefly a particular point of his work. With much emotion and anxiety, I made this intervention which consisted in drawing Didier Anzieu's attention to a number of contradictions in the manner in which he related certain aspects of his theorization of the skin-ego with the ideas of Esther Bick on the psychic skin and those of Donald Meltzer on the dimensions of psychic space.[1] With his habitual openness of mind and generosity, Didier Anzieu recognized the pertinence of these remarks, asked to read the university research study from which these questions had arisen and, to our great surprise, wrote to us a few weeks later to tell us that this work deserved to be published and that he was proposing it to the publisher Dunod for the collection "Psychismes" of which he was the founder. We were extremely moved, but also entertained great doubts because it is probably extremely rare for such a publication to precede the completion of university training. And yet this was the case for the signing of a contract for this first project. The publication came a few years later, during which time we were able to further our practical experience as psychologists, started psychoanalytic training, and benefited from the valuable support of Didier Anzieu and René Kaës. The book immediately met with success on publication and the following year obtained the "Prix Psychologie" awarded by the *Journal des psychologues*. Our psychoanalytic clinical experience, as well as our subsequent research studies contributed thereafter to its rewriting in 2001, for the second edition. And today this will be its third version.

The overall architecture of the previous text has been preserved but certain formulations have been clarified and nuanced, while models have been improved and given greater complexity. We have introduced many additions and developed new points. The references have also been expanded and updated. We have indicated where this is the case by referring to many other studies, present, recent or old, as well as to our own studies on psychic development, early psychopathology, psychic transmission and its stumbling-blocks, trauma, the effects of disability, intersubjectivity and the genesis of thought, the rhythmicity of experiences, the infantile and baby aspects of the self, parenting and the weaknesses of the parent–child relationship, internal parenting, and so on.

We have enriched the illustrations, but have retained all the previous clinical observations because they still seemed to be enlightening and capable of withstanding the examination of theoretical models.

While our discussion articulates a certain number of models that are available in the psychoanalytic conceptual domain, it also takes into account and discusses certain theories elaborated in other or adjacent fields to psychoanalysis, such as the studies on attachment, developmental psychology and interactionist or cognitive approaches.

Finally, our discussion continues to accord a central role to the relationship with the object and to the transformation of experiences, particularly painful ones, in this relationship to the object as a condition of development. Such a position coincides with the majority of current conceptions which, in different epistemologies and fields of practice, deal with the question of the emergence and development of psychic life with reference to a model of intersubjectivity. These conceptions highlight how thinking, the sense of existence, and identity rely on conditions that have their origins in intersubjective experiences.

A final word, now, to draw attention to a point that is clarified more closely in the introduction. Interest in the baby, in the birth of subjectivity, has led many authors, in the past but also in the present, to reduce the baby's experience to the mother–baby relationship. The adjective "mothering" (rather than "maternal") has been retained in order to consider the attention and primary care given to a baby, the primary environment that he encounters, a term which, in spite of its "gendered" aspect, refers as much to the mother as the father, and to every important person in the baby's life, every adult that gives him his/her love, that is attached to him and helps him to grow. But most of the time we use the term "parental", and we deliberately highlight the "parental" before the "maternal" and the "paternal". Indeed, it is first and foremost the parental that guarantees the conditions for a harmonious, creative and secure development of the baby. The parental contains the maternal and the paternal, and contains the links between each of them within each parent. Parental functions – maternal and paternal – are primarily psychic functions which characterize the internal parenting of each parent, and of each subject, in the same way as psychic bisexuality does.

Lastly, we defend the idea that experience with babies and knowledge of the baby are very useful for clinical work and for clinical practice with all patients – children, adolescents or adults. We hope that reading the following pages will play a part, for each reader, in developing his/her curiosity about the experience of babies and the conditions of the emergence of thought, and will foster his/her attention to the infantile and baby aspects of patients, irrespective of the forms of his/her practice, because it is always these aspects that are affected most when psychic suffering is intense and cannot be contained. All psychic care consists, in large part, in hearing and containing the suffering of infantile or baby aspects, and in helping the child or baby in each patient to develop his thinking and to grow.

Albert Ciccone
December 2018

Note

1 This discussion can be found in the book edited by Didier Anzieu titled *L'Épiderme nomade et la peau psychique* (Anzieu et al., 1990). It is also taken up again and developed in Chapter 7 of this volume.

Preface to the 1st edition

Birth to Psychic Life rather than Birth *of* Psychic Life. Psychic life pre-exists, in effect, the newborn infant in the form of a psychical apparatus that is specific to the couple, family and group that form the background of psychic life, the matrix on which it nourishes itself and from which it will have to detach itself. It is within this common psychical apparatus that the child finds his place as a psychic being and can, if everything goes well, build his own personal psychical apparatus.

Over the last few decades, a significant body of literature has appeared on the relationship between the baby and the mothering environment, on its maturational and pathogenic effects, and on the particularities of their treatment. It had become necessary to make both an analysis and synthesis of it in order to make it as useful as possible for practitioners (psychologists, child psychiatrists, psychotherapists, psychoanalysts) and for researchers. This was this considerable task that Albert Ciccone and Marc Lhopital undertook and saw through successfully at the University of Lumière Lyon 2, and we are pleased to publish their book at Dunod. The authors have scrutinized, condensed, commented on and criticized this literature, and compared it with their clinical experience. They have chosen an original and fruitful study plan. Taking as their starting point a short article by Esther Bick on the constitution of the psychic skin in infants, during the first year of life approximately, they have identified six statements that govern successively the six postulates of their book: the introjection of an external object (the breast) ensuring the link between the parts of the self; the correlative constitution of a psychic space; the assimilation of the containing object with the skin; thanks to this psychic skin, the acquisition of the distinction inside/outside and of the processes of splitting; in the case of failure, the continuation of pathological projective identification and consecutive confusions of identity; and the formation of a "second skin" in reaction to the real or fantasized inadequacy of the containing object.

Like any study that delineates its field and the issues at stake in it in order to better treat its object, this one puts into latency and presupposes some of the major conditions of birth to psychic life: that the human "mothering environment" is a relationship between subjects in which each one plays his role from the beginning; that this intersubjective organization only produces its effects of "birth" if, and only if, a principle of "unsticking" and linking establishes from the outset, a third element between the baby and its primary object; and finally that this environment is only a psychic environment by virtue of the speech-representations, half-said and prohibited, that are exchanged in it.

Didier Anzieu, René Kaës

INTRODUCTION

In *Une peau pour les pensées*, Didier Anzieu states that

> Psychoanalysis has shown a great deal of interest in the investigation of psychic contents – fantasies, anxieties, screen memories, etc. – as the means and conditions of access to the psychic conflicts and neurotic symptoms that result from them. It did not give much consideration to the problem of the container, which was taken for granted, until it encountered cases – narcissistic personalities, borderline cases and certain psychoses – where the psychic container was so clearly damaged or deficient that the first reaction was to declare them unanalysable. How is the container constituted […]?
>
> (1986a, p. 75, translated for this edition)

We will attempt, if not to answer this question concerning the earliest states of psychic life, at least to identify its main terms, while emphasizing the importance of the psychic envelope and the role of the containing function of the external-internal object in the development and functioning of the psyche.

It was the encounter with the thought of Esther Bick, and particularly her considerations concerning the psychic skin (Bick, 1968, 1986),[1] which, in the day-to-day clinical experience of early psychopathology, inaugurated our project of looking, from a psychoanalytic point of view, at the conditions of the birth to psychic life. We will approach this question by studying, among other things, the relationship between the subjective states at the beginning of psychic life and the subjective states in psychopathology. We will explore how knowledge and understanding of psychopathological states tell us about the development of psychic life and, conversely, how the understanding and representation of the first forms of psychic life equally tell us something about psychopathology.

0.1 Principal propositions concerning psychic birth

The aim of this work is to attempt a reconstruction of the genesis and early alterations of the psyche in order to account for the conditions of birth to psychic life. While our discussion is based to a large extent on the thinking of Melanie Klein and her successors, we will endeavour to highlight the interfaces and links between various models. These interfaces do not erase the differences but reveal a "common substance". The theoretical support of certain authors will help us in this work of linking. This is the case, for instance, of the theoretical model of Piera Aulagnier which will help us to, among other things, make connections between the conceptions of Esther Bick and those of Didier Anzieu.

Melanie Klein's thinking was an invaluable contribution extending the scope of Freud's work, and her studies permitted considerable advances in the knowledge of mental life, in particular its primary states. Furthermore, Melanie Klein's theses, from 1946 onwards, defending, with increasing insistence, the early existence of the ego and object-cathexes were accepted, confirmed or taken up again, as Jean-Michel Petot (1982) has pointed out, and remain very relevant today. Melanie Klein drew attention to the early relationship established between the baby and his mother, the "innate and unconscious sense" of the existence of the mother's breast, the manifest relationship to the external world (1952ab), at a time when the studies of René Spitz (1965) and of genetic psychology, for instance, were spreading the idea that the smile is only intentional at three months, or that the baby does not recognize its mother's face before the age of eight months, etc. Research in experimental or genetic psychology, or other lines of research, and in the domain of the skills of the newborn baby, or of the foetus,[2] have since confirmed the pertinence of Melanie Klein's ideas and how they were ahead of their time.

Starting with Kleinian thought, which we will link up with other conceptualizations, we will identify the three psychic constellations, recognized by several authors, that are attendant upon this event that is psychic birth (we will see why the terms can vary and why we are proposing certain formulations that seem to us more adequate): the *auto-sensual* or *adhesive* or *autistic position*, the *symbiotic* or *paranoid-schizoid position* and the *depressive position*. We will stress the dynamic nature of psychic organization oscillating at a very early stage from one position to the other and from a narcissistic pole to an object-related pole. The central role played by the depressive position in this dynamic will be highlighted, and especially depressive anxiety, experienced in a more or less narcissistic and catastrophic or object-related mode, depending on the degree of complexity of the psychical apparatus as well as on its level of integration which determines the nature of the experience of loss. In this connection we will propose the notion of melancholic position which, alongside the auto-sensual, symbiotic and manic positions, offers the psyche a possibility of defensive withdrawal when faced with depressive pain.[3]

This picture we are putting forward of the psyche oscillating between different positions, one of which is predominant at each stage of its development, will allow us to conserve the idea of primary narcissism or a first phase of auto-sensuality, as well as of normal symbiosis, even though, in the light of studies on the skills of the newborn baby, these notions could be reconsidered. We feel it is appropriate to maintain the idea of these developmental stages, but it is necessary to clarify further the picture we have of auto-sensual and symbiotic psychic states, and in particular to reconsider the notion of primary narcissism, which cannot be reduced – as it often is, based on Freud's (1914b, 1940a) remarks – to the idea of an objectless stage in which subject and object are undifferentiated. The normal auto-sensual and symbiotic phases, like autism and symbiotic psychosis, do not correspond to states of closedness. Openness to the object is obviously present in them, but the relationship to the object is of an essentially narcissistic nature. Thinking in terms of the *positions* of the psyche within each mental state or during each phase of development is more appropriate, in our view, for accounting for these psychic movements, these oscillations between cathexis and decathexis, openness and closedness, as evidenced in the newborn infant and the autistic child or psychotic child – and as evidenced in every subject in his development as well as every subject presenting a psychopathology.

The term position was introduced by Melanie Klein[4] to denote a psychic constellation regrouping particular anxieties, their related mechanisms of defence, and a way of relating to the world generated by these anxieties and by the manner of protecting oneself against them. These constellations, these psychic positions, appear from the beginning of psychic development and are reactualized throughout life, as Melanie Klein (1948b, 1952a) said – and that is why she uses the term position rather than that of stage or phase of development –, in connection with situations particularly linked to the uncertainties of psychic development or to disturbing or traumatic contexts. And the psyche oscillates between different positions, both in the course of its development and in more or less fixed psychopathological states. Within this oscillation, one position dominates, thereby determining the singularity of a mental state or phase of development and making it possible to denote this or that stage or this or that psychopathology. But the psyche is never immobilized in a constant state, in one exclusive position, in an immutable mode of functioning. It always oscillates between more or less important states of closedness and more or less pronounced states of openness. Such a model can be applied just as much to psychic development as to psychopathology. And this model converges with the conceptions of many authors to whom we will be referring in this book, who consider that in every personality "normal" and "pathological" aspects, "neurotic" and "psychotic" or "autistic"[5] parts, zones that are open to the world and development, and zones that are closed and resistant to any growth, coexist.[6]

We fully adhere, and our clinical experience constantly supports this adhesion, to this idea of a possible coexistence within the personality of non-psychotic parts, which are concerned about their development and respectful of their dependent relations, and psychotic parts, or autistic enclaves, which are saturated with omnipotence and maintain the illusion of independence. We will present the psychotic and autistic processes that can be deployed even in non-psychotic personalities, and will indicate, among other things, how thought can be prey to autistic manoeuvres.

We will describe how the construction of subjectivity and the sense of identity are based on normal processes of identification and mechanisms of defence, but whose persistence and, above all, distortion, under the effect of forces inherent to the baby himself and/ or pressures stemming from the environment, determine the psychopathological evolution. The modalities of identification at the basis of subjectivity and the sense of identity are represented by *identification through adhesivity* in the bidimensional auto-sensual space, *identification through projection* in the tridimensional symbiotic space, and *identification through introjection* in the quadridimensional individual space. The defensive modalities, apart from these identificatory processes which can also have defensive functions, essentially concern *dismantling* in the auto-sensual position, *splitting* and *idealization* in the symbiotic position, and *repression* in the depressive position.

These identificatory and defensive processes may be in the service of development, but also of resistance to growth. We will develop, for instance, the idea of projective identification with internal objects to account for incorporation fantasies that are necessary for introjective identification, or to account for disturbances of the sense of identity, dissociation or depersonalization. We will look at the process of transition from one modality of identification to another, and will put forward the idea that each modality of identification contains qualities related to states or processes that are anterior to it ontogenetically: "projectivity" contains "adhesivity" and "introjectivity" contains "projectivity". We will further suggest that the relation of proportionality between these different qualities determines the success of the identificatory movement and the authenticity of the sense of identity.

Concerning the modalities of identification, we will distinguish and denote by different terms the psychic process and the state of mind to which its utilization leads. The term "identification" will denote the process, and the term "identity" (adhesive, projective or introjective) will denote the state of mind.

We will place emphasis on the function of the containing object and on the introjection of the containing function in the construction of subjectivity and the sense of identity. We will thus examine psychic development in its relation to the development of the *psychic envelope*. The containing object – "momentary or optimal" – as we will define it, is a container not in the sense of a recipient but of an "attractor" (Houzel, 1985b, 1987) which attracts the instinctual and emotional life of the baby. The optimal container gathers up the scattered sensuality and creates the conditions for maintaining "consensuality" (Meltzer et al., 1982). Moreover, it is a transformer of raw experiences that cannot acquire psychic status. (René Kaës speaks of a *"conteneur"* – Kaës, 1976a, 1979.)

We will often have recourse to the description of phenomenological observations as we wish to maintain close links between the conceptual approach and the reality of daily clinical practice.

Introduction

Just like José Bleger (1971), we consider phenomenological observation as "that which is realized from within phenomena, as they are perceived, experienced and lived or organized by those who are an integral part of the phenomenon" (p. 50, translated from the French). Bleger distinguishes between the phenomenological and the naturalist point of view and gives the following example to explain this distinction: a mother and her child are in a room; the mother is going about her activities and the child is isolated in his game, each of them acting independently without speaking to each other or looking at each other. At a certain moment the mother leaves the room, and the child stops playing immediately to go out with her. Bleger points out that, from the naturalist point of view, and if we only consider the level of interaction, we can say that in the first sequence of this observed situation, there is no interaction or communication, and we may be led to suppose that each partner – the mother and the child – is an isolated and individual person. On the other hand, from the phenomenological point of view we can say that the mother and the child, albeit apparently isolated, are in fact in a state of shared symbiosis.[7]

The representation and comprehension of intra- and interpsychic processes draw widely on spatial metaphors, which is helpful for representation but can also create misunderstandings. We will have to try in particular, on several occasions, to elucidate in the object-relationship what concerns the relationship to the internal object and the external object respectively. Phenomenology seeks to account for the link between intrapsychic processes, such as identificatory processes (adhesive, projective, introjective), and their behavioural correlates, their equivalents in the subject's relationship to external objects. Just as the internal world is built through the internalization of experiences and of relations to external objects, the external world presents itself as a stage for the dramatization of the internal theatre. The object is thus often both outside and inside (which is reflected by the expression "external-internal" or "internal-external", sometimes used in the following lines).

We will emphasize on several occasions the two conditions underlying the alteration of psychic development. The alterations of psychic development, the "accidents" of birth to psychic life, result from the encounter between a mothering environment at pains to fulfil its function of having to psychically contain and nourish the newborn baby, and a newborn baby whose capacity to benefit from the psychic qualities of its mothering environment or of stimulating them is in abeyance. This constitutional "handicap" (heightened sensitivity, major intolerance for frustration, excessive destructivity, etc.) is partly dependent on proto-emotional experience *in utero*. The relationship to the object has a central role in the development of personality which consists in introjecting emotional experiences in the relationship to the object, in intersubjectivity. More than the object, it is the relationship to the object that is introjected.

Concerning the nouns that denote this first, primary object that the baby cathects, as for the primary environment that he encounters, we attach to them the adjective "mothering". This qualifier reflects the primary care from which the baby who has just been separated from his mother's body, from the maternal uterine matrix, benefits, in order to be born into the world. Although this term is "gendered", we are using it first and foremost because it is not so easy to ditch social representations of parenting, and further because the primary care in question reconstructs a postnatal "symbiotic" matrix, extending the intrauterine matrix universe, a psychic matrix from which the baby and the parents separate, the baby developing his subjectivity and the parents their parenting. The feeding situation of the baby at the breast (or at the bottle) represents, as we shall see, a prototypical situation of this "containing" parental function assured by the object or mothering environment. "Mothering" and not "maternal", for this environment which protects the baby, dispenses this primary care and permits psychic birth and growth, concerns both the mother and the father and every important person in the baby's life, every person who gives their attention, their love, every person who raises the baby and to whom the baby is attached. The authors to whom we refer, whose contributions we take up or extend, are very often (too often) focused, sometimes exclusively even, on the mother and the mother–baby relationship. Our concern will always be to extend their considerations to parenting and always to place the "parental" function before the "maternal" function; for the light they throw on the mother–baby relationship, on maternal qualities, on the mother's state of mind and on possible maternal insufficiencies or psychopathologies, etc., applies in the large majority of cases to the father and mother alike, and so we will transpose their reflections to the parental function and to the parent–baby relationship. We will also see how the "containing" function allies and articulates maternal and paternal qualities, psychic qualities that

Introduction

belong to each subject, characterizing the internal parental objects and constituting the "psychic biparenting"[8] of each of them.

We will mention the place of the family history, the place of the internal objects of each parent in the identificatory destiny of the child. Further, we will evoke the processes of psychic transmission, the parental projections that the baby inherits and that have an impact on early subjective experiences, determining in part the movement of subjectivation. In this way, we will throw light on certain psychopathological manifestations or symptomatogical constructions from a transgenerational viewpoint.

Let us now present Esther Bick, before focusing on her theses concerning the notion of "psychic skin", theses that will constitute an internal framework for our model.

0.2 Presentation of Esther Bick

0.2.1 Infant observation

Esther Bick belonged to the second generation of members of the Kleinian movement, including analysts such as Hanna Segal, Wilfred Bion and Herbert Rosenfeld. As a psychoanalyst, a pupil and then a close friend of Melanie Klein, she introduced, in 1948, "infant observation"[9] into the core of child psychotherapy and psychoanalytic training at the Tavistock Clinic in London. In 1960, Martha Harris, who succeeded Esther Bick, developed and democratized this set-up by making it available to a large range of child practitioners. In the same year, Esther Bick's infant observation was also made part of the Institute of Psychoanalysis training course in London. This observation involves observing an infant and his family once a week in the home setting over a two-year period following the infant's birth. Esther Bick, and then others, supervised the work of students in weekly seminars. She ran such seminars until the end of her life. Thus, over a period of 30 years she studied a dense body of clinical material and developed a very rich understanding of the infant's psychic life.

Surprisingly enough, the relations between psychoanalysis and direct observation (of the infant) have been ambiguous, with psychoanalysis often preferring the reconstruction of a mythical child on the basis of adult analysis, leaving a prominent role to speculative imagination. However, psychoanalysts have always carried out direct observations. Freud (1914a, 1916–1917, 1920) himself emphasized on several occasions the interest of observing children directly or of analyzing a neurosis dating back to early infancy. He himself conducted direct observations: apart from the observations of auto-erotic behaviour characteristic of infantile sexuality (Freud, 1905) and the analysis by proxy of Little Hans (Freud, 1909) – which may be considered as the equivalent of a direct observation –, we can also mention the famous observation of the "wooden reel game" with his 18-month-old grandson (Freud, 1920). Melanie Klein (1952ab) observed infants and commented on infant observations.[10] Anna Freud (1965) also recommended the direct observation of children. Susan Isaacs (1952) clarified the methodological principles of observation and emphasized the close and intimate links between observation and psychoanalysis. Bion (1967a, 1970, 1974–1977) played a role in enlarging the metapsychology of psychoanalytic observation. Other psychoanalysts practised infant observations: we may cite Donald Winnicott (1941, 1957) and Margaret Mahler (1968), among many others.[11]

But it was Esther Bick who systematized infant observation and gave it its framework and impetus as an experience in psychoanalytic training. In 1964, she published an article called "Notes on infant observation in psycho-analytic training" (Bick, 1964) in which she explains the importance that she ascribes to this experience of infant observation in the training of psychoanalysts. She points out in this article how difficult it is to observe, that is, to "collect facts free from interpretation" (p. 254). Observation teaches caution and reliance on consecutive observations for confirmation of the meaning of the facts. The observer learns to "watch and feel without jumping in with theories" (ibid.). He also learns to discard fixed notions about how to handle a baby and discovers the unique character of each mother–baby or parent–baby couple. He learns to appreciate how a parent takes care of her baby and finds her own solutions. He learns to find the right distance that allows him to be sufficiently in contact with the situation and not to introduce distortion. This implies a capacity to discern the transference and countertransference movements, the projections of the parties involved – the family members and the observer himself – which nourish and intensify the internal conflicts of each of them. The observation of a baby in his family is an experience whose emotional impact is intense and requires a great deal of working through, which is part of training in the psychoanalytic method. The observer learns, moreover, how

Introduction

the detailed observation of signs, of a subject's overall behaviour, is an important part of psychoanalytic work. This experience will also help him to understand the (current) infantile feelings of patients, to see the baby or the child that a patient was, and it will confirm the relevance of analytic reconstructions, particularly of his early development.[12]

Esther Bick wrote very little herself. The transmission of her teaching was essentially oral. Since 1988, the French translation of the *Collected Papers of Martha Harris and Esther Bick* (1987) has been available under the title *Les Écrits de Martha Harris et d'Esther Bick*. But infant observation according to Esther Bick's method has been constantly evolving in France, Europe and beyond, and many texts give an account of this method as well as its applications[13] (in the treatment or prevention of psychopathologies or risk situations).

The method features three stages:

- the first is observing. The observer receives the emotional impact of the observed situation. He lets himself be impregnated by the situation, while trying not to interfere in the spontaneous unfolding of the parent/baby relationship;
- the second is note-taking. This involves a work of reconstruction. The observer, alone, gives shape to the traces left by the impact of the situation. He is invited to note all the details he can remember in simple language and without theoretical or interpretative codification;
- the third is the seminar. This is a period of group elaboration. The group (observers and psychoanalyst) put themselves in the service of the observation and the observer in order to develop an understanding of the observed situation, and of the impact of the situation on the observer.

In the following stage, the observer, transformed by all the previous work, returns to the family, and these stages are repeated rhythmically. The observer's psychic capacities to receive and contain the situation, his or her capacities to understand will be developed and thereby offer valuable support to the parent–baby relationship.

The first essential rule recommended by Esther Bick is, as Michel Haag (1984) relates, the "*tabula rasa*", the "I don't know" attitude. Michel Haag reports these remarks by Esther Bick:

Introduction

> The fundamental thing is to really learn to observe, not to jump to conclusions or to use "clichés", and to learn to see completely different things because one child is never the same as another [...]. Without the attitude: "I don't know, I will see in the light of the facts", no work with anyone, whatever his capacities, is really fruitful.
>
> (Bick, cited by Haag, 1984, p. 25, translated from the French)

The second essential rule taught by Esther Bick concerns the fundamental requirement that the observer only be a receiver and never initiate a change of any kind; he must not interfere in the observed situation, must respect the parent–child relationship, and must not impinge intrusively on a sensitive and vulnerable relationship.

The practice by the observer of these two major precepts has a beneficial influence for parents and baby alike. Manuel Perez-Sanchez (1981), among others, notes the degree to which the observer has a containing function for the parent–baby relationship. The observer who is able to receive the complaints and comments of the mother or father, without giving advice, is felt to be a support. Indeed, advice given with the aim of helping is usually experienced as a criticism by the parent concerning his or her parental capacities, as one more demand. That is why the observer who does not intervene, who does not interfere, who shows by the quality of his presence that he is psychically available to receive projections, worries and emotional turbulence, can serve as a support for the sometimes disconcerting experience of being a mother or father. The profound respect of the relationship between the parents and their baby underlying the practice of infant observation is clearly reflected in the texts that describe this practice.

This position advocated by Esther Bick seems to us to be a good model for what must be the clinical position of every psychotherapist, of every psychoanalyst. Being able to listen to the other person, being in contact with the internal world, without immediately clinging defensively to some pre-established perspective, to a pre-existing theorization, is the state of mind that the psychoanalyst must constantly strive for. Bion always insisted on the need for the analyst to discard theoretical constructions to be able to listen to – and think about – what the analysand is saying (see Bion, 1974–1977). He emphasized the need for the analyst to be "without memory and

Introduction

desire", explaining how desires, memories and the attempt at immediate understanding destroy the analytic state of mind (Bion, 1967ab, 1970, 1974–1977, 1997[14]). Furthermore, Bion (1967a) considered that analysis is based on "doubt", and that it is essential to preserve this attitude of "philosophical doubt" to permit the continuation of the analysis. Likewise, according to Bion (1974–1977), mental growth occurs at the price of a state of continual psychic breakdown: each time something new is perceived, everything that has already been seen deserves to be reconsidered; living in this perpetual state of crisis is a condition for mental development. That is why we share the idea that true clinical listening occurs at the price of discarding any pre-established perspective, at the price of a requirement akin to what Esther Bick calls the *"tabula rasa"*. However, this experience still has to be tolerated. It involves accepting an extremely difficult and painful discipline, for it requires one to continually endanger internal relations that have been woven and which sustain knowledge and certainties. It requires a capacity to tolerate catastrophic anxiety (in the sense Bion (1965, 1966) gives to this term).

Let it be added that the observation of infants and parenting, in this state of mind, teaches one to be sensitive to the essential aspects of a caregiving relationship, in the sense of "taking care", of being attentive to the foundations of a "caregiving position" and of "caregiving concern" (Ciccone, 2012c, 2014), and thus to building models of psychic care. Observing how a parent encounters a baby (and how the baby is sustained in such a movement of openness) or how a parent helps a baby give up a violent or aggressive impulse, or how a parent psychically "reanimates" a baby who is withdrawn, cut off from the world, or alternatively how a parent goes about consoling a baby in distress, is an invaluable source of information regarding the question of what is really healing in caregiving, and regarding training for every practitioner of psychic care, for every psychoanalyst. Such an experience helps to understand and to feel what is essential in the work of psychic care, and to build models for thinking about psychoanalytic care.[15]

0.2.2 The article of 1968 on psychic skin

After Melanie Klein's description of the primary splitting and idealization of self and object, Esther Bick's description of the psychic function of the skin constitutes, as Donald Meltzer points out

(Meltzer et al., 1975), the second convincing addition to Freud's conception concerning the beginning of mental life, that is to say the idea of "primary narcissism".

Freud (1905) had initially described the evolution of the libido from autoerotism – the sexual impulse separates itself from the functions of self-preservation, and therefore from the external object, and derives satisfaction from the subject's own body – to object-love. In the context of his investigations into psychotic states (Freud, 1911b), describes a stage between the phase of autoerotism and that object-choice, namely, the stage of narcissism. If, during the auto-erotic phase, the independent sexual impulses derive satisfaction from the body, each for its own needs, during the narcissistic phase they reunite and turn towards the ego, which is already constituted at this period (Freud, 1912–1913). Narcissism thus sees the ego take itself as its own love-object, before choosing external objects. In 1914, in his article "On narcissism: an introduction" (Freud, 1914b), Freud discusses the notions of ego-libido – sexual energy taking the ego as its object – and distinguishes primary narcissism from secondary narcissism. There exists an original libidinal cathexis of the ego, which corresponds to primary narcissism, while secondary narcissism represents the withdrawal of the libido from people and things in the external world and its recathexis in the ego, as evidenced in schizophrenia – or paraphrenia, to use Freud's term.

Autoerotism, which corresponds to the initial state of the libido, is thus distinguished from narcissism, the state that follows it. From this point of view, narcissism coincides with and represents the constitution of the early ego. Freud makes the following remark, which was to nourish many subsequent contributions, in particular those of Klein and her collaborators (Klein et al., 1952):

> We are bound to suppose that a unity comparable to the ego cannot exist in the individual from the start; the ego has to be developed. The auto-erotic instincts, however, are there from the very first; so there must be something added to autoerotism – a new psychical action – in order to bring about narcissism.
> (Freud, 1914b, p. 76–77)

Later, Freud (1915a, 1916–1917) erased the distinction between autoerotism and narcissism, describing as narcissistic the early original psychic state from which object-love only emerges later on, the

Introduction

prototype of which is the intra-uterine state. Autoerotism is therefore envisaged as the sexual activity of the narcissistic phase of fixation of the libido. The descriptions that Freud gives of absolute narcissism, or of absolute primary narcissism (1940b [1938]), may lead one to suppose that this state is objectless, which apparently does not correspond to the idea that Freud had previously given of autoerotism, namely, that it is based on self-preservation and constituted by the effacement of the object when faced with the organ.

Melanie Klein's addition follows the presentation of the case of Schreber (1911b) in which Freud speaks of "abnormal alterations of the ego" inducing distinctive disorders of psychosis. Melanie Klein (1946) is led to put forward the notion of splitting in the early ego and of primary idealization of self and object. The operation of splitting, aimed at managing the anxiety resulting from the action of the death drive, reveals the qualities of good and bad object and inaugurates the beginning of object-relations. These emerge from the beginning of postnatal life when the "early ego" already has a few basic elements of cohesion and integration.

Esher Bick's contribution lies in her description of the *psychic function of the skin* in the development of subjectivity. She shows that the baby needs to have the experience of a containing object with whom he can identify in order to feel sufficiently contained within his own skin. This will allow him to tolerate physical separation and to protect the self from the disintegrating effect that it could have. Esher Bick describes the consequences of a disturbance of this experience in establishing a "second skin" function. She defines this *identification with a containing object* as a prerequisite for the process of splitting and idealization of the self and object.

Here is the essence of Esther Bick's (1968) text titled "The experience of the skin in early object-relations":[16]

> The thesis is that in its most primitive form the parts of the personality are felt to have no binding force amongst themselves and must therefore be held together in a way that is experienced by them passively, by the skin functioning as a boundary. But this internal function of containing the parts of the self is dependent initially on the introjection of an external object, experienced as capable of fulfilling this function. Later, identification with this function of the object supersedes the unintegrated state and gives rise to the fantasy of

internal and external spaces. Only then the stage is set for the operation of primal splitting and idealization of self and object as described by Melanie Klein. Until the containing functions have been introjected, the concept of a space within the self cannot arise. Introjection, i.e. construction of an object in an internal space is therefore impaired. In its absence, the function of projective identification will necessarily continue unabated and all the confusions of identity attending it will be manifest.

The stage of primal splitting and idealization of self and object can now be seen to rest on this earlier process of containment of self and object by their respective "skins".

The fluctuations of this primal state will be illustrated in case material, from infant observation, in order to show the difference between unintegration as a passive experience of total helplessness, and disintegration through splitting processes as an active defensive operation in the service of development. We are, therefore, from the economic point of view, dealing with situations conducive to catastrophic anxieties in the unintegrated state as compared with the more limited and specific persecutory and depressive ones.

The need for a containing object would seem, in the infantile unintegrated state, to produce a frantic search for an object – a light, a voice, a smell or other sensual object – which can hold the attention and thereby be experienced, momentarily at least, as holding the parts of the personality together. The optimal object is the nipple in the mouth, together with the holding and talking and familiar smelling mother.

Material will show how this containing object is experienced concretely as a skin. Faulty development of this primal skin function can be seen to result either from defects in the adequacy of the actual object or from fantasy attacks on it, which impair introjection. Disturbance in the primal skin function can lead to a development of a "second skin" formation through which dependence on the object is replaced by pseudo-independence, by the inappropriate use of certain mental functions, or perhaps innate talents, for the purpose of creating a substitute for this skin container function.

(Bick, 1968, p. 114–115)

Introduction

In this fundamental text of Esher Bick we will identify six postulates that will represent six basic statements or six axes — the most essential ones concerning the subject we are concerned with — on the basis of which, or around which, we will develop our reflection:

- first postulate:
  In their most primitive form, the parts of the personality felt to have no binding force amongst themselves are held together thanks to the introjection of an external object experienced as capable of fulfilling this function;
- second postulate:
  The introjection of the optimal object, the mothering object (the "breast"), identified with this function of a containing object, gives rise to the fantasy of internal and external spaces;
- third postulate:
  The introjected containing object is experienced as a skin. It has a function of "psychic skin";
- fourth postulate:
  The introjection of an external containing object, giving the skin its frontier function, is a prerequisite for the operation of processes of splitting and idealization of self and object;
- fifth postulate:
  In the absence of the introjection of containing functions, projective identification continues unabated, with all the consequent confusions of identity;
- sixth postulate:
  Disturbances of introjection, resulting either from the inadequacy of the actual object or from fantasized attacks on it, can lead to the development of a "second skin" formation.

Notes

1 The article of reference is that of 1968, "The experience of the skin in early object-relations"; the text of 1986, "Further considerations on the function of the skin in early object-relations", a posthumous publication of a paper presented at the pre-congress of 1975 of the British psychoanalytic Society, develops earlier discoveries.
2 See, for example, Vurpillot, 1972; Brazelton, 1973, 1979, 1982; Bower, 1977; Mehler et al., 1978, 1988; Trevarthen, 1980, 1989b; Trevarthen and Aitken, 1996; De Casper and Fifer 1980, De Casper and Spence,

Introduction

1986; De Casper and Granier-Deferre,1994; Herbinet and Busnel, 1981; Pinol-Douriez, 1984; Field and Fox, 1985; Lecanuet et al., 1989, 1995; Nadel and Camaioni, 1993; Busnel, 1997; and many others.

3 Kleinian and post-Kleinian authors attribute a primordial role, in the development of the human being, to depressive pain and psychic suffering. Donald Meltzer (1978) drew attention to the difficulties Freud had in taking psychic suffering into account as such, and not simply as the equivalent of an absence of pleasure.

4 The term appeared in 1928, in "Early stages of the Oedipus conflict", but it was above all used from 1935 onwards, when Melanie Klein described the depressive position (in "A Contribution to the study of the psychogenesis of manic-depressive states"). Nevertheless, it was only later, after having fully conceptualized the other central position, the paranoid-schizoid position (Klein, 1946), that she was to explain the choice of this term (Klein, 1948b, 1952a).

5 Such as Wilfred Bion (1957), Frances Tustin (1972, 1981b, 1985c, 1990), Salomon Resnik (1986a), David Rosenfeld (1997).

6 See also Ciccone, 2018.

7 On the conditions and modalities of clinical observation, see Ciccone, 1998c.

8 See Ciccone 2011, 2012bc, 2014, 2016a.

9 Infant observation: infant includes both the newborn baby and the very young child.

10 Concerning infant observations carried out by Melanie Klein, it is worth noting an unpublished manuscript, "Notes on baby", presented and commented on by Joseph Aguayo (2002), in which Melanie Klein recorded periodic observations of her grandson, following his birth in 1937 and during his early childhood. It is one of the first detailed and long-term infant observations carried out by a psychoanalyst (an observation that could not be published for obvious reasons, though some extracts were used in her 1952 article, "On observing the behaviour of young infants"). We can see Melanie Klein's capacity to observe shrewdly what was unfolding before her eyes, her sensitivity to the feelings of the baby, and her touching manner of helping him to overcome his states of distress. These notes show how much attention she paid to the impact of the environment on the baby, to the resonances between the emotional experiences of the baby and those of the parents. We mentioned earlier to how Melanie Klein was ahead of her time: as Aguayo shows, some of her observations in this document anticipate theorizations that others made later, for instance,

Introduction

those of Winnicott on the "spatula game" (Winnicott, 1941) and on the "transitional object" (Winnicott, 1953), or those of Bowlby on "instinctive behaviours" and the "fear of the stranger" in his attachment theory (Bowlby, 1969). Remember that Winnicott and Bowlby were both in supervision with Melanie Klein at the moment when she was doing these observations (see, Grosskurth, 1986).

11 Margaret Mahler signalled the importance of her own studies on normal children and their mother, which enriched her analytic work with neurotic adults and children, and above all confirmed her hypotheses in the domain of infantile psychoses. She drew on the remarks of Edward Glover (1956) to the effect that analysts are able to make direct observations of infantile behaviour and, within the limits of their prejudices, to draw conclusions from them about primary mental processes. It is worth recalling that in the 1960s, in France, Myriam David and Geneviève Appell (1966), in association with John Bowlby, observed mother–infant relations, within a more ethological perspective, but using a methodology that was sometimes very similar to that of Esther Bick.

12 On this theme of the interest of infant observation in psychoanalytic training, see the later article by Martha Harris (1976). For further development and illustrations concerning the interest of such an experience for training and psychoanalytic practice, see Ciccone et al., 2012; Ciccone, 2014.

13 Perez-Sanchez, 1981, 1987; Haag, 1984, 2002; Miller et al., 1989; Sandri et al., 1994; Lacroix, Monmayrant et al., 1995; Ciccone et al., 1998; Delion et al., 2004, 2008; etc. See also, concerning the observation of young children, of 2 years of age or more, as it is also practised in the Tavistock Clinic training, and its applications, Adamo and Rustin, 2014.

14 *Taming Wild Thoughts* (1997) is a posthumous book edited by Francesca Bion, which includes the paper "The grid", written in 1963, and the transcriptions of two recordings of Bion dating from 1977.

15 Based on the observation of babies and the work of parenting, one of us has thus proposed different models of psychoanalytic psychic care: the model of the "encounter", the model of "drive integration", the model of "psychic reanimation" and the model of "consolation" (Ciccone, 1998a, 2012c, 2014).

16 A large part of this text can also be found in *Explorations in Autism* (Meltzer et al., 1975) of which Michel Haag (1984) has provided a complete French translation.

PART I

FIRST POSTULATE

> In their most primitive form, the parts of the personality felt to have no binding force amongst themselves are held together thanks to the introjection of an external object experienced as capable of fulfilling this function.

This statement will lead us first of all to define introjection and to consider the relations between this process and the construction of the psychical apparatus.

Then we will turn our attention to the nature and qualities of the first external objects providing this containing function. We will therefore make a long detour in order to study autistic manoeuvres. We will then discuss primitive anxieties and psychic elements in their earliest form.

1
INTROJECTION AND ITS RELATIONS TO THE CONSTRUCTION OF THE PSYCHICAL APPARATUS[1]

The concept of introjection is fundamental for the help that it provides in representing the very construction of the psychical apparatus, and then its functioning. Introjection works in association with projection and, indeed, the process of introjection/projection may be considered as a genuine form of "psychic respiration" (Guignard, 1985).

We will first try to circumscribe this concept of introjection, before going on to use a phenomenological approach to elucidate it. We will then seek to explain an essential distinction differentiating introjection from incorporation. This distinction, which will reappear in different forms throughout this book, is essential for appreciating the functioning of psychic life, and thus of mental health.

1.1 Conceptual approach

The term introjection was introduced in 1909 by Ferenczi in symmetry with that of projection. Projection characterizes the expulsion by the paranoiac of his ego of impulses that have become unpleasant. Introjection is defined by the fact that the neurotic seeks to take into his ego as much of the external world as possible. This "inclusion" within the ego of the objects of the external world results from the extension to the external world of interest that is autoerotic in origin. This conception led Ferenczi to consider all object-love as an extension of the ego or an introjection:

> In principle, man can only love himself; if he loves an object, he takes it into his ego.
>
> (Ferenczi, 1912, p. 317)

Freud takes up this notion of introjection, introduced by Ferenczi, in "Instincts and their vicissitudes" (1915a). He describes the relations between projection and introjection which are involved in the differentiation of subject/object and ego/external world. The subject strives to introject what is good, which he takes into the ego, and projects what is bad, which he equates with the external world. This idea is stated once again in "Negation", where Freud (1925) emphasizes the connection between introjection and the experience of oral incorporation (he had already described the connection between incorporation and identification in 1915 in an addition to the *Three Essays on the Theory of Sexuality* (1905), in "Mourning and melancholia" (1917) and in *Group Psychology and the Analysis of the Ego* (1921)).

Freud draws attention to introjection in the analysis of melancholia in 1917. Introjection corresponds to the withdrawal into the ego of the libido linked to a love-object as a result of an actual slight or disappointment. This libido withdrawn into the ego serves to establish an identification of the ego with the abandoned object. "Thus the shadow of the object [falls] upon the ego", as Freud says (1917, p. 249).

Narcissistic identification with the object makes it possible to avoid abandoning the loved person, in spite of the conflict between the "critical activity of the ego" and the "ego altered by identification". Freud takes up this process again in *Group Psychology and the Analysis of the Ego* (1921). In *The Ego and the Id,* Freud (1923) wonders whether introjection is not a precondition for giving up the object, thereby rendering the loss more tolerable. It would seem, then, that the introjection he described in melancholia, with its attendant pathological conflict, coloured by hate and sadism, between the ego-ideal and the ego identified with the object through introjection, in fact reflects a failure of introjection.[2] I will come back to this point further on.

In order to form a picture of the process of introjection it is necessary to draw on bodily, sensory or biological metaphors. In her text "Certain functions of introjection and projection in early infancy" (1952a), Paula Heimann takes up the comparison made by Freud on several occasions between the mind and the cellular organism (see Freud, 1920, 1921, 1923). The life of the cell, like that of the body, is maintained by virtue of two fundamental mechanisms: the incorporation of extraneous but useful matter, and the expulsion of matter that is specific to the organism, but harmful. The mind obeys the same rule and its development is subject to the two essential processes of introjection and projection, which no longer concern the interior of the body, but psychic interiority.

Piera Aulagnier (1975), in her own way, describes the fundamental importance of the processes of introjection and projection in the construction of the psyche, and their connection with sensory mechanisms. In the model she proposes, the activity of the "originary", that is to say emerging psychic activity, is based on the sensory model which is characterized by a continuous oscillation between "taking-into-self" and "rejecting-outside-self". Piera Aulagnier extrapolates this double mechanism to all the sensory systems whose function entails the "taking-into-self" of information, a source of excitation and of pleasure, and the attempt to "reject-outside-oneself" that same information when it is a source of unpleasure. In psychoanalytic terms, "taking-into-self" and "rejecting-outside-self" may be translated by the *cathexis* and *decathexis* of that of which we are informed, and of the object of excitation, the source of this information. We can say that, following an experience of meeting and forming a link with an external object, introjection consists in establishing this object within the mind. More than the object, it is the *link with the object* that is introjected. It is the assimilation of the "experience of togetherness", as Martha Harris (1977, p. 270) puts it, that makes it possible to face up to the rupture due to absence.

Furthermore, the internalization of objects through the process of introjection has identificatory effects. We can therefore speak of *introjective identification* to describe the experience of the ego that takes possession of objects through identification. Not only does the ego take possession of objects but it develops itself, deploys itself and grows through introjection. Introjection thus plays a role in constituting the ego.

These comments will gradually become clearer in the course of the book. Let us now try to describe from a phenomenological point of view this process involved in the concept of identification.

1.2 Phenomenological approach

Introjection consists, then, for the ego, in setting up the object within itself. This process has the consequence of abandoning the object in the concrete world, and introjection can occur when the situation of object-loss arises: the abandoned, absent object is set up within the ego; it is introjected. Likewise, the infant can abandon the external object, the external source of gratification, if he has established a gratifying internal object. Thus, for example, the baby who sucks his thumb "remembers" his past pleasures in suckling at the breast and feels in actual contact with the desired breast.

Infant observation according to Esther Bick's method can provide material that helps us to study and understand the conditions in which introjection seems to occur: it sometimes even makes it possible to observe the moment when processes of introjection come into operation. Martha Harris gives an example of this through sequences of an infant observation.

> Between the age of 3 and 5 weeks, this baby had to suffer the fact that his mother momentarily had less milk. Following this period, he seemed to want to be nourished permanently and when he was not at the breast, he often placed his curled tongue between his lips, thereby filling his mouth. Around the age of 4 months, he seemed to experience terrible distress at the end of each feed, and was visibly frightened that the breast might be withdrawn from him. At this period, he liked to taste solid food and having put food in his mouth by himself, he would push it to the back of his mouth with his thumbs, sucking them greedily while looking incredibly depressed. Sometimes, after these sequences, he seemed to enter into contact with something and would talk to himself in a dialogue that had the intonation of his mother speaking to him and of himself responding; this cheered him up.

Martha Harris suggests that when the intense thumb-sucking, which occurred when the infant was still being nourished, gave way to the little inner conversation,

> he had, as it were, abandoned his attempt to insist on having a false object, a thumb-nipple that would have belonged to him and could have nourished him each time he so wanted, and that instead of this false object he turned towards an internal remembering and had a dialogue with the internalized mother. It was apparently at this point that he had introjected

Introjection and the psychical apparatus

> an experience with the mother, whom he had allowed to have a separate existence in the external world, but with whom he was able to speak in his internal world.
>
> (Meltzer and Harris, 1980, p. 362, translated from the French)

I (A.C.) have observed in an infant aged two and a half months a sequence that seems to reveal the beginning of a process of identification.

> During a family reunion, the infant was sitting on her grandfather's knees and was having an intense conversation with him in a game from which they were both deriving great pleasure. The grandfather was holding in each of his hands one of the baby's hands and he brought his face close to the infant's face while caressing his own cheeks with the baby's hands. This contact between faces was accompanied by joyful vocalizations on the grandfather's part. Then the two faces moved apart and the baby was giggling with joy while gazing intensely at the happy expression on her grandfather's face. The game, in which these two phases alternated, continued for several minutes and the infant and her grandfather continued to derive evident pleasure from it. After this intimate and intense exchange, an uncle took the baby and put her on his knees with her back against his front in such a way that the baby could see all the members of the family involved in a lively discussion in which the grandfather was now taking part. At this point the baby was babbling intensely, laughing, and seemed caught up in an inner dialogue in which one could recognize intonations expressed by the grandfather's voice during their exchange. During this "self-dialogue" in which the baby seemed, in a sort of hallucination, to be reliving the earlier exchange with the grandfather, she accompanied her vocalizations with uncoordinated movements of her arms and hands in an attempt to bring them together.

Through these attempts at establishing links, the baby is staging the internalization of the privileged relationship that she has just woven with this object of the mothering environment in the form of the grandfather. She is trying to "psychicize" this experience. In his quasi-hallucinatory play, she is dialoguing with that which is in the process of becoming an internal object.

It should be noted, moreover, that each time the grandfather speaks, taking part in the lively family discussion, the baby stops her play instantaneously, stops moving and is extremely attentive to her grandfather's voice, but without looking at him. She only resumes her activity again when he stops talking. It seems that, in the course of the process of introjecting the external object or experience, the baby is engaging in a sort of verification or comparison between the actual object and the future internal object, a sort of adjustment of this object that is in the process of becoming an internal object.

Manuel Perez-Sanchez (1981) describes the signs of protest of a one-month-old baby that he was observing as a movement of projection. The baby would kick with its feet and press its face against the breast when it could not find the nipple that it was searching for or when it was suckling a breast from which nothing came. This movement of projection consisted in trying to get rid of the "bad breast".

He explains the fact that, around the age of three months, pleasant experiences of breastfeeding are followed by peaceful moments in which the baby looks around, observes, is interested and happy, in the following way:

> [The baby] *has incorporated his mother's calmness and security* – symbolically speaking, the "good breast" or the "good mother" – and *he is therefore capable of projecting around him* [...] placing his interest on everything that surrounds him, because he has something inside.
> (Perez-Sanchez, 1981, p. 50, author's emphasis)

The baby can be generous and give himself to others because he has introjected a good and secure experience. This process functions in the same way for everyone, child or adult, but the difference with the adult is that he or she can retain the introjection for a long time, whereas the baby needs the presence of the object. If the mother is no longer paying attention to him, he quickly feels uneasy and cries. After moments of physical contact with his mother, of warm interaction, of gratifying exchanges, the baby who can smile to the observer, whose presence is no longer persecuting, shows that "*something has been introjected, assimilated, or incorporated: in concrete terms, a 'good mother', which he is capable of projecting as a 'good object' by means of his friendliness*" (ibid., p. 62, author's italics). This state can gratify the mother and stimulate in her the desire for another exchange reinforcing her sense of being a good mother: "In her turn, the mother introjects the 'good baby', feeling that her identity is that of a 'good mother of a good baby'" (ibid.).

1.3 Introjection and incorporation. Introjective identification and projective identification (with the internal object)

We have discussed the origins of the elaboration of the notion of introjection, origins that concern among others Freud's contributions on mourning and melancholia. We have pointed out that what Freud says about introjection, in the case of melancholia, seems to describe a failure of introjection more than a real introjection. This point is essential.

If we follow up this idea, it will lead us to differentiate between the different processes of internalization with regard to their nature, their qualities, the fate they reserve for internal objects, and thus the subjective experience that they produce. These processes concern *introjection*, on the one hand, and *incorporation* on the other.

When Freud describes melancholic introjection (1917, 1921, 1923), he is clarifying the process of *narcissistic identification* (having, in the preceding decades, identified the hysterical aspects of identification).[3] Through narcissistic identification, the object-cathexis regresses to the oral phase of the libido which still belongs to narcissism. To give up the object, the ego adopts the features of the object, it introjects it, identifies with it, likens itself with it. This secondary identification gives greater complexity to a form of identification that Freud calls "primary" (1923), and which is operative at a period when object-cathexis and identification cannot be distinguished, at a period, then, we could say, when the ego does not know the object, when the ego that cathects the object *is* the object.[4] When the ego discovers the object, it can then negotiate the cathexes coming from the id; it can either accept them or reject them. In the case of abandonment or of object-loss, the ego will be able in particular to set up the object within itself, introject it, identify with the object through a secondary narcissistic identification, the secondary nature of which is debatable with regard to what we are describing as introjection, which, as we shall see, in fact corresponds to an "incorporation".[5] By identifying with the object in this way, the ego forces itself upon the id as a love-object and tries to make good the id's loss by saying: "Look, you can love me too — I am so like the object", as Freud puts it (1923, p. 30).

Thus in the case of object-loss, the ego can have recourse to the earlier measure: equation of the ego and the object. At the same time as the object is abandoned outside, it is copied and sedimented on the inside. We can therefore say that *there is no mourning*. Here mourning merely signifies acceptance that the object is not outside. But melancholic "introjection" does not imply a work of mourning; it even impedes mourning (that is to say the appropriation of the sense of loss). The introjection that Freud describes corresponds, therefore, to a failure of introjection. Identification with the object is a way of mastering the id, of seducing it.

By identifying in this way with lost object-cathexes and sedimenting them within itself, the ego can then find itself menaced and torn between different identifications which, alternately, will monopolize consciousness. The ego thus identifies with objects that both constitute and alienate it, that capture it. While we're on the subject, Freud speaks of *"multiple personalities"*, which may be understood as signs of a real "internal group", as we will refer to it further on (Chapter 4): the multiple personality is the seat of a conflict between different inner characters (what is involved is a real domestic dispute between paternal, maternal, fraternal objects, etc.).

We can thus say that if the ego is constituted by the object, and if narcissism results from the incorporation of objects (the ego and consciousness no longer originate only in perception — see Freud, 1887–1902), these objects can also alienate the ego. Such objects will have to be described not as introjected internal objects but rather as *incorporated internal objects*, incorporated objects constituted not through introjective identification but through *projective identification*. This is what we are going to show, and it is a fundamental distinction. Let us now continue this line of reflection by drawing on the work of Maria Torok and Nicolas Abraham (1987), who have made a very valuable and enlightening contribution with regard to this differentiation between introjection and incorporation.

In her article, "The illness of mourning and the fantasy of the exquisite corpse", Maria Torok (1968) is led to differentiate between *introjection* and *incorporation* in studying the process of mourning. She explains how an object-loss leads to the incorporation within the ego of the object with which the ego partially identifies, making it possible to wait for libidinal adjustment to occur. For her, what is operative in mourning is first and foremost incorporation and not introjection. This incorporation is part of the normal manic reaction of mourning, a reaction which for Freud (1917) is absent from normal mourning, but which other authors, in particular Karl Abraham (1924)[6] or Melanie Klein (1940), recognize as inherent to the normal process of mourning.

What differentiates introjection from incorporation? First of all, Maria Torok points out, introjection is a process and incorporation is a fantasy (Maria Torok and Nicolas Abraham (1972) propose the term "inclusion" to denote the process linked to the fantasy of incorporation). Moreover, introjection does not concern the object, but rather the drives and their vicissitudes of which the object is the aim and the mediator.

Introjection, Torok writes (1968, p. 113), "transforms instinctual promptings into desires and fantasies of desire, making them fit to receive a name and the right to exist and unfold in the objectal sphere".

Introjection does not imply loss. For loss may constitute an unmastered obstacle for introjection. The object is then set up within the ego to compensate for the failed introjection: this is incorporation proper. Incorporation occurs when introjection has failed.

Furthermore, the introjection of desire, of the drive, mediated by the object, occurs openly, whereas the incorporation of the object hides from view, including that of the ego, secrecy being imperative.

The introjection of the instinctual drives leads to an enlargement and enrichment of the ego and puts an end to dependence on the object, whereas incorporation of the object creates or reinforces "imaginal" ties. Introjection has an instantaneous and magical character, akin to hallucination. Its aim is to bring about a magical recuperation of an object that has vanished. Incorporation is a lure that presents itself as the equivalent of an immediate introjection, but one that is purely hallucinatory and illusory.

Introjection and incorporation are thus at odds. The incorporated object shows how the drive and desire have been banished from introjection. But both movements are nonetheless linked, especially at an archaic level, and the fantasy of incorporation must be considered as the sign not only of a failure of introjection but also as a (failed) *attempt* at introjection: the fantasy of incorporation is a way of expressing the desire for introjection. The fantasy of incorporation is, in fact, as Maria Torok points out, the first image by means of which the ego represents its own birth to itself, its own constitution as ego. The fantasy of incorporation is not the reflection of a request to be granted or hunger to be satisfied but as the "disguised language of as yet unborn and unintrojected desires" (ibid., p. 115).

Finally, if introjection produces internal objects, constitutes objects as internal objects, incorporation, for its part, produces *imagos*. The imago portrays everything that has resisted introjection and that the ego has appropriated through incorporation. The imago always serves, says Maria Torok, to prohibit a (sexual) desire. It was established after a satisfaction was initially granted but then withdrawn, and she recalls that, even before being introjected, a desire has become retrospectively reprehensible and shameful. The imago is responsible for torments and sufferings through which desire for the object is revived, desire that is satisfied in them, says Maria Torok. (The models of *crypt* and *phantom* that Abraham and Torok would subsequently develop can easily be recognized in these remarks.)

In their article "Mourning or melancholia" (1972), Nicolas Abraham and Maria Torok write:

> When we ingest the love-object we miss, we shun the consequences of mourning [...]. Incorporation is the refusal to reclaim as our own the part of ourselves that we placed in what we lost the part of oneself contained in what has been lost; incorporation is the refusal to acknowledge the true import of the loss, a loss that, if recognized as such, would effectively transform us. In fine, incorporation is the refusal to introject loss. The fantasy of incorporation reveals a gap within the psyche; it points to something that is missing just where introjection should have occurred.
> (Abraham and Torok, 1972, p. 127)

The introjection that accompanies language, words, sees "the successful replacement of the object's presence with the self's cognizance of its absence" (ibid., p. 128). In incorporation, on the other hand, the object-thing, the unnamed thing is taken itself (in fantasy).

Introjection is compared to learning a language, incorporation to purchasing a dictionary.

In the same vein, Shirley Hoxter writes:

> An introjected object can survive the death of the external object and continue to be a source of life. It can foster further growth [...]. But an object retained in a concrete system of incorporation is a mere possession: once lost it is gone forever.
> (Meltzer et al., 1975, p. 189)

Nicolas Abraham and Maria Torok relate the example of a kleptomaniac boy that one of them had in analysis. This boy had a sister two years older than him who died at the age of eight. Before dying, she had "seduced" him. At puberty, this boy took to stealing bras because his sister would have needed them at the age of 14, he said, after making a slip of the tongue in which he gave himself the age that his sister would have had.

The sister was sheltered alive in the boy's psyche; he carried her within him, alive inside a crypt, a crypt consisting of the shameful secret around forbidden sexual games, a secret shared with this lost object. This boy had incorporated his sister, but the ties linking him to her were not introjected, and his representation of her was impaired. According to the model of the crypt and of the phantom elaborated by Abraham and Torok, the fantasy of incorporation, the authors say, perpetuates a clandestine and shameful pleasure by transforming it into an "intrapsychic secret".[7]

We would like to put forward the following hypothesis, formulated as follows: introjection produces a *representation*, whereas incorporation produces a *perception*. With introjection, we are in a representative world: the introjected object is a representation (a thing-presentation). With incorporation, we are in a quasi-hallucinatory world: the incorporated object is experienced as a perceived rather than represented object.

In spite of the indications and clarifications furnished by Maria Torok, we will retain the expression "introjection of the *object*", connected with Kleinian language, which accounts for the way that the environment is internalized. But we will stress the idea that, more than the environment, it is *experience* that is internalized; more than the object, it is the *link to the object* — with the drive vicissitudes that underpin it along with the desires and conflicts that are operant within it — that is introjected. Introjection concerns objects but also *object-relations*.[8]

In connection still with the suggestions of Abraham and Torok, and in order to take the modelization of early identificatory processes further, we will formulate another hypothesis: it may be said that what Abraham and Torok describe with regard to incorporation is based on a process of *projective identification*. The difference that they highlight between introjection and incorporation overlaps with the difference between introjective identification and projective identification.

The introjected object is an integrated object; it enriches the ego. The incorporated object alienates the ego. When the object is incorporated, its qualities are felt and experienced as qualities of the ego. The ego integrates with its structure the introjected object, but it subjects its identity to the constraints of the incorporated object. If the ego integrates the introjected object, it is gathered together (in whole or in part) within the incorporated object: the subject identifies projectively with the incorporated object, deploying the fantasy of having entered the body of the other person. In other words, if the introjected object is the fruit — and the effect — of an integrating (introjective) identificatory process, the incorporated object is the fruit — and the effect — of an alienating (projective) identificatory process.

It is worth recalling, moreover, that Melanie Klein (1952a), who considers that projective identification rests essentially on urethral and anal sadism (projecting substances and bad parts into the maternal body), links projective identification with oral sadism (emptying the maternal body of what is good and desirable), which she describes not in terms of incorporation but rather of the *sadistic and voracious introjection of the breast*. She explains that suckling as an "act of vampirism", which consists in exhausting the breast, permits the infant to nourish the fantasy of finding a way to get inside the breast, and then inside the mother's body.

Furthermore, and as we shall see later on, projective identification, from a psychogenetic point of view, precedes introjective identification (it is not a matter of a succession of exclusive identificatory modes, but of the primacy of a certain type of identificatory process at a given moment of development, or in a particular situation of psychic work). This, indeed, is what seems to occur in mourning where projective identification – in other words, the incorporation of the lost object, in Maria Torok's terms – precedes introjective identification, that is to say successful mourning. And we know that projective identification is a characteristic of the manic position, which is coherent with the picture defended by Maria Torok or Melanie Klein of a normal manic reaction in the work of mourning.

It may be said that the process is the same for any form of mourning, that is to say, for any form of learning, for any teacher/pupil, nurturer/nourished or analyst/analysand relationship. Before introjecting, that is to say, internalizing, integrating, mental food, knowledge, etc., each subject incorporates, in other words identifies projectively with his teacher, nourishes the fantasy of entering his body and behaves as if he were the teacher. It is only subsequently that incorporation yields to introjection, that projective identification gives way to introjective identification.

If projective identification is not too destructive, the experience of the one who receives it may be expressed as follows: "I speak, I think, and I am as if I were the other person". If destructivity is particularly active, degradation is added to projection because of envy, which gives: "I speak, I think, I am as if I were better than the other person". The subject places himself inside the other person, without recognizing need or dependence, and steals his thought by acting as if it were his own, as if instantly and magically he had become as powerful, as knowledgeable and as adult as the other person (as he imagines him or her). The subject has incorporated the object; he has introjected nothing. What is involved here is pathological projective identification, incorporation as described by Abraham and Torok.[9]

Incorporation thus appears to be necessary to introjection, just as projective identification is necessary to introjective identification. The transition from one to the other, that is, the transition from the status of imago or of incorporated object to the status of introjected internal object, represents the essence of the process of mental development, and of the process of care, and more particularly of the analytic process. However, this transition remains particularly complex. We will try to throw light on it on successive occasions.

Let us take our reflection further. We will come back later to the process of projective identification (Chapters 11 and 12), but we can already say that three forms of projective identification will be identified: the first consists in communicating with the other person by making him experience and feel emotions and feelings that are uncontainable, incomprehensible and unrepresentable for oneself – beta elements (Bion, 1962ab) –, and in thus being dependent on the psychical apparatus, the apparatus for thinking of the other person; the second consists in getting rid of a part of oneself, of bad, persecutory feelings, but also of good, helpful feelings, by evacuating them into an object and attributing them to this object; the third form of projective identification consists in penetrating the object in fantasy (anal and urethral sadism), and in nourishing the illusion of being the object, of having emptied it of its substance, of having incorporated it (oral sadism), which is reflected by a disturbance in the sense of identity. The first form represents a normal process of projective identification, which may become pathological if it is exclusive or excessive. The second and third forms represent a pathological projective identification in itself, but one that functions in the normal development of every psyche. The second form is an effect – and a cause – of persecution. The third form is an effect of envy. Only the first form requires the presence of two protagonists; the second and third forms can operate in the absence of the real external object.

In effect, projective identification can occur almost exclusively with internal objects, as in delusional states where the subject lives within a magic world,[10] or in "false-self" organizations, where the subject incorporates the qualities of another, or rather the superficial characteristics of the qualities of another, at the price of the abandonment or murder of his own self. It nonetheless concerns external objects on account of the *acting out* directed towards them – as, for example, in parasitism – or on account of the ties of dependence in which they are involved – as in the exercise of "alpha function" as described by Bion (1962ab).

We can now clarify our hypothesis and say that incorporation is underpinned by a process of *projective identification with an internal object that has the status of an incorporated object*. In 1966, Donald Meltzer developed the idea of projective identification with internal objects (we will come back to this in Chapter 11). This corresponds to what Didier Houzel (1985b) considers as a form of "narcissistic introjection", which is different from introjective identification proper, and functions at the level of the boundary between the internal space of the self and the internal space of internal objects.

If we accept the clarifications offered by Nicolas Abraham and Maria Torok, we can say that the internal object with which the self is in projective identification (like the deceased sister continuing to live on in the psyche of the boy cited in the example above) has a status of *imago*. Nicolas Abraham (1987), in an essay aimed at removing the confusion between the concepts of identification and introjection, describes identification with an external object or with an imago in terms of narcissistic identification when this identification is not used to introject a relationship, but realizes the ideal lent to the imago. However, "this [narcissistic identification] is not in the order of introjection but rather of projection" (Abraham, 1987, p. 130, translated for this edition). This lends support to our hypothesis that incorporation corresponds to a process of projective identification with an internal object or rather an imago.

The process of projective identification with an internal object – or an imago – consists in getting inside an object that is itself situated within the psyche and which represents an incorporated object, both in the absence and the presence of the real external object. This may be a way of avoiding separation, mourning, or a first stage in the work of mourning (corresponding to the manic phase of the work of mourning), as Donald Meltzer explains:

> for the child in projective identification, experience of separation can be completely obviated by turning to intrude into his internal object in the absence of the external one.
> (Meltzer, in Meltzer et al., 1975, p. 231–232)

Incorporation, projective identification with an internal object, is a potentially alienating process. It can lead, as we have seen, to the formation of a "false-self", to delusion, etc. André Green (1988) describes well these states of alienation to an internal object, of possession by an internal object that destroys the subject, states that we also come across in the "false-self" organization, depressive and delusional manifestations, psychopathy, etc. Green highlights the distinction between an object fundamentally linked to narcissism, the loss of which would be irreparable or highly damaging and would entail a major risk of depression, and an object "less welded to the ego", more independent, more external to it, which would be more replaceable, more substitutable. He is clearly describing here a distinctive characteristic between the *alienating incorporated object* and the *integrated internal object*.

Furthermore, while it has been said that incorporation precedes introjection in the work of mourning, we think it is also possible to apply this model to the development of thought. Before being able to think, that is to say to represent the absent object, the baby, prey to bad sensations due to need combined with the absence of the object that is a source of satisfaction, hallucinates the breast in order to evacuate these bad feelings. He hallucinates the breast – when he can, for if his anxiety is too catastrophic or lasts too long, no mental activity can emerge – and the experience of satisfaction, the *gestalt* of satisfying experiences, in a movement of auto-generation on the part of omnipotent narcissism. In fact, he is himself the breast; that is to say, the psyche is gathered inside the breast-that-is-within-itself-and-auto-generated by it, and that represents an incorporated object. We spoke above about the proximity between the fantasy of incorporation and hallucinatory processes: hallucination, just like delusions or dreams, can be understood as a state of more or less total projective identification with an incorporated internal object. It is only after a long work of introjection and construction of internal objects that are sufficiently integrated, fortified and helpful, that these hallucinatory processes will gradually give way to thought, that is to say, to the possibility for the psyche to represent to itself the absence, the object that is absent and preoccupied by an elsewhere that is still unrepresentable, without this absence or the unrepresentability of this elsewhere constituting a danger of annihilation for the psyche.

A process of "normal" projective identification is thus necessary for all introjection. Every psychic object undergoing a process of introjection is subject, initially, to such a process of projective identification, which will gradually yield in order to guarantee a non-alienating destiny for the psychic object.

1.4 Conclusion

> These mechanisms of introjection and projection represent not only an essential part of the function of the ego, they are the roots of the ego, the instruments for its very formation.
> (Heimann, 1952a, p. 126)

Introjection "fabricates" ego; it has an identificatory effect and results in an "egoification of the object", as Jean Florence (1978) would say. This introjective identification by means of which the ego appropriates objects and their attendant ties with their charge of impulses, desires and conflicts, is constitutive of psychic objects and creates objects that have a particular quality: they are living objects that nourish and develop the ego.[11]

Identificatory introjection establishes the object in the ego and integrates it with the ego; but at the same time, it "unwelds" the object from the ego. Indeed, in order not to be too alienating, the internalized object must not be too linked to narcissism, too "welded to the ego", to use the expression of André Green (1988) mentioned earlier. Otherwise, the internalized object will have the status of an incorporated object, with alienating, confusing and symbiotic effects. It may be said that the introjected object *is transformed* by the ego, whereas the incorporated object *transforms* the ego and alienates it (see Ciccone, 1997a, 2012a). The boundary between the introjected internal object and the incorporated internal object situates the zone of transition, of inflection, from introjective identification to projective identification, and, in a certain way, from mental health to psychopathology.

Moreover, though the definition of introjection can presuppose a distinction between one ego and another ego, between an inside and an outside, it must be emphasized, and Paula Heimann, along with others, and later Esther Bick, show this clearly, how much this process is inherent to the very formation of the ego. The incipient ego is defined by the first introjections of another psychic entity. Thus "the infant's first sucking is then neither an id-activity nor an ego activity; it is both, it is an activity of the incipient ego" (Heimann, 1952a, p. 128). Likewise, all psychic progress is considered to be the result of the increasing introjection by the infant of his immediate circle (or more precisely of object-relations and their vicissitudes).

Introjection and introjective identification are linked metonymically to oral experience (while projection and projective identification take up the anal perspective of the object-relation). Orality is the seat of the baby's first perceptions. The sensations of receiving via the mouth, of sucking, swallowing and vomiting, leave their mark on all the other experiences. Furthermore, oral experience attracts and concentrates all the other concomitant sensory and emotional experiences in their situation of being – or feeling – contained. We will speak further on of the "attracting containing object" (Houzel, 1985b, 1987) and of "consensual experience" (Meltzer et al., 1975).

First postulate

This experience of "being gathered together", during sucking, for example, gives the baby the feeling of being contained in a container. This feeling, heightened by the progressive introjection of the container, or of the containing function, is the prerequisite for all later introjection. It constitutes the basic sense of identity and underlies individuation and the distinction between internal and external spaces.

At this stage of mental life the process of introjection is not defined as the fantasized transition of an object from an outside towards an inside, but as the very construction of the boundary delimiting the inside and the outside through the loan of the containing function that the emerging psyche makes from the external object, which is only external from the observer's point of view. The containing function will be introjected and established on the inside due to the very fact that it will delimit the inside.

In other words, the introjection of an object, of a content, presupposes the introjection of a container, of a containing object, of a containing function.[12]

We are now going to explore the characteristics of this containing object, in its first or primary form.

Notes

1 This chapter was written solely by Albert Ciccone.
2 It is worth recalling here the work of Béla Grunberger (1975) in which he describes the permanent conflict between the ego and the ego-ideal reflected in melancholic depression.
3 On the notion of identification in Freud's thought, and its relation to current conceptions concerning the modes of projective identification, see Ciccone, 2012a.
4 As Freud was to say in 1938: "'The breast is a part of me, I am the breast'. Only later: 'I have it' – that is, 'I am not it'" (1941b [1938], p. 299).
5 In his study of the object-relation, Brusset (1988) notes that in melancholia the identification of the ego with the lost object, just like identification with the ideal object in mania, occurs in a *primary mode*. This is characterized on the one hand by the deployment of a fantasy of oral incorporation and, on the other, the predominance of an affective, emotional process whose logic is to exclude representation.

Introjection and the psychical apparatus

6 See, also, in the Freud–Abraham correspondence (Falzeder, 2002), Abraham's letters dated 13 March 1922 and 2 May 1922.
7 On the crypt, the phantom and their relations with projective identification, see Ciccone, 2012a.
8 We may recall once again the work of Bernard Brusset (1988), for example, who has developed a conception of the psychic personality considered as the result of the internalization of object relations.
9 As Anne Alvarez (1992) says: "In 'introjective identification' the new identity is not stolen, but earned or even received as a gift from a friendly well-treated object" (Alvarez, 1992, p. 178).
10 Herbert Rosenfeld (1970) considers that delusional states evidence projective identification with internal "delusional objects".
11 I have shown elsewhere how the proposition that the mode of identification (introjective, projective, adhesive) determines the nature and the destiny of the psychic object must be completed, within an intersubjective perspective opening on to psychic transmission, by the proposition that the nature of the object itself is decisive with regard to the mode of identification employed by the ego to take possession of this object in order to internalize it (Ciccone, 1997a, 2012a).
12 A comparison could be made between what André Green (1975, 1983) describes concerning the introjection of the "framing structure" of maternal care through the mother's "negative hallucination" and what we are saying about the introjection of the containing function – but on the condition, obviously, that one speaks of mothering care (and not "maternal") and the "negative hallucination of the mothering object" (and not of the "mother"). This negative aspect represents the background necessary for the positive aspect of the object relation.

2

THE FIRST CONTAINING EXTERNAL OBJECT

The momentary object

In her text, "The experience of skin in early object-relations" (1968), Esther Bick writes:

> The need for a containing object would seem, in the infantile unintegrated state, to produce a frantic search for an object, – a light, a voice, a smell or other sensual object – which can hold the attention and thereby be experienced, momentarily at least, as holding the parts of the personality together. The optimal object is the nipple in the mouth, together with the holding and talking and familiar smelling mother.
> (Bick, 1968, in Harris and Bick, 1987, p. 115)

This statement will lead us to denote and describe two types of containing object which we will differentiate: the *"optimal object"* and the *"momentary object"*. The momentary object, which is a sensual object, must make way, as a containing object, for the optimal object the prototype of which arises from the experience of feeding, in a satisfying and secure sensory and emotional context.

The need for a containing object is constant. Until the baby has internalized the optimal object, he will not be able to turn to this object within him during the absence of the real external object. He will therefore "cling" to a sensation, to a momentary sensual object. He will give up this sensual fixation thanks to the sufficiently repeated and sufficiently good experience of secure sucking, an experience that he will then be able to introject, a sort of prototype of containing experiences.

2.1 Momentary object and autistic object. Auto-sensuality and autism

Before the optimal object is internalized by virtue of this repetition of the containing experience, along with sufficient rhythmicity, the infant clings to a momentary object. This statement will lead us to develop the notion of "autistic object" elaborated by Frances Tustin and to look at autistic manoeuvres. Indeed, the detour via pathology often facilitates the understanding and representation of normal processes; the exploration of autistic manoeuvres will thus enable us to appreciate the function of the processes of recourse to the momentary object. Before considering the notions of autistic object and manoeuvres, we must clarify the picture Tustin gives of autistic states. From 1972 up until her last contributions in 1994 she was constantly affirming and clarifying her ideas.

Let us note from the outset the differentiation Tustin made between what she first called "normal autism" and "pathological autism", and then "auto-sensuous state" and "autistic state". In the introduction to the French edition of her book *Autistic States in Children* (1981b), Tustin explained her reasons for having used the word "autism" to describe both normal and pathological states of infancy. She thought she had wrongly given the impression that she considered infancy as a passive, inactive state, rather than as the state of active quest that it quite clearly is. Considering that the word "autism" had been associated so much with pathological states, Tustin thought that it could no longer be employed to describe normal states. She therefore suggested that the terms "autism" and "autistic" be reserved for pathological states and that the terms "auto-sensuality" and "auto-sensual" be used to denote normal states (see also Tustin, 1991a). We share this observation and this epistemological choice. That is why, as we shall see, we will use the notion of "auto-sensual position" to name what had first been called by some, in particular following the contributions of Tustin, "autistic position". Equally, as will become clear in the following chapters, we will rename the paranoid-schizoid position described by Melanie Klein as the "symbiotic position", for the terms "paranoid" and "schizoid" are too redolent of psychopathology.

But these terminological reflections in no way detract from the pertinence of the descriptions of the mental state that characterizes the baby, with the anxieties he faces, the defences he uses, and the mode of relating to the world that these generate.

2.1.1 Definition and description of autism

The conceptions of Frances Tustin, along with those of Donald Meltzer which we will also have the opportunity of presenting in detail, are authoritative in the field of the psychoanalytic approach to autism. They are a reference for many practitioners of autism and provide support on a daily basis for practices of various orientations (therapeutic, pedagogical and educational). The French school has drawn inspiration extensively from Tustin's thought and her great experience, and its main representatives (Geneviève Haag, Didier Houzel), whom we will also mention on several occasions, have worked directly with her and trained with her.

2.1.1.1 The autism debate

Before presenting some of Tustin's conceptions, it is worth recalling just how much of a "hot topic" autism is, an object of often passionate theoretical or ideological debates. Tustin's conceptions, and psychoanalytic conceptions in general, developed and continue to develop in a context in which there is a multiplication of studies, in particular Anglo-Saxon, in the neuropsychological or neurophysiological field; studies that nourish controversies, in particular concerning the aetiological question, between the advocates of a psychogenetic causality and those of an organic causality of autism. Much is at stake since the question concerns parental guilt. But these controversies are often misplaced because causality is a very complex notion that should never be envisaged in a simplistic or linear fashion – in any case, this is not how it is viewed by the psychoanalytic point of view on autism developed by Tustin, Meltzer and their pupils.[1] It is reasonable to suppose that the debates – theoretical, often ideological, and always political – around autism simply concentrate and focus on this pathology, for various reasons, all the conflictual questions raised by the approach of psychopathology in general, and infantile psychopathology in particular. Autism, in fact, remains a rare disorder,[2] but the questions that it raises may be considered as paradigmatic for all the questions raised by psychopathology in general and infantile psychopathology in particular. Autism may thus be considered as a focal point for epistemological debates on psychopathology; hence the scale of the debates around autism and their sometimes groundless character.

To say a few brief words now on the neuropsychological and neurophysiological propositions and theories that have given rise to many studies, especially in recent years,[3] that develop essentially cognitive hypotheses, leading to the conception of autism as a so-called neuro-developmental disorder. The authors of these research studies describe in a detailed and precise manner the multiple disorders of autistic children, highlighting the *cognitive deficits*, which are considered as basic disorders and explained in terms of organic, neurophysiological dysfunctioning (Wing, 1976; Damasio and Maurer, 1978; Rutter, 1981a, 1983; Rogers and Pennington, 1991, etc.). Some adhere to a clearly developmental perspective and produce comparative studies of autistic development and of normal psychological development with a view to better underscoring the impairment of the higher cognitive functions in autism (Wenar et al., 1986; Sauvage et al., 1988).

Current neuropsychological conceptions set out, with a view to explaining autism, to define specific deficits of certain cognitive or social capacities (cognitive capacities, social capacities or the cognitive capacities involved in the development of social relations are impacted). The altered capacities concern representation, imitation, understanding, symbolic play, joint attention (Hammes and Langdell, 1981; Ungerer and Sigman, 1981; Baron-Cohen et al., 1985, 1992; Sigman and Mundy, 1987; Hobson, 1989, 1993, etc.). Certain studies emphasize specific and narrowly focused deficits considered as central for explaining autistic disorder. Several explanatory models are thus available, each organized around one or several specific cognitive deficits. Jean-Louis Adrien (1996), for instance, has outlined a few of them.

We thus have the model of the deficit of *joint attention* (Sigman and Mundy, 1987; Mundy and Sigman, 1989; Mundy, Sigman and Kasari, 1994). Joint attention is a notion that we owe to Jérôme Bruner (1975) and refers to attention focused by two people on the same visual object. Joint attention consists in sharing an event with another person, in attracting the attention of another person towards an object with the aim of achieving shared contemplation.

The capacity for joint attention can be observed, for instance, in the baby gazing in the direction of his partner's gaze, or who points his finger to show the partner an object that is a source of interest (protodeclarative pointing),[4] or who uses "the referential gaze"[5] (alternately gazing at an interesting object and at the adult nearby). We know, for instance, that at eight months the infant is capable of localizing the source of his partner's attention in space, if the latter is in his field of vision (Scaife and Bruner, 1975), and at 18 months, irrespective of where this source is (Butterworth and Cochran, 1980). Joint attention deficit in the autistic child, as conceived by Marian Sigman and her collaborators, consists in an alteration of the reciprocal affective exchange, in the sense in which Colwyn Trevarthen (1979) speaks about it when he describes intersubjective emotion sharing.

We also have the model of a failure to develop a *theory of mind* (Baron-Cohen, Leslie and Frith, 1985; Frith, 1989; Frith, Morton and Leslie, 1991). The theory of mind (a term coined by Premack and Woodruff, 1978) denotes the recognition of mental states in oneself and others, the recognition of a way of thinking in others that is different from one's own. A certain number of experimental situations make it possible to test the existence and functionality of a theory of mind in the child. One of the best known is perhaps the "Sally-Ann" test (developed by Wimmer and Perner, 1983). In this test a skit is enacted involving two dolls (Sally and Anne), each of which has an object that they put in a certain place; one of the dolls goes away; meanwhile, the second takes the object of the first doll and hides it in another place; when the first doll returns, the children being tested are asked where she will look for her object; the children, of course, answer that she will look for it in the place where she herself left it, given that she is not aware of the substitution. This test, and others with variants, demonstrates the clear development of a theory of mind in the child at four years of age. Simon Baron-Cohen and his collaborators have demonstrated the lack of such a capacity in the autistic child. Even if the cognitive level of the autistic child tested is high, and even if his capacities for recognizing social relations are adequate (apart from those based on a theory of mind), his aptitudes for developing a theory of mind are disturbed (Baron-Cohen, 1991). Furthermore, studies on the origins of the theory of mind highlight the way in which it implies a capacity for "pretence" (Leslie, 1987).

Another model of central deficit in autism is that of the deficit of *emotional regulation* (Trevarthen, 1989a). In this model, the affective indifference of the autistic child is considered as the sign of a fundamental and early deficit in the production and regulation of emotions. Such a central deficit, whose origin is held to be biological and due to brain regulatory system dysfunction, produces impairments of all the functions that rely on emotional sharing, such as joint attention and imitation.

Other studies describe an array of dysfunctions pertaining to different capacities (imitation, emotion sharing, the development of a theory of mind), the prototypical capacity of which would be one that consists in *forming and coordinating representations*, as these dysfunctions are always underpinned by a biological defect (Rogers and Pennington, 1991). Still others highlight a deficit in the *development of* the "*interpersonal self*" (Hobson, 1993): this is an early elective deficit concerning the intimate experience of oneself in relation to others, that is to say the experience of intersubjective emotional contact (Trevarthen, 1979), of affective bonding (Stern, 1985). Others, finally, insist on specific disorders of *imitation* (De Myer et al., 1972; Sigman and Ungerer, 1984; Jones and Prior, 1985; Stone et al., 1990; Nadel, 1992).

In short, whatever predominance is ascribed to this or that deficit, the conception of these researchers is always a deficit-based conception, and the deficits affect functions or behaviours that are linked to each other and interdependent, such as social interest, representation, imitation, pretend play, protodeclarative pointing, joint attention, emotional sharing and the theory of mind.

All these neuropsychological studies provide skilful descriptions of the different symptoms of the autistic child. Most of them had already been described, as we shall see, with just as much skill, and often greater complexity, by psychoanalysts who were interested in autism, even if they were not named in the same way. If certain neuropsychological points of view dispute psychoanalytic theories (particularly by insisting that autism should always be considered as a neurological disability), others concur without difficulty with psychoanalytic theses (Hobson, 1989, 1993).

But the psychoanalytic point of view is based, of course, on a different conception of psychic reality, and is more concerned with affective, emotional and fantasy life, without however excluding biological reality. Tustin, for example, always allowed for the fact that potential organic disorders could be at the origin of certain forms of autism. Moreover, in her psychogenetic conception she speaks of a predisposition linked to the genetic constitution or to intra-uterine experience (Tustin, 1990), of the "hypersensibility" of the baby (Tustin, 1981b, 1990), just as Meltzer speaks of "inadequate equipment" (Meltzer et al., 1975), terms that plainly contain the idea of a particular constitutional functioning which may originate partly in biological reality. In this context, autism is seen as the effect of a reaction to a situation of major, primitive or agonistic anxiety, irrespective of the reasons that lead to such a scale of anxiety and to the predominance of such a reaction.

Autism as a *defence* is thus often contrasted with autism as a *deficit*, the first proposition being the presupposition of the psychoanalytic point of view, the second of the neuropsychological and organicist point of view. The autistic reaction is considered by psychoanalysts as a measure of protection against a danger experienced as catastrophic. But it needs to be added that if it is a defence, the autistic manoeuvre consists above all in a "compensatory" utilization of the weak defences available: it is a matter of "making do with less than enough", as Anne Alvarez (1992, p. 189) says.

Although the explanatory theories and models diverge, they nevertheless often try to establish areas of convergence. Psychoanalysts increasingly take into account the specific modes of processing information and of sharing mental states in the child or the autistic subject (see, for example, Hochmann, Ferrari et al., 1992; Misès and Grand, 1997; Alvarez et al., 1999; Amy et al., 2014, 2016), and cognitivists sometimes take into account the emotional dimensions in subjective experience and in intersubjective relations (see, for example, Hobson, 1993). Though the models can be linked up and prove complementary, they nonetheless remain in tension and nourish contradictory debates that are sometimes violent, but potentially creative.[6]

2.1.1.2 *The model of Frances Tustin*

Let us move on now to the conception of autism developed by Frances Tustin (1972 to 1994b). Frances Tustin defined autism as a state where auto-induced sensuality reigns, and where attention is directed almost exclusively towards sensations and bodily rhythms. The child's interest is caught by external objects, but they are experienced as part of his own body or as closely associated with it. They are taken as an extension of bodily activity governed by sensation. "Sensation-objects", which are not recognized as distinct from the body, subsequently foster the perception of the "not-me", under the protection of "mothering" care. This early period during which external objects are experienced as "sensation-objects" was first called *primary normal autism* (we will come back to this notion in Chapter 5), and then *phase of auto-sensuality*.

The changeover into "pathological" autism, or into autism itself, results, for Tustin, from an intense and premature awareness in the infant of separateness from the mother's body at a moment when his neuropsychical apparatus is not sufficiently developed to enable him to deal with this experience. This "psychological prematurity" arises from an encounter between a "hypersensitive" child and a mothering environment that is hard put to dampen the shocks due to awareness of bodily separateness.[7] The infant experiences this separation as a loss of a part of his own body and is invaded by primitive dreads, such as falling, being emptied, exploding and being annihilated. Tustin assumes that if the environment cannot contain the experiences of bodily separation that confront the baby with an environment where "black holes" open up, that leave him in a state of "nameless dread" (Bion, 1962a), the baby is then led increasingly to use the sensations of his own body, to manipulate/engender autistic objects and to create autistic shapes.

Autistic protective manoeuvres are devised to organize everything in terms of comforting auto-sensuality. The external world, instead of being a stimulating factor for the child's development, becomes an object of negation or confusion with the sensation-object. The utilization of autistic objects and shapes entails a delusion of perfect satisfaction and integrity, and leads the child to reject his mothering object because it is never as available, magical and mechanical as his idiosyncratic creations.

For the autistic child, the sense of security depends on the illusion of exerting absolute control over a fragment of his body or an object that he feels is a part of his own body. Only that which can be controlled and manipulated in a "tangible" way seems to him real and safe. This is why emotional states, for example, which cannot be manipulated concretely, will seem unreal to him or will be felt to be very dangerous bodily substances. For an autistic child emotion is either an enigma – he cannot see what the issue is – or a concrete danger and he turns away from it. The same goes for imaginary or fantasy-based productions and capacities in these domains (which draw in particular on memory, reflection and play) are thus relatively unexploited, unused.

Autistic pathology is the mark, then, of a non-encounter between the child and the world, a failure in the establishment of a primary human contact capable of relieving the child of the normal terrors with which every newborn is faced, terrors that are experienced in an exaggerated way due to the constitutional hypersensitivity of the child. These terrors stem from experiencing the loss of the object as a loss of the body, as an amputating and annihilating catastrophic separation. The chief threat in autism is that of "non-being"; the child protects himself against the terror of not existing any more, which is different from the fear of dying. As Tustin (1990, p. 39) says, "losing the sense of existence is far worse than dying".

Autistic manoeuvres engender the illusion of being encapsulated in a shell. This "auto-generated encapsulation" immobilizes psychic functioning and, consequently, halts cognitive and affective development. Moreover, encapsulation "preserves" the traumatic experience (as David Rosenfeld (1986) says) from the bodily separation with the object, an experience that can be evoked or treated again if a suitable situation to do so presents itself, for example, a psychotherapy.[8]

2.1.2 Autistic manoeuvres

Frances Tustin describes the manoeuvres to which the child has recourse when the containing function of the mothering environment is faulty or when the child turns away from his mothering environment. She distinguishes between the utilization of autistic objects and autistic shapes (which she was to call autistic *sensation-objects* and *sensation-shapes* (Tustin, 1990)).

2.1.2.1 Autistic objects or sensation-objects

Autistic objects are experienced by the child as belonging to his own body. They are always hard objects and it is the sensation of hardness that is important for the child. They can be represented by external objects or by hard bodily substances produced by the child in his body (hard faeces, dried snot). Tustin distinguishes autistic objects from confusional objects (we know that she differentiates between encapsulated autism and confusional autism). If autistic objects are hard, confusional objects tend to be soft. The function of autistic objects is to maintain the illusion of a shell and completely obstruct any awareness of the "not-me"; confusional objects, on the other hand, lead to the illusion of being enveloped in mist; they blur awareness of the difference between me and not-me, but do not obliterate it completely.

These kinds of object and this way of using objects are normal in infancy when the baby makes little distinction between his body and the external world, between his mouth and the breast that is experienced as an array of sensations (justifying the expression "normal" autism). "Sensation-objects" provoke illusory delights from which the environment will have to distance the infant in order to attract his attention towards desire for the "breast", for the world, for other people. If this attraction fails or is impossible, such a use of objects may become fixed and pathological. The difference between normal auto-sensual objects and pathological autistic objects lies in the stereotyped and fixed use of the latter and the absence of associated fantasies. Pathological autistic objects are not associated with any fantasies or, if so, with very crude fantasies, akin to physical sensations. They have their origin in hidden auto-sensual activities and Tustin speaks of infants who suck their rolled-up tongue or the inside of their cheeks, or who wriggle their bottom in order to feel their faeces in their rectum, and so on. The autistic object diverts the infant from the actual breast and is used to accommodate unbearable frustration. But it represents a major handicap for the development of thought, memory and imagination which normally compensate for the inevitable absence of total satisfaction. The autistic object does not attain the status of object; rather, it represents a sensation aimed at filling the "black hole", at saving the infant from the devastating experience linked to the loss of the nipple that is felt to be an integral part of his mouth.

2.1.2.2 *Autistic shapes or sensation-shapes*[9]

Autistic shapes are sensations that the child creates, most of the time secretly, from soft bodily substances or bodily movements, and which constitute a sort of tranquilliser. They are reassuring and soothing and, after an explosion of anger or ecstasy, extreme states that are unbearable for the autistic child, these shapes give him the impression that they are caressing, flattering and calming him. Unlike autistic objects that are hard, autistic shapes are soft and amorphous. These auto-generated and idiosyncratic shapes fascinate the child who has absolute power over them. They avert perception of bodily separation.

Just as Frances Tustin distinguished between autistic objects and confusional objects, we propose to differentiate *autistic shapes* from what we will call *confusional shapes*. While the autistic form procures a soothing sensation diverting consciousness from the terrifying "not-me", the confusional shape blurs perception of this same "not-me".

As for autistic objects, such shapes or "trace-sensations" are used in the development of the normal baby. They are fabricated, in the baby as well as the older child, from bodily movements, but above all from bodily substances such as the soft faeces in the rectum, food in the mouth, snot in the nose, saliva, and so on, as well as equivalents of these substances such as sand, modelling clay, etc. What is important is not the substance or its equivalent in themselves, but rather the fact that they produce shapes. In normal development, interest is quickly directed towards the real object that produces or induces these shapes, resulting in the formation of concepts. The object takes part in an exchange and can be shared. Normal shapes can be identified and "classified". In the autistic child, these shapes structure sensual experiences, but in an aberrant or ineffective way. They cannot be exchanged and shared with others, and do not lead to any conceptual elaboration.

2.1.2.3 *Auto-sensual clinging to proprioception, to "thought" (or psychic excitation)*

Let us now differentiate among autistic manoeuvres, in order to better delineate them, the recourse to autistic objects and shapes employing external objects or detached parts of the body or parts in appendage, and the autistic utilization of interoceptive sensibility and, more precisely, of proprioception, a manoeuvre that we refer to by the term *auto-sensual proprioceptive clinging*. We will distinguish two forms of proprioceptive clinging: the first (tonic clinging) may be likened to the use of autistic objects; the second (kinaesthetic clinging) is a way of creating autistic forms.

- *Clinging to the hypertonia* of contracted musculature is revealed through a muscular shell to which the child clings in order to feel unified and gathered together in his mental life. They lead to the formation of the "muscular second skin" of which Esther Bick speaks. The hardness of the contracted musculature (which provokes movements of postural withdrawal giving a typical appearance to certain autistic children) has the same function as the hardness of the autistic object, as envisaged by Tustin.
- *Kinaesthetic clinging* includes all the motor rhythms: swaying (of the whole body or of certain segments like the head, the hands, the legs, etc.), gestural stereotypies, repeated and continuous contractions/relaxations of certain visible or hidden muscular groups (at the level of the face, the inside of the mouth, the neck, the inside of the throat, the thorax, the belly, the diaphragm, the sphincter muscles, etc.). Their purpose is to create autistic shapes as defined by Tustin.

We will also mention *self-destructive clinging* (a term that we will distinguish from self-aggressive, just as auto-sensuality is distinguished from autoerotism: self-destruction occurs prior to self-aggression, which implies a higher level of object-cathexis of the subject's own body). Self-destructive activities are in the service of a cathexis of the boundary and constitute, as Margaret Mahler (1968) says, a "pathological attempt *to feel alive* and whole" (p. 71, author's emphasis). We shall see that self-destructive manoeuvres represent boundaries between autism and symbiotic psychosis, particularly all the destructive manoeuvres consisting in "penetrating violently inside" (sticking fingers in the throat and biting them, hitting the eyes, etc.), which reveal access to a picture of the inside, an inside filled with catastrophes.

Autistic or auto-sensual manoeuvres concern, in our view, not only the bodily sphere, but also mental representations. This is true of *forms of clinging to "thought"* or to pseudo-thought. Tustin (1984a) presents, for example, the case of a little girl creating autistic shapes from arithmetical numbers, the equivalents of bodily substances. But what we want to describe as *clinging to thought* is a little different, even if it includes the autistic use of mental productions as equivalents of bodily productions. This clinging to pseudo-thought consists, for example, in manoeuvres – used even by subjects who are neither autistic nor psychotic – which have the aim of fixing attention on a particular mental image or on a repetitive imaginary scenario. This type of mental manoeuvre can be used at the moment of going to sleep or in the case of solitude or rather of traumatic isolation. This clinging to an idea or image is aimed at protecting the ego against annihilation anxieties, but diverts it from an authentic activity of thinking. Such clinging may concern cognition itself, which links up with Tustin's example: the object of knowledge, just like the very process of acquiring knowledge, can be cathected autistically and distorted, deprived of the potential of growth that they contain. Clinging to "thought", in a more complex form, can find expression in what we will call the "intellectual second skin", a characteristic notably of certain personalities organized around a "false-self", who fetishize knowledge (see Chapter 15).

More than this clinging to thought, the autist resorts to *clinging to psychic excitation*. Psychic excitation is obtained by some form of mental activity or bodily activity such as compulsive masturbation, the purpose of which is to maintain the survival of psychic life by means of permanent excitation.

Bodily autistic manoeuvres always have a psychic equivalent; sensory excitation always finds expression in psychic excitation. But in manoeuvres of clinging to psychic excitation, or clinging to/ by means of a mental activity, as we are trying to describe them, sensory activation is not predominant; it is either absent or uncathected. Think, for instance, by way of illustrating these manoeuvres further, of states of trance, or of the mental state generated by certain substance-addictive behaviours.

All these auto-sensual manoeuvres are used by a great number of people, normal or neurotic (or other), up to a certain point. Only their overuse reveals or leads to autism. Furthermore, these manoeuvres are not included in autoerotic behaviours. Autoerotism is absent in autistic states, as will become clear below.

2.1.3 Autism, auto-sensuality, autoerotism and transitional phenomena

Autoerotism, as we understand it, is somewhat akin to the idea that Freud (1905) gave in his *Three Essays on the Theory of Sexuality* of an autoerotism constituted by the separation of the sexual drives from the nonsexual functions on which they were first based. But it is even more akin to the idea advanced in "Instincts and their vicissitudes"

(1915a) of a "purified pleasure-ego" constituted by the *introjection/ incorporation of objects that are sources of pleasure*. The consideration of such a process was the sign of a new conception with regard to what Freud had called the autoerotic ego – the sense of autoerotism here being different to the one we are presenting.

Autoerotism may be defined as a mental and physical measure whose aim is to obtain a bonus of solitary pleasure in the absence of the external object, but based on the recollection of an internalized experience of pleasure and comfort. *Autoerotism is thus inherent to introjection*: the baby who sucks his thumb recalls the gratifying absent object; the real object is replaced by an imaginary object, by a representation. Autoerotism goes hand in hand with a work of representation, of symbolization. Autoerotism thus concerns secondary narcissism, as Freud (1914b) describes it in "Narcissism: an introduction" on the subject of neurosis. Tustin (1986) suggests, moreover, modifying Freud's (1914b) postulate that autoerotic impulses exist from the beginning (we pointed this out in our introduction); postulating rather that "auto-sensuality" exists from the beginning and is differentiated progressively in the course of normal development into autoerotism and auto-sadism.

In autism, the internalization of a good gratifying object, the memory of which is helpful in the case of frustration or distress, has not taken place or does not function. Autoerotism is replaced by auto-sensuality. When the autistic child sucks his thumb, it serves less to recall an experience of pleasure or of internalized safety than to cathect a cluster of oral sensations necessary for psychic survival. This concerns a state of primary narcissism where it is more a matter of survival than of pleasure or frustration. Moreover, in autoerotism, thoughts and fantasies linked to an earlier libidinal object-cathexis are active. On the other hand, in auto-sensuality autistic manoeuvres are characterized by the absence of any authentic "thought-activity" – we will look at the status of "thought" in autistic states further on (Chapter 10). Geneviève Haag sees autoerotism as belonging to normal symbiosis, in what she calls the "internalization of the linking factor of symbiosis".[10]

Autistic objects, autistic shapes, proprioceptive clinging and self-destructive clinging, along with psychic clinging, represent a handicap for the development of the child. Their aim is to conceal the not-me, to cancel out or blur the distinction between me and not-me. In this respect they are situated poles apart from transitional experiences (Winnicott, 1951, 1971) which form a bridge between me and not-me and are of help to the child. Transitional objects are associated with fantasies, while autistic and confusional objects are only associated with sensations. Transitional objects reveal the introjection of a satisfying relationship with a real object. The child has the feeling, even if it is weakly established, of having something good inside him and can tolerate the absence of the mother or of the mothering object because the transitional object keeps it alive in his mind, and he retains the memory of this prior link.

Confusional and autistic manoeuvres are not based on memories or thoughts and even impede them from developing; above all, they have the function of avoidance, protecting the child against dangers stemming from the not-me that are experienced concretely. While transitional experiences promote cathexis of the not-me, autistic and confusional manoeuvres divert attention and interest from the not-me; they disavow separation and the external world. Transitional phenomena support symbolization and the deployment of thought, while autistic manoeuvres impede all work of symbolization and extinguish thought (in any case, any thought of the object; the child cathects the current sensations procured by the autistic manoeuvre, and perhaps the memory of past bodily sensations, but not the memory of the object; the memory, or the "hallucination", does not concern the object of satisfaction but sensation or bodily perception).

Let us now illustrate this model of the auto-sensuality of autistic and confusional manoeuvres with the literary example of the novel by Patrick Süskind (1985) titled *Perfume: The Story of a Murderer*. One of us has proposed a reading of this novel highlighting the central role of auto-sensuality (and not autoeroticism) in the organization of the psychic functioning of the main character, Jean-Baptiste Grenouille (Lhopital, 1992, 1997).

> Grenouille was to become a macabre murderer whose quest consisted in trying to appropriate the smell of his victims. The story of Grenouille may be reconstructed as that of an undesired and rejected infant experienced as a repugnant object, who was entrusted to wet nurses but could not receive or attract sufficient attention, or any satisfying maternal love. Faced with the emptiness of non-cathexis, with the menace of agonistic despair, but exercising his appetite to survive, if not to live, Grenouille had the choice of the defensive means of

his economy of survival. In his quest for any sign permitting him to cling to the world of the living, one of his senses was from the outset highly stimulated in him, even to the point of vertigo, namely, smell. Grenouille was born among fish waste, under the stall run by his mother, in a narrow street Paris that was saturated with strong smells to the point of being nauseating. He channelled all his sensoriality and his whole capacity for attention into this mode of survival that his scent became: through his nose and the strong smells that he inhaled, Grenouille felt gathered together, reunited; he felt he existed. If he was completely left behind and neglected, if he was no more than a nose clinging from the outset to the smells that surrounded him, he *was* at least this sniffing nose. It was as if, in order to survive, Grenouille was obliged to *smell* in order not to experience agonistic distress any longer. It was that or chaos, that or death: *being nose* for want of being born in the desire of another.

This clinging to a sensory mode is an autistic auto-sensual mechanism, as described by Tustin. It is also the effect of the unisensory reduction produced by the dismantling of the perceptual apparatus, as Meltzer speaks of it (Meltzer et al., 1975) (see Chapter 5). It may be said that Grenouille resorted very early on to autistic defences as his only means of survival. He was to grow up autistically clinging to this nose, whose capacities to identify every kind of smell, every kind of perfume, would be exacerbated to the point of madness. Smell as an autistic object gradually assumed the status of a fetish object. His psychic envelope was organized essentially as an "olfactory envelope" (Anzieu, 1985) (see Chapter 7). His "psychic skin" seems initially to have been little more than the "adhesive identification" (Bick, 1986; Meltzer et al., 1975) (see Chapter 5) that made him stick himself to sensory forms of excitation, for want of having been hosted in the psychic space of an object who desired and expected him. This adhesive identification, this deployed auto-sensuality, this clinging to the surface qualities of objects which would turn into fetishization led the author of *Perfume to* describe Grenouille as a "solitary tick", an animal that one day "abandons caution, drops and scratches and bores and bites into that alien flesh" (Süskind, 1985, p. 25). This would be Grenouille's fate. With this illustration, we have clarified the characterology of auto-sensuality and further circumscribed the issues at stake in autistic manoeuvres. We will now pursue a more phenomenological approach and provide clinical examples.

2.2 A phenomenological approach to autistic and auto-sensual manoeuvres

These autistic and auto-sensual manoeuvres that we have just described can easily be identified in clinical observation. We are now going to give a few examples of this, first in the autistic child, then in the autistic baby or one who is going through autistic states, then in the psychotic adult, and finally in neurotic children and adults.

2.2.1 In the autistic child

The autistic children that we have met in institutions (child psychiatric day hospitals), or that we have had in treatment, only very rarely resorted or resort to external autistic objects. We can give the example of a ten-year-old autistic child who compulsively used a (metal) key which she constantly held in her hand when she was in her family. Each day, on arriving at the institution, she would hand the key to her mother or to the person who was accompanying her, and on leaving she would clamour for this object vehemently. This example illustrates the utilization of an object that has a boundary status between the autistic or confusional object and the transitional object, insofar as the object is unique, on the one hand, and that the child can separate from it on the other; and, finally, that a relational function, and thus a potential fantasy scenario, are associated with its manipulation.

It is common to observe many children clutching hard objects which impress a tactile sensation at the level of an extended zone of the body and not only at the level of the palm of the hand. This zone often concerns the front side of the body. Movements of rubbing the tummy, for example, have the function in these children of compressing the "front" against a hard object. We know that Tustin (1981b) considers that the perception of the body in these children is split into a "soft front" and a "hard rear". The endangered "soft front" is protected when it is compressed between the "hard rear" and the hard surface of an external object.

Though external autistic objects seem to us to be relatively infrequent, bodily appendages used as autistic objects are much more common. Whether it is a matter of dried snot in the nose, of nails that the child sticks into the palm of his hands to the point of hurting himself, while refusing to have them cut, or of the tongue that the child compresses against the inside of his mouth or against his cheeks or between his teeth, it is the sensation of hardness that he is seeking, as Tustin explains.

Recourse to autistic shapes is very common in autistic children.

> Florian, for example, a six-year-old autistic child, spends long periods turning between his fingers a flower that he is holding by the stem, while staring intensely at the circular movement of the petals. When he was younger, he was fascinated by the sensory effect caused by light rays passing through the spaces between the wooden spindles of a stair banister. At the same time, he would scrawl regular vertical lines on the walls, and scanning this graffiti visually, in moments of disorganizing panic, procured him soothing sensations. Denis, a ten-year-old autistic boy, is fascinated by the waving movement of threads of wool that he is holding in one hand and leaves blowing in the wind, and also by the whirling movement of dead leaves blown around in the wind. Many children use motor rhythms that consist in compulsively flapping their hands in front of their faces.

This visual clinging to unisensory shapes is used to search for a rocking motion characteristic of autistic shapes. The rocking motion is obtained through the alternation of what could be called a *"full" sensation* with an *"empty" sensation* – a line/an absence of line, light stimulation/shadow, etc., or through a whirling movement.[11]

We have differentiated *autistic shapes* from what we have called *confusional shapes*. If the autistic shape diverts consciousness from the terrifying not-me, the confusional shape blurs the perception of the not-me. This is how we understand, for example, the head-swaying of certain autistic children – and even non-autistic children – before going to sleep, or head-banging against the wall during sleep. The function of these manoeuvres is to confuse perceptions of external objects, but also "perceptions" of internal objects. Compulsive head-swaying blurs internal perceptions, reveries and thoughts which are felt to be a threat to the precarious integrity of the self.

> We will also relate the example of an autistic adolescent, René, in whom perceptual blurring is caused by pressing his index finger against the outer layer of the eye-ball – with such pressure that a skin lesion at the level of the eyelids is now irreversible – thereby modifying the spherical shape of the eye and blurring sensory reception. René only resorts to this manoeuvre when he comes into eye contact with another person. His relationship to inanimate objects, as well as his relationship (other than visual) to animate objects, does not elicit this kind of manifestation. Only the visual relationship, which fosters contact with the internal world of the other person, a worrying and even terrifying world which is a source of claustrophobic anxieties (being imprisoned in the object) and agoraphobic anxieties (being penetrated by a threatening or devastating object), elicits compelling manoeuvres of perceptual blurring insofar as primary clinging by means of the gaze probably was and is still lacking.

Proprioceptive clinging – of the "muscular second skin" type – and kinaesthetic clinging are always used by autistic children. The permanent contraction of certain muscular groups gives the characteristic aspect of the posture of certain autistic children: arms out to the side with a 90° elbow bend, clenched fists, extended lower limbs, toe-walking. This position on the tips of the toes[12] results in a bouncy gait engendering inner rhythmic sensations that are highly valued by the autistic child. All rhythmic movements, the swinging of a part of the body or of the whole body, are signs of *autistic clinging* or *confusional clinging*, depending on whether they are devised to deny or blur perception of the external world or of the internal world.

Here is a final example of confusional clinging which highlights the difficulty family members have in coping with autistic anxieties and how autistic manoeuvres can "contaminate" and be maintained.

> This example concerns a family met by one of us (M.L.) in the context of family therapy. The family group was characterized by an impairment of the stimulus-barrier system, an

impairment enacted particularly by the mother who, for past reasons linked to her history and current reasons linked to her child's severe autism, was struggling with a rift in her own psychic envelope. She was a woman who was always on the edge of breakdown as she could not rely on her husband whom she discredited; and she would destroy any attempt by him to contain the situation.

During the interviews, this mother often came across as being very unstable and excited; she could not sit still on her chair and her legs often trembled. Whenever her daughter was too agitated or manifested her discontent or her anxiety through screams or tears that were always intense, she would pick her up suddenly, as if to tear her away from her agitation, and propose to put her on her lap. She would then put the child on her knees, sitting or lying on her tummy, while her legs continued to tremble. The child was thus pervaded by these trembling movements. She calmed down and it was noticeable that she was staring at the ceiling. She also emitted a continuous sound, vibrating to the rhythm of her mother's trembling. Noting the calming effect of this response, the mother was reassured about her mothering qualities and said that the child liked that very much.

We may suppose that, at a very early stage, this child had experienced the persistence of a momentary containing object, a sensual object that she had created and that was proposed to her each time instead of the optimal object. The mother could not draw on any internal resources of containing parenting (Ciccone, 2012b, 2014) – and nor could the father – for reasons that were in part her own, but also because her parenting capacity was affected, "contaminated", by the severe autism of her child. As she herself was clinging to her motor rhythms, in order to survive, she could only offer her child her own kinaesthetic modes of clinging, her own autistic manoeuvres, whose illusorily soothing functions she verified each time. The child was indeed momentarily soothed, but by the sensual and caressing effect of the autistic and confusional shapes procured by the vibrations of her voice and the tremblings of her body, confusional shapes that made her absent from herself, that blurred the perception of her inner ill-being, as well as the perception of the otherness of her object or of her mothering environment.

2.2.2 In the autistic baby

If the clinical observation of autistic manoeuvres in the child is relatively simple, the clinical and phenomenological approach to autistic manoeuvres and states in the baby is more difficult and more delicate. We are now going to dwell on this for a moment, drawing on the experience of one of us (A.C.), who took part for a long time in a multidisciplinary consultation in a neonatal unit, whose purpose was to provide neuropsychic monitoring for newborn babies at risk. This consultation is systematically provided for all children whose perinatal conditions were particularly difficult (great prematurity or dysmaturity, respiratory distress requiring assisted ventilation, etc.), endangering the quality of subsequent development. The children are seen for the first time at an age varying between six and eight months. Each year, out of about 100 babies observed in this context, the idea of a current autistic state, or of transitory autistic withdrawal, or of the spontaneous emergence of an early autistic withdrawal, is deemed to apply to about 15 of them. We will therefore present a few examples of babies going through current, transitory or resolutive autistic states.

If we are retaining the term "autistic" to describe these states even when they are transitory and resolutive, it is obviously not for "diagnostic" purposes, given that it is very difficult to affirm the existence of an autistic state in the very young baby, but rather in order to account for a mental state that goes beyond the ordinary auto-sensual withdrawals that can be observed in every baby.

We will mention first a child with severe cerebral motor infirmity (CMI). Some of the other children, whether cited or not as an example, suffered from a more or less serious perinatal brain injury which, for some of them, had more or less irreversible consequences. A prior clarification is necessary. The light thrown on these contexts is simply an attempt to account for a *psychic state* in children who, in addition, may suffer from brain pathologies (it is obviously neither a matter of explaining organic disorders psychogenetically nor of denying the influence of the somatic context on psychological development). But psyche and soma are linked and in an even more salient way in the baby. An impairment of neurological, neuromotor and/or neurosensory equipment results in an impairment of the appreciation of reality which may lead to psychological symptoms equivalent to those that are met with in psychogenetic pathologies. Furthermore, the psychic state has an impact on the use that the child makes of the deficit and on the evolution of the organic pathology (we have seen pathological electroencephalographic signs in abandoned babies normalize after they were adopted; some squints in infants disappear, while others persist; some babies use their squinting to avoid making eye contact with another person; other babies "cling" to more or less discrete organic pathologies, etc.). Finally, in everyone, but in an even more evident and understandable way in babies, psychic turmoil makes use of the means available to the psyche to express itself: the body, motricity, the soma, the biological and neurophysiological systems, and so on.

Here are a few examples, then, where, in this chapter, priority will be given to clinical and phenomenological observation.

> Adrien (18 months) is a twin. While his brother is in good health, Adrien suffers from tetraparesis. His face is ungracious, his head is often thrown back, his tongue lolling out, and his eyes are affected by a convergent squint. Adrien uses primitive defences like sucking his tongue and focusing intensely on light. Concerning his habit of sucking his tongue, caution is required concerning the meaning given to this behaviour, because a child with CMI is unable to bring his hand to his mouth on account of motor impairment. This is not the case for Adrien who also uses the rhythmic manoeuvre of hitting himself in the mouth with his fists.

We have noticed several times in very young babies (less than two months) this behaviour that consists in hitting themselves more or less hard in the mouth. We understand it as a defensive manoeuvre aimed at getting rid of the "bad sensation" due to the absence of the nipple in the mouth. The absent breast, as Bion (1962a) says, is felt to be a bad breast present. The baby who hits himself in the mouth rhythmically with his fist, just like the autistic child who puts his fingers, and even his whole fist, into his mouth, is evoking the "gaping hole" into which he feels he is in danger of being sucked and "falling forever". This hole is the greedy mouth which cannot cling to any nipple/mouth, and which will lead the child who has become autistic to use autistic objects to fulfil this function of mouth-hole.

> Adrien, moreover, "excites" his mouth and tongue with objects that he holds in his hand. This behaviour is reminiscent of the reaction of newborn babies in whom one is testing buccal reflexes ("cardinal point" reflexes) by stimulating the mouth on both sides, and who turn their heads towards the point of stimulation while making a rooting movement, moving the lips and tongue in search of the nipple.

Adrien's use of objects seems to reveal an attempt to control the painful situation of the "absent nipple".

> Sofiane (11 months) was born prematurely and had perinatal asphyxia. Sofiane avoids eye contact and is visually attracted to lights. He also makes throat noises and babbling is absent. His psychomotor development is retarded and Sofiane is unable to move around by himself (no crawling or walking on four legs), though he has no central neuromotor problems. He is interested in objects, sometimes brings them to his mouth, but does not follow them with his eyes if he throws them away and does not look for them ("sign of oblivion" – Carel and Michel, 1985). If he sees an object that interests him, he fixes his gaze, maintains his attention, but his interest soon turns into an excess of external, but above all internal, excitation. Sofiane then gets agitated and shakes the object, making throat noises and staring at a light. Sofiane sometimes has nystagmus (probably linked to a vestibular impairment).

We can see the autistic-like manoeuvres that Sofiane uses in states of anxiety as well as in states of excessive excitation: manoeuvres of avoiding eye contact and sensory clinging. We may suppose that the intermittent nystagmus is used by Sofiane as a means of avoiding eye contact. Furthermore, in the state of auto-sensual withdrawal, twitching eyes produces secret autistic forms such as throat-clearing or tongue-sucking to which the child who is experiencing an excess of excitation clings (the excess is perhaps not obvious for the observer, but the fragile, hypersensitive psychical apparatus of the autistic child has tolerance thresholds that are difficult to evaluate).

> Didier (eight months) was an abandoned child awaiting adoption. His mother probably had an intellectual impairment. Her

pregnancy was not followed medically and the mother did not even know that she was pregnant. She abandoned the child at birth. He was premature and had perinatal asphyxia and respiratory pauses (paraclinical examinations did not, however, reveal any anomaly). Didier is accompanied by a child educator from the institution where he is placed temporarily. He sucks his tongue, takes hold of objects only on contact with them, does not throw them away but hits his temple with them, and has poor control of his movements. His upper limbs are held out and bent at the elbow (flexion withdrawal of the upper limbs and shoulder abduction). The need to contain himself and cling to himself is manifested by a slight hypertonia of the hands (fists clenched, thumbs-in-palm), discrete hyperkinesia and clinging to objects. Didier is not interested in faces and it is difficult to make eye contact with him. He does not seem to react to strangers. He does not look at himself in the mirror. Didier spends long periods rubbing his hand on a piece of plastic. When the educator, on whose knees he is sitting, is talking, she makes a lot of gestures and her hands are therefore no longer "holding" the child who, at those moments, throws himself backwards, makes withdrawal movements of the upper limbs, sucks his tongue intensely, and focuses his eyes on the light. In fact, he focuses more on the reflections generated by the educator's hand passing in front of the light. When Didier is "held" properly, wedged in the educator's arms, his skills are much better; he can take interest in people, manipulate objects, etc. Equally, when he is lying on the table being examined, he makes eye contact, babbles and looks at himself in the mirror.

In Didier we can see avoidance of contact and of relating, his sensory clinging, his way of containing himself and clinging to himself (in particular through the hypertonia of his limbs and hands, hyperkinesias, and the auto-sensual use of objects). It is conceivable that the reflections generated by the educator's hand passing in front of the light produce autistic shapes, just like the piece of plastic caressed by his hand. These autistic shapes soothe the child, who is invaded by a sensation of being "let down", of not being held psychically, of no longer being unified in his mental life. On the other hand, when Didier is "held", "contained", his presence in the world is much improved. Likewise, when the examiner's face is close to his, Didier can make eye contact because the situation is more symbiotic.

Didier was seen again at the age of 11 months, after two months of adoption. Psychomotor progress was striking, his relational and interactive attitudes show that he can benefit from the psychic qualities of his environment thanks, among other things, to a decrease in sensory and kinaesthetic clinging. However, some autistic manoeuvres persist: upper limb withdrawal (without spastic hypertonia), visual clinging to lights inconstant. On the other hand, he no longer sucks his tongue. These manoeuvres are elicited especially when he is offered a new object. Likewise, if he already has an object in his hand, he clutches at it even more when being offered others. The beginnings of stereotypy can be noted: while the adoptive mother is speaking, Didier places his hand several times between his face and that of his adoptive mother, makes a few rotation movements, and smiles.

The adoptive mother indicates that Didier prefers the face-down position and that when he is a bit excited he cannot tolerate being on his back and only calms down when he is on his tummy. She also points out that Didier never lets go of a little plastic giraffe that he clutches in his hand, and clamours desperately for it if he is separated from it and cannot find it again.

Adoption and the setting-up of a containing and secure environment seemed to give fresh impetus to a new developmental process in Didier. Certain autistic manoeuvres have disappeared but reactions of withdrawal and clutching are still there, particularly when faced with new situations. For example, when Didier clutches at an object even though he is being offered another, it is as if the first object provided him with comfort when faced with the anxiety-inducing situation caused by being confronted with an unknown object. His relationship to the world thus sometimes remains very "sensory", in spite of the curiosity that he is capable of showing. For example, when Didier is interested in what his adoptive mother is saying, one has the impression that he perceives her verbal output as a rotating and rhythmic sensual movement which he tries to control and to put in his mouth. The lack of distinction between hand and mouth seems to lead him to the illusion that he is producing the rhythmic sounds of speech with his hand.

The first containing external object

Moreover, Didier's preference for lying on his tummy illustrates Tustin's idea that the autistic child protects his soft front with his hard rear. When he is "disorganized", Didier feels that his "soft substance" is delivered up to the terrifying not-me. To protect himself and to push away the danger of liquefaction, to struggle against the fear of spilling himself outside, he has to press his soft front against a hard surface: his back on one side, the ground (or his mother's knees) on the other. Thus contained, gathered together physically and psychically, Didier feels reassured.

Finally, what the adoptive mother says about Didier's relationship to the plastic giraffe object is evocative of an autistic object, but the character of uniqueness (the object is not replaceable) seems to suggest a shift towards transitionality.

> Lauriane (ten months) does not belong to the category of newborn babies at risk. She was referred to the multidisciplinary monitoring consultation for baby development due to the concerns of paediatricians about her. At nine months, she was showing signs of psychomotor retardation, "motor anomalies", as well as bouts of vomiting. Lauriane appears to be a hyperkinetic child, attentive but dispersed. She seems worried and clutches her doll tightly. While being examined, she is agitated with trembling and emotional dystonia, and it is difficult to distinguish between hypertonia and anxious excitation. The trembling gets worse when the child is naked on the examination table. She smiles, but not in a context of interaction. She seems to be "in her own world", as her mother says. Locomotion is reduced to preliminary crawling movements. Prehension is impeded by anxiety which leads to oppositional hypertonia and amplifies her trembling. During the interview with the mother, Lauriane seems to "play" with objects (small giraffe, rattle) which she has in her hands, but she gives the impression of clinging to these objects, to her "own world", and strong trembling can be observed. The mother says that this trembling occurs systematically in Lauriane when she wakes up and notices that her mother is not with her.
>
> Lauriane seems to go through periods of autistic or post-autistic withdrawal. The warning signs are the psychomotor retardation and bouts of vomiting. Although the doctors only began to show concern when Lauriane was nine months old,

the mother was able to give valuable indications about the vigilance, relational quality and psychic state of the child in the very first months of life, suggesting that the autistic withdrawal occurred very early. The observation of the child shows no cathexis of motricity and of her own body. This motor inertia is accompanied by postural traits: shoulder retraction, neck extension, refusal of prehension, lower limb withdrawal in the upright position (jumper-support inconstant). Even if a neurological factor (the consequence of possible unidentifiable brain damage) perhaps plays a part in the (spastic) hypertonia, it does not explain everything because many children have suffered much more obviously from hypoxia and do not have hypertonia.

As we have already pointed out, we are not envisaging exclusive relations of causality but are trying to account for the mental state of a child irrespective of the somatic context. We understand postural withdrawal and motor inhibition, which have effects of retardation or stagnation on psychomotor development, as defensive manoeuvres of the child to keep the terrifying not-me at bay. The smile that has no value as communication, "games" with objects which seem to "cut" Lauriane off from the perception of the world, seem to attest to a withdrawal into her own "world", into a strange private space, full of goodness knows what "sensations" and "thoughts" or images that help to keep her unified in her mental life. The trembling to which she frequently has recourse, irrespective, as we have already said, of the part played by neurological factors, produce what Tustin describes as autistic shapes, which rock the child and reassure him, carry him and contain him when he is faced with the "black hole" due to the early discovery of bodily separation. We have seen that this trembling appears or is amplified when Lauriane is naked (not contained by a substitute skin), when she is manipulated by a stranger (intense phobic anxiety when faced with what is unfamiliar, unknown), when she wakes up and her mother is absent, or when her mother is talking to someone else and is not psychically present. Lauriane's hypertonia is used as a "muscular second skin" to which she clings in order to avoid "falling forever".

Trembling and autistic shapes, hypertonia and the "second skin" are the effect of auto-sensual clinging based on a process of adhesive identification (see Chapter 5). While these manoeuvres protect the child from the repetition of a terrifying awareness of not-me, of bodily separation, awareness that comes at a moment when the psychical apparatus is unable to handle it, and while they contain or keep the child suspended in his mental life, they, at the same time, turn him away from object-relations, from the psychic container that could offer him his mothering environment, and thereby compromise his mental growth.

Concerning Lauriane, but also most of the other children cited here as examples, it would be necessary to speak about the familial and historical elements that potentially throw light on the pathology of the baby, but that would take us beyond the scope of this chapter, which is more concerned with clinical symptomatology and phenomenological observation.

2.2.3 In the schizophrenic adult

Stimulated by the contributions of Frances Tustin and Donald Meltzer on infantile autism, Piera Aulagnier (1985a) has made, within the logic of her own theorization, an extremely interesting contribution. Reflecting on the phenomena that are observable in analytic work with adults with a schizophrenic constellation, Piera Aulagnier sees what she calls a "particular type of 'hallucinated sensation'" as an equivalent of transitory autistic withdrawal. She describes an abrupt and violent reaction occurring in the session: all of a sudden total silence sets in and the patient's facial expression suddenly changes and becomes immobilized, accompanied by frequent changes in the breathing rhythm. What Piera Aulagnier finds particularly striking is that the analyst feels, at that particular moment, that he has been subjected to a verdict of non-existence, that for the patient he is no more than an object that is part of the furniture. She explains these violent reactions as follows:

> A "noise" and not a statement bearing meaning, an undefinable smell, a proprioception concerning the inside of the subject's own body, have suddenly irrupted into the analytic space, have totally invaded it [...]: the subject is this noise, this smell, this sensation and he is simultaneously this fragment and this only fragment of the sensory body mobilised, stimulated by what is perceived [...]. Everything is concentrated on a zone, or rather, on a sensory point.
>
> (Aulagnier, 1985a, p. 151, translated for this edition)

Faced with the irruption of an unthinkable affect, "the psyche can only avoid its own annihilation [...] by hallucinating, not an object but a sensory perception, [...] a 'stand-in for an object'" (ibid., p. 153). Piera Aulagnier likens these sensory perceptions to the autistic shapes-traces-contours described by Frances Tustin. She adds that the patient can only speak of this "hallucinated sensation" and of this "past experience" after the hallucinatory experience, on awaking, she says, and the discourse of the schizophrenic concerning his hallucinations is therefore based on this "sensory testimony" which becomes "evidence of the truth of the delusional construction" (ibid.) According to Piera Aulagnier, in such moments of hallucinatory withdrawal – equivalent to an autistic withdrawal – the subject very probably re-experiences affects attendant upon the first experiences of distress and murderous rage which are experienced/suffered by the newborn baby.[13]

Faced with the void, the abyss, nothingness, the "black hole", the danger and even the unthinkable dimension of the not-me or of the outside-self, faced with the impossibility of thinking in the moment about this experience, the hallucinated sensation or the autistic shape/trace constitute themselves as the ultimate recourse, as an expensive but necessary means of not "falling": during this transitory episode this is the only mode of being/experience that can preserve the attribute of existence, the sense of existing.

Salomon Resnik (1986a), in a reflection on "autistic space", presents the case of an adult female patient (we think she is a schizophrenic patient, though the author says nothing about this), an architect by profession, whose psychoanalytic process succeeded in reconstructing phenomenologically the different stages that had led her to find herself confined within a sort of autistic fortress that was supposed to protect her from the world. With regard to her, he describes the autistic experience as an "anaesthetic", "analgesic" experience in which claustrophobia "is not felt" as long as one remains inside the "autistic bloc". He speaks of the "autistic atmosphere" characterized by the possibility of switching suddenly and abruptly from the "frozen" state to that of "burning fire".[14] He describes the paralysis of the cognitive and affective world leading to the construction of a fortress, to the suffocating control of exchanges and "commerce" with the world. He explains how the potential for communication contains the risk of breaking up, of falling to pieces, of falling into the unfamiliar orbit of the other in an infinite plunge:

If there is no mother-world to receive her, with which [the patient] can connect through the mediation of a third party, a father/bridge, the earth becomes a place of fear and terror.
(Resnik, 1986a, p. 181, translated for this edition)

2.2.4 In neurotic children and adults

In 1972, Tustin said that she found "pockets" of shell-type autism in many neurotic children, manifested by disorders such as phobias, sleeping disorders, mental anorexia, selective mutism, skin diseases, psychosomatic disorders, school difficulties, alterations of language, and delinquency. Inside these pockets, transitional experiences are not developed; imagination has remained primitive and is only exercised in games involving bodily objects or their equivalents in the external world.

In her book *Autistic States in Children*, Tustin (1981b) states that in working with neurotic children she has invariably come upon a "'pocket' of functioning in which awareness of reality was so blocked or distorted that it justified the term psychotic" (p. 225). For her, treating certain neurotic problems implies a struggle to help these children live within the boundaries of their own body and to tolerate the "disillusionment that they had not an 'extra bit' to their body (particularly to their mouth) that gave them omnipotent control and power over the outside world" (ibid.). Another aspect of pathology in certain children with an autistic enclave is their inability to regulate their impulses and reactions. The "turbulence of basic sensuality" in these children – lacking limits and a stimulus barrier that are ordinarily established with the help of a containing parental environment – means that they "are attached to the functioning of their parts, bodily organs and rhythms which are experienced as fixated, inanimate and mechanical objects" (ibid., p. 226).

Tustin finds confirmation of these hypotheses in psychosomatic disorders and hypochondria, since in these different cases sensuousness "has become unduly directed towards organs and bodily processes" (ibid., p. 226–227) and is not transformed into dreams, fantasies or play. In disorders such as encopresis and enuresis, Tustin suggests that children obtain "surreptitious satisfaction" from their bladder and bowel, thereby bypassing the restrictions – inherent to toilet training – imposed by the father and the mother as separate individuals with their own limits. Furthermore, the absence of transformation of sensations into percepts and concepts in a part of the personality of certain subjects can lead to learning difficulties or school phobias. Finally, Tustin recognizes an "enclave of shell-type autism" in anorexia nervosa.

In an article of 1985, Tustin (1985c) draws on some of her discoveries – concerning the nature of autistic anxieties and the use of autistic objects and shapes – to understand certain apparently inaccessible adult neurotic patients. These patients have a part of their personality that is hermetically sealed off, a "hidden enclave of autism" which, according to Tustin, the psychoanalyst needs to become aware of as soon as possible. In her following books (Tustin, 1986, 1990), she once again describes "autistic capsules" or "autistic barriers" in neurotic patients. This term, which she had already employed in 1972, highlights forcefully how autistic protective measures block development. When these patients are in the vice of their autistic capsule, they seem impenetrable, anaesthetized, self-sufficient, and they control the analysis. Tustin gives examples of more or less secret autistic terrors and practices in these patients. The autistic capsules are at the origin, for instance, of obsessional and phobic disorders, but also of manic-depressive disorders and psychosomatic symptoms.

Autistic capsules protect against hypersensibility and despair. They are a means of defence against traumatic experiences, particularly early infantile traumas, and against feelings of depression, great vulnerability and helplessness. Tustin, points out, for example, how intense the feeling of traumatic loss is in these patients, a feeling that is hidden by their hard autistic capsule:

> They are grieving about the loss of they know not what. They have an agonized sense of loss and brokenness, which is unthinkable and inarticulate.
>
> (Tustin, 1990, p. 155)

These patients are difficult to treat because they have the capacity to drag the other person into their silent dramas. They threaten to "break their therapists' hearts" because they themselves are "heartbroken" (ibid.).

> Their "heartbreak" goes beyond what we usually mean by the term. The feeling of brokenness goes into the very fabric of

> their being [...]. The "original agony" of the breakdown was when the sensuous experience of the "oneness" of the "teat-tongue" was felt to break into "twoness". Since the rhythm of sucking had become associated with the beating of the heart, it was the "teat-tongue-heart" that was felt to be broken. Of course, all this was wordless, and to put it into words seems clumsy and even absurd. But it helps us to understand that for these patients bodily awareness of their separateness had been experienced as an interruption of their "going on being". Their sense of "being" was felt to be threatened. Annihilation stared them in the face, and very desperate steps had to be taken to combat it. To combat it and cover over their brokenness, they developed the plaster cast of autism [...]. This concretized experience of encapsulation spells death to the psyche.[15]
>
> (Tustin, 1990, p. 156)

Tustin stresses the necessity, when treating these patients in psychotherapy, of modifying these autistic barriers in such a way that human relations can develop. This modification is obtained by dint of the analyst's patience and attention, but also his rigour and firmness in making sure that the patients gradually agree to give up their more or less secret autistic manoeuvres and take interest in human communication. The damaged psyche can then be treated and the neurotic anxieties and defences elaborated.

Other authors have emphasized the existence of autistic processes in non-psychotic pathologies. Sydney Klein (1980), for instance, – whose theses Tustin takes up – describes autistic phenomena in neurotic patients. He gives the example of patients who are well established socially and professionally and who entered analysis for professional reasons and as analytic candidates, or for minor difficulties. The patients Sydney Klein speaks of are characterized by a state of impenetrable encapsulation of a part of their self, a silent and implacable resistance to change, and a lack of real emotional contact with themselves and with the analyst. The atrophy of their emotional life is attended by a desperate and tenacious clinging to the analyst who represents the only source of life. These patients present intense anxiety at the slightest sense of separation. They have therefore developed, for instance, an exaggerated sensibility to the analyst's tone of voice and facial expression out of persecutory fear of hostile reactions on his part. Just as Tustin has reiterated,

Sydney Klein thinks that the sooner the analyst becomes aware of this encapsulated part of the patient that cuts him off from the rest of his personality as well as from the analyst, the less danger there will be of the analysis becoming an interminable intellectual dialogue, and that the patient's possibilities of reaching a stable equilibrium will increase accordingly.

Other studies have taken up or extended Tustin's views. David Rosenfeld (1986), for example, has described how the autistic encapsulation of a trauma has the effect of preserving and sealing it off it until it can be subsequently processed and transformed, in the best of cases. Yolanda Gampel (1983, 1988) has made the same finding. Nina Herman (1987, 1988), like others who cite Tustin, has drawn attention to the utilization of autistic objects by neurotic subjects. Didier Houzel (1988a) has envisaged autistic enclaves in child psychoanalysis and given an example in the context of school phobia. David Rosenfeld (1997) has studied the relations between addictive behaviours or psychosomatic disorders and autistic processes. The notions of "psychic clinging to thought" and "intellectual second skin" that we are proposing to describe certain autistic manoeuvres in "false-self" organizations of non-autistic and non-psychotic personalities also extend these views of Tustin.

2.2.5 Thinking as an autistic object

We have considered autistic manoeuvres as procedures to which autistic children and autistic babies, but also psychotic adults and neurotic adults or children, can have recourse. Autistic objects, autistic shapes and autistic clinging bring into play concrete objects, bodily appendages or bodily functions, but also mental functions. Although autistic manoeuvres are conceived of as processes functioning in a register prior to thinking, we want to stress and illustrate the possible utilization of thinking itself — or of pseudo-thinking — as an autistic object. We have spoken of clinging to psychic excitation and clinging to thinking. We will turn our attention now to the second of these.

Autistic children have an inner activity of "thinking";[16] some of them, even mute, develop an inner language. Indeed, the quality of the understanding of language that some autistic children can display, the restoration of the ability to speak that can be observed in certain autistic children in intensive psychotherapeutic treatment, for example, suggests that a form of inner language can be elaborated even in the autistic state. The autistic state should not be considered as immobilized in a position in an immutable fashion, but rather as permanently oscillating between a state of auto-sensual narcissistic withdrawal and periods of openness to experiences of object-relating – this is valid for the child who has become autistic and for the baby who is subject to transitory autistic withdrawals, and also for the newborn child going through the primary phase of "auto-sensuality". The massive nature of autistic manifestations and their exclusivity in relation to periods of normal psychic functioning will determine whether pathological autism sets in or whether a gradual overcoming of transitory states of autistic withdrawal occurs.

This picture of the psychical apparatus in the "autistic mentality", it might be said, makes it possible to suppose that outside the "autistic position" (see Chapter 5) or the zone of "autism proper" (Bremner and Meltzer, 1975), a zone where the activity of thinking is absent, a certain activity of thinking and a certain amount of language can develop. These beginnings of thought, these embryos of internal objects, which emerge during openness to experiences of object-relations, during furtive episodes of adequate mental presence, during interactive exchanges between the child and its mothering environment, exchanges in which an alpha function (Bion, 1962b), even if precarious, is operative, can be utilized for manoeuvres of psychic clinging such as those to which we have already referred. Geneviève Haag, for example, explains the mutism of certain autistic children who possess an inner language as a manoeuvre of clinging to their inner "thinking" whose expression through language would open up breaches leading to catastrophic anxieties in their precarious psychic envelope (personal communication).

Donald Meltzer, who studied mutism in autistic children (Meltzer et al., 1975), does not seem to mention these manoeuvres that may be described as psychic clinging. From a point of view that is at once topographical (transversal study within the autistic mental state) and evolving (longitudinal study of mental development based on the state of autism proper), Donald Meltzer describes the reasons for autistic mutism, from "autism proper" to post-autistic zones, as corresponding to:

- the failure to develop dream thoughts;
- the failure of processes of identification with speaking objects;

- the pregenital oedipal jealousy which interferes with the verbal coition of internal objects and renders them silent;
- the prolonged immaturity which results in a handicap in learning to speak;
- the underdevelopment of the distinction between animate and inanimate, human and non-human, which impedes the growth of internal objects that are a suitable audience for speech;
- the lack of stimulation of a desire to communicate, and the sole presence of a desire to control or to provoke the obedience of objects for which gestures and signals suffice.

To this list may be added *psychic clinging to "thinking"*.

In every subject, thinking can be used as an autistic object, when it has the exclusive function of maintaining the survival of the mental universe. We have evoked the clinging to thinking used as a manoeuvre to struggle against anxieties to do with falling asleep or isolation.

> An excellent example of clinging to thinking as a means of survival in a situation of traumatic isolation can be found in Stephan Zweig's novella, *The Royal Game* (1942), concerning the character of Dr B. Faced with the void, with the absolute nothingness produced by the traumatic isolation imposed by his torturers, Dr B., who manages to steal a book on chess, clings to the descriptions of chess games. For him, this is a way of holding out and of "holding himself together", of resisting barbarism and mental torture, of struggling against the threat of annihilation and mental breakdown that they generate. The exacerbation of the character's use of the visual register and of obsessive mental activity, in order to "play" chess games "in his head", illustrates the recourse to a mode of autistic clinging to thinking, with the risk of "madness" that it involves.

We have also mentioned the clinging to thinking that constitutes an "intellectual second skin" characterizing certain forms of false-self. It can be said that all fanatical adhesion to an ideological discourse may involve such autistic clinging. This hypothesis of psychic clinging to thinking can also serve to throw light, for example, on the "scientist" mode of listening that can sometimes be observed in the provision of care in general, and in psychiatric medicine in particular, under the influence of the ambient positivism and of its effects of desubjectivization. The reduction of the mind to the brain, the reduction of the human to the biological, as well as the reduction of care to standardized protocols and objective evaluation that leave no room for the singular approach of subjectivity, are signs of clinging to an ideological and omniscient way of thinking, one of the essential functions of which is to protect against the inevitable mental pain that results from being faced with psychopathology. Clinging to a theoretical model that excludes the subject makes it possible to avoid encountering the intolerable and scandalous suffering of the other – and thus one's own – and thus to safeguard one's own narcissistic integrity. The patient as an object of study, a desubjectivized and dehumanized object, is an object in the service of the narcissism of the carer.

Theorization in general, and psychoanalytic theorization in particular, can also be subject to adhesive behaviour consisting in sticking to "ways of thinking", to models, in order to conceal a state of emptiness or inner confusion. Conceptualist hype, where the brilliance of the exposition fascinates, may conceal profound inner disarray and correspond to a massive need for incorporation. Sticking adhesively to thought or to mentors, switching on tape recorders as soon as they utter the first word, and then being "full of admiration" and functioning oneself like a tape recorder repeating the discourse heard, is the mark of a mode of functioning akin to autistic clinging, between autistic clinging and projective identification (incorporation): it is as if one were trying to stick oneself inside another person. Thinking is then cathected (adhesively) like an all-powerful fetish that seals breaches and plugs holes. Adhesive clinging to fetishized and omniscient thought remains a peripheral activity, generating a false-self, and results in an "affected manner of speaking" that does not come authentically from the depths of an integrated experience, in surface effects that give the illusion of a surface and function as an envelope.

2.3 Primary anxieties

We have likened an aspect of the momentary object, which is a sensuous object, with the object and autistic shapes. The momentary object is characterized, moreover, by the unisensory reduction that it operates. In this respect it is akin not to the autistic object proper, but to the perception that the autistic child has of objects outside himself. This perception and this experience result from what Francisco Palacio-Espasa (1980) calls a "mutilating simplification" of the object. Likewise, dismantling (Meltzer et al., 1975), a characteristic defence mechanism of autistic functioning which results in scattering the object into a multitude of small parts, each bearing a single sensory quality (smell, colour, etc.), leads to a partial and piecemeal perception of external objects. We will return later to these characteristic processes of autistic functioning (Chapter 5).

We would simply like to draw attention here to the link that can be established between the momentary object and autistic functioning. This link manifests itself on the one hand in the function of the momentary object, which recalls the function of the object and of autistic shapes in their relationship to the menace of the not-me, and, on the other, in the nature of the momentary object which evokes the perception that the autistic child has of the objects of the external world – and of the internal world – after the operation of the processes of mutilating simplification or of dismantling. The momentary object does not have the status of a representative internal object, unlike the optimal object, which we will describe in the next chapter. Let us look now at the anxieties from which the momentary object, and then the optimal object, preserve the newborn child.

Klein (1932, 1946, 1948a) had spoken of primary "life-annihilating" anxieties stemming from the inner work of the death drive. Winnicott (1952b, 1956a, 1958a, 1960a, 1962a) described the feelings of "disintegration", the "unimaginable" anxieties of the baby, linked to the threat of "annihilation": being fragmented, falling forever, not being in touch with one's body, having no orientation. He took up these ideas again in 1974 and described "primitive agonies": return to an unintegrated state, infinite falling, loss of psychosomatic collusion, failure to live in the body, loss of the sense of reality, loss of the capacity to establish a relationship with objects, etc. These normal experiences of early life cannot be experienced/registered due to the lack of a sufficiently integrated ego. When they occur in an excessive manner and are not contained by the environment, they may retain a central place in later development. Indeed, a defensive organization may be set up to struggle against the fear of the return of an experience that has already happened but not yet been experienced, and which will be reflected in the adult by a "fear of breakdown". These primitive anxieties may be likened, as Renata Gaddini (1981) has done, to the anxieties triggered by what Bion (1965, 1966) calls "catastrophic changes", accompanied by a sense of disaster and breakdown.

According to Michel Haag (1984), Esther Bick presents the birth trauma as consisting of *claustrophobic anxiety* (passing through the birth canal), followed by agoraphobic anxiety (upon emerging into infinite space). These anxieties, which the baby will never again experience with such intensity, will determine his subsequent states of panic. Bick compares the baby invaded by agoraphobic anxiety to a cosmonaut who, in space, loses his space suit (Michel Haag points out that the slightest leak in the spacesuit of a cosmonaut would cause his immediate disintegration owing to the rupture of his skin and blood vessels). Bick (1986) also emphasizes the "dead-end", "falling" and "liquefying" anxieties experienced by the baby. His primordial terror is that of falling to pieces, of spilling out into boundless space.

Tustin evokes primitive terrors in terms of flooding, waterfalls, whirlpools, eruptions, etc. She attributes the liquid and gaseous nature of the first sensations of the self to the intrauterine experience of the foetus floating in amniotic liquid. She considers, moreover (Tustin, 1986), that the autistic child has not gone beyond this sensation of floating and that coming into contact with reality is tantamount to a real "coming down to earth", in the strict sense of the expression.

These primitive bodily anxieties, normal postnatal anxieties, are soothed and relieved by adequate "holding", both physical and psychic, of the baby by the mothering environment. The absence or shortcomings of the external containing object will lead to an excessive activation of these anxieties.

This description of the mental state of gestation, a gaseous and liquid state, perpetually in danger of serial overflowing, of volcanic explosion, of falling forever, etc., leads us to turn our interest to the nature of psychic elements in their earliest form.

Before doing so, it is worth stressing, with Cléopâtre Athanassiou, the essential role of these primitive anxieties as a factor of development:

> It is the fear of falling forever, of total self-liquefaction, that drives the baby to hang on, to bond, etc., to build ego-functioning

and identity in his relationship to an object, however primitive it may be.

(Athanassiou, 1982, p. 1191, translated for this edition)

2.4 Psychic elements in their most primitive form

In an attempt to delineate the constitution of psychic elements in their most primitive form, we will employ, among the available metaphors, the notions of drive, pictogram, agglutinated nucleus and agglomerate.

2.4.1 The drives

Freud considered, as we have seen, that the auto-erotic drive impulses exist from the beginning. It may be said of the drives that they represent the original psychic dynamic. Freud defines the drive as follows:

> An instinct appears to us as a concept on the frontier between the mental and the somatic, as the psychical representative of the stimuli originating from within the organism and reaching the mind, as a measure of the demand made upon the mind for work in consequence of its connection with the body.
> (Freud, 1915a, p. 121–122)

The drive, which has its origin in a somatic process, is a "bit of activity" whose aim is always satisfaction, that is to say the suppression of the state of excitation located in an organ or a part of the body. This excitation acts as a constant force, making it impossible for the subject to evade it. The reduction of tension, experienced as a satisfaction, is found in the bodily modification.

In addition to this bodily, somatic, origin of drive impulses, we will emphasize their "volcanic" aspect on the one hand and their scattered, diffuse and chaotic aspect on the other. The volcanic aspect is evoked by Freud when he speaks of "drive eruption" and compares the drives to a series of isolated waves, separated in time, whose relation to one another is comparable to that of successive eruptions of lava. This image is reminiscent of our earlier descriptions of the original state of the mind, in the form of explosive gas or overflowing liquid. Tustin (1986) moreover, says clearly that it is the drives which, in their primitive state, seem to be experienced as gushing water or dangerous gases.

Concerning the scattered, diffuse and chaotic character of the first psychic elements, these are poorly accounted for by the notions of "independent sexual drives" and "organ pleasure". The sexual drives, according to Freud's first images of the primordial drives, are manifold, arising from diverse organic sources, and manifest themselves in the first instance independently of one another, the aim pursued by each being to obtain "organ pleasure". There is therefore no unification, but rather a fragmentation into part-drives each searching for local satisfaction. The ego-drives, which are identified with the drives of self-preservation, are opposed in psychic conflict to the sexual drives, and their aim is the satisfaction of needs of vital importance.

The scattered and chaotic aspect of the primary psychic elements is better illustrated if we consider not only their instinctual drive but also their sensory character, as Piera Aulagnier does, for example, with her notion of pictogram. The image of a stream of multiple and dispersed sensations to which the baby is subject in the very first stages of life and at the dawn of his mental life is very well described by Tustin:

> The infant is the stream of sensations from which constructs emerge as nameless entities.
> (Tustin, 1972, p. 60)

The infant experiences himself, in this state of abundant sensoriality, Tustin says, as a series of organs unrelated to one another within a whole, and at certain moments he can be entirely "mouth" or entirely "tummy" or entirely "hand", and so on. These are skin sensations which will gradually afford him the impression that these organs are gathered together in a bag, in an envelope. But before realizing that he has a skin and that his bodily substances do not flow out, the infant "seems only to have the sensation that the substances of his body have no conceivable end or limit" (ibid).

The drive, which is envisaged by Freud as a frontier concept between the mental and the somatic, has an organic source and, owing to the work that it imposes, a psychic destiny. It is this bodily source and this psychic destiny of the drives that lead them to be considered as representing the psychic elements in their most archaic form. This pathway from a bodily origin to a psychic destiny was taken up in the notion of pictogram developed by Piera Aulagnier (1975), who points out that the definition given by Freud of the drive is applicable at every point to the one that she is proposing for pictographic activity.

2.4.2 The pictograms

> The pictogram is the representation of a duality constituted by a sensory source, a source of excitation, and an object, the cause of the excitation. It is the primordial experience of an experience of pleasure which, for Piera Aulagnier, is the condition and cause of the cathexis of a physical activity that the psyche discovers in its power – an experience of a pleasure that it obtains, which is the necessary prerequisite for the cathexis of the activity of representation and of the image that results from it.
>
> (Aulagnier, 1975, p. 24)

The pictographic representation arises from the meeting between a sense-organ and an external object that has the power to stimulate it, but it has the particularity of being unaware of this duality of which it is comprised. The image of the "complementary object-zone" presents itself to the psyche as a reflection of itself, engendered by itself, guaranteeing it the existence of a relationship of identity between the bodily zone and the object, between the emerging psyche and the external world. The pictogram, which is an "image of bodily things" is simply the "first representation that psychical activity gives itself of itself" (ibid., p. 30).[17]

In her article, "*Le retrait dans l'hallucination: un équivalent du retrait autistique?*" Piera Aulagnier (1985a) illustrates the notion of pictogram in a particularly illuminating way with regard both to primitive psychic elements and to autistic psychic functioning and primary anxieties:

> Imagine someone who suddenly falls into a precipice and is left hanging on with just one hand to the sole and fragile outcrop of a rock. During this time, he will only be this union "palm of the hand-piece of stone" and he must only be that if he wants

to survive. As long as this tactile perception persists, he feels assured that he is living, that he is not already plunging into the void. And in order not to plunge, he must avoid thinking about himself plunging; but equally he must not fantasize about the omnipotence of a persecutor whose desire would be to cast him into the void. The tension of his hand and its clinging both manifest the eruption into psychic space of a representation "hand-rock", the only one present, and the sum of psychic work carried out to maintain the exclusion of the fantasized representation and of the ideational representation of the experience he is going through.

(Aulagnier, 1985a, p. 152, translated for this edition)

We consider this pictographic activity to be at the heart of the mental functioning of the autistic child, whose primordial concern, as Tustin points out, is one "of avoiding becoming 'nothingness' [...], of struggling to have a sense of existence" (Tustin, 1981b, p. 13–14, translated from the preface to the French edition), a sense that he obtains from autistic objects, autistic shapes and autistic manoeuvres. Mutilating simplification (Francisco Palacio-Espasa, 1980), sensory dissection and reduction (Hoxter, 1975), and self-mutilation of the psyche through clinging to the pictographic representation (Piera Aulagnier, 1985a) are for the autistic child survival measures aimed at avoiding his own annihilation, just like in the example of the subject who falls into a precipice and is left hanging by one hand to the sole outcrop of a rock.

2.4.3 The agglutinated object or nucleus, the agglomerates

Other authors have proposed hypotheses and metaphors concerning the constitution of the primary psychic elements. We will only discuss here José Bleger's (1967) figure of the agglutinated object or nucleus and Daniel Marcelli's (1985) notion of "agglomerate".

José Bleger develops the idea of a primary "agglutinated object" which he defines as

a conglomerate or condensation of very early outlines or formations of the ego in relation to internal objects and to parts of external reality [...], all without discrimination but also without confusion.

> Confusion arises when discrimination is lost, whereas in agglutination there is strictly speaking no confusion, since discrimination has not yet been attained. The agglutinated object includes the most primitive psychological structure, in which there is a fusion of internal and external [...], and its persistence constitutes the psychotic nucleus of the personality.
>
> (Bleger, 1967, p. 34)

The agglutinated object or nucleus brings together a large quantity of frustrating and gratifying experiences, of various intensities, undergone at different moments at the beginning of life, and integrates in an undifferentiated and indiscriminate manner aspects of external reality with a small nucleus of the ego. The agglutinated nucleus implies a non-differentiation between the objects and parts of the ego that are linked to them (as in the pictogram where the object and the complementary zone are undifferentiated).

Daniel Marcelli's notion of "agglomerate" is partly derived from José Bleger's notion of agglutinated object or nucleus. Early experiences of pleasure and satisfaction or unpleasure and pain form what Marcelli calls agglomerates in which three poles are juxtaposed: a provocative object, a perceptual-sensory or motor activity and an affective quality. These three poles are inextricably linked with one another. Marcelli divides these agglomerates into two categories: the soothing or pleasant ones and the exciting or unpleasant ones. The first would later be understood as the "bringing into connection of a good, gratifying and soothing object fragment and a lovable ego fragment" and the second as the "bringing into connection of a bad and dangerous object fragment and an ego fragment in tension, aggressive, full of hate" (Marcelli, 1985, p. 413, translated for this edition). Marcelli adds that these agglomerates, which unite an object fragment, a fragment of perceptual-sensory activity and a fragment of affective quality, do not require the real presence or existence of the external object:

> For the baby, whether the object fragment exists in reality or not, it is just as real from the moment a perceptual and sensory activity and an affective experience are united by creating an object fragment.
>
> (Ibid, p. 416, translated for this edition)

These fragmentary objects are simplified objects so that they can be recognized and cathected. They are represented by the baby's tongue, lips, mouth, skin and hands, as well as the mother's nipple, breast, skin, fingers and gaze. The various affective experiences, unrelated to one another, form fragments that are first united, stuck together and agglomerated, thanks to the perceptual and sensory functioning which has a function of glue, with fragments of object. Later, according to Daniel Marcelli, these fragments of affective experiences will become ego-fragments.

We will take these ideas into account, but we will emphasize the place of affect, which, in our opinion, must not be reduced to a mere agglomerated element on the same level as the object and perceptual and sensory activity. It is affect, and the nature of affect, that determines the constitution of these first nuclei of the ego. We will come back to this question (Chapters 8 and 10).

2.4.4 Other metaphors

Still other metaphors have been proposed to account for the primary psychic elements or rather the primary forms of thought that emerge from these primordial forms. Bion (1957), for instance, speaks of "ideograms" to describe primitive forms of thinking. These ideograms seem to be equivalent to the perceptions/thing-presentations to which Freud referred (1915b). Ideograms are images derived from the links between sense impressions on the one hand and consciousness on the other.[18] Bion (1962ab) further introduces the notion of "beta element" to describe archaic raw and unthinkable experiences which seek transformation in order to be thought.

Didier Anzieu (1987a) proposes the metaphor of the "formal signifier", following the notion of "demarcation signifier" advanced by Guy Rosolato (1985). Demarcation signifiers are tactile and somatic in nature and concern preverbal communication. Formal signifiers reflect primitive forms of experiences, often frightening ones, concerning bodily and spatial transformations.[19] Didier Anzieu likens formal signifiers to pictograms, but we would say, rather, that they constitute a first stage in the symbolization of pictograms (see Ciccone, 2012a). Likewise, demarcation signifiers are available for symbolization, for the advent of a preverbal communication with linguistic signifiers.

Also worthy of mention here is the notion of "pre-narrative envelope" put forward by Daniel Stern (1993) to describe primitive thoughts; although it coincides in some respects with the notions of agglutinated object and agglomerate, it already constitutes a symbolized figure, a first "concept".[20] The pre-narrative envelope designates a first form of representation of a unit of subjective experience consisting of a constellation of invariant elements concerning different modalities of experience: a sensation, a perception, an affect, a bodily movement, and so on. The ensemble describes the experience and gives a tension, a trajectory, to the subjective unit (this is the case, for instance, for the unit of the subjective experience of hunger, then of feeding, and then of the alleviation of hunger, etc.).

These different metaphors already describe the first forms of thought, of movements of thought starting from primitive psychic elements.

2.4.5 Conclusion

These notions of drive, pictogram, agglutinated nucleus, agglomerate and others are thus metaphors which seem to us to have the potential to depict and offer models for the first psychic representatives that constitute, if not the first thoughts, then at least the matrices or prototypes of the first thoughts which we will call, after Bion (1962b), "proto-thoughts". We will reflect further on the fate of these proto-thoughts – and will also return to some of these notions – when we explore the emergence and development of the principal activity of the psyche whose genesis we are studying, namely, the activity of thinking (Chapter 10).

These "primitive thoughts" provide an initial representation in outline of the embryos of internal objects which are gradually constituted by virtue of the process of introjection, as we have described (Chapter 1). The creation of this psychic "substance" takes place in the *relationship to the object*, in intersubjectivity, and principally in the symbiotic relationship. We will return further on to symbiotic states (Chapter 6). For the time being, we would just like to point out that it is in experiences of normal shared symbiosis – experiences of intense communication, exchanges of looks and smiles between the baby and its mothering environment – that psychic substance "is fabricated", as Geneviève Haag (1987b, 1988b) puts it. These experiences, which she describes as "creative symbiotic elations",[21] repair the most primitive narcissistic wounds, detoxify the most archaic anxieties, accord psychic status to earlier experiences of separation hitherto felt to be an amputation of the bodily ego and thus give the emerging psyche the elements necessary for the activation of thought processes.

In the next chapter, thanks in particular to Bion's ideas concerning "alpha-function" and the "container-contained apparatus", we will see how these psychic interactions – early intersubjective interactions inaugurating the functioning and deployment of thought – unfold.

Notes

1 On this subject see the chapter titled "Autism: the controversies" in Anne Alvarez's book *Live Company* (1992, p. 184–199).
2 It should be noted that autism remains a rare pathology, even if certain currents of thought are trying to extend it to a very large number of cases, by introducing, for instance, a category called "autistic spectrum disorder", as the *American Psychiatric Association* has done in its new classification of the DSM V (2013), a classification which corresponds not only to the advances in scientific research but also to the ideological issues and economic and political pressures mobilized by autism.
3 For a panoramic view of these studies, see Lelord et al., 1989, 1990; Bailey et al., 1996; Adrien, 1996. Or, more recently, Rey et al. (2016), for example, who make a review of theories and interventions in neuropsychology and conclude, like all serious authors on this subject, by emphasizing that multidimensional intervention is always necessary.
4 Though protodeclarative pointing (Bretherton and Bates, 1979) is absent or rare in autism, forms of "nonsocial" pointing, such as the proto-imperative pointing utilized to obtain an object or pointing for naming, are, however, present (Baron-Cohen, 1989; Baron-Cohen et al., 1992, 1996).
5 Or "social reference". On this notion see Sorce and Emde, 1981; Klinnert, 1985; Sameroff and Emde, 1989.
6 On the controversies concerning autism and the relations between the psychoanalytic approach and the neuropsychological or cognitive approach, see also the studies of Denys Rybas (2004, 2013) or Jacques Hochmann (2009). On the harmful aspect of the ideological splits concerning autism, see Geneviève Haag's reflections in her conclusion to her recent book (Haag, 2018). It is also worth noting

how the psychoanalytic and neuropsychological viewpoints can be articulated creatively in the publications already cited of the CIPPA (International Coordination of Psychotherapists and Psychoanalysts and Associate Members Caring for People with Autism), which give a sample of the work of the majority of current French psychoanalysts who are interested in autism (Amy et al., 2014, 2016).

7 Didier Houzel (1991, 1993) speaks of awareness of the "separability" of the object, rather than of "separation".

8 Concerning the semiological identification of the big groupings of pathological autism, Tustin (1972) has distinguished between abnormal primary autism corresponding to a massive deficiency of contributions due either to an environmental factor (affective deficiency) or to an internal factor (sensory deficiency), secondary shell-type autism, akin to the clinical picture described by Leo Kanner in 1943 and 1944, and regressive secondary autism akin to early infantile psychoses (symbiotic psychosis, schizophrenia). In 1981, Tustin reviewed this classification, retaining the following "nosography": primary "encapsulated" shell-type autism, secondary "segmented" shell-type autism, primary "entangled" or confusional-type autism, and secondary "fragmented" or confusional-type autism (Tustin, 1981b).

9 "Shapes" has been translated into French sometimes as "*formes*", sometimes by "*traces*" or by "*contours*". The meaning is that of a "vague contour", with connotations of something archaic and primitive (see Geneviève Haag's note in the French translation (1984a) of Tustin's article "Autistic shapes").

10 The first stage of this internalization is characterized by variants of sucking, which also internalizes attention. Sucking permits a representation of feeding, including the visual relationship. When this does not work, rhythmic manoeuvres are used and form a container prior to the symbiotic container. The second stage (around three to four months) is characterized by the joining of hands and interaction between the two halves of the body. The baby plays with its hands, feet and boundaries. This autoerotism is a form of "self-mastery". In autistic children, the latter does not achieve psychic status: they go on clinging to this attempt at self-mastery. Finally, the third stage (around four to five months) is characterized by a first awareness of separation. (Personal communication.)

11 On the whirlpool movement in autism, see Houzel, 1985a.

12 We know of some children who have undergone, by surgeons hostile to any form of psychodynamic approach and strongly encouraged

by the families, mutilating and painful interventions that are useless at the functional level, on Achilles tendons. Their equinus was not of neuromuscular origin, and other autistic manoeuvres were swiftly established after the surgical operation.

13 Piera Aulagnier (1986) was to re-examine this notion, hesitating – which was coherent with her theoretical model – to speak of "hallucinations" to refer to processes at work in the originary space. We think it is worth retaining this term of "sensory hallucinations" provided that the status of hallucination – along with those of fantasy and thought – in autistic experience is clarified; this is what we will attempt to do further on (Chapter 10).

14 Elsewhere, Salomon Resnik (1985, 1986b, 1999) envisages the psychotic state as a "freezing" of experience, history and thought.

15 These patients are of the same type as those described, from quite another perspective, by René Roussillon (1999) in connection with "identity/narcissistic" related pathologies where the subject is struggling with early agonistic experiences and it is the sense of a "lack of being" that dominates the clinical picture. René Roussillon draws on Winnicott's thinking, and Tustin points to the similarity between her thinking about autistic capsules in neurotic patients and what Winnicott (1974) describes regarding the fear of breakdown and primitive agonies.

16 We will return later to the nature of this "thinking" (Chapter 10).

17 If it comes first in the genesis of the psyche, we should not forget that pictographic activity, which, according to the model and terminology of Piera Aulagnier, finds its realization in the originary process and in the originary space, will never cease and will always be present in all psychic work that is actualized in the primary space according to the primary process, then in the secondary space according to the secondary process. "Concerning the originary", Aulagnier (1986) writes, "there is one point that I want to underline particularly: irrespective of whether this process – the only one that can transform the signs of somatic life into signs of psychic life – lasts for three hours, three days or three weeks, its activity will nonetheless persist throughout our existence" (p. 119–120, translated for this edition).

18 It is worth mentioning the notion of "audiogram" proposed by Suzanne Maiello (2000), who puts forward the hypothesis that the first psychic elements are constituted by auditory, sound and rhythmic traces (as the Greek root *id* signifies "see", the term "ideogram" refers too much to a visual dimension).

19 Tobie Nathan (1990) has taken up this notion and extended it with the notion of "formal containers" in order to describe kinaesthetic and coenesthetic experiences of modifications of the body, and rhythmic bodily movements.
20 We will see how Stern's model converges with that of Bion on the formation of primary concepts (Chapter 10).
21 Personal communication.

PART II

SECOND POSTULATE

> The introjection of the optimal object, the mothering object (the "breast"), identified with this function of containing object, gives rise to the fantasy of internal and external spaces.

We will begin by defining the "optimal containing object", describing its qualities and the nature of the processes in which it participates.

This postulate will lead us subsequently to consider the notions of psychic space and internal world.

3
THE OPTIMAL CONTAINING OBJECT

The external *containing object* plays a fundamental role in the birth of psychic life. Its function continues to be primordial throughout the building up of the psychical apparatus, the construction of the internal world and subjectivity. In other words, even when it has been introjected and established within the mind, the containing function of the actual object is no less required.[1]

Indeed, even when the external object has been internalized, its loss threatens the internal object with disintegration. That is why, for instance, after separating from his parent in order to confront a new situation – taking his first steps, entering an unknown place – a child returns systematically, after each attempt and going a little further each time, and throws himself into his parent's arms. He comes back to check that he or she is still there, that the separation has not destroyed the actual object, has not caused his or her disapproval, that the parent/external object is still living and authorizes the separation. But above all, the child returns towards this parent to *repair the symbiosis*. In these symbiotic exchanges he is busy fortifying his internal object threatened by separation from the actual object. Once it has been restored and fortified, the internal object provides the child with support and a shelter in which he can take refuge in order to try out the new situation again calmly, this time venturing further into unexplored territory. This is how the child makes progress in his mental development. The containing object is thus itself contained by the object that it contains.

To return now to the primary containing object. Drawing on the work of Esther Bick, we have differentiated the *momentary containing object* and the *optimal containing object*. Remember that the prototypical optimal object denotes a complex sensory and emotional constellation formed by the experience of the nipple in the mouth and of sucking, by the sensation of being held and carried, by the sensory information that is derived from this experience, and by the emotional quality in which this experience is steeped. This internalized ensemble produces a representation, a primary psychic object that represents the optimal object. This primary representation is a pictogram whose external pole is of course the maternal breast or its substitute; but it is, above all, as Didier Anzieu points out (1974b, p. 145, translated for this edition), a "breast capable of all metonymic substitutions". It is "a milk-breast, a mouth-breast, a cavity-breast, a faeces-breast, a penis-breast", among yet others. And it is also a complex object: a "container that contains itself at the same time as the baby", as Anzieu says (ibid.), and which gathers together "all the known phantasied contents of the baby, including other virtual babies". And it is also a "combined mother-father", Anzieu adds, a characteristic to which we will return in more detail further on. This primary breast-object is defined by the presence of the mothering object, her contact, words, smell, warmth, care, manipulations, games and milk, which restore the internal well-being of the baby dissolved in phantasy and heal him.

Furthermore, the external containing object is not a container in the sense of a recipient, but rather of an "attractor", as Didier Houzel has pointed out (1985b, 1987). It attracts all the baby's drive and emotional life; it gathers together all the scattered sensuality and all the attention of which the baby is capable and creates the conditions for maintaining a state of "consensuality".[2] Just as a magnet attracts and organizes iron filings or as a valley attracts and organizes the water flow, so the containing-attracting object gives the drives and emotions a stable form and a meaning.[3]

Finally, the external breast-object is split, in part object-relations, into a "nourishing breast" and a "toilet-breast", as Donald Meltzer (1967) designated them. The function of the "toilet-breast" is to contain the projection of the baby's psychic suffering, suffering that is at the origin of the need for a welcoming and containing external object.

The external containing object has a psychic function as a transformer of raw experiences that cannot be assigned with a psychic status. (René Kaës (1976a, 1979), as we shall see, speaks of "container" to underline this active aspect.) It creates the conditions for the emergence of thought and supports the development of the baby's capacity for thinking.

3.1 The qualities of the container

3.1.1 A protected space

Following Donald Meltzer (Meltzer et al., 1982), we will describe four indispensable qualities of the external object if it is to provide its containing function:

- first, "the container has to have boundaries which, while they may be concretely represented, are fundamentally the boundaries drawn by selective attention" (Meltzer et al., 1982, p. 199) – in other words, the boundaries of the containing object concern, on the one hand, its representable materiality and, on the other, its capacity to focus attention on current experience, that is to say the psychic capacity of the object to be "present", not to be "elsewhere" ;
- second, "the container must be a place of comfort, sheltered from irrelevant stimulation coming from the interior of the body" (p. 200) – this comfort of the container concerns sensory qualities (warmth, softness of voice, etc.) and emotional qualities (stillness, serenity, availability, etc.);
- third, the container is characterized by "privacy" which Meltzer defines as "something that is the product of the history of the relationship between container and contained, something that had its inception in a very imperfect way but grows naturally as the history lengthens" (ibid.) – this intimacy of the baby at the breast is a quality that depends on the previous one, that is to say, comfort;
- fourth, the container is characterized by "exclusiveness", the sense it gives of "uniqueness".

Elsewhere, Meltzer (1987a) uses the concept "private life" to account for this relationship between the mother and child that is very "withdrawn from the world" and protected by the father, a relationship guaranteeing the creation of a space in which the child can grow and develop. He also speaks of a "warm greenhouse" to depict this protected space.

3.1.2 A primary preoccupation

Winnicott described the qualities that the mother must have to foster the infant's healthy psychic development. Other than the characteristics of adaptability of a "good enough" mother who must preserve the "infant's illusions" (1951, 1971), and "physical" qualities concerning "holding", "handling" and the "presentation of objects" (1960a, 1962a), Winnicott defines the psychical characteristics of the containing external object through his notion of "primary maternal preoccupation" (1956a). He puts forward the hypothesis of a primary maternal preoccupation whose importance he shows in the construction of the very early foundations of the ego. This particular psychic state is described as an "organized state [...] which could be compared with a withdrawn state or a dissociated state, or a fugue, or even with a disturbance at a deeper level such as a schizoid episode in which some aspect of the personality takes over temporarily" (1956a, p. 302). The mother must be able to reach this state of "heightened sensitivity" in her attitude towards the infant and to recover from it afterwards. Winnicott speaks of an "ordinary devoted mother" who is able to put herself in his place and to respond to his needs, and does not hesitate to use the term "normal illness" to characterize this psychic state. The mother will "recover" from this state as the child "releases" her.

Winnicott also discusses cases where the mother's task cannot be achieved correctly. He describes how maternal failures interrupt the infant's "going on being" and can lead to a threat of annihilation, which is a very real primitive anxiety that endangers the very existence of the self:

> without the initial good-enough environmental provision, this self that can afford to die never develops. The feeling of real is absent and if there is not too much chaos the ultimate feeling is of futility [...]. If there is not chaos, there appears a false self that hides the true self, that complies with demands, that reacts to stimuli, that rids itself of instinctual experiences by having them, but that is only playing for time.[4]
> (Winnicott, 1956a, p. 304–305)

One of us has suggested replacing the formula "primary maternal preoccupation" with "primary *parental* preoccupation" (Ciccone, 2012bc, 2014, 2016a). In effect, primary preoccupation for an infant is both paternal and maternal. For one thing it concerns the father as much as the mother, and for another, within each of them it draws on qualities of parenting that combine maternal and paternal aspects, which constitutes what the above-mentioned author has called "psychic biparenting" (to which we will return later).

3.1.3 An adequate rhythmicity

The containing and reassuring quality of the optimal object implies a *rhythmicity* of the exchanges between the mothering object and the baby, a ritualization of maternal care. The rhythmicity of the experiences gives an illusion of permanence. Absence is only tolerable and maturational if it alternates with a presence in a rhythmicity that guarantees the sense of continuity; discontinuity is only maturational against a background of permanence, and rhythmicity gives an illusion of permanence.

Rhythmicity also makes it possible to anticipate experiences, to anticipate reunion, and thereby supports the development of thought – of the idea of absence. Rhythmicity in the occurrence of repeated experiences is a structuring factor for the development of the capacity for thought (see Chapter 10). For this reason, the object must not be absent for a period of time that exceeds the baby's capacity to retain a living memory of it. Winnicott (1971) laid stress on the traumatic aspect of separation which, beyond a certain time, produces a sense of loss and plunges the baby into an experience of agony. The object must not betray the promise of reunion, and the reunion must occur rhythmically, at a rhythm that guarantees continuity (if it is necessary to feed a baby every three hours, it is not only for physiological reasons).

Rhythm is thus central to a basis of security.[5] Basic security is the effect of – or implies – a rhythmicity, a rhythmic experience.[6]

3.1.4 A capacity for attunement

The containing object must also be able to "tune affectively" with the baby in their interactions. Daniel Stern (1985) describes *"affective attunement"* as exchanges in which the parent expresses through his/her behaviour an affective or emotional experience of the baby whose properties he/she reproduces (intensity, rhythm, form), which gives the baby not only a representation of his subjective state – affective attunement is a first form of symbolization – but also, and above all, the experience of an intersubjective sharing of affect, of the emotional state. The more significant the experiences of affective attunement are, the more the baby will develop the conviction that subjective states can be shared, and thus communicated.

Affective attunement is not simply an echo or mirror reflection or imitation of what the baby is expressing; it is a *translation* of the affective experience of the baby.

3.1.5 A claiming activity

The containing object must also have a function of awakening, of inviting the infant to participate in the relationship, in communication, of *active claiming*, as described and illustrated by Anne Alvarez (1992) – we will come back to this further on. It is not just a matter of being a sensitive and attentive receptacle for the baby's experiences, but of actively claiming him. It is not just a matter of consoling his states of distress, but of always leading him towards a higher level of contact, of relating, of presence in the world.

3.1.6 A capacity to be used

Let us also add the object's *"symbolizing" function* or function as a *"pliable medium"*, of which René Roussillon (1991, 1995, 1999) speaks. René Roussillon develops the notion of "pliable medium", borrowed from Marion Milner (1955), to describe the function of external objects, "things" (René Roussillon gives modelling clay as an example), in the primary process of symbolization of the subject (we will come back to this in Chapter 10): the object (thing) must be sufficiently pliable, which implies specific qualities (indestructibility, extreme sensibility, indefinite transformability, unconditional availability, its own animation, and so on) in order to be a mediator of symbolization, so that it can be used to produce symbolization (and to symbolize symbolization itself).

These qualities obviously apply first and foremost to the primary object, to the mothering object, to the parent. The mothering object must have a symbolizing function; it must be able to lend itself to symbolization, to thinking. It must therefore present the qualities of a "pliable medium"; it must be able to be "used" in its form and in its interiority, and survive this "use" – to use the terms of Winnicott, who introduced the notion of "use of the object" (1971). It must be able to tolerate being attacked and destroyed, and to resist destruction. It is on this condition that the object will be discovered as a real object, differentiated from the object in phantasy.

3.1.7 A harmonious biparenting

The optimal containing object, moreover, must combine harmoniously the *maternal and paternal functions*. The notion of "good combined parents" developed by Salomon Resnik (1986ac, 1994, 1999) – following that of "combined parents" which is based on Melanie Klein's work (1929, 1930, 1932, 1940, 1945, 1952a, 1957, 1961) on persecution-phantasies linked to the primal scene – accounts for this blend between the maternal function that contains the experience and the paternal function that structures, coordinates and organizes it. Donald Meltzer (1976) had spoken earlier of a "combined internal object" to refer to good parents who work together in order to take care of the children and protect them. The maternal and paternal functions must be harmoniously combined in the internal space of the containing object (and in the social space of the relations to the primary external objects) so that the child can introject an image of "good combined parents".

One of us has followed up this metaphor by describing "psychic biparenting" (mentioned above) which is based on "psychic bisexuality" and, in its most archaic primary forms, "psychic bisensuality" (Ciccone, 2003c, 2011, 2012bc, 2014, 2016a). This internal biparenting is constituted harmoniously if the creative interplay between the maternal and paternal poles has first occurred outside, within each parent and between the parents themselves. The "maternal" aspects of biparenting concern welcoming, receptivity, containing capacity, pliability, and the "paternal" aspects of firmness, rigour and consistency.

Internal biparenting is linked in each parent with the infantile aspects of the self, creating an internal "psychic bigenerationality". It is at the heart of this internal bigenerationality that the introjected parental aspects, if they are harmoniously combined, will take care of the infantile aspects of the self.

3.1.8 A capacity for thinking

The aforementioned qualities describe both concrete and psychic aspects of the mothering containing object. We will conclude by

Second postulate

looking more precisely at the *specifically psychic function* of this object. The object must be able to *think about the baby's experiences*, experiences that he cannot think about himself, in order to help him to gradually think about them by himself.

It was Bion (1962ab, 1970) who was to give a very precise and pertinent depiction of the interaction between the emerging psyche of the baby and the parental psyche, an interaction that is constitutive of the child's psyche. The breast, the different metonymies of which we have looked at, is for Bion a "thinking breast".

Bion puts forward three principal notions to describe this intersubjective process of thought: "maternal reverie", "alpha function" and the "container/contained apparatus", all three of which are intimately linked to the notion of projective identification (which will be described in detail in Chapters 10 and 11). We are going to develop these points in the next part.

To summarize, Bion postulates that the birth and quality of the psychic life of a human being are dependent not only on the mother (or the mothering object), but also on the mother's psychic life, and more particularly on what he calls her "capacity for reverie". Reverie describes the state of mind that is receptive to all the baby's projections and capable of receiving his projective identifications, whether good or bad. "Alpha function" transforms the unthinkable contents (which Bion calls "beta elements") into elements that are available for thought ("alpha elements"). By means of her alpha function, the mother detoxifies the baby's projections in her interpretative reverie. Alpha function thus makes it possible to match the projected contents with a container so that these "containing/contained" elements can be reintrojected and so that the infant's own apparatus for thinking is gradually developed.

The containing function is thus an active function which consists in receiving and transforming into thoughts the projected raw experiences. René Kaës (1976a, 1979), for example, emphasizes this active dimension by distinguishing two aspects of the object in exercising the containing function: the container (*contenant*) proper, which offers itself as a passive receptacle in which the baby's sensations–images–affects can be deposited, and the containing function (*conteneur*) which corresponds to the active aspect, to maternal reverie according to Bion, to the exercise of the alpha function.[7]

It may thus be said that the baby initially thinks with the apparatus for thinking of another person. His own apparatus for thinking, his own alpha function, constituted in and through this intersubjective psychic interaction, will enable him later to interpret his own emotional and subjective experiences. Mental growth depends on the internalization of the "containers-contents" formed by the process of projective identification. The object, by virtue of its alpha function, takes the first step in the activity of thinking: the baby splits and projects a part of his personality that is in a chaotic and confused state: the adequate object into which the emotional experience is expelled contains this part of the baby's personality, and in her "reverie" initiates the process of symbol-formation and of thinking.

We can therefore understand the importance of the feeding situation – and the fundamental importance that Esther Bick ascribes to it – and we can see its prototypical character: indeed, it is in the prototypical situation of feeding that this interaction between a baby in a state of disorganization and a mothering object who will transform his chaotic experience into one of integration is operative. A baby that is hungry has an experience of disorganization, of catastrophe; he is agitated, screams with despair, and struggles with a major experience of anxiety. When he is being fed, this bad feeling disappears and is replaced by a good gratifying feeling. He has the experience of being gathered together thanks to the attraction that the nourishing object exerts on him. The junction between the different sensory modalities – holding, envelopment, the interpenetration of gazes, the contact of the nipple in the mouth, tender and soothing words and the inner sense of plenitude – gives the baby an experience of being gathered together internally, a sense of ego, a sense of existing. This generates a first organization of the body image, a basic sense of identity. If this experience is good enough and repeated in a sufficiently rhythmic, and thus sufficiently predictable way, the baby will gradually internalize it and will be able to rediscover it if needs be (always with the help of another person who is sufficiently attentive and interpretative). For example, when the baby is hungry, the feeling he has will always be one of annihilation and he will have no choice but to evacuate this feeling by means of motility (being agitated, screaming and crying). If the parent understands the baby's distress and takes him in her arms, comforts him, speaks to him, the baby will calm down. And yet he will still feel hungry. But this bad sensation will be detoxified of catastrophic anxieties. It will be transformed into a tolerable feeling and may even pave the way for the baby to be able to represent the absent object, the feeling of plenitude to come. This is the beginning of thinking.

Furthermore, and to put things in another way, the situation of feeding provides the experience of a multi-sensual conjunction. Now if this experience has been internalized, in the case of distress or disorganization, the reminder of just one of the sensual modalities may suffice to give the baby the experience of being gathered together again, an experience of integration. This is a clear sign that the optimal containing object (the complex ensemble that it represents) has been internalized and that the baby has the capacity to call on this internalized object, to draw on his own capacity to think – on the condition that he is helped by the real external containing object, who will simply remind him of a more or less partial aspect of the global complex situation.[8]

If the legitimate normal early anxieties are not recognized, contained, thought about and transformed by the mothering environment or if the baby cannot benefit from the work of containing, they may disturb or intoxicate the subsequent process of development. Here is an example.[9]

> A mother gives birth to a baby a few weeks after the death of her own father. We can imagine and notice, through her discourse and account of the experience, the effects of the mother's mourning on the quality of her mental presence for the child. A few weeks after the birth, the child was diagnosed with a serious cardiovascular illness and the doctors did not know if he would survive. The child survived, developed some difficulties due to his cardiovascular problem and to the traumatic effects on his environment of the discovery of this illness, a trauma that was added to the grief that the mother was already experiencing.

It may be assumed that the baby – who is struggling to live, to breathe (due to his cardiovascular difficulties), who encounters a grieving mother, herself affected by death and overwhelmed by the child's imminent risk of death, by the sword of Damocles hanging over his head – has been subject to agonistic experiences of dramatic intensity, and repeated so often that they have left traces in the "memory of the body".

The optimal containing object

During a consultation, when this child was four years old, the parents complained about the appearance of enigmatic and distressing behavioural and somatic symptoms. I was initially led to understand these as signs of an internal breakdown in this child, and this was subsequently confirmed during the consultation. Indeed, during the consultation, it became apparent that, like every child but perhaps earlier than most children, the child had discovered death, the sense of death. He had heard it spoken about often enough in a context of drama and pain without understanding everything. But he had understood something, namely, the irreversibility of time.

Before, he thought that time was reversible (when one is big one can become small again, etc.). But now he had understood that time is irreversible. "When you are a granny or a grandpa, after you die", he said. "I don't want to die", he added. He asked his mother if she was going to die, etc. Then he played with a teddy and said to it: "You are ugly but I don't want you to die", and he asked his parents and his sister to tell the stuffed animal that it was ugly. This child was born after a sister who was described as an ideal baby, a "beautiful dream baby", whereas he was ugly. We can understand that he was repeating to the teddy words that he had probably heard as a baby, or in any case that reflected the ambient state of mind that he had encountered at that time.

It can be said that the discovery of death caused a recathexis of the traces of agonistic experiences that the child had experienced as a baby, experiences that those around him found it difficult to think about and transform at the time. And so the child experiences in his body breakdowns that are expressed in various symptoms. These perceptions mobilize an activity of thought and representation that can take place within a care setting, in the context of family care and treatment. The child can put into words what he had hitherto only been able to feel in his body, and words can be said to him about the breakdown that he has probably already experienced as well as the fears of dying that he may already have experienced in the distant past but which he fears may return.

Let us turn our attention now to this notion of "alpha function", which offers a detailed account of the intersubjective interactions at the basis of the activity of thinking in the baby.

3.2 Alpha function

Among the qualities required by the optimal object for ensuring its function as a container of psychic life, the capacity for "reverie" and for "alpha" functioning play a particularly important role. The notion of "alpha function" accounts for the inter- and intrapsychic, inter- and intrasubjective processes that are operative in the interactions between the mothering object and the baby, between the psychic container and the contents. The alpha function supports the "capacity for reverie" of the object whose task is to ensure the psychic birth of the baby.

It was in 1962 that Bion put forward the idea of an alpha function converting sense data into "alpha elements", providing the psyche with the material of thoughts. The mother's alpha function enables her to detoxify the baby's projections; he will then be able to reintroject the alpha elements, whose gradual assemblage will allow for the formation of a "contact-barrier" and the advent of his own alpha function. This contact-barrier provides the basis for the formation both of unconscious phantasies and for the "organ of consciousness" of which Freud (1900) speaks.

These Bionian concepts describe with great precision the very genesis of mental life. Alpha function operates on all the sense-impressions and on all the emotions of which we are conscious. It enables these to be apprehended as such and registered, chiefly in the form of visual images. It converts the sense-impressions and emotions into alpha elements, mnemic elements capable of being stored and of meeting the conditions of dream-thoughts, of unconscious waking thought, and thereby of conscious thought. Thus the alpha function transforms sense-impressions and emotional experiences in order to make them available for thought. Bion writes:

> The infant personality by itself is unable to make use of the sense data, but has to evacuate these elements into the mother, relying on her to do whatever has to be done to convert them into a form suitable for employment as alpha-elements by the infant.
>
> (Bion, 1962a, p. 116)

As they proliferate, the alpha elements come together to form the "contact-barrier" (Bion, 1962b).[10] This marks the point of contact and of separation between the conscious and unconscious elements and permits their distinction. The nature of the contact-barrier (agglomerated alpha elements or ordered logically or geometrically, etc.) will determine the selective passage of elements of consciousness to the unconscious and vice versa. The quality of this *contact-barrier* – which we understand as the *condition of the process of repression* – will affect dreams, memory and the characteristics of memories.

If alpha function is disturbed, or inoperative, sense-impressions and emotions remain unchanged and are felt to be "things-in-themselves",[11] raw and non-productive elements whose only fate is to be evacuated. These are "beta elements". They are stored but, unlike alpha elements, they represent not so much memories as "undigested facts", "raw experiences". Unlike alpha elements, beta elements cannot be rendered unconscious, memorized and made available for thought.

The disturbance or even the destruction of alpha function and the prevalence of beta elements characterize psychotic thinking. The psychotic subject is grappling with "things-in-themselves" rather than with their visual or verbal representations. As beta elements cannot be made unconscious, there is no repression, suppression or learning. The psychotic subject is thus incapable of discrimination; he cannot help but be aware of every slightest sensory excitation, but this hypersensibility does not constitute a conscious contact of the psychotic with himself or with others as living objects, who become inanimate objects. Indeed, even if they are described as, and felt to be, materially present, they assume non-living qualities.

We can thus begin to get an idea of the adverse, if not disastrous, consequences for the baby of a serious disturbance of alpha function of the object or of the mothering environment.

Let us see now how what Bion calls the "container-contained" apparatus functions, and how the alpha function of the object operates. The baby feels the need for a breast, by virtue of a sort of "innate preconception", of an "empty thought"[12] that is waiting to be "filled" or "saturated" by the realization of the breast:

> the need for the breast is a feeling and that feeling itself is a bad breast; the infant does not feel it wants a good breast but it does feel it wants to evacuate a bad one.
>
> (Bion, 1962b, p. 34)

Second postulate

In effect, the "bad breast" is felt to be a "thing-in-itself", a "proto-thought" which presents the characteristics of a beta element. This beta element has to be evacuated. The assimilation of food and the evacuation of the bad breast are indistinguishable. The "desired breast" can be felt to be an "idea of the absent breast" rather than a "present bad breast" when the bad-breast-element-beta, projected into the breast of the object, is transformed and converted into an alpha element and reintrojected; this good-breast-alpha-element will function as a representation of the breast distinct from the realization of the breast as such.

In other words, a content (the "bad breast") is projected into a container (the maternal breast) where it is "mated" with this container, before being reintrojected in the form of a "container-content". This apparatus becomes the infant's own apparatus for thinking.

If we generalize the experience of a feed, we can see with Donald Meltzer that,

> without an apparatus that can nourish itself on truth, the baby finds itself in the necessity of being nourished by the psychic life of the mother [of the mothering object]; the baby's experiences are confused in nature, and when it is bombarded by sense data of an emotional experience that it cannot understand, it is obliged to evacuate this experience into the mother who must be capable of containing it, modifying it and restoring it to the baby in a relatively meaningful form of order or of harmony, from which the catastrophic anxiety has been removed or, at least, diminished.
>
> (Meltzer and Harris, 1980, p. 357, translated from the French)

This function that the object accomplishes for the baby, alpha function, constitutes the first step in the activity of thinking of the baby himself, who initially thinks with the apparatus for thinking of his object. This activity of thinking thus rests on a process of projective identification whereby the baby splits and projects an unthinkable content, a confused emotional experience. The object/receptacle into which this content is projected contains this part of the baby's personality, and through its activity of "reverie" begins the work of symbol formation, the work of thinking.

Normal psychic development depends on the possibility for the baby to project intolerable feelings, for instance the feeling that it is dying, into the object, into the "breast", and to reinject them after their sojourn in the breast has rendered them more tolerable for its psyche:

> If the projection is not accepted by the mother the infant feels that its feeling that it is dying is stripped of such meaning as it has. It therefore reintrojects, not a fear of being made tolerable, but a nameless dread [...]. The establishment of a projective-identification-rejecting-object means that instead of an understanding object the infant has a wilfully misunderstanding object – with which it is identified.
>
> (Bion, 1962a, p. 116–117)

The normal, useful and creative character of projective identification, which represents an interaction between the rudimentary consciousness of the baby and the parental psyche, is dependent on what Bion calls the parent's "capacity for reverie".[13] We will come back further on to the description of projective identification and its normal or pathological qualities (Chapters 11 and 12). Let us add that this process that takes place between the psyche of the parent and the emerging psyche of the baby is similar to that which occurs between the analyst and the patient, when the latter is in a state of confusion and incapable of thinking about a disturbing or devastating emotional experience and relies on the analyst's capacity to accept and transform his projective identifications.

Furthermore, Bion (1962b) thinks that, in parallel with the realization of alpha function, there exists an envious and destructive part of the self which accomplishes a travesty of this function, elaborating alongside the contact-barrier what he calls the "beta-screen". The "beta-screen" is made up of "bizarre objects", defined as beta-elements with a tincture of personality, that is, to which ego and superego traces are added. Bizarre objects stem from the transformation of elements of the contact-barrier into alpha-elements divested of the characteristics that distinguish them from beta-elements. This transformation follows upon the destruction and the dispersion of the contact-barrier under the effect of the "reversal of direction of alpha-function". The beta-screen is the product of the psychotic part of the personality and creates dissociative, confusional or hallucinatory states. It also has the characteristic of inducing in the other an emotion or an attitude expected of him. The beta-screen can thus have effects of incomprehension and misunderstanding.

To return now to the capacity for reverie of which Bion speaks, which represents an indispensable quality of the container that both reveals and is dependent on the mother's own alpha function.

> When the mother loves the infant what does she do it with? Leaving aside the physical channels of communication my impression is that her love is expressed by reverie.
> (Bion, 1962b, p. 35–36)

Bion considers this reverie as the psychological source of supply of the infant's needs for love and understanding. He defines it as follows:

> Reverie is that state of mind which is open to the reception of the infant's projective identifications whether they are felt by the infant to be good or bad. In short, reverie is a factor of the mother's alpha-function.
> (Bion, 1962b, p. 36)

The parent's capacity for reverie plays a fundamental role in the development of the baby's capacity to tolerate frustration, and thus in the development of his sense of reality. Indeed, when intolerance of frustration exceeds a certain threshold, the baby evacuates this traumatic experience into the parent by means of projective identification, and the parent, through her capacity for reverie, restores the emotional experience to the infant with reduced amounts of catastrophic anxiety; in this way the sense of reality is strengthened. Just as his sense of reality is strengthened, so is his sense of his own existence:

> The mother's capacity for reverie is the receptor organ for the infant's harvest of self-sensation gained by its conscious.
> (Bion, 1962a, p. 116)

If the object's capacity for reverie is deficient, the baby's capacity to tolerate frustration is sorely tested and additionally burdened.

In our view, the reverie of the mothering object enables her to give an interpretation to the baby's projections. By means of this interpretation the object contains the experience, and the baby will then be able to reinject it while drawing on the object's interpretation to construct his apparatus for interpreting, his apparatus for thinking, his psychic apparatus.

This process functions in the same way in the analytic situation. It should be added that the "interpretation" that the parent or analyst gives, in their "reverie", concerns their own emotional experience. As Donald Meltzer (1984ac) says, when the analyst gives the patient an interpretation concerning a dream, for example, what he is describing, in fact, is the significance not of the patient's dream but of his own dream, of the dream that he is having in the session, of what comes to him in the form of dreams and fantasies from the deepest aspects of his own mind concerning the emotional significance of the situation. The analyst's capacity for reverie, a support for the countertransference and condition of psychic construction in the patient, illustrates the same function as the parental capacity for reverie, the condition of the psychic birth of the baby: this is alpha function.

Didier Houzel (1986) likens the "reverie" of the parent to the "metaphorical interpretation" of the analyst when he proposes to link up disconnected elements of the material by means of a comparison ("that resembles", "that makes me think of", "for me, that evokes") an associative link with the characters of the psychic world. This link is not only a substitution of one signifier for another, but an "internal transformation of the psychic objects, making it possible to create new objects that subsume several aspects of a primary experience that were hitherto scattered" (p. 162). Didier Houzel considers that the capacity for reverie realizes the second level in the work of unifying the parts of the self. The first level of integration is brought about by the manoeuvres of clinging to an external object described by Esther Bick, the prototype of which is clinging to the nipple. The second level is thus realized by the capacity for maternal reverie which permits the mentalization of experience and provides the psychic means to keep the scattered parts of the personality linked together, which implies the possibility of "letting go" of the nipple. The third and last level is linked to the activity of symbolic thought.

The manifestations of an operative alpha function, of a capacity of adequate reverie, can be observed regularly in daily life. Geneviève Haag (1983), for example, reports the frequently heard remarks made by parents commenting on the normal clinging behaviour of their baby, such as: "Don't cling like that ... I'm not going to drown you ... I'm not going to let you down". Such ordinary comments reflect a close intuitive understanding of what the child is experiencing. Geneviève Haag considers that this attitude, namely, "the constant interpretation of – and the response, both physical and verbal to – the fundamental needs of the baby, and, in particular, his anxieties" (Haag, 1983, p. 263, translated for this edition), organizes the early links between the parent and their baby. We would say that it is thanks to their capacity for reverie that the parent, if he/she is sufficiently contained in their mental life, can detoxify the ordinary primitive anxieties of the baby.[14]

In unusual situations, this time, we can observe the spectacular capacity of certain mothers or of certain fathers of babies who are going through a transitory autistic state to try to reach their infant in the depths of his autistic withdrawal and, as it were, "reanimate him psychically". These mothers and fathers manifest a powerful desire to attract and catch the baby's gaze, to help him to be in contact with the living breast. With remarkable spontaneity, they can help the infant to develop the illusion of creating an object full of life. On the other hand, other mothers, other fathers, who feel particularly hurt by the baby's withdrawal, particularly terrorized by the absence of eye contact, show great difficulties in going towards and entering into contact with their baby. The baby who "refuses" to make eye contact with the parents, to create the feeling of parenthood in the mother or the father, to give them the feeling that they are good parents, mobilizes intense early anxieties in them. If these anxieties are not detoxified, or insufficiently detoxified, the parent(s) will not be able to contain them. As a result, they will be unable to receive and contain the specific anxieties of the baby who will have no other recourse than to maintain his autistic withdrawal, a desperate means of clinging to life, more or less transitorily.

In her book *Live Company* (1992), Anne Alvarez also describes the dynamic qualities of the containing object (the parent or the therapist) and emphasizes the *claiming activity* – already mentioned earlier – of the object, who must not only satisfy or modify or transform the needs of the baby but also actively "claim" him, contributing or adding something to enrich his development. The function of claiming implies, of course, bringing a depressed or withdrawn child back to a normal level of presence, reanimating him psychically as we were saying; but it also implies bringing a child who is already at a normal level to a higher level of emotional experience (joy, surprise, astonishment, pleasure, and so on). The parent claims the baby's attention, calls on the baby to relate and communicate, and to be born as a psychic individual.[15]

3.3 Alpha function and mental life before birth. The "history of birth"

At this stage in our reflections, a clarification is necessary. Our attention is focused on the conditions and realization of the differentiation of a singular psychic space. This is dependent on the introjection of a container with particular qualities and according to a precise process, which we have just described. This introjected container will have the function of delimiting an internal space and an external space, on the one hand, which is what we are going to look at now, and of developing this space by nourishing, protecting and promoting the growth of the objects that it contains, on the other hand.

However, neither the baby in whom the process of introjecting an external containing object is as yet insufficiently advanced, nor the foetus in the uterine matrix, are exempt from mental or rather "protomental" life.[16] Indeed, it is conceivable that the sensory and motor systems enable the foetus to have access to sensori-motor information that reaches the undifferentiated psyche, participating in its construction, in the form of what Piera Aulagnier (1975) describes as pictograms, with which are associated what Donald Meltzer (Meltzer et al., 1985) calls "protoemotions", a term that we can understand, by analogy with the term protomental, as denoting representations of the psyche in which emotion is not differentiated from sensory perception. Without wanting necessarily to detect indications of the appearance of an increasingly early ego, close to birth and even before birth, during intrauterine life, we can nonetheless envisage the fog of the psychic life of the foetus well before the time, as a baby, when he is confronted with the necessity of introjecting an optimal containing object ensuring his mental and physical continuity. It is legitimate to consider, as Donald Meltzer (1984b, 1986, 1987a, 1992; Meltzer et al., 1985, 1988) does on several occasions, inspired by the "scientific fiction" elaborated by Bion (1973–1974, 1977ab, 1979) about foetal life, that emotional experiences, their symbolic representation and their impact on the structuring of the personality begin in utero.

It is worth pointing out that studies on foetal sensory and perceptual skills, which reveal foetal capacities for discrimination, show the *transnatal continuity* in perceptual experience. These research studies attest to foetal capacities to discriminate certain stimuli, in particular the mother's voice, capacities for memorizing and recognizing acoustic sequences and language stimuli, emphasize the reactivity of the foetus to the "voice addressed", and explore other skills besides.[17] Concerning the emotional aspects of foetal life, the ultrasound observations realized according to the methodology of Esther Bick by Alessandra Piontelli (1987, 1989, 1992ab) or Romana Negri (Negri et al., 1990; Negri, 1995, 1997) – whose work was supervised by Donald Meltzer – follow up observations of babies after their birth, show the *behavioural continuity between the foetus and the infant* and make it possible to construct or argue in favour of hypotheses concerning the richness of the emotional life of the foetus and the impact of foetal life on the development of personality.

In his "bionian tale of foetal life and of the caesura of birth" (Meltzer and Sabatini Scolmati, 1985) – a tale that should be understood not as a theory but simple as conjecture, a model for exploring clinical phenomena – Donald Meltzer describes the alpha function in the protomental processes of the foetus from the moment the latter has attained a sufficient degree of neuroanatomical complexity. The alpha function in the foetus links up the formal *gestalts* of the sense organs with protoemotions, forming the first "symbolic representations" of the significance of these protoemotions. As protomental experiences are blurred, impossible to coordinate, "cushioned", this primitive symbolism is first and foremost "auditory and rhythmic in its form, with a physical aspect comparable to dance" (Meltzer and Sabatini Scolmati, p. 95, translated from the French).

In his scientifico-poetic language, Donald Meltzer pursues his reconstruction as follows. He suggests that the dream processes derived from this primitive symbolism remain peaceful and do not give rise to any reversal of alpha function, as long as no foetal distress appears. But when the term of pregnancy approaches and the walls of the uterus (of the "claustrum") retract, various kinds of distress provoke a reversal of the alpha function; this is reflected in the production of "bizarre objects" which are evacuated in the form of psychosomatic disturbances and hallucinations. The foetus then seeks an object to contain these psychic disturbances, and its auditory impressions suggest the existence of "extra-terrestrial" objects capable of providing such a service. Its efforts in this search will result in breaking the claustrum. But the external world then comes as a great shock. The intensity of external stimuli makes them painful, either in a primary way or in a way that is secondary to the emotions they arouse. Alpha function is then once again reversed, and the bizarre objects are evacuated in the form of screams, streams of urine and faeces. But this evacuation now meets with a receptive-containing object capable of re-establishing the beta elements, of transforming them, of restoring alpha elements to the baby and of permitting him thereby to have "interesting dreams".

When the baby has found this object, he is faced with new problems insofar as he notices that the object is not always present, that it is not always satisfying, that it is both thrilling and a source of despair:

> The natural tendency of the baby [...] is then to *split the object into good and bad*. But this also *splits his self into segments* that are attracted to these objects and identified with them when they are either internalized (introjective identification) or penetrated (projective identification), or both. The development of the structure of personality has begun.
> (Meltzer and Sabatini Scolmati, 1985, p. 96, translated from the French)

Notes

1 Melanie Klein was one of the first to insist on the importance of the relations to the actual object in the development of the psyche. She emphasized on many occasions the role of good and bad experiences, in reality, which confirm the phantasies of a good and bad object, which reinforce trust in the good aspects of the self or alternatively the fear of the talionic superego. "From its inception, analysis has always laid stress on the importance of the child's early experiences, but it seems to me that only since we know more about the nature and contents of its early anxieties, and the continuous interplay between its actual experiences and its phantasy-life, can we fully understand *why* the external factor is so important" (1935, p. 285).

2 In the sense that Meltzer (Meltzer et al., 1982) gives to this term which we have already discussed and will return to later (Chapters 5 and 7).
3 Didier Houzel (1994) drew inspiration from the notion of attractor as described by the mathematician René Thom in connection with his "catastrophe theory" (Thom, 1972). Concerning this force of attraction exerted by the mother's face, voice and breast, see Klaus and Kennell, 1982.
4 On the false self, see Chapter 15.
5 Tustin (1986) spoke of "rhythm of security".
6 One of us has worked particularly on this question of rhythmicity in the experience and development of the baby (Ciccone, 2005, 2013a, b, 2014, 2015, 2016c).
7 Note that this distinction by René Kaës was taken up by Didier Anzieu (1986b, 1990) who, curiously, subsequently inverted it (1993a, 1994), attributing to the containing function (*conteneur*) the characteristics of the container (*contenant*), and vice versa.
8 Berry Brazelton (1973), for instance, in his assessment scale of the skills of the newborn baby, prioritizes the functionality of the means of soothing an agitated and crying baby (from the mere presentation of the face, associated subsequently with words, then with the contact of a hand, etc., to holding the baby in one's arms and rocking) to measure his aptitude to be comforted, that is, in metapsychological terms, to appreciate the quality of the processes of internalization or of introjection that he has carried out.
9 Extract from Ciccone, 1995a.
10 Bion was inspired by the properties of the contact barriers described by Freud in 1895.
11 The term "things-in-themselves" is derived from Kant's (1781) thought, where it refers to objects as they are, independent of observation, contrary to objects of experience or sensible intuition.
12 Term also inspired by Kant.
13 The container-contained apparatus is constantly, in the course of development and throughout life, subject to internal tensions. Bion, with his conception of "catastrophic change" (1965, 1966), has described the relational tension between a container and a content. This tension can be found, for instance, between an idea and the statement that is supposed to contain this idea. Bion (1967a, 1970) has shown the necessity of an adequate container when faced with the violence of new forms of thought. Each new idea that is developed, threatens, with its expansive thrust, to destroy the psychic container, hence the

importance of an external container that is neither too rigid nor too flexible in order to strengthen the internal container and allow the new idea to develop.

14 We can find very illustrative and lively clinical examples of the ordinary containing function of the object in an article by Martha Harris (1970) titled: "Some notes on maternal containment in 'good-enough' mothering".

15 See the studies on the establishment of early relations in which researchers, filming the first contacts between mothers and their baby, highlight the intense claiming activity of mothers to get their baby to open his eyes and to begin relating to them (McFarlane, 1977; Klaus and Kennel, 1982).

16 Term borrowed from Bion (1961), which denotes a state in which the physical and mental spheres are undifferentiated.

17 See Mehler et al., 1978, 1988; De Casper and Fifer, 1980; De Casper and Spence, 1986, De Casper and Granier-Deferre,1994; Herbinet et al., 1981; Lecanuet et al., 1989, 1995; Busnel and Granier-Deferre, 1989; Busnel, 1997.

4

PSYCHIC SPACE[1]

The picture that Melanie Klein develops throughout her work of an internal world full of objects with complex relations between them, and her picture of the exchanges between the ego and the objects, and more particularly of the transactions of the ego within the objects themselves (based in particular on her conceptualization of projective identification), has led Kleinian and post-Kleinian authors to develop a visual representation of *psychic space*. The notion of a containing object, moreover, implies the conception of a spatiality of the psychic world. Bion was thus led to speak of psychic space, mental space, emotional space and a space of thought (Bion, 1963, 1965, 1970). Money-Kyrle (1968) has envisaged the construction of an internal spatio-temporal system, the result of an internalization of external objects. Resnik has often utilized the expression "mental space", and one of his books, moreover, bears this title (Resnik, 1994). But it is Meltzer who has worked on this notion most, and who has developed a picture of the structure of the space of the psychic world, with all its complexity, and of life in the different places of this internal space.

4.1 The four worlds and their spatialization

Psychic space is divided initially into two worlds: the internal world and the external world. These world are full of objects which themselves possess an internal world. Donald Meltzer (Meltzer et al., 1975; Meltzer, 1984a, 1992) thus describes four worlds: the internal world, the external world, the interior of the external world and the interior of the internal world. To this he adds the "nowhere world", a black hole; into which every psychic element that approaches it is in danger of disappearing. Concerning the terminology, on the subject of these various chambers in the "geography of the psychical apparatus", he points out elsewhere (Meltzer, 1967) that the terms "internal" and "external" apply to the psychic worlds, whereas the "interior" or "exterior", the "inside" or the "outside" are terms that serve to define the relationship with the interior or exterior of the body of an object (internal or external). Each object can thus be identified regarding its "geographical localization in fantasy". The complex relations between each of these worlds are established by virtue of the perpetual movement of projection/introjection. According to this view, derived from Melanie Klein's thought and conceptualization, the model of the psychic universe is organized according to a very particular spatial complexity.

Didier Houzel (1985b) has thrown light on the three frontiers of psychic space. The first frontier separates the interior space of the self and the interior space of external objects; these two spaces are primarily the locus of the operation of projective identification, where a split-off part of the personality is projected into the object that it cathects. The second frontier concerns the interior space of the self and the interior space of internal objects; it is the seat, on the one hand, of introjective identification, and of projective identification into internal objects, on the other, which is a form of "narcissistic introjection", different from true introjection. We have already spoken about this process and we have suggested that this movement of narcissistic introjection, or of projective identification with internal objects, underlies phantasies of incorporation and differentiates incorporation from introjection (see Chapter 1). Finally, the third frontier distinguishes the internal space from the external space. It is this frontier that has been the subject of research such as that of Esther Bick on the psychic skin or that of Didier Anzieu on the skin-ego.

The topographical complexification of psychic space is accompanied by a multidimensional development, as envisaged by Donald Meltzer (Meltzer et al., 1975). In his chapter "Dimensionality in mental functioning", Meltzer proposes a developmental point of view of spatial dimensionality in the view-of-the-world. He describes the one-dimensionality, two-dimensionality, three-dimensionality and, lastly, the four-dimensionality of psychic space, while explaining the nature of mental experience at these various levels.

- *One-dimensionality* characterizes a world full of objects whose only quality is that of being attractive or repellent, a world in which time is indistinguishable from distance and where the self, by moving away from an object, only moves simultaneously towards another by pure chance, a world from which emotionality is almost absent. The one-dimensional world, according to

Meltzer, is that of "autism proper", which is characterized essentially by an absence of mental activity, by a reduction of experience to a series of events not available for memory or thought.[2]

- The *two-dimensional state* corresponds to a state prior to the distinction between internal space and external space. Objects are perceived as undifferentiated from the sensual qualities of their surfaces. Relating is a relationship of sticking, consisting of mirror imitation, echolalia and superficiality.[3] No process of projection can occur for lack of a differentiated internal space. Two-dimensionality represents an impairment of memory and desire, for the relationship to time is essentially circular, since the self would be unable to conceive of enduring change, and therefore of development or cessation. Any threat to this changelessness tends to be experienced as a breakdown of surfaces, with the emergence of the primitive catastrophic anxieties to which we have already referred (liquefaction, falling endlessly, explosion, and so on). The autistic state can clearly be recognized here.

- *Three-dimensionality* marks the appearance of the interior space of the self and of the object, of projective and introjective processes, of the differentiated organization of the external and internal worlds with the emergence of thought. With three-dimensional space the conception arises of natural orifices (which are no longer provoked by tearing, as in two-dimensionality), as well as of a "sphincter function". The self struggles to protect and control its orifices in order to have access to mental continence. Time is no longer indistinguishable from distance as in one-dimensionality, nor circular as in two-dimensionality; rather it is apprehended as a movement from an interior to an exterior, taking on a definite directional tendency.

- Lastly, the *fourth dimension of mental space* corresponds to the psychic stage linked to the introjection of good parents, who will weave a story internally. Four-dimensionality characterizes the struggle against narcissism and the reduction of the omnipotence ascribed to good objects as well as intrusive persecutory objects that require absolute control. It marks the advent of a new type of identification, namely introjective identification whose predominance (compared with projective identification) will allow for the establishment of a mode of object- relating in the place of a type of exclusively narcissistic identification.

How does the transition from one organization to the other occur? Cléopâtre Athanassiou (1982) has offered us some very precious elements for understanding this. With the help of a schema that we have reproduced below, she illustrates the evolution of psychic space in its different dimensions (Athanassiou studies the evolution from one-dimensionality to three-dimensionality), as well as the development of the first forms of identification inherent to this evolution.

Here is this schema (Athanassiou, 1982, p. 1192–1198):

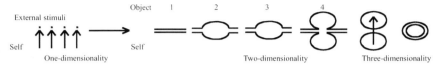

Let us consider first the transition from one- to two-dimensionality. One-dimensionality corresponds, in the baby, according to Athanassiou, to a series of integrations/disintegrations. The baby clings to successive sensory stimuli. Between these "points of clinging" where the baby is gathered together in its mental life, there is simply a state of emptiness without any experience of identity. The transition to the experience of a two-dimensional world, in other words the establishment of a "surface identity", takes place progressively through the repetition of this "point centring" so that the effect of a first centring can persist until a second centring occurs. This effect of "continuous centring" gives the surface sensation to which the psyche organized in a two-dimensional mode can adhere. Attention is maintained from one point to another and the self does not disintegrate immediately each time the object disappears, as is the case in one-dimensionality.

The transition from two- to three-dimensionality takes place through a progressive unsticking – the first control of the experience of psychic separation – of the adhesive contact, at the centre of a zone of intense sticking. Gradually, the two psychic layers that are partially unstuck each circumscribe a space, contained in a container. With the appearance of this third dimension (the interior space), the processes of inclusion and thus of projective identification can operate; each space, that of the self and that of the object, can receive and contain the other. In the three-dimensional state the rapport between the self and the object is reversible. For example, when the baby is held by his mother in a sufficiently enveloping way to feel contained in an envelope to which his own envelope adheres completely, and he sucks his thumb, at that moment "the thumb in the mouth is the self in the object; but it is also the nipple/object in the containing self" (Athanassiou, 1982, p. 1196, translated for this edition). The differentiation between the ectoderm of the self and the endoderm of the object – the two surfaces are no longer identical or twinned as in two-dimensionality –, between the skin of the self and the skin of the object, is dependent on the creation of a space that Cléopâtre Athanassiou describes as the space of the paternal function. This space allows the self to constitute itself as separate from the world of adhesive relations and to activate the processes of projective and introjective identification. The self can then feel sure that it contains the object, in other words, that it can construct its own nucleus of identity.

We would like to propose a modification and a complement to the schema of Cléopâtre Athanassiou in order to illustrate more precisely the functioning and complexification of the modes of identification, beginning with their most primitive aspect. In the next part we will come back to the idea that adhesive identification functions in the two-dimensional register, projective identification in the three-dimensional register and introjective identification in the four-dimensional register. Athanassiou locates projective identification in the three-dimensional state, with which we are completely in agreement. But we understand her description of three-dimensionality as indicating that the fourth dimension – where the interior space of the subject is separate from the interior space of the object, each caught up in, and constructing, its own historicity – has already been established. We locate three-dimensionality starting from drawing n° 3 in Athanassiou's schema, and above all in n° 4, which symbolizes *two distinct spaces connected by a common skin*. It is here, it seems to us, that projective identification is operative, with the confusion of spaces that it implies (of which Athanassiou gives a good description) and with the adhesive effect that can be observed clinically. This sometimes leads to errors of interpretation because, at the level of phenomenological expression, the adhesive effect of projective identification sometimes gives it the appearance of adhesive identification (see Chapters 7 and 12).

The projective identification described by Athanassiou, which she locates in what we consider to be the fourth dimension of mental space, corresponds in our view to the *projective aspect of introjective identification* (a part of the self sojourns in the object – experienced as *separate* – then is introjected and strengthens the nucleus of identity). Real projective identification, however, is linked to a fundamentally symbiotic mode of relating, and is operative in a context of confusion of spaces – of the self and of the object – experienced as delimited by a "common skin" (Mahler, 1968; Anzieu, 1985).

Here, then, is the new schema that we are proposing, based on Cléopâtre Athanassiou's schema, and in the light of the discussion above:

Psychic space

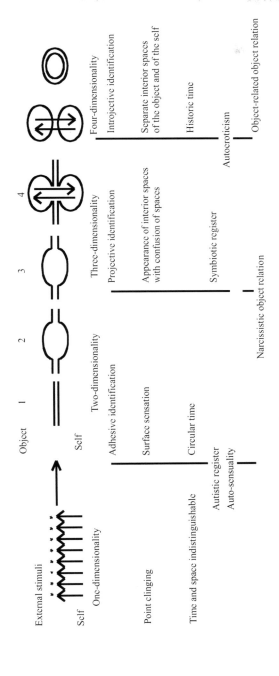

An essential point must be emphasized here that we will return to on several occasions. This schema illustrates, among other things, how all introjective identification necessarily comprises a projective movement. It also illustrates how projective identificatory processes, and the symbiotic relationship in which they take place, imply that a *normal basic adhesivity* functions and keeps the two psychic spaces "attached". We would say that *introjectivity contains projectivity*, and that *projectivity contains adhesivity*. The transition, for the object from a status of adhesive object (autistic or "autisticized" – see Ciccone, 1996b, 1997a, 2012a) to a status of confused object (symbiotic) and then of a separate object remains difficult to form a conception of, and can no doubt be considered in terms of a modification or reversal of the proportionality of the different identificatory components (adhesive, projective, introjective) constituting the relationship with the object. It may be said, moreover, that the object is never totally separate. The projective component of introjective identification always maintains a confusional aspect in every "separate state". Nevertheless, the connection uniting two separate objects – even if there is always a symbiotic nucleus in separation – and the connection uniting two objects linked by projective identification are of a very different nature, and the ensuing sense of identity for each of them does not have the same consistency in each case.

After this description of psychic space, from both a structural and development point of view, and before focusing more particularly on the notion of the internal world, it is worth noting how Donald Meltzer (Meltzer et al., 1982; Meltzer, 1984a, 1988, 1992) describes the existence of spatiality in internal objects too, and in particular in what may be considered as a prototypical internal object, the fruit of the internalization of the primary object, which Meltzer calls the "*claustrum*", when it is occupied by the ego or parts of the ego which seek omnipotently a refuge to protect themselves from different anxieties. This object is thus the locus of projective identification, or rather, *intrusive identification* as Meltzer prefers to say, who describes various chambers in this claustrum. Each chamber, when it is penetrated by intrusive identification, gives the ego a particular characterology. Three main chambers are defined: the head-breast, the genital chamber and the rectal chamber, and Meltzer describes life inside each of these chambers. Life in the head-breast gives an effect of grandiosity; life in the genital chamber is characterized by erotomania; and life in the rectal chamber is governed by sadism, violence and tyranny. Moreover, life in each of these chambers generates specific claustrophobic anxieties.[4]

4.2 The internal world
4.2.1 Internal sociality

The conception that we owe to Melanie Klein of the internal world gives this world the very concrete aspect of a social organization, of an *internal groupality*.

> Mental space and the notion of the internal world constitute [...] a theatrical and kaleidoscopic experience where all the characters called "internal objects" will assume different functions and will try to speak to each other, to express their agreement or disagreement, or separate from each other [...]. Every individual is a living group,

writes Salomon Resnik (1985, p. 50, translated for this edition), who considers the individual as "a more or less tuned multiple entity depending on the degrees of integration of the ego" (ibid., p. 53). Resnik (1985, 1986c, 1989, 1999) refers to the multiple nature of each person, drawing on the "social" perspective that Klein gave to the subject's interiority, a subject as a community of internal objects. He recalls that Bion, in his teaching, always thought "in group terms" in connection with the multiplicity of the human being; Bion spoke of the psychotic as a group-patient, a "group-personality", says Resnik (1986b, 1989).[5]

The concept of an internal world had already been used by Freud (1911b, 1921) but in a metaphorical sense – his chapter titled "The internal world" (see Freud, 1940a [1938]) remained unfinished. Abraham (1924) had conceived of it more concretely. But, as Meltzer (1984a) points out:

> Melanie Klein's work undeniably introduced into the concept of psychic reality, with the internal objects and the parts of the self that inhabit this reality, a cosmology, a sociology one might say, much more concrete than Freud or Abraham had ever conceived of or intended. By establishing this very concrete differentiation between interior and exterior, Melanie Klein's work established a link with an aspect of the history of psychology

that, over the centuries, had been the monopoly of theology; that is to say treats many of the qualities and significations of the gods and devils that had belonged to the matrix of theology as qualities of internal objects, placing them – as far as their psychological meanings are concerned – within the mind and the body.

(Meltzer, 1984a, p. 542–543, translated from the French)

Salomon Resnik (1994), moreover, stresses how the notion of internal object gives depth to mental space, introduces a third dimension and implies the idea that the space of the internal world is inhabited by an "ego in relief" (in contrast to the representation of a two-dimensional image projected onto a screen).

What does the internal world and the objects that inhabit it consist of? The inner world, Klein writes, consists of

innumerable objects taken into the ego, corresponding partly to the multitude of varying aspects, good and bad, in which the parents (and other people) appeared to the child's unconscious mind throughout various stages of his development. Further, they also represent all the real people who are continually becoming internalized in a variety of situations provided by the multitude of ever-changing external experiences as well as phantasied ones. In addition, all these objects are in the inner world in an infinitely complex relation both with each other and with the self.

(Klein, 1940, p. 362–363)

The inner world is "the product of the child's own impulses, emotions and phantasies" (Klein, 1955, p. 141). The experiences originating in external sources exert an influence over internal relations and events, just as the internal world influences the perception of the external world. It is the immediate and combined action of introjection and projection that builds the inner world at the same time as it outlines an image of the external world.

The life of the inner world begins with essentially bodily sensations and expressions, and initially presents a concrete aspect. Indeed, the infant feels that, inside his body, there are parts of people, that they are alive and active, affect him, and are affected by him. Paula

Heimann (1952a) regards these internal objects as real "citizens of the inner world". The ego maintains emotional relations with them that are similar to those it has with people in the external world. All the relational interactions between an object and the ego can occur within the mind. Concerning the topographical localization of internal objects, they are situated in all the agencies. They can be introjected into the superego, modifying its severity or its tolerance; they can inhabit the ego, having an effect on its character, etc.

> This inner world of life and events is the creation of the infant's unconscious phantasy,[6] his private replica of the world and objects around him.
> (Heimann, 1952a, p. 155)

The infant will be affected as much by the manifestations of his inner objects, imagined by himself though they are, as by those of the real people outside himself.

Internal objects are first perceived as people or parts of people living inside the infant. He has introjected them through experiences with external objects. These internal objects are not an exact replica of external objects, insofar as they are both subject to and created by the infant's phantasies; gradually, in the course of ego-integration, internal objects lose their concrete quality and take on an abstract quality.

> Phantasies about living entities within the self develop into ideas and mental work with concepts.
> (Ibid., p. 157)

The clarification that internal objects are not an exact replica, but a "private replica" of external objects, emphasizes the work of *transformation* that is imposed on the mind in the deployment of the processes of appropriation, integration, the constitution of psychic objects, in other words, in the work of subjectivation.

4.2.2 Three-dimensionality as the inauguration of the internal world and thought

The potentiality of an internal world, extraordinarily full of animate objects with a relational life, *depends on the introjection of an optimal containing object* which marks the three-dimensional organization of psychic space. Indeed, it is with three-dimensionality that the interior spaces of the self and the object appear, and into which something can be projected and reintrojected. This communication, which implies the projection into the object of parts of the self and the reintrojection into the self of the object, or aspects of the object, is evidence of the beginning of the constitution of the internal world and of the birth of thought. We have given examples, derived from infant observation, illustrating this transition (Chapter 1).

The three-dimensional representation of the object and, through identification, of the self, gives each of them a container separating the spaces. This representation implies that the object is no longer perceived as a sensual surface alone and that it attests to its capacity to contain its own differentiated space. The idea of orifices in the object and in the self then arises. Thus, the potentiality of a container is linked to the establishment of what Donald Meltzer (Meltzer et al., 1975) calls a "sphincter-function". The three-dimensional state permits the birth of thought, for it implies the possibility of an absent object, that is to say defusion with the object and its inclusion in psychic space, its internalization in the form of a first representation. The object, from the three-dimensional perspective, is "separate enough to be desired and taken in to the self rather than being affixed to" (Wittenberg, 1975, p. 94).

The transition from a two-dimensional world to a three-dimensional world can be illustrated by the following example. It concerns a three-year-old autistic child that I (A.C.) observed in the context of a family therapy:[7]

> Aurélien spent most of the time in the family therapy sessions on the "periphery" of the experience of the consultation. He was "elsewhere", with a vague look on his face, looking absent, or plunged into a fusional possession with an object that he "observed" from all angles for very long periods of time (which induced his father to speak about his uncanny feelings faced with this mysterious child who seemed to "see the world differently from us", to "see reliefs and perspectives that we cannot make out", etc.), or who would be hiding under the desk, under a chair, his eyes covered with his hands or with his mother's hands that he was holding in front of his face. The need to hide his eyes occurred during moments when the quality of his mental presence was better. In

fact, Aurélien frequently sought eye contact, but could not stand being looked at by therapists. When he made eye contact with one of his therapists, Aurélien hid his eyes, got down under the desk, or he "lost" himself, focusing on a virtual point in the distance through the window. He could only tolerate being looked at, in a non-persecutory exchange, on the condition that he had a proprioceptive support, a tactile support during these experiences of interpenetrating communication. He was provided with this support in positions such as when he was on his mother's knees, with his back against her belly, with a hand behind his mother's head (behind her eyes); or when he was lying on his back with his legs entangled with his mother's; or when he was behind his mother (behind her eyes) and "supporting" her neck, her head and her eyes.

Moreover, Aurélien very often imitated, so furtively that only a very shrewd observation could identify it, intimate attitudes of one or the other therapists: rubbing the chin, touching the moustache, scratching the head, crossing the arms, holding the hands, etc. These mimetic behaviours were usually dissociated from the "bodily discourse" that Aurélien expressed at such moments.

Aurélien dramatized the fragility of his psychic skin which led him to stick to surfaces — the sensory surface of objects whose qualities he mutilated, the behavioural surface of the people whose personal attitudes he imitated, the spatial surface of the room whose contours he sought to reduce. However, the first outlines of a three-dimensional organization could be observed. Indeed, the attraction of the gaze highlighted the beginnings of a representation of an interior of the object. This interiority which attracted him terrorized him at the same time and generated catastrophic anxieties that could only be contained through the reinforcement of his external envelope (proprioceptive support, tactile contact with the external object-mother). Without this recourse, the only solution for him was to project immediately outside, through the window, the bits of himself imprisoned in the bits of the object (the therapist's head).

From this point of view Aurélien's mimetism manifested not so much a need to reduce the two-dimensionality of the object to its surface qualities as a desire to experience the interiority of the object. These outlines of projective identification attest to the birth of a three-dimensional space, a space where the terror due to the perception of interiority leads to the need to stick himself to the internal surface of the object (lodge himself at the back of the head, behind the eyes) or to expel the fragments of himself engulfed by the fragments of the object. Meltzer (Meltzer et al., 1975) explains how, for an autistic child, looking inside the therapist's eyes can be immediately transformed into peering through the window, when the notion of interiority is not yet felt and no degree of projective identification can as yet be attained. Aurélien, in his psychic development, was just beyond this point, that is, at the point when outlines of three-dimensionality are present, when projective identification is very similar to adhesive identification, when interior and exterior are delimited and indistinguishable, when interiority is apprehended as confused sensations of emptiness and/or of fullness, when the problem of the classification of spatial experience (interior/exterior, empty/full, etc.) arise. In such moments, the infant who is looking inside the object and then peers at the void outside through the window, is trying, as Salomon Resnik (1986a), to empty immediately with his eyes an intolerable fullness, "a fullness that is full of emptiness" (Resnik, 1986a, p. 188, translated for this edition).

The establishment of a "sphincter-function" was represented by Aurélien in a game with a little box that he opened and closed untiringly; a game that appeared notably after attempts to approach one of the therapists. He was thereby enacting a work of psychically cathecting sphincter control, a work of elaboration of mental continence. The appearance of internal space is accompanied by claustrophobic anxieties (remaining imprisoned in the object) and agoraphobic (being intruded upon by the object and anxieties to do with bursting and being scattered into bits) which explain the compelling need to control the "psychic sphincters", to control exchanges with objects in the external world.

If two-dimensionality represents an ontogenetic stage, insofar as it is a privileged structuring of mental space at a moment when interiority cannot be totally experienced and thus represented, the two-dimensional flattening of the external-internal world also seems to be a possible defensive solution during experiences that endanger psychic life. In other words, as we shall see further on, the auto-sensual position (two-dimensionality, adhesive identification) is always a possible alternative, even in more complex psychic states where more elaborate positions are likely to predominate. We will see that it is contact with depressive anxiety that leads the ego to adopt this or that position, depending on the context.

Defensive recourse to two-dimensional flattening and adhesivity is illustrated, for example by Cléopâtre Athanassiou (1988) in an article titled "Le remaniement des souvenirs".

> Athanassiou gives, among others, the example of a three-month-old baby in good health who, after a playful exchange with his mother, and when she turned away from him to pay attention to the father, immediately "went absent" from everything, stopped moving and stared at a reflection of light on a radiator, showing indifference to everything surrounding him. When his mother re-established contact with him, he was cheerful again. Suddenly overcome with tiredness, the mother withdrew once again from the relationship. This time the baby began to scream. The mother interpreted these screams as an expression of hunger and so she tried to feed him; but the baby kept screaming. Not daring to imagine that the baby simply wanted to communicate with her, the mother suggested that he wanted his nappy changed. While doing this, she talked to him again, communicated with him, with the result that the baby cheered up again.

Cléopâtre Athanassiou comments on this observation and points out that the emotion linked to the loss of the object was present from the outset, but it went unnoticed by both the baby and those around him for everything was flattened on the surface of an object: the gleaming radiator. The second separation provoked screaming because the baby hoped he would be able to avoid recourse to this radical defence to relieve his suffering, he hoped that a containing and understanding object would help him; but as he no longer had his first defence, his position was very painful. Thus, during the second traumatic phase, the baby perceived that an object could contain his emotions linked to loss and give them meaning. Since this object was not available within the mind, it was in the external world that the baby made his appeal. Until then, his emotions, evacuated by adhesivity and two-dimensional flattening, had remained untransformed, unthinkable, like a "nameless dread" (Bion, 1962a).

> Adhesivity does not deal with terror; it can only annihilate for a moment. Only space in its three-dimensionality can be the site of a transformation.
>
> (Athanassiou, 1988, p. 81, translated for this edition)

The transition from the domain of what is not containable, and thus thinkable, to what becomes so, corresponds to the transition from a two-dimensional to a three-dimensional structuring of the internal-external world. The three-dimensionality of mental space, the establishment of a "sphincter-function" and the possibility of utilizing the processes of normal projective identification are all conditions inaugurating the actuation of the activity of thought.

Furthermore, the transition from a two-dimensional to a three-dimensional world, a condition and sign of the deployment of thought, introduces a conflict that Donald Meltzer has theorized as the "*aesthetic conflict*", and we can say that the example of Aurélien, seen above, is an illustration of this: Aurélien was both attracted and terrorized by interiority; he was attracted by the gaze, by the experience of the object's interiority, but this interiority was a place of anxiety, and even of terror. Meltzer (1984b, 1986; Meltzer and Harris Williams, 1988) put forward the hypothesis that the first conflict that the baby encounters on coming into the world results from the aesthetic impact that his object has on him and on his sensoriality, and of the enigmatic character of the interior of the object which contrasts with its exterior beauty. Meltzer treats the aesthetic conflict as a major issue of the depressive position, which he considers as, first, anterior to the paranoid-schizoid position (which is a defensive position into which the subject withdraws in order to escape the aesthetic impact and the pain of the aesthetic conflict). The baby is attracted by its dazzling object to such an extent that he sometimes has to close his eyes; but this object is elusive, giving and withdrawing, giving good and bad things in an enigmatic way, so that the baby finds himself submerged by the ambiguity of the messages he receives, by the complexity of the sensory and emotional experiences it is subjected to. He will thus ask himself questions about the interiority of the object. The attraction by the "beauty" of the object is a condition for the appearance of questions about the "interior beauty" of this object. This interest in the aesthetic qualities of the interior is evidence of the birth of thought.[8]

Notes

1 Chapter written by Albert Ciccone alone.
2 However, in the description that Meltzer gives of autism proper elsewhere (Bremner and Meltzer, 1975), mental space is described as *two-dimensional*. This is the idea we want to focus on (see Chapter 5).

3 Esther Bick has described, in 1975 (text published in 1986), how adhesive identification is two-dimensional (see the next chapter).
4 We will come back to these points in more detail when describing the processes of projective identification (Chapter 12).
5 Enrique Pichon-Rivière (with whom Salomon Resnik worked) had introduced the notion of *internal group* (Pichon-Rivière, 1971), but from a perspective that was still dependent on a psycho-sociological perspective, as René Kaës (1993) points out, who himself has developed this notion in his research based on Freudian theory and employing a model that is different from post-Kleinian authors (Kaës, 1976b, 1983, 1988a, 1993, 1994).
6 Except in citations, we do not follow the distinction, proposed originally by Susan Isaacs (1952), between fantasy and phantasy. In French we always use the term *fantasme*.
7 See also the example given by Suzanne Maiello (1988) of the treatment of an autistic child in whom she discerned the beginnings of a tri-dimensional organization of internal-external space.
8 We will come back, in Chapter 8, to this notion of aesthetic conflict.

PART III

THIRD POSTULATE

> The introjected containing object is experienced as a skin. It has a function of "psychic skin".

This third postulate will lead us, through the exploration of notions associated with that of "psychic skin", to consider its construction from an ontogenetic point of view.

We will first study the process of adhesive identification on which the emergence of the "psychic skin" is based, which will lead us to outline the representation of an "auto-sensual position".

Secondly, we will define the symbiotic state, with reference to Margaret Mahler's depiction of the symbiotic phase with the phantasy of a common frontier, and we will describe the "symbiotic position".

Finally, we will discuss the idea of the skin-ego elaborated by Didier Anzieu, a skin-ego depicting the constitution of a "psychic skin", with the advent of a "depressive position".

5

ON ADHESIVE IDENTIFICATION

Genesis of the psychic skin

The genesis of the psychic envelope and of the basic nucleus of identity rests on a primitive identificatory process: *adhesive identification*. This may be considered, as Donald Meltzer does (Meltzer et al., 1975), as a first form of what Freud (1910, 1915a, 1921, 1923), called *narcissistic identification*, the second, less primitive form, being represented by the process of *projective identification* described by Melanie Klein and her successors. Adhesive identification is located in two-dimensional space, and projective identification in three-dimensional space (*introjective identification*, on the other hand, comes into play with four-dimensionality).

The relinquishment of narcissistic identification in favour of introjective identification – the principal economic problem of analysis, as Jean Bégoin (1984) points out – represents the unavoidable precondition for psychic development leading to mental health. Adhesive identification will thus have to give way to projective identification, then to introjective identification. These identificatory stages are defined by the prevalence – and not the exclusivity – of an identificatory mode.

We will define adhesive identification by locating it in the mental state that it determines, or to which it is linked, namely, the "auto-sensual state". This state characterizes autism, as we have seen (Chapter 2), and it is also experienced temporarily and sporadically, by the baby in the very first moments of life, which has led some to speak of a "normal autistic state" for the baby. We have given an account of the transition from this mode of expression to that the "auto-sensual state", following Tustin in this respect, for the term "autistic" has a connotation that is too pathological (see Chapter 2). In (pathological) autism, adhesive identification can be observed as if enlarged by the lens of a microscope. Adhesive identification, in the auto-sensual state, operates in association with dismantling.

Adhesive identification and dismantling represent early defence mechanisms linked to a mental organization that may be described as the "auto-sensual position" (or "adhesive position", to use Esther Bick's terms). This corresponds to what Daniel Marcelli (1983) had described as the "autistic position". We adhere to the hypothesis put forward by Daniel Marcelli of such a psychic position – which we call "auto-sensual" – which, from an ontogenetic point of view, is situated at the dawn of personality and groups together characteristics of the same order as those that are specific to the autistic position defining autism.[1] The observation of pathological processes offers a path of access for the understanding of normal processes, and the observation of autistic processes helps us to understand a certain number of ordinary processes in the development of the subject, and here of the baby. There is nothing in pathology that does not exist in normal development, but obviously to a lesser degree. The processes become pathological when they are massive, exclusive and associated with other toxic processes, and distort their initial function, when they impede the development of the subject and the unfolding of subjectivity (see Ciccone et al., 2018).

Concerning the notion of "auto-sensual position" or "adhesive position", it takes up the conceptions developed by Daniel Marcelli concerning what he called the "autistic position". However, we differ from Daniel Marcelli's thinking on two points. The first concerns the notion of position, a term used by Melanie Klein, which can be understood as a coherent psychic constellation grouping together the anxieties, their attendant defence mechanisms, and the resulting object relation. Melanie Klein chose the term position to denote the phases of development because "these groupings of anxieties and defences, although arising first in the earliest stages, are not restricted to them but occur and recur during the first years of childhood, and under certain circumstances in later life" (Klein, 1952a, p. 236). Positions are thus manifestations of fundamental attitudes towards objects and refer as much to phases of development as to the fixation-points of pathologies. We will distinguish between the notion of position and that of stage or phase of development, but in a different way to Marcelli who attributes the notion of position to the field of psychogenesis and that of stage to the field of ontogenesis. We defend a model in which the psyche does not remain fixed in an exclusive state, but fluctuates, attracted by more or less contrasting or antagonistic tendencies. Within each phase of development, of each ontogenetic state/stage, the psyche occupies and experiments with several positions, some more narcissistic and others more object-related. Among the different positions, one will be predominant within each phase of development; the same is true for each psychopathological mental state.

The second point on which we differ from Marcelli concerns the pathologization of normal processes. In our view, psychopathological derivatives can be understood not only as an amplification and a fixation of normal defensive processes, but also and primarily as a morbid distortion of these processes put in the service of the struggle against development and growth. *Pathologization essentially amplifies the destructive aspect of normal processes.* We will have the opportunity of coming back to these points but, before considering this autistic or auto-sensual position, we would like to say a few words on normal auto-sensuality, previously called "normal autism", and add some clarifications.

5.1 Normal auto-sensuality

Daniel Marcelli, with his ontogenetic hypothesis of a normal autistic position, is in keeping with the ideas of Margaret Mahler (1968) who envisaged a normal autistic phase, and of Frances Tustin (1972, 1981b) who used the terms normal primary autism, and then phase of auto-sensuality. Esther Bick, as Michel Haag (1984) indicates, had spoken of an "adhesive position" prior to the paranoid-schizoid and depressive positions.

Mahler situated the period that she described as "autistic" during the first two months of life. She described it as a sort of "quasi-hermetic shell" that keeps external stimuli outside and protects the privileged cathexis of proprio- and interoceptive sensations. "Normal autism" represents a stage of "absolute primary narcissism" characterized in the infant by a "lack of awareness of a mothering agent" (1968, p. 10). The aim of the autistic phase is to preserve the internal homeostasis. The infant finds himself in a "state of primitive hallucinatory disorientation in which need satisfaction seems to belong to his own omnipotent autistic orbit" (ibid., p. 7). She adds that cathexes, which are essentially turned towards the inside of the body, must be displaced towards the external sensorial afferents, towards the sensory-perceptual pole, a displacement that marks access to the normal symbiotic phase.

Tustin described "normal primary autism" or "phase of auto-sensuality" as a state in which objects are no longer distinguished from the flow of sensations that they produce and which give the infant the feeling that he exists (for the infant, the rhythms and vibrations that accompany the feeding situation *are* the breast, the rhythms and vibrations felt on contact with the mother's body *are* the mother, and so on). These "illusions" protect the infant against experiences revealing exteriority, and thus separation, before his neuro-psychical apparatus can bear it. The infant thus finds himself, during the phase of normal primary autism or of auto-sensuality, enveloped in a sort of protective "postnatal womb" (Tustin, 1981c, p. 6.).

These formulations of Mahler and Tustin can be retained if, first, we replace the term "normal autism" by that of "auto-sensuality" and, second, if we bear in mind that, at this stage, the outside, the external, while not being perceived-recognized as such, is nonetheless cathected,[2] and every exchange (every action or reaction to a stimulus) is situated in the framework described by Piera Aulagnier (1975) with her notions of pictogram and self-engenderment, or Winnicott (1947, 1951, 1962a, 1971) with his notion of an object "created" by the child. Moreover, as we have already pointed out, we do not adhere to a picture that fixes or immobilizes the infantile psyche in an exclusively auto-sensual position. Our conception is that from birth the *psychic state of the infant fluctuates between an auto-sensual position*, as we will define it, *and an openness to a mode of relating that is already object-related.*[3] All the authors who observe newborn infants, whether they refer to psychoanalytic theory or belong to the interactionist current, whether they are ethologists, developmentalists or cognitivists, provide observation material and elements of understanding that are incompatible with the idea of an exclusively auto-sensual phase characterized by a complete absence of object-cathexis. Winnicott's conception of the found-created object and transitionality helps us to advance along this tricky epistemological and metapsychological path: the "object-cathexis" of the auto-sensual position, with its paradoxical character, corresponds to this creation of the object by the infant – which is in keeping, as we have already pointed out, with Piera Aulagnier's idea of self-engenderment. The object is cathected as soon as the infant is able to have the illusion of having created it, provided it does not impose its otherness too suddenly. And knowledge of the object is very early.

Tustin, moreover, notes:

> Of course, the state of normal primary autism is not complete; there are moments of fluctuating awareness of the external world but, as development occurs through a process of leaps, there is a definitive stage when the infant becomes aware in a more constant way of his separateness from his mother and begins to adjust his behaviour to adapt to her intentions.
> (Tustin, 1981c, p. 8, translated from the French)

In *The Protective Shell in Children and Adults,* Tustin (1990) declares that there is no absolute normal autism and that, as Melanie Klein had always maintained, the infant has awareness of separation from the mother and the capacity to integrate experiences of relating to the external world.

The conception of normal primary autism should not, in our view, be called into question on the condition that this phase is denoted by the term "auto-sensuality". It is the picture of such a mental state that must be clarified. This auto-sensual mental state is characterized for us, like any other mental state, moreover, by an oscillation between a dominant position – the "auto-sensual position" – and other positions, such as those that we are going to explore. In the phase of auto-sensuality, it is the auto-sensual position that will predominate. The other positions tried out by the psyche will give it object-experiences that will gradually enable it to avoid resorting to the auto-sensual position. The onset of (pathological) autism and its intensity will be dependent on the time spent, during the phase of auto-sensuality (previously called normal autism), in the auto-sensual position, and on the degree of toxic adherence to this position, which distorts it by amplifying the defensive function against all development and against entering into any form of contact with otherness.

The auto-sensual position, that is, the ex-"autistic position", is a defensive position in ordinary development against anxieties inherent in the perception of external reality. It protects the self but without impeding its openness to the world, which can occur gradually in small doses.

> The "autistic position" is a more than "normal" attitude in the sense that it represents a defence of the still fragile, ego, a defensive armour, a "skin" that contains a self "*in statu nascendi*" and keeps it distinct and separate from a foreign and dangerous reality …: otherness.
> (Resnik, 1986a, p. 174, translated for this edition)

The pathologization of this experience results from – or leads to – a closedness that resists on a lasting basis any contact with otherness. It is expressed in the clinical pictures of early autism. It stems, as we have shown in relation to Tustin's work (Chapter 2), from becoming aware too suddenly of exteriority, for the psychic apparatus cannot bear this experience of separation which is experienced in an exaggeratedly catastrophic way for intrinsic reasons and which cannot be buffered by the environment.

In all cases, the illusion of the created object must always be maintained throughout the process of disillusionment (Winnicott, 1951, 1971). As René Roussillon (1981) explains, a sudden experience of disillusion is not the equivalent of disillusionment, but corresponds to a loss of illusion – which results in a meta-illusion, that is, an illusion about illusion (the illusion that one can do without illusion). The mothering environment must "actively" protect the infant's illusions to avoid early experiences of disillusion that he cannot bear without his mental state being damaged. Lack is only maturational if it is tolerable. The object is obliged to go away, but its absence must not exceed the period of time during which the infant can retain a living image of it within himself. Otherwise, a rift is created in the continuum and a primary defence develops that may be an autistic defence and give rise to transient autistic states such as those we have considered (Chapter 2). We would like to repeat again that *weaning is only maturational if the breast has provided the child with sufficient nourishment and security.*

We have already spoken about the need that the baby feels to recover his lost internal object through warm and gratifying experiences with the real object, and we have spoken of the weak capacity of the very young infant to conserve introjections (Chapters 1 and 3).

Interactionists have observed the same phenomenon. Anne Decerf, for instance, writes:

> During early mother–infant interactions, the infant occupies the relational space through intense movements of presence and discreet withdrawal, which are coupled on the mental stage by a continuous presence of the mother's face. It is as if memory were capable of taking over from the perceptual function momentarily deprived of its contents following a partial rupture with the external world. On its return, the perceptual representation takes over from the memory trace and its interim representative functions, while confirming its adequacy to represent the one who is absent: the child "re-finds" his mother.
> (Decerf, 1987, p. 509, translated for this edition)

This interpretation seems quite correct to us, even if it tends to reduce the experience to a "mechanical" aspect. In fact, the internal mother, the lost internal object, whose loss requires a recuperation of the real object to strengthen the identification, does not only concern a mental image, a perceptual representation and a memory trace. It concerns *emotionality*, an emotional complex consisting in a euphoric feeling of having inside oneself a good-experience -satisfying-and-living-mother. This feeling of having internalized a good gratifying relationship nourishes the infant inwardly during the absence of the real object, and helps him to bear this absence for a certain time. The creation of mental images or memory traces of representative or perceptual activity only corresponds to the fragmentary aspect of the introjection of the experience, the "mechanical" aspect to which the living experience cannot be reduced.

5.2 The auto-sensual position: adhesive identification, dismantling

It may be noted, then, that the auto-sensual or adhesive position is a position occupied by the psyche, in a privileged albeit nonexclusive way, at the dawn of personality, before the primacy of the paranoid-schizoid (or "symbiotic") and depressive positions, that is to say, in the period of primary narcissism, and which subsequently presents itself as the predominant means of recourse in autistic mental states. It is governed by the two most archaic psychic processes: *adhesive identification and dismantling*. Adhesive identification is a notion that was introduced by Esther Bick, essentially in her oral teaching (see her presentation of 1975 published in 1986). It was developed by Donald Meltzer (1975) and his collaborators (Meltzer et al., 1975). Dismantling was described by Meltzer in 1969 in a communication titled "The origins of the fetishistic plaything of sexual perversion" (see Meltzer, 1972). He comes back to it in more detail in *Explorations in Autism: A Psychoanalytic Study* (Meltzer et al., 1975).

Adhesive identification denotes both a primitive identificatory process which, from an ontogenetic point of view, operates prior to the constitution of an internal object, and a defensive mechanism to which the psyche can resort at any point in its development and whose essential consequence consists in the two-dimensional flattening of the internal-external world[4] (this dual perspective, developmental and defensive, also applies to the process of projective identification). The defence of adhesivity consists above all in clinging[5] to avoid the menace inherent to each experience of separation, of individuation. We have seen, with Tustin, Winnicott and Bick, the nature of the anxieties from which the infant, like the autistic child, has to protect himself (see Chapter 2). It is in order to struggle against these anxieties that the newborn infant has recourse transiently, and the autistic child more or less insistently, to adhesive identification.

Adhesive identification produces a type of dependence in which the object's separate existence is not recognized. It does away with any sort of gap or distance between the subject and the object. Adhesive identification leads much to "mimicry of the surface appearance and behavior of their objects object than of their mental states or attributes" (Meltzer, in Meltzer et al., 1975, p. 230). The autistic child thus has a compelling need for the surface of things, their appearance, to be unchanging. The slightest change is equivalent to loss and provokes extreme reactions of panic, disarray and annihilation. Adhesive identification does not tolerate any solution of continuity between the object and the ego; they are indistinguishable. It is two-dimensional and is therefore opposed to the existence of a containing object, that is to say a three-dimensional object, and constitutes a fundamental impediment to thought:

> Thinking *about* means being *outside*, while, in a state of fusion, no perspective, no three-dimensional view, thought can arise.
> (Wittenberg, 1975, in Meltzer et al., 1975, p. 94)

The second defensive mechanism described by Meltzer in the autistic mental state is dismantling. The dismantling of the self as a psychical apparatus corresponds to a suspension of attention leading each of the senses to wander towards its most attractive object of the moment. This dispersion occurs very passively, as if the psychical apparatus were falling to pieces. Since each sense, internal or external, attaches itself to the most stimulating object, suspended attention is directed — or rather carried — towards a variety of objects, for it would be an extraordinary coincidence if the same object were, at any given moment, the source of the most captivating sensations for each sensory and perceptual modality. Dismantling scatters objects into a multitude of small bits, each of which has a particular sensory quality. It reduces objects to a multiplicity of unisensory events, where animate and inanimate become indistinguishable, which cannot be used to form thoughts. Just like splitting, dismantling — which corresponds to a process prior to splitting — scatters both the object and the self, which finds itself dismantled into separate perceptual capacities (seeing, hearing, touching, feeling, and so on).

Dismantling is a passive process, uncharged with persecutory anxiety, pain or despair. This is why autistic children — in the state of "autism proper" —, that is to say, when they are exclusively in an auto-sensual or "autistic" position, do not usually suffer from depersonalization or fragmentation anxiety, anxieties originating in the first experiences of ego-coherence.

> When the self is dismantled into its sensual components by the suspension of the ego-function of attention, a coherent ego ceases temporarily to exist [...]. This primitiveness, we suggest, is essentially mindless.
> (Meltzer, in Meltzer et al., 1975, p. 14)

The active process corresponds to the capacity for attention that makes it possible to link up and coordinate sensory perceptions. As the disintegration of the ego by dismantling is produced passively[6] and by means of "natural splitting" via the suspension of attention, reintegration will occur very easily and without depressive pain.

> When the ego is reunited by an attractive object, so does perception of objects reintegrate. For this reason, the Autistic State Proper is highly reversible in a momentary way, and does not

constitute a disease but is more equivalent to an induced stupor. However, the employment of this mechanism does deprive the child of much development experience (in a quantitative sense) and may retard ego development in a very characteristic way.
(Meltzer, in Meltzer et al., 1975, p. 203)

The converse experience of that of the dismantled object is called by Meltzer the experience of the "common sense" type object, the experience of "consensuality", following the Aristotelian notion of "common sense", taken up by Bion (1962a).

The dismantling of which Meltzer speaks seems to us to represent a mechanism that is very similar to what Mahler describes (1968, p. 65–67) as a "negative hallucinatory behavior", a "massive withdrawal of cathexis from the perceptual *sensorium*" and a "hallucinatory denial of perception". We understand the example that Mahler gives of the infant who "turns a deaf ear" to his mother and to the entire world, yet who can listen to the sound of a record turning, fascinated by the rotating movement on which his attention is focused, as an illustration of the mechanism of dismantling, associated with adhesive clinging.

Francisco Palacio Espasa (1980) describes a third solution, for the autistic child, to the unbearable anxiety arising from frustration and from the absence of a containing external object or containing experience: *retreating towards an idealized internal object*.[7] This mechanism should be envisaged, it seems to us, not as an alternative to adhesive identification or dismantling, but as a corollary of adhesive identification. The internal status of this object – a status that implies that a container, however archaic it may be, has been constituted and is operative – leads us to think of this object, and above all the nature of this object, as the consequence or effect of the process of adhesive identification. Moreover, Palacio Espasa suggests replacing the term "idealized internal object" with the term "object ideal" (Manzano and Palacio Espasa, 1983) in order to stress the potential character of this object linked to its poverty of phantasy.

This defensive measure of retreating towards an internal object, whose nature is to be conceived as a consequence of the work of adhesive identification, leads us to draw attention to the fact that adhesive identification is a *psychic process* and, as such, requires the presence of an external object to be realized. In this connection, Palacio Espasa differentiates between "unconditional adhesive projective identification", which helps to preserve a state of omnipotent completeness, even in the absence of the external object, and "conditional adhesive projective identification", which requires the presence of a cathected external object to maintain the phantasy of completeness. We will see that this second form of adhesive identification which, according to Palacio Espasa, characterizes children suffering from symbiotic psychosis, in fact corresponds to projective identification, which is operative in symbiotic states and sometimes gives rise, from a phenomenological point of view, to adhesive effects (see Chapters 7 and 12).

We will distinguish, then, as we will do for projective identification (Chapter 12) – between adhesive identification as a *psychic process* and the *effects* that it produces *regarding the state of mind and the relationship to external objects*. We will describe the characterology of adhesive identification as well as its manifestations in relation to external objects. It is important to note, as Meltzer (1989b) has suggested, that adhesive identification, as well as every identificatory process, describes first and foremost a *relationship between the self and internal objects* – Donald Meltzer (1972) had already made the same remark on the subject of projective identification. This adhesive relationship distorts and transforms internal objects. We would say that adhesive identification "autisticizes" internal objects (Ciccone, 1996b, 1997a, 2012a). It produces two-dimensional objects, without an interior, without mental activity, phantasy or affect.

The autistic child's object ideal of which Francisco Palacio Espasa speaks is the effect of a process of adhesive identification and represents such an autisticized internal object. This object is characterized by its poverty and simplicity, at the level of both the representations and affects that are associated with it. These internal characteristics reflect and influence the perception that the child has of the external world:

> This internal poverty projected on to the surrounding world allows the child to carry out a *mutilating simplification* of his perception and experience of certain objects outside him; as a result, their own existence becomes more recognizable and acceptable.
> (Palacio Espasa, 1980, p. 358, translated for this edition)

This notion of mutilating simplification, or of *invalidating simplification* (Manzano and Palacio Espasa, 1983), is very useful for understanding and representing the internal world of the autistic child. This type of functioning is not, however, only found in autism.

Adhesive identification and dismantling represent, therefore, fundamental defensive measures that are employed in autistic states or in autistic parts of the personality, but also by the baby at the dawn of his mental life to protect himself against catastrophic anxieties caused by traumatic awareness of separation. But the persistence of these processes leads to the development of an internal world full of *autisticized internal objects*: dismantled, unisensory, simplified, mutilated and invalidated objects.

A final point should be made concerning a terminological and epistemological aspect. Esther Bick, as Geneviève Haag (1986) indicates, preferred to speak of adhesive *identity* rather than of adhesive identification, for this term seemed to denote more exactly a very primitive existential modality, prior to the constitution of an object and even of any form of mentalization (the term identification contains, in effect, the idea of a relation to an object that is already somewhat differentiated and constituted).[8] However, we will retain the term identification insofar as adhesivity, as we have already said, can be used defensively or regressively in various more complex positions than the auto-sensual position. On the other hand, we will use the term *adhesive identity* to denote the *mental state* produced by the process of adhesive identification, a process that leads to a transformation of internal-external objects. We will make the same distinction with regard to projective identification: the term *projective identification* will be used to designate the process, while the term *projective identity* will refer to the state of mind.

5.3 Phenomenology of adhesive identification

We will now consider adhesive identification from a phenomenological point of view; its extreme psychopathological forms on the one hand and its more subtle effects on the other, for instance, in the baby who is going through the normal auto-sensual phase.[9]

5.3.1 In autistic children and psychotic children

Geneviève Haag (1984a) describes behaviours in autistic children which evidence the process of adhesive identification. She gives as examples the difficulty in taking hold of the nipple and of sucking, the inability to chew, the failure to grasp objects, the "sign of the object that is burning", the appropriation of an adult's hands to accomplish manipulations, echolalia, the suspended gaze and the realization of the "cyclops effect". All these behaviours, which concern or evoke the act of *taking* (with the mouth, hands or eyes), are the result of a massive inhibition in the autistic child of the "drive for mastery" (Freud, 1905), of prehension, and thus of the apprehension of the world.

Concerning the difficulties in taking hold of the nipple and the inability to chew that results, Geneviève Haag, drawing on the observation that a baby who is poorly held is himself unable to grasp anything with his mouth, puts forward the hypothesis that certain depressed or immature mothers, who are lacking sufficient support, make it extremely difficult for their child to be able to grasp the nipple because they themselves are poorly held and carried. The baby who does not suck much or sucks poorly scarcely experiences this rhythmic kinaesthesia in the interpenetration of bodies, and if he is "hypersensitive", as Tustin said, or particularly vulnerable (because he has suffered at birth, for instance), his auto-sensuality is at risk of quickly becoming organized along surface sensory lines, without ever being able to achieve a sense of security. He will manifest "permanent self-gripping".

The "sign of the object that is burning", which Daniel Marcelli (1983) calls the "sign of the burning cube", and which we link to the failure to grasp objects, describes the phenomenon whereby the autistic child moves his hand slowly towards an object, withdraws it, moves it towards the object again, brushes it with his fingertips, taps it, grasps hold of it and then gets rid of it immediately without being able to manipulate it, as if it were burning hot. Marcelli sees this sign as an indication of adhesive identification which results in the hand that has just taken hold of the object becoming a sort of new disturbing organ. In effect, the infant does not understand that two objects can have a spatial relationship between them such that they share a common frontier (as is the case with a baby who is just a few months old – see Bower, 1977). Thus, the hand and the object grasped form a strange, unknown and frightening neo-reality. Moreover, to this is added the action of dismantling that impedes coordination and the hierarchization of the different sensory perceptions.

The autistic child's habit of "getting an adult to do something for him" describes the frequent habit of taking hold of an adult's hand and using it as a prolongation of his own arm.

> Taking hold of another person's hand constitutes a refusal to perceive the boundary of his ego, the will or the need to include the other person in an ameboid prolongation of this same ego.
> (Marcelli, 1983, p. 23, translated for this edition)

This behaviour is characteristic of adhesive identification, where the child uses another person's hand as if it had no life or will of its own, where the child does not recognize the separate existence of the other person; he includes him within a limitless ego as a new appendix, for fear that a precipice might open up between him and the other person into which he would run the risk of falling endlessly. Marcelli considers this behaviour as a corollary of the absence of "pointing" (see Chapter 2); in effect, pointing implies knowledge and tolerance of the distance between the subject and the object of desire. Margaret Mahler (1968) described this behaviour as a prototype of "psychotic personation" which reflects the belief that everything that the child thinks is also automatically and simultaneously thought by the other. These autistic children, she says, "with signals and gestures, command the adult to serve as an executive extension of a semi-animate or inanimate mechanical kind, like the switch or lever of a machine" (p. 68). This coincides with Meltzer's idea (Meltzer et al., 1975) that what drives the mental activity of the autistic subject is essentially the wish to obtain the obedience of his objects.

Echolalia is the symptom par excellence of the adhesive identity in the domain of language.

> The echo does not respect the prosody heard, but flattens it or distorts it, "emptying it" in general emotionally.
> (Haag, 1984a, p. 324, translated for this edition)

To echolalia must be added echopraxia, which, in the domain of body language, corresponds to what echolalia is in verbal language.

Finally, suspension of the gaze, as well as the realization of the "cyclops effect" (an effect produced by looking deeply into another person's eyes, with the two faces very close together, which gives the illusion of a single eye in the middle of the forehead), both frequent in autistic subjects, does away with space, or the depth of space, both in the external world and in the body image.[10]

Donald Meltzer (Meltzer et al., 1975) describes the characterological traits illustrating the adhesive identity in autism, in contrast to the projective identity, as dependence, separation- dilapidation, empty-headedness and caricature.

Dependence gives the child more or less tyrannical control over the object, whose separate existence is not recognized – this is related to the habit of "getting the adult to do something for him". Unlike projective identification, which tends to produce a delusion of independence due to a lack of differentiation between adult and infantile capacities, adhesive identification produces dependence "by sticking to the other person". While separation in the child who is employing projective identification is a threat for his omnipotence, though it can be avoided by introducing himself into his internal object in the absence of the external object, in the child employing adhesive identification this separation leads to breakdown, as if he were torn away and rejected by the object – the separation and disappearance of the object are equivalent. Whereas one of the characteristics of the projective identity concerns the delusional illusion of being able to know and see the interior clearly, exactly the opposite is true for the adhesive identity; thus, the autistic child imitates the surface appearance and behaviour so that he often seems to be empty-headed.[11] Unlike people who use projective identification intensely and who present the world with an aggressive caricature of their objects, the autistic child, through mimicry which corresponds to adhesive identification, offers an unaggressive caricature but one that has the quality of a reduced model; it is a perfect imitation of the behaviour, but without interiority, without thoughts.[12]

To this characterology of the autistic mental state that Meltzer describes, we would like to add the idea, in particular concerning dependence, that *adhesive identification leads to a dependence* not on the thought or on the apparatus for thinking of the other, but *on the psychic consistency of the other*. Adhesive identification puts the subject in contact not with the content of the thought of the other but rather with its "plastic "qualities to which he adheres.

It is also worth noting that in autistic children, in our view, adhesive phenomena are rarely observed in the "pure" state. Most of the time they contain projective elements and they are sometimes on the boundary between adhesive identification and projective identification, as we have seen in the case of Aurélien (Chapter 4).

We will illustrate this point with the help of another example, that of Maud, a four-and-a-half-year-old autistic child that one of us (M.L.) followed in the context of a small therapeutic group of autistic and psychotic children. Maud, who was unable to establish and maintain a relationship with others and with the group, was in the habit of drooling on a small table in the middle of the room and of sticking her cheek to it, while thrusting her right hand into the back of her mouth. Maud could enter into eye contact, but frequently let herself fall on the ground and only stood upright if one of the therapists supported her neck with his or her hand. Her attitude during many sessions thus consisted in sticking her body onto animate or inanimate supporting objects, or in clinging to herself by putting a hand in her mouth, or in letting herself fall onto the floor in spectacular ways. These manifestations led the therapists to verbalize about "a little girl who said she would never be able to attach herself well to the mummy-group and that she had to stick herself to the table and to herself so as not to fall, that it was perhaps not worth becoming attached to the group, for there would then be a risk of being dropped, and so on". Physical and psychic dilapidation was only avoided by the tactile and proprioceptive support offered by the therapist's hand.

These behaviours of sticking to the surface of animate or inanimate hard objects are evidence of the defensive utilization of the process of adhesive identification against the catastrophic anxiety of separation–dilapidation. However, we would say that Maud's clinging was not purely "adhesive". Indeed, the use of her own bodily products forming a "glue" reveals an obscure awareness of the separate external world and thus a beginning of three-dimensional organization, or disorganization. Furthermore, self-clinging or self-mastery by means of thrusting a hand into the mouth indicates a sliding from autistic auto-sensuality towards a persecutory symbiotic register (the interpenetration of looks with Maud, which had been possible for a long time, were already a sign of this symbiotic component). In destructive symbiosis, as Geneviève Haag often points out, "being stuck to" gives way to "colliding violently with" (see Haag, 1985b).

Projective aspects are thus often mixed with adhesive identification – we have seen that adhesivity is constitutive of projectivity, and we have discussed paths of transition from one to the other (Chapter 4). Moreover, access to a mode of identification is not incompatible with the return to an earlier mode of identification, and this may be spontaneous and reversible. Some psychotic children, for instance, who manifest a capacity to establish symbiotic ties, identified projectively, sometimes have recourse to adhesive manoeuvres such as compulsive echolalia and mimicry. This is the case in situations where they are made aware of separation from the object in a way that they experience as very sudden and as indicating that the object rejects their projective identifications. These children, with whom dialogue is entirely possible and coherent, suddenly begin to stick to the adult's words, which they repeat frenetically when he asks them specifically to express a desire, or when he manifests his anger about a form of behaviour that he is led to reprimand, or alternatively when he indicates that it is time to separate.

5.3.2 In the baby

The idea of adhesive identification is present in substance in the article by Esther Bick, "The experience of the skin in early object-relations" (1968), when she writes:

> The need for a containing object would seem, in the infantile unintegrated state, to produce a frantic search for an object – a light, a voice, a smell, or other sensual object – which can hold the attention and thereby be experienced, momentarily at least, as holding the parts of the personality together.
> (Bick, 1968, p. 115)

This idea is taken up again, and adhesive identification is named and described, in her paper of 1975 (Bick, 1986), where she considers the different sensory organs by means of which the baby clings to a stimulating object as equivalents of the mouth clinging to the breast. Sensual, sensorial or kinaesthetic clinging in the newborn baby in the grips of a state of disorganization is evidence, as it is in the autistic child, of the adhesive work accomplished by the psyche to avoid catastrophic anxiety. Baby observation makes it possible to identify easily behaviours or attitudes illustrating the processes of adhesive identification and dismantling.

When the child is submerged by an experience of anxiety and he finds no adequate response in his immediate environment, or when he cannot benefit from the qualities of the surrounding environment, he finds himself in a painful situation from which he can only extract himself by relying on his own defensive capacities. The very young baby has two essential ways of withdrawing in situ from anxiety: *immobilization* and *perpetual movement* (see Ciccone, 1995a). These two manoeuvres are manoeuvres of clinging to auto-sensuality.

Immobilization is a radical way of suspending existence. "I'm not there" the child might say to himself, "so I cannot experience anything". The immobilization of all psychic life manifests itself in, among other ways, clinging to a sensation: a proprioceptive or kinaesthetic sensation (the baby clings to his contracted musculature – his eyes shut, his fists closed, his arms bent), a visual sensation (clinging to a source of light), an auditory sensation (fixation of attention to a sound, noise or music), and so on. We can, for instance, easily observe a baby of just a few weeks old, and who is removed too suddenly from the mother's breast for an examination, beginning to stare at a source of light or a corner of a white ceiling, as if he were absent (dismantling and adhesive identification). It sometimes takes several warm stimulations by the mother or the examining doctor before the baby resumes contact. If the stimulation is itself too sudden, the baby then starts screaming in a terrible attack of rage, for at that moment he feels the violence of the separation from his mother. As long he is "absent", he can avoid any feelings of separation. If he resumes contact in a way that does not guarantee him the impression that he is sufficiently held in the relationship, in a symbiotic relationship, he experiences the sudden separation after the event, which triggers the attack of rage or despair.

Perpetual movement is another defence used by the young baby. It is easily observed, for example, when one undresses a baby in the first weeks of his life and he begins to move his legs about alternately as soon as he is naked. The parents sometimes say, on observing this reaction, that "the baby is pedalling", that he will become a racing cyclist, etc. In fact, the baby is protecting himself by this perpetual movement from a bodily experience of dispersion triggered by the fact of being naked. Some babies scream as soon as they are naked and giving him a bath is a real ordeal. Everyone knows how it is sometimes necessary to hold a baby very tightly, enveloped in nappies, to reassure him.

Other situations of perpetual movement of a part of the body can readily be observed; for example, that of the baby who is only a few weeks old and who, when the breast or the bottle is not available, starts hitting his mouth rhythmically. This gesture can also have the meaning of motor discharge of the tension due to waiting, or many other meanings besides related to the meaning of the psychopathological symptoms that are self-mutilations (Ciccone, 2014). Likewise, immobilization and perpetual movement have the characteristics of many autistic symptoms: swaying, stereotypies, motor rhythms, manic agitation, fascination for sensations or images like the specular image, and so on. Selma Fraiberg (1982) has described in babies subject to situations of great deficiency a form of defence that she calls "freezing", which can be understood as a particularly pathological amplification of the immobilization observed more frequently in an ordinary baby. Freezing consists for the severely deprived in immobilizing posture, motility, the voice, the gaze, and in clinging to the mother in mute terror. This reaction of frozen immobilization collapses after a certain period of time and is replaced by disordered agitation – perpetual movement reappears, but in a particularly exaggerated way – reflecting the state of panic and disintegration against which the freezing afforded protection.[13]

These manoeuvres of immobilization and perpetual movement used by the baby to protect himself against anxiety are transient measures which, if they persist and are not replaced by relationships, interrelationships with a human being, with the parent, can become toxic. The majority of parents, as we have already said, spontaneously interpret their newborn baby's anxieties, putting his agonistic experiences into words, and contain him in this way: "I'm not going to drop you, I'm not going to drown you", etc., the parents say. They are real therapists for the child. If these normal agonistic anxieties are not adequately contained by the environment or if the baby, for intrinsic reasons, cannot derive benefit from the parent's efforts to contain him, these anxieties, as we have seen, will impact the process of development and leave traces.

Michel Haag (1984) recounts the supervision by Esther Bick of his observation of a three-day-old newborn infant, a sequence of which illustrates adhesive identification.

After the feed, the baby, who was being held in his father's arms, wrinkled his forehead while screwing his eyes up very tightly. The father, wondering if the baby was disturbed by the light, shielded the baby's eyes with his hand so that he was in semi-darkness, but this did not stop the baby from screwing them up energetically. He withdrew his hand and Michel Haag noticed movements of the muscles of the baby's jaw that were moving at the same rhythm as that of the previous feed.

Esther Bick explains the two ways in which a baby can deal with the fear of falling: either he continues to move about all the time or he holds himself by stiffening his muscles.[14] The continuous jaw movements and the self-clinging to the facial muscles are signs of adhesive experiences. The baby observed by Michel Haag had recourse to these manoeuvres "because he was removed from the breast *and was no longer held by the breast* since the nipple was withdrawn" (Bick, cited by Haag, 1984, p. 164, translated from the French).

The sequence observed by Michel Haag continues as follows: the father put the baby in his cot and his face assumed an expression of a peaceful sleep full of inner happiness; his eyes were closed but without effort and his jaws were immobile.

Esther Bick points out that the baby can assume this expression because in his cot he feels *completely held*. Then she generalizes from the following example:

When we are dealing with mothers whose holding is inadequate [...], the baby has to hold on to other things, for example to a light, a strong light, or to a sound, or to objects in the room.
(Bick, cited by Haag, 1984, p. 165, translated from the French)

Esther Bick explains, for example, that if leaving the house is problematic, if holidays are always spoilt for the parents in such cases, it is because "it is to the *environment* that the baby is stuck, clinging" (ibid.). Leaving this environment makes everything to which the baby was holding disappear.

Geneviève Haag (1984a, 1985a) describes the first gaze of the normal baby, particularly in the first six weeks, as a very "suspended" gaze, as if "clinging", while "the gaze of a smile, between 2 and 4 or 5 months, is a gaze of very intense interpenetration, accompanied by quite a joyful state when everything goes well, that is when the persecutory aspect of this interpenetration is in the background". This suspended, clinging gaze of the first two months of life evidences the adhesive identity.

Geneviève Haag develops elsewhere the idea that, in physical games of self-mastery, the baby "plays at feeding" with his whole body around the sagittal axis:

> The left side of the baby seems more often to represent the baby's body, or even what may be happening inside him, and the right side seems more often to represent the maternal function in different aspects of holding; or, if this holding is lacking or lacking in quality, to be devoted more to "clinging".
> (Haag, 1985a, p. 109, translated for this edition)

The movements of sticking, and later of joining – hand-mouth, hand-foot and, later, foot-mouth – seem to represent a bodily enactment, or a bodily extension of the psychic process of adhesive identification (sticking-clinging), and then of projective identification (joining-grasping).

We will give an example of these physical games of feeding drawn from the observation not of a baby but of an adult with autism, as if we were looking through a microscope – a microscope of pathological amplification and of stereotyped repetition – at details of behaviours that can be seen in babies and that Geneviève Haag calls "intra-bodily identifications" (Haag, 1987b, 1988abc, 1990a, 1992, 1997).

> We will describe two autistic manoeuvres of this patient (he uses many others) in therapy with one of us (A.C.). The first stereotypy comprises the following gestural sequence: joining his hands while crossing his fingers / withdrawing his right hand / hitting the back of his left hand with the palm of his right hand / joining his hands once again / etc. The second manoeuvre consists in hitting his thigh with a closed fist/ sliding his fist over his knee down to the ankle / hitting his thigh

again / etc. The violence of these manoeuvres is at the origin of skin and bone lesions responsible for joint deformations at the level of his hands and knee.

Apart from the self-destructive clinging to pain and the aspect of kinesthetic clinging engendering autistic traces-sensations, aspects belonging to autism which we have described as auto-sensual manoeuvres devoid of phantasies, it seems possible to decode in these gestural sequences a scenario of self-mastery that fails, and therefore cannot be psychicized. The hands that cannot stay joined with crossed fingers is evidence of the fact that the baby-part cannot hang on to the breast-nipple part. The fist sliding untiringly from the knees is evidence of the fact that the baby-part cannot be held and retained by the breast-nipple support. The baby who cannot attach himself, hang on to the breast, develops hostility and anger that is reflected in the violence of hitting. These manoeuvres, moreover, are often accompanied by verbal attacks which involve "cutting off the head", "killing", "flogging", and so on. The stereotypies cease each time the patient is able to look at the other person with an interpenetrating quality. If one attaches oneself with the gaze, if one is held by the gaze, then one no longer slips. This patient who had become autistic, and who is now an adult, still clings adhesively to these attempts to stick to a supporting object.

Outside the domain of pathology, the enactment of such scenarios can be observed in the physical games of the baby consisting, for instance, in joining and detaching parts of the body in connection with the arrival of the bottle or the mothering object, as Geneviève Haag illustrates.

Another privileged area for the bodily manifestation of normal adhesive identification lies in tactile contact at the level of the back, or "back-contact". Geneviève Haag (1987b, 1988abc, 1991, 1992, 1997) accords a primordial place to the integration of back-contact in psychic development. This integration, which occurs essentially by the gaze, when it is joined with tactile experience, plays a part in the constitution of the first psychic skin. It is back-contact, associated with the interpenetration of gazes (eye contact with the mother's face) and with mouth–nipple interpenetration, and enveloped by mothering words, which affords the baby the basic feeling of security and integrity. The internalization of this reassuring back-contact, and especially the junction between back-contact and interpretations, ensures the development of the sense of identity. Geneviève Haag concurs with the considerations of James Grotstein (1981), among others, on the "background object of primary identification" – which he subsequently preferred to call background *presence*, as Geneviève Haag (1991, 1992, 1997) points out – to back up her conceptions concerning the importance of back-contact in psychic integration (see also Sandler's (1960) notion of "background of safety"). The internalization of the background object plays a fundamental role in the constitution of the psychic skin and individuation, in the "duplication" skin of the object/skin of the self, in the construction of the body image, and bodily and psychic separation.

The prototypical situation drawing together the different sensory junctions (contacts at the level of the back, of the eyes, of the mouth, to which is joined contact via speech) is nothing other than the situation of feeding, suckling, as we have seen, where the baby, if he is held properly, has his first experiences of what Esther Bick (1968) called an "optimal containing object". Sometimes, as we were saying earlier (Chapter 3), in the case of disorganization, the mere recall of one of the consensual modalities is sufficient to gather the psyche together, to rediscover a sense of identity. To emphasize once again the essential role of back-contact, it is worth noting that in a baby or an older child in disarray, it is often the restoration of back-contact (putting the child on one's knees with his back against one's belly, caressing his back) that helps him to calm down and feel secure again.[15] We would say that, in these reparative moments, prior to symbiotic reparation, it is first – and this is what makes it possible to recreate symbiosis – the *basic adhesive envelope* that is restored. This basic envelope is constituted of the adhesivity that is necessary for the functioning of the projective processes characteristic of symbiosis.

We will conclude this phenomenological investigation of adhesive identification in the baby by evoking examples of experiences related by Daniel Marcelli (1983) showing that the very young baby is more sensitive to the contours of an object than to the variations of its situation in space. The baby does not use all the sensory information available to him, but is content to focus his attention on the geographical contour of the object as if it were reduced to a projection plane on a wall. Thus, while he has no difficulty in discerning two objects with no common frontier, relations of contiguity, of adherence between objects, can be a source of perplexity and concern (see the sign of the burning cube in the autistic child). Likewise, Anne Decerf (1987) reports experiences showing that the visual exploration of the baby first focuses on its geometric contours before reaching the interior of a structure, regardless of the geometrical figure (see Salapatek, 1975; Maurer and Salapatek, 1976). For example, before seven weeks, the gaze of an infant scrutinizing a face fixes more on the perimeter of the face than on elements within it. All this illustrates clearly, we think, the two-dimensional character of the adhesive identity.

Adhesive identification plays an essential role in the development of the young baby. It permits familiarization with the proximal sensory afferences on the basis of which the baby will be able to build up his differentiated body and psychic ego. However, the pathological amplification of this process of defence will result in the persistence of an illusion of absence of limits and will profoundly impede the baby's possibilities for development. It is the introjection of an "optimal containing object" that will help the baby to build up a nucleus of identity leading him to give up the auto-sensual position or adhesive position.

Notes

1 Thomas Ogden (1989, 1994) has suggested the same notion, drawing on the same references; he speaks of a "contiguous-autistic position".
2 The object is cathected before it is perceived, according to the famous formulation of Serge Lebovici (1961).
3 See also, in connection with the equilibrium between the first narcissistic and object-related cathexes, Rosenfeld, 1964a; Cosnier, 1970; Carel, 1988. The point of view that primary narcissism is the seat of a fluctuation between openness and closedness is one that is shared, for instance, by André Green (2000).
4 See the illustration that we gave of it based on an example offered by Cléopâtre Athanassiou (Chapter 4).
5 The Anglo-Saxon term, employed notably by Meltzer, is "to cling", which means to grip, to hang on, to adhere, to stick in order to resist separation. On this subject see the much earlier study by Imre Hermann (1945) on the "clinging instinct", a study that inspired John Bowlby (1969) in his theorization of the attachment instinct.
6 The notion of passivity simply accounts for the absence of energy that is necessary for dismantling; it does not mean that the infant might

suffer from this archaic splitting. The subject is just as much an "actor" in psychic dismantling as he is an "actor" in perceptual gathering together.

7 Melitta Schmideberg (1930), Melanie Klein's daughter, had drawn attention to this mechanism in schizophrenia. Melanie Klein (1935, 1946) saw it as a means of defence against depressive and persecutory anxieties, and as a basic mechanism in schizophrenia – we will come back to this (Chapter 8).

8 Tustin (1984a, 1986), following this same idea, suggests employing the term "adhesive equation" or taking up again the expression "mimetic fusion" or "imitative fusion" inspired by the work of Eugenio Gaddini (1969).

9 We are also referring to the examples already given concerning two-dimensionality which illustrate the process of adhesive identification (Chapter 4).

10 Concerning the suspension of the gaze, it corresponds to an "absence" in the world, but may also express a visual clinging (which reduces and flattens the world) while the peripheral vision analyzes images – peripheral vision is devoted to this function more frequently in autistic subjects (Bullinger, 2015). Avoiding eye contact is thus sometimes a sign of using peripheral vision for the purposes of control.

11 As Salomon Resnik says, in autism, "the void begins to occupy the place of absence" (Resnik, 1986a, p. 31, translated for this edition). See also Resnik, 1994, in particular Chapter 4, where the author takes up and develops this statement with reference to cases of obsessional, psychotic or borderline patients, in whom he describes the flattening of mental space.

12 The characterology of the adhesive identity, in contrast to the projective identity, could be envisaged from the point of view of the countertransference. Projective identification provokes in the one who is the "victim" of it, feelings of being "pumped", emptied, exhausted, a parasite, and mobilizes hostile feelings as if one were dealing with a "pot of glue"; adhesive identification, on the other hand, produces the feeling of being automated, inanimate, reduced to a useful object or of being inexistent.

13 We will return in Chapter 13 to the pathological defences in the baby described by Fraiberg in situations of danger and extreme affective deprivation.

14 Concerning the segmentary hypertonia of the newborn, Bick opposes *clinging* to *grasping*. Clinging, adhering, is of a two-dimensional

order – "as yet there is no mind", she says –; grasping is of a three-dimensional order – "the mind is there" (Bick, cited by Haag, 1984, p. 102–103, translated from the French).
15 The restoration of back-contact is primordial in the approach to autistic children (see the cases of Aurélien, Chapter 4, and Maud, Chapter 5).

6

ON SYMBIOSIS

A common skin

6.1 Normal symbiosis

Normal symbiosis has already been mentioned several times in the preceding chapters. We have spoken of symbiotic elation as a state in which psychic substance is "fabricated". We have stressed the necessity of rediscovering and restoring symbiosis at times of painful and destructive separations. The reparation of the symbiotic bond allows separation to take place subsequently without heartbreak and without a sense of dislocation: each one can separate, taking with him a part of the experience shared with the other; the bond with the other is then introjected. We have insisted on the normal basic adhesivity that is constitutive of the backcloth against which the symbiotic bond can be built.

Symbiotic experiences are essential throughout life; they help to resolve a good number of critical situations that the vicissitudes of existence reserve for us. They are essential in grouping; indeed, it may be said, that the first organizer of the group, namely, "group illusion" (Anzieu, 1971), comprises, in addition to adhesive elements (constitution of a group skin), symbiotic elements in the construction of an undifferentiated group identity. They are essential in therapeutic care; we are indebted to Harold Searles (1965, 1979) for the notion of "therapeutic symbiosis": a phase of symbiotic relating between the psychotic patient and the analyst is necessary for a therapeutic process to get going. Normal symbiosis can therefore be found in many places and has its origin in this early period of psychic development that Margaret Mahler described as the symbiotic phase. In what does it consist?

In *On Human Symbiosis and the Vicissitudes of Individuation: Infantile Psychosis* (1968), which brings together, with additions, most of the studies that she had carried out since the beginning of the 1950s on infantile psychosis and on the development of the infant and the process of individuation, Margaret Mahler describes psychic development in three stages. The first stage is represented by the "normal autistic phase", situated in the first two months of life; the second stage is represented by the "normal symbiotic phase", occurring from the second to the eighth month approximately; and the third stage by the "separation-individuation phase", which extends over the first three years of life.

The normal autistic phase corresponds to the states that we described in the previous chapter, and that we are renaming, with Tustin, the "auto-sensual" phase (for the following phase, we will retain the term "symbiotic", which is much less connoted pejoratively and does not necessarily refer to a pathological state).[1] The symbiotic phase reflects increased sensory awareness and capacity to relate to the environment. The child displaces libido from internal sensations to the skin and the peripheral organs. This displacement of cathexis is of fundamental importance for the formation of the body-ego.

The symbiotic phase is characterized by a state of "omnipotent psychosomatic fusion" between the rudimentary ego and the object-representation:

> The infant behaves and functions as though he and his mother were an omnipotent system – a dual unity within one common boundary.
>
> (Mahler, 1968, p. 8)

This *common boundary*, this membrane or mother-infant symbiotic matrix, contains "not only the pre-ego self-representations but also the still undifferentiated libidinally cathected symbiotic part-objects" (ibid., p. 15). In the symbiotic phase a psychic ego is differentiated from a symbiotic object, an object for the satisfaction of needs. The ego has a confused awareness of this symbiotic object, which is no longer merely an assuager of needs, but also becomes an object of desire: during the symbiotic phase "the affect of *longing* replaces the objectless tension state with the feeling of 'craving' which already has psychological meaning" (Mahler, 1968, p. 220).

Bion (1962a) saw this "longing" as a sign of the development of thought, the capacity to tolerate waiting, in other words the capacity to tolerate frustration which determines the transformation of the absence of the object into a thought about this object.

Béla Grunberger (1975) describes the transition from an "absolute narcissistic regime" to a fundamentally opposite regime consisting of frustrations and instinctual drive tensions, a regime in which the infant begins to use in multiple forms the visceral and sensory external and internal organs: this is the phase of "integrated narcissism". This transition illustrates the transition from an auto-sensual state to a symbiotic state. The narcissistically deprived character of the phase of "integrated narcissism" requires the object to repair the narcissistic injuries in order to positivize the "negative balance sheet" of instinctual life. Margaret Mahler considers, moreover, the holding attitude of the mothering agent, her "primary maternal preoccupation" described by Winnicott (1956a), as the "symbiotic organizer".

Normal symbiosis, which is at its height around the fourth and fifth months of life, thus represents a mental state dominated by hallucinatory fusion within a common boundary between the ego and the symbiotic object. It is towards this state that the ego regresses, or in this state that the ego is fixed in cases of symbiotic psychosis.

But in psychosis, as we have noted for every transition from a "normal" state to a "pathological" state, the defences are amplified and distorted; destructivity is increased, which alters or impedes psychic development. We will see that in symbiotic psychosis, destructivity is always associated with symbiosis. One can say that in the normal, developmental symbiotic phase, the symbiosis is "open", while in symbiotic psychosis, the symbiosis is "closed".

Indeed, in ordinary development, it is as though at birth, after the separation of the bodies, a postnatal symbiotic matrix were formed reuniting the baby and the parent (the father is just as concerned by this primary symbiosis as the mother), from which the baby and parent will separate, the baby developing his subjectivity and the parent developing his capacity for parenting. Neither the parenting of the parent nor the subjectivity of the baby are given from the outset, but are developed and singularized on the basis of this symbiotic matrix. Normal primary symbiosis is thus open. It contains the possibility of differentiation and openness to the world.[2] This is not the case – or less so – for symbiotic psychosis, where the symbiosis is closed; it obliterates the perception of the world and impedes openness.

Now that these essential clarifications have been made, we can now envisage the psychopathological state of symbiotic psychosis. Indeed, just as the study of autism teaches us about normal auto-sensuality and adhesivity, so the study of symbiotic psychosis teaches us about normal symbiosis.

6.2 Symbiotic psychosis, symbiotic position, syncretic object

To describe symbiotic psychosis is to describe pathological symbiosis. What we learn about normal development from studying pathology, as we have seen for the auto-sensual position, is that pathology amplifies normal processes (as if they were being observed under a microscope), but pathologization also involves a distortion and dysharmonization of these processes, which is essentially the work of destructivity, of the death drive. We have emphasized this distortion in the adhesive position at the heart of autism; we will do the same for projective identification (see Chapter 11), the preferred mode of identification during the symbiotic phase and in pathological symbiosis. *Pathologization accentuates the destructive aspects of normal processes.* This is why Geneviève Haag, for example, often speaks of symbiotic psychosis in terms of "destructive pathological psychosis" (see Haag, 1985b).

Symbiotic psychosis reflects for Margaret Mahler the incompletion of individuation, in other words, the incompletion of the sense of individual identity. The psychic representation of the object remains merged with the self and participates in the illusion of omnipotence. Symbiotic psychosis is characterized by the fear of separation which crushes the infant's fragile ego. Mahler prefers to speak of a *"reaction to separation"* rather than of "separation anxiety" in the phase of normal development during which an "'intrapsychic availability' of a mother image that can bring gratification and assuage pain" (Mahler, 1968, p. 234) has developed, so that the absence of the actual object puts the normal baby in a state of waiting and helplessness, with anxiety as a consequence. On the other hand, the psychotic infant, in his state of omnipotence, has not elaborated this internal image. Thus, separation provokes extreme reactions: panic fear, attacks of anger and rage, and destructive behaviour. With these clarifications, the sign of "separation anxiety" is to be considered, in the psychotic child, as a sign that his state has improved.

Symbiotic psychosis is conceived by Mahler as a defensive organization in response to the catastrophic experience engendered by the slightest experience of separation. However, the symbiotic organization comprises in substance a supplementary anxiety: *fear of being re-engulfed* by the symbiotic object. This additional anxiety can lead the infant who develops a symbiotic psychosis to resort to autistic mechanisms to protect the fragile individual identity acquired, which is in danger of destruction by being re-engulfed by the object. The psychotic child is thus prey to unbearable panic related to separation and a terrifying fear of being re-engulfed. The anxieties about being re-engulfed underlying symbiotic functioning are, as Francisco Palacio Espasa explains, persecutory anxieties of two types:

> Fear of being re-engulfed linked to the projection of desires for fusion; and fear of being devoured, linked to the projection of cannibalistic oral impulses. In fact, these two types of anxiety are closely bound up with one another and with claustrophobic anxieties — fear of remaining confined within the mother's body.
> (Palacio Espasa, 1980, p. 367, translated for this edition)

Illustrations of pathological symbiosis can be found, for instance, in Gisela Pankow (1983), who explains how, according to her, the parents of schizophrenics need the body of their child to make up for the limitations of their own bodies and to feel secure in their own skin, all this within a symbiotic bond. Piera Aulagnier (1985b) also describes the mother–infant relationship in schizophrenia as responding to the necessity of

> being half of oneself, the other half being detained by an object who himself can only preserve his unity at this price [...]. Maternal omnipotence, which so often occupies the foreground, conceals, and can always make room for a "half mother", a mutilated half, searching for its complement, a search the child understands to be a requirement he must satisfy.
> (Aulagnier, 1985b, p. 282, translated for this edition)

(This is akin to the conceptions of Searles concerning schizophrenia.) Joyce McDougall (1986, 1989) also proposes representations (phantasies of "one body for two", of "one psyche for two"), not only in psychotic functioning but also in the psychosomatic functioning of the personality, which illustrate perfectly certain manifestations, physical and psychic, of pathological symbiosis.

These representations can be maintained; they are still pertinent and are readily confirmed by clinical experience. However, it must nonetheless be added and noted that while a parent may manifest a symbiotic need and keep a child in such a psychopathological position, the psychosis of a child can itself generate a parental reaction consisting in closing the relationship and maintaining a pathological symbiosis. Symbiosis can produce psychosis, but psychosis can also produce symbiosis – we will have occasion to return to this point.[3]

The characteristic aspect of pathological symbiosis, which distinguishes it from normal symbiosis, is represented by the "destructive investment in the [...] combined psychotic mental representations" (Mahler, 1968, p. 233). The fusional relationship is cathected to a large extent with *destructive energy*, which is in keeping with our picture of psychopathological deviations. Moreover, destructive impulses and fears of attacks are projected outside.

Thus, symbiotic functioning belongs to a paranoid-schizoid register. We propose, moreover, to name the paranoid-schizoid position described by Melanie Klein (1935, 1946), characterized by persecutory anxiety, the processes of splitting and projection, and the part-object relationship, the *"symbiotic position"*; for, contrary to the terms "schizoid" and "paranoid", the term symbiotic does not refer to a psychopathological context. The symbiotic position, or paranoid-schizoid position, represents the position dominating the normal symbiotic phase, and appears to be the preferred means of defensive recourse in symbiotic psychotic pathologies. The primacy of adhesive identification yields to the primacy of projective identification, associated no longer with dismantling but with splitting.[4] The splitting of the object goes hand in hand with a splitting of the ego through the internalization of a persecuting object and an idealized object. The paranoid-schizoid or symbiotic position is impelled by the tendency towards fusion with the ideal breast and omnipotent denial of the persecuting breast. Projective identification operates to maintain the illusion of a common boundary between the subject and the object. The subject experiences the need to feel "hosted" in the psyche of his object. As Salomon Resnik often says, the psychotic patient feels a compelling need to lodge himself inside the other person.

> The psychotic suffers from agoraphobic anxieties and this is why his basic ideology is to live inside an object to defend himself against an extremely threatening outside and to preserve both a fragile and hard ego which is always in danger of breaking into pieces.
> (Resnik, 1986c, p. 62, translated for this edition)

If the autistic position, from the point of view of the object-relation, "autisticizes" the internal-external object, as we saw in the previous chapter, and if the depressive position "transitionalizes" it, we would say that *the symbiotic position "syncretizes" the object:* between the *status of autisticized object* and that of *transitional object* – not in the sense of the object in external reality, but of the object in the object-relation – the *"syncretic object"* appears.

Francisco Palacio Espasa (1980) describes a syncretic object, but he likens it to the autistic object. This confusion stems from the conceptions of José Bleger (1967) concerning the agglutinated object or the agglutinated nucleus, from which Palacio Espasa drew inspiration. Bleger suggested the idea of an agglutinated nucleus – to which we have already referred (Chapter 2) – to describe the psychic substance in the position prior to the paranoid-schizoid position, which he baptized the "glischro-caric position" (from *glischro*: viscous, and *caryon*: nucleus). This position is supposed to be reminiscent of the auto-sensual or adhesive (autistic exposure). However, while the notion of agglutinated nucleus seems to account for the state of the ego and of the object relation in the primal space or the auto-sensual position, it seems to us that what Bleger describes regarding the glischro-caric position does not correspond to the characteristics of the auto-sensual position: Bleger defines the glischro-caric position as being dominated by confusional anxiety; the operative defences are splitting, immobilization, fragmentation; the fixation points concern epilepsy and confusional states; and the relation to the object is symbiotic in nature. The glischro-caric position seems to us, therefore, to be equivalent to the symbiotic or paranoid-schizoid position. In our view, it does not represent an earlier position vis-à-vis the paranoid-schizoid position, but rather a first state within the paranoid-schizoid position itself. Moreover, "syncretism", which characterizes the relationship in this position, a term Bleger borrowed from Henri Wallon (1941), is presented by Wallon as an element of the emotional stage, a stage reached from the second month of life onwards with the appearance of "affective symbiosis".

The syncretic object as conceived by Palacio Espasa (1980) – combining "both ego, the parental objects and the object in itself in an agglutinated and indiscriminate way" (p. 378, translated for this edition) – represents more of an agglutinated object in Bleger's sense. For our part, we propose to define the syncretic object, which we will call quite simply a *symbiotic object,* as a split object, each pole of which, persecuting and idealized, attracts fusionally, symbiotically, a split-off part of the self. Contrary to the agglutinated or autisticized object, characterized by indiscrimination and non-differentiation, it is discrimination, and consequently splitting, that organize the syncretic and symbiotic object. Our contention is that in normal symbiosis it is the idealized pole that attracts the greatest part of the ego, while in destructive symbiosis it is around the persecuting pole that the ego agglutinates, either due to a failure of the idealized pole or due to the incapacity of the nuclei of the ego to discriminate the idealized pole.

The ambiguity of Bleger's conceptions concerning the glischro-caric position and the agglutinated object, which describe a borderline state between an adhesive position and a symbiotic position, allows us to lend support to Mahler's idea, taken up by Palacio Espasa, that the distinction between autism and symbiotic psychosis is sometimes difficult to objectivize. Margaret Mahler notes that autistic symptoms and symbiotic symptoms are often present at the same time. What differentiates the autistic picture from the symbiotic picture is the predominance of autistic or symbiotic defences. In an article titled "De l'autisme à la schizophrénie chez l'enfant" (1985b), Geneviève Haag tries, drawing on the work of Tustin and Meltzer among others, to highlight the common traits between autism and the schizophrenic psychoses, which she denotes by the term "pathological symbioses",[5] and to study the paths of transition from one state to the other. In the table below, we have regrouped the different findings presented by Geneviève Haag.

Autism	Pathological symbiosis
• Unintegration	• Explosive and destructive disintegration
• Archaic anxieties (falling, annihilation, liquefaction, nameless dread)	• Archaic anxieties overloaded with intense persecutory anxieties
• Interpenetration avoided	• Aggressive hyperpenetration, tyrannical, sometimes hallucinated mastery of the object, agitation
• Autistic withdrawal	• Rest in autistic withdrawal, defensive autistic manoeuvres against hyperpenetration
• "Being stuck to"	• "Being violently intruded upon"
• Encapsulation utilized to obviate awareness of bodily separation giving rise to the sensation of having lost a powerful part of the body	• Fragmentation, confused and disoriented penetration, utilized to obviate awareness of bodily separation
• Adhesive identification	• Pathological projective identification
• Passive dismantling through relaxation of attention (prior to the first psychic container)	• Active fragmentation, oral-sadistic attack on the body (beyond the first psychic container)
• Non-constitution of the first container (rhythmic in nature) leading to the quasi-permanent maintenance of body rhythms	• Loss or fragility of the first container (rhythmic in nature) leading to frequent recourse to body rhythms
• Vertical splitting of the body image	• Body image more "unified" at the level of the sagittal axis
• Little sadism	• Primary sadism, basic aggressivity
• Particular sensibility to the emotional states of the object, depressive concern for the object	• Sexualized and destructive excitability in attempts to achieve closeness and reparative dependence, due to "non-differentiation of zones" and to "oral-sexual short circuits"

Source: Haag, 1985b

In an article written ten years later, Geneviève Haag and her collaborators elaborated a "grid for the clinical identification of the evolving stages of the autism treated" (Haag et al., 1995). The evolution of autism as far as the symbiotic organization, and then individuation, is envisaged in it with even greater complexity. Four stages are described, from the autistic state to individuation, thus including the symbiotic phase: the first stage is that of the *"successful" autistic state,* an autistic state proper, which, according to the authors, is never complete and continuous; the second evolutive stage is that of the *beginning of the symbiotic phase*, with recovery by the child of a first "psychic skin", of a first sense of a circular envelope; the third stage is that of the *established symbiotic phase*, with vertical splitting of the body image and internalization of the hemi-bodies, then horizontal splitting and internalization of the anal and sexual zones; the fourth stage, finally, is the *stage of individuation*, with an experience of separation as a total sphincterized body. To help get our bearings developmentally, the first stage (successful autism) corresponds analogically to the first two months of life; the second stage (beginning of the symbiotic phase) to the period of the third to eighth month; the third stage (established symbiotic phase) to the end of the first year of life; and the fourth stage (stage of individuation) to the second year of life. For each stage, Geneviève Haag and her collaborators enumerate very precise and precious clinical elements concerning the emotional and relational expressions, the state of the gaze, the state of the body image, the state of language, the state of graphism, the exploration of space and of objects, temporal identification, as well as reactivity to pain and the immune state.

The evolution of (treated) autism until individuation consists, then, in traversing a symbiotic phase during which processes and skills are deployed that can be observed in the normal development of an infant of 3 to 12 months approximately. We are going to indicate some clinical reference points given by Geneviève Haag and her collaborators to describe this period from the stage of the "beginning of the symbiotic phase" to the end of the stage of the "established symbiotic phase", for they are very illustrative of the symbiotic state and symbiotic modes of functioning.

The *emotional and relational expressions* are characterized, in this symbiotic period, by tantrums during separations or frustrations (and not only when stereotypies are impeded or the relationship is forced, as was the case during the earlier stage of autistic withdrawal). The key issue here is one of wresting. Possessive and jubilatory facial attacks can be observed, with an alternation between jubilation and fear in visual contact. The child frequently presents hypomanic states, with a mixture of excitement, emotion and enthusiasm. He also manifests envy. Manic-depressive alternations may then appear, with the possibility of a perverse development if the manic phantasy predominantly involves aspects linked to anal masturbation (see Meltzer, 1966, 1992). Awareness of separation is outlined, even if infantile omnipotence persists. Real relational moments with tender exchanges become possible.

Concerning the quality of the *gaze*, the authors note an alternation between a hyperpenetrating gaze and an elusive gaze (it is no longer avoidant or peripheral as in the earlier phase). Looking deeply into the other person's eyes can sometimes be observed through the "cyclops effect" to which we have already referred. The underlying phantasy is one of entering through the eyes and sticking oneself behind the head. The gaze becomes a vehicle of orality (eating, being eaten by the eyes). A squint, used to avoid perception of otherness and distance, is sometimes observed. Gradually, exchanges of looks are normalized.

The state of the *body image* appears through manoeuvres consisting in including oneself in containers, marking the ongoing construction of a sense of envelope, of a psychic skin (defective in the earlier stage where the infant continued to cling to stereotypes to struggle against primitive anxieties of falling, of liquefaction). Containers are searched for and evaded at the same time, owing to "tightening anxieties", claustrophobic anxieties. The mouth (which was "amputated" in the earlier stage, producing a soft, flabby moth, with drooling) is reintegrated in the body image: explorative manoeuvres with the fingers or with mouth sounds can be observed. The body image is built up in the form first of a "pipe-ego" (see Tustin, 1986) (frequent interest in pipes and what happens inside them). There then appears the issue of "vertical splitting", with "hemiplegic" attitudes or behaviours (fusion of one hemibody with the hemibody of another person – "lateralized adhesive identification"), then that of "horizontal splitting" of the body image, with cathexis of the lower half of the body, anal and sexual zones.

Language, while inexistent or echolalic in the purely autistic state, develops in the form of vocal games in which the infant experiments with the internalization of bonds of communication through autoeroticism. He internalizes relational "returning loops"[6] in the theatre of the mouth (see Meltzer, 1985). Gradually demutization occurs, in half-words, in doublets (work of vertical splitting), or in vowels (the vowel is likened to the "soft" quality that the infant seeks, and the consonant to the "hard" quality that he avoids – see Tustin, 1981b; Haag, 1994). Then, the melodic phase is imitated, words are repeated and vocabulary develops.

Graphism, non-existent or extremely rudimentary in the earlier stage, and without any rhythmicity, becomes possible if the infant is first held physically, and takes the form of rhythmic sweeps, of unrolled spirals (see Haag, 1990b). Then the axis of traces is verticalized, horizontalized, and the infant shows an interest for separated half drawings, stuck together again, in one axis or in another, as well as for duplication. Graphism, done first of all in preference on hard supports, becomes possible on detachable[7] supports, and the use of colours (with their emotional significance) is increasingly frequent.

The *exploration of space and of objects*, which is very weak in the earlier stage (where objects were essentially taken as autistic objects), now develops, with exploration of hollow spaces, folds, protrusions, containers, contours, angles (projections onto architectural space of the characteristics of the envelope and of the vertebral axis – see Haag, 1997, 1998). The infant is interested in comparisons between symmetrical objects, then develops activities of embedding, of interlocking. Space is thus apprehended in three dimensions.

Finally, concerning *temporal identification*, Geneviève Haag and her collaborators, who had described in the autistic state proper a one-dimensional time (time is abolished, the child is lost clinging to a unisensory element), or two-dimensional (circular time, ritualizations with the "return of the same"), now speak of an oscillating time (with a belief in its reversibility) which alternates with circular time first, then establishes itself and alternates gradually with linear, continuous time.

We have now described a few elements of this symbiotic phase, as presented by Geneviève Haag and her collaborators, on emerging from autism proper. This stage is organized as *pathological symbiosis*, as the authors indicate, who emphasize the similarity of its forms of expression with the *symbiotic psychoses*.

Mixed pathologies are thus frequent, as Margaret Mahler had pointed out. We have mentioned on several occasions examples of autistic children in whom adhesive, two-dimensional processes already contained symbiotic elements. We have referred to cases of symbiotic children who, faced with the panic due to separation or to the mere mention of separation, had recourse to defensive autistic manoeuvres, such as confusional swaying and compulsive echolalia. The elements contributed by Geneviève Haag and her collaborators throw light on these imbrications, these paths of transition between autism and symbiotic psychosis. Pure autism, just like pure symbiotic psychosis, is only to be understood as virtual states.

6.3 The processes of separation–individuation

The way out of symbiosis lies in the realization of the process of separation–individuation. Before recalling how Margaret Mahler conceives this process, let us look at the evolution described by Geneviève Haag and her collaborators (Haag et al., 1995) of autistic states in order to indicate some elements of observation characteristic of individuation.

After the symbiotic phase, in the evolution of the "treated" autism, the "stage of individuation" opens up. In this stage the sense of separation is confirmed and the processes of introjection are stabilized. Relational exchanges are more assured, as well as moments of tenderness, with a real concern for others. The bond is internalized. Primitive anxieties are assuaged and the capacity for separation solidified. Violent bouts of anger and manifestations of oedipal rivalry can be observed. Language becomes more complex, with a grammatical organization and the appearance of "No". A socialized gestural language ("Well done", "Goodbye") also appears. Specular recognition is confirmed. At the level of graphism, one sees the appearance of the closed circle (constituted, unified and separate psychic envelope), radial forms (see Haag, 1993), and figurative traces. One also sees the initiation of games of hide-and-seek (sign of the permanence of the object), decanting, closing/opening, "offering behaviours" (consisting in putting objects in someone else's hand and taking them back again), which are re-experimentations of the first "returning loops". Temporality is characterized by the perception of a linear time, a "time of separation", with a notion of the inevitable flow of time.

To return now to Margaret Mahler and her description of the way out of symbiosis in normal development. Mahler divides the process of separation–individuation into four stages:

- the first stage involves a first displacement of libidinal cathexis from internal sensations towards external stimuli and exteroceptive activity. The first reactions to strange objects then appear, evidencing the "dawn" of the symbiotic matrix;
- the second stage (towards the end of the first year) is characterized by a second displacement of cathexis towards broader sectors of external reality under the impetus of the maturational thrust of locomotion.

> At that point, a large proportion of the available cathexis shifts from within the symbiotic orbit to investing the autonomous apparatuses of the self and the functions of the ego – locomotion, perception, learning.
>
> (Mahler, 1968, p. 19–20)

It is during this phase that the birth of the infant as an individuated individual occurs;

- the third stage (which extends over approximately the second 18 months of life) is that of "*rapprochement*": the infant becomes aware on a more lasting basis that his mother is a separate object from him and that he risks losing her;
- the fourth stage sees the realization of the acquisition of the "permanence of the libidinal object" in the sense that Heinz Hartmann (1964) understands it. Margaret Mahler stresses the discrepancy between the acquisition of the permanence of the object, of which Jean Piaget (1935) speaks, which occurs before the end of the first year, and the much more gradual acquisition of the permanence of the libidinal object as conceived by Hartmann, which remains fragile until around the thirtieth month. It is during this fourth stage that the infant can retain the image of a parent who has both gratifying and frustrating, good and bad, aspects.

The process of separation-individuation is therefore dependent on and contemporary with the elaboration of the depressive position, to which we will return further on (Chapter 8). It establishes introjective identifications and opens mental space up to its fourth dimension, that of historicization.

Notes

1 We will even rebaptize the "paranoid–schizoid" position with the term "symbiotic position".
2 On this point, see Ciccone, 2014.
3 On the traumatic effects on parents of coming to terms with psychopathology in a child, see Ciccone, 2012a, 2016b, 2017, 2018.
4 We shall not be developing the notions of splitting and projective identification here, as they are the subject of the fourth and fifth postulates.

5 Tustin links schizophrenia, regressive secondary autism, confusional autism and symbiotic psychosis (see in particular Tustin, 1987).
6 "Returning loops" are motor images of a returning relaxation of the "tension towards". The realization of these return loops implies a rhythmicity of the relationship to the object, of emotional movement, and relies on useful projective identifications. These return loops gradually constitute circularity, the first level of representation of the bodily organization. They play an essential role in the construction of the body image and of space (see Haag, 1991, 1993, 1995, 1998).
7 Duplication and the detachable support are evidence of the division of the layers of the first psychic skin.

7

ON THE SKIN-EGO

A complete psychic envelope[1]

The conception of a psychic function of containing and transformation participated in the creation or development of the metaphor of the "psychic envelope". We have seen how Esther Bick introduced the notion of *psychic skin*, and we are going to consider the notion of skin-ego proposed by Didier Anzieu, a little later, in 1974.

But the notion of the psychic envelope had its incipient outlines in early psychoanalytic texts. As early as 1895, in the "Project for a scientific psychology" (Freud, 1950 [1895]), for instance, the idea of ego-boundaries is presented, of an inside and an outside of the ego. In *The Ego and the Id*, Freud (1923) spoke of the ego as an entity corresponding to the projection of a surface.[2] Later, Paul Federn (1952), for example, studied "ego boundaries" and the ego's variations in psychoses, dreams, and sleeping and waking states. Bion, as we have seen, particularly developed the notion of the "containing object", of the "containing function" of the object, after which Esther Bick suggested the notion of "psychic skin".

Didier Anzieu subsequently modelized the notion of "skin-ego", and this was to prove extremely fruitful and give rise to conceptualizations related to psychic envelopes in the psychoanalytic approach to all subjects, but also groups, families and institutions. Anzieu's work inaugurated or confirmed a real effort to take into consideration what may be called the "envelope function" (Ciccone, 2001), for the notion of an envelope is a metaphor that describes not an object in itself but a psychic function; it is the depiction of a function.

We will define the notion of the skin-ego and present the functions of this psychic envelope with the psychopathological effects specific to the defects of each of these functions. We will go on to consider its psychogenesis and situate it in relation to the models that underlie our reflection, notably that of Donald Meltzer. We will then discuss the similarities and differences between the notions of "skin-ego" and "psychic skin" and describe the structure of the psychic envelope and the pathologies linked to its alterations. Finally, we will emphasize the contributions of the theorization of psychic envelopes to metapsychology and to the psychoanalytic understanding of psychopathologies.

7.1 The hypothesis of the skin-ego

Didier Anzieu (1974a, 1985) built his hypothesis of the skin-ego on theoretical findings from four different sources. He refers to the studies of ethologists and psychoanalysts: (Harlow, 1958, and his experiments on the object of attachment in baby monkeys; Bowlby 1969, and the "instinct of attachment"; Winnicott, 1951, 1962ab, and his descriptions of the needs of the baby), to certain studies on the observation of human groups (Turquet, 1974, and his notion of a "relational boundary of the I with the neighbour's skin"), to certain studies on projective tests (Fischer and Cleveland, 1958, and their isolation of the variables "envelope" and "penetration" in the Rorschach test), and finally to the psychosomatic and psychodynamic investigation of skin disorders (see Pomey-Rey, 1979 – Anzieu links the gravity of skin alteration to the quantitative and qualitative importance of the psychic disturbance).

These four series of findings led Anzieu to the hypothesis of a skin-ego. To formulate it, Anzieu begins with the prototypical situation of feeding. During the feed, the baby has three concomitant experiences: that of a differentiating contact through the nipple in the mouth and incorporation; that of a centre of gravity through repletion, and that of important tactile stimulations due to being held, carried, held tightly against the mother's body, manipulated, and so on, all this in a bath of words. These tactile experiences, which correspond to the conditions satisfying the instinct of attachment, lead the baby to differentiate a surface comprising an external side and an internal side, distinguishing the outside and the inside, and a volume in which he feels bathed. This surface, which Anzieu calls "interface", and this volume give the infant the sensation of having a container. Thus, through experiencing his body in contact with his mother's, and in the context of a secure relationship of attachment with her, the baby acquires the perception of the skin as a surface, which engenders, on the one hand, the notion of a boundary between the inside and the outside and, on the other, a basic feeling guaranteeing him the integrity of his bodily envelope, a feeling that will help him to gradually master the orifices.

This feeling of the integrity of the bodily envelope gives the ego a narcissistic envelope and the mind a basic sense of well-being, hence the idea of the skin-ego:

> By "skin-ego" I am referring to a mental image used by the child's ego during its early stages of development to represent itself as an ego containing psychical contents, based on its experience of the surface of the body. This corresponds to the moment when the psychical Ego differentiates itself from the bodily Ego in operative terms but remains mixed up with its figurative terms.
>
> (Anzieu, 1985/2018, p. 43)

It is the instinct of attachment which, according to Anzieu, if it is satisfied sufficiently and early enough, provides the baby with the basis on which the "integrative impulse of the ego" can manifest itself – a term borrowed from Pierre Luquet (1962) – which consists in establishing barriers, filtering exchanges, etc., providing the basis for the development of the skin-ego on which "the very possibility of thought is founded".

7.2 The functions of the skin-go

Didier Anzieu first describes nine (1985/2018), then eight functions of the skin-ego (1993a, 1994, 1995). In keeping with the generally accepted idea that psychic processes are based on biological functions,[3] Anzieu presents these functions of the skin-ego as based on the functions of the skin.

1. The skin-ego has a function of *maintaining* the psyche. This function is developed through internalization of maternal "holding":[4]

    > The skin-ego is a part of the mother – especially her hands – which has been interiorized and now maintains the psyche

in a functional state, at least while the baby is awake, just as the mother keeps its body in a state of unity and solidity. [...]. What matters here is not the phantasmatic incorporation of the nourishing breast but the primary identification of a support-object which the infant can cling to and be held by; it is the drive to attachment or clinging that is satisfied rather than the libido.

(Anzieu, 1985/2018, p. 106–107)

Anzieu, who was inspired, among others, by the work of James Grotstein (1981) of whom we have already spoken, (see Chapter 5), describes very well, in the setting-up of this function of maintaining the psyche, a process akin to that evoked by Esther Bick (1968), namely, the introjection of the optimal external object as the indispensable precondition for establishing a binding container, holding together the scattered parts of the emerging psyche of the infant. The disturbance of this function activates anxiety related to the loss of the support-object and hampers autonomization. The second function follows on from the first.

2. The skin-ego has a function of *containing*. It envelops the whole psychical apparatus. It represents a bark of which the instinctual id is the nucleus. It contains the drives, giving them boundaries and specific insertion points in mental space. This containing function is exercised, before being interiorized, by maternal "handling".[5] The deficiency of this function gives rise to two types of anxiety: on the one hand, anxiety due to diffuse, permanent and unidentifiable instinctual drive excitation which leads the subject to seek a substitutive bark in physical pain or in psychic suffering; and on the other, anxiety to do with having an inside that empties itself, thoughts that escape, etc., when the envelope is interrupted in its continuity by holes and functions as "a sieve skin-ego", to use Anzieu's term.

3. The skin-ego has a function of a protective *shield against stimuli*. It consists of a duplicate structure, just like the skin, where the external layer of the epidermis protects the sensitive layer, which is the seat of free nerve endings and of the tactile corpuscles. Further on, we will consider the structure of the skin-ego and pathologies linked to a structural alteration of this envelope. We

Third postulate

will see that Anzieu describes many situations corresponding to a defective stimulus barrier system.

4. The skin-ego ensures the function of *self-individuation*. It affords the feeling of being unique and the possibility of recognizing and affirming oneself as a differentiated and different subject. This is what the schizophrenic is lacking, for example.
5. The skin-ego has an *intersensorial* function. It avoids the independent, anarchic functioning of the various sense organs and leads to the constitution of a feeling of "common sense". When this function is deficient, anxiety to do with body fragmentation ensues.[6]
6. The skin-ego fulfils the function of *supporting sexual excitation*. On this supporting surface the erogenous zones are localized, the difference between the sexes is recognized, and their complementarity is desired. The alteration of this function may lead to the development of a narcissistic envelope if the cathexis of the skin is more narcissistic than libidinal, or alternatively to difficulties for the subject in achieving a sexually satisfying relationship, or to a predisposition to sexual perversions if the sexual zones are sites of algogenic rather than erotogenic experiences.
7. The skin-ego has a function of *libidinally recharging psychic functioning*. It maintains the internal tension of energy and the unequal distribution between the psychic sub-systems. The failures of this function have as their corollary the fear of seeing the psychic apparatus explode (see the epileptic fit) or the fear of Nirvana (reduction of tension to zero).
8. The skin-ego fulfils a function of *registering tactile sensory traces*. This function is reinforced by the mothering environment's role of "object-presentation".[7]

> The ekin-ego is the original parchment which acts as a palimpsest, preserving the crossed-out, scratched-through, overwritten drafts of an 'original' pre-verbal writing made of traces on the skin.
> (Anzieu, 1985/2018, p. 114)[8]

The anxieties connected with this function are, on the one hand, that of being marked by shameful and indelible registrations originating in the superego, like skin redness or eczema, etc., and, on the other, that of being unable to fix memory traces.

9. Finally, the skin-ego has a function of *self-destruction of the skin and of the ego*. It is a negative function, an "anti-function", which is based on auto-immune organic phenomena, carrying out unconscious attacks against the psychic container, reversing the aim of the drives. It is a toxic function of the skin-ego (and was subsequently withdrawn from the list of skin-ego functions by Anzieu).

In the new edition of *The Skin-Ego* (Anzieu, 1995), this list is maintained (without the ninth function), even though it underwent some changes in the intermediary versions. Indeed, in his chapter in a collective book titled *Les contenants de pensée* (Anzieu et al., 1993), Anzieu very briefly proposes a few modifications to this list at the level of the labelling of the functions and of their order of succession. The function of stimulus barrier is called the function of "constancy". The function of individuation moves from the fourth to the sixth place. The function of intersensoriality is called the function of "correspondence". The function of supporting sexual excitation is named the function of "sexualization" and moves from the sixth to the seventh place. The function of libidinally recharging psychic functioning becomes the function of "energization" and moves from the seventh to the eighth place. The function of registering tactile sensory traces becomes the function of "significance" (*signifiance*) and occupies the fourth position. Finally, the function of toxic self-destruction is withdrawn from the list: it is an anti-function that belongs to the "work of the negative". Here, then, is the new list of the classification of the functions of the skin-ego: *maintenance, containing, constancy, significance, correspondence, individuation, sexualization and energization*. This categorization is once again developed in *Le Penser* (Anzieu, 1994), where he deploys analogies between the functions of the skin, of the ego or of the skin-ego, and of thinking or of the thinking-ego. This list is neither exhaustive nor definitive, and Anzieu (1985, 1995) proposes to match other functions of the ego with the functions of the skin, for example, the function of storage (fats …) compared to the memory-function of the ego; the function of production (hair, nails …) and the function of emission (sweat, pheromones …), which are likened to the function of producing ego defence-mechanisms. Anzieu also proposes to match certain tendencies of the ego or of the skin-ego with the structural characteristics of the skin touching upon the complexity of its constitution, and its volume with that of other organs, and so on.

7.3 The psychogenesis of the skin-ego

How is the psychogenesis of the skin-ego envisaged? Didier Anzieu (1985) distinguishes three stages in the integration of the skin-ego, organized, for the first two, around a specific phantasy:

- the first stage is marked by the domination, in the mind of the newborn infant, of an "intra-uterine"[9] phantasy. This last denies birth and expresses the desire to return to the maternal womb, a desire characteristic of primary narcissism. Fixation to the intra-uterine phantasy characterizes, according to Anzieu, the autistic envelopes, to which the baby withdraws and protects himself in order to escape functioning in an open system. The autistic envelope is a "closed system, that of an egg that does not hatch";
- the second stage, that of the "interface", is dominated by the phantasy of a "common skin" between the mother and the infant. This common skin maintains the two partners in a state of mutual symbiotic dependence, ensures communication without an intermediary and reciprocal empathy. The experience of separation at this stage induces phantasies of torn-off, stolen and bruised skin;
- the third stage reveals a path towards an increasingly open system of psychic functioning. The infant has acquired a skin-ego that is his own, according to a twofold process of internalization: internalization of the interface that becomes a psychic envelope containing psychic contents, and internalization of the mothering surround that becomes the inner world of thoughts, images and affects.

When we come to describe the structure of the skin-ego, we will see, at each stage of its development, how this envelope which will become a skin-ego is organized.

The skin-ego, virtual at birth, emerges, then, from a basis of primary identification with the support-object, whose phantasmatic representation is that of skin that is common to the baby's body and the mother's body. Their respective bodies are situated on each side of an interface, which furnishes the infrastructure that is necessary for the ego to constitute itself through the internalization of this interface.[10] But if the ego is to be able to continue its process of structuring, it must first break with the primacy of primal tactile experience and constitute itself as a "intersensory space of registration", realizing the synthesis between the different senses and organizing the various types of sensations into the beginnings of thought. At this point, Anzieu introduces the hypothesis of what he calls "the taboo on touching". Tactile communications are repressed under the effect of the taboo on touching. They are therefore not destroyed but recorded and retained as the backcloth, as a "first psychical space into which other sensory and motor spaces can be slotted" (Anzieu, 1985/2018, p. 167). Thus, if the skin-ego is initially tactile, the visual envelope, the olfactory envelope, the gustatory envelope and the sound envelope will fit into this tactile envelope.[11]

We would like to point out a contradiction in Anzieu's remarks. He presents tactile experiences as constituting the primary psychic space; the tactile envelope, into which the other envelopes fit, is first, primal. However, in his chapter on the "sound envelope", Anzieu presents the sound space as the "first psychic space", so that the sound envelope is therefore the most primitive psychic envelope. The sound (and olfactory) envelope represents the *self*, around which the ego differentiates itself – the self preexists the ego[12] – on the basis of tactile experience. In this case, the sound space may be said to precede the visual, visual-tactile, locomotor and graphic spaces.

We will resolve this contradiction by proposing another temporal model of the constitution of the different sensory envelopes, and by considering that the containing-attracting object "attracts" all sensoriality in an undifferentiated manner. On this view, the primary consensuality is a *confused sensuality*. To the chronological linear model we prefer a star-shaped model that represents the progression from nondifferentiation towards a simultaneous differentiation of the different sensory envelopes, each at its own rhythm. The skin-ego and consensuality subsequently result from a harmonious interlocking of these different envelopes. The alteration of an envelope will result in the alteration of the skin-ego.

To return now to the prohibition on touching, which is the basis of the development of thought. The prohibition on touching does not require a definitive renunciation of echo-tactile communication, but only a renunciation of echo-tactile communication as a principal mode of communication. The prohibition on touching, that is the prohibition on the primacy of the pleasures of the skin, and then the hand, transforms concrete tactile experience into "basic representations to serve as the background against which systems of intersensory correspondence can be set up" (Anzieu, 1985/2018, p. 150). These intersensory correspondences first have a figurative aspect, maintaining a symbolic reference to touching; they then gain access to an abstract level, freeing themselves from this tactile reference. Thus the ego, which functions first as a skin-ego structure, passes over, if the skin-ego has been sufficiently integrated, to a system of functioning as a "thinking-ego".[13]

7.4 Epistemological confrontations

7.4.1 Construction of the skin-ego and spatial structuring of the psychical apparatus

Didier Anzieu (1985) establishes a parallel between the psycho-genesis of the skin-ego and the structuring of mental space in its different dimensions, as Donald Meltzer presented it, that is, in terms of a two-, three-, and then four-dimensional organization (see Chapter 4). Let us now discuss this parallel:

- the three stages of the integration of the skin-ego are characterized by the *intra-uterine phantasy* (for the first stage), the *phantasy of a common skin* (for the second), and by the *constitution of the skin-ego* (for the third);
- it is important to bear in mind that two-dimensional space is that of adhesive identification (Bick); that three-dimensional space is that of the paranoid-schizoid position (Klein) or symbiotic position, and is dominated by projective identification; and that four-dimensional space, finally, is that of the depressive position (Klein) and is dominated by introjective identification. It is in the fourth dimension of psychic space that the transition occurs from a narcissistic relationship to the object relationship;
- in addition, we have seen in connection with the conceptions of Margaret Mahler (Chapter 6) that the auto-sensual position and two-dimensionality characterize the autistic phase; that the paranoid-schizoid or symbiotic position and three-dimensionality characterize the symbiotic phase; and that the depressive position and four-dimensionality characterize the phase of separation-individuation.

The intra-uterine phantasy that Anzieu describes, fixation to which organizes the autistic envelopes, seems to us to correspond to the adhesive or auto-sensual position and to the primary phase of development that Mahler called the phase of "normal autism".

The second stage, on the other hand, raises a problem for us. Anzieu clearly considers that it is marked by a phantasy of common skin and by symbiotic dependence which follow on from a state dominated by an autistic-type organization. This second stage is thus reminiscent of Mahler's symbiotic phase with the common border, and corresponds to Meltzer's three-dimensional space and to Klein's paranoid-schizoid position, where projective identification dominates. But Anzieu makes the object-relation rest, in this second period, on adhesive identification, and locates it in two-dimensional space. Adhesive identification and two-dimensionality characterize, as we have seen, the auto-sensual position, and this should be linked to what Anzieu defines as the intra-uterine phantasy organizing autistic envelopes, and not to the phantasy of a common skin, to which, as Anzieu himself says, the organized psyche in the mode of autistic envelopes does not have access. Indeed, when he describes autistic envelopes, he understands them as pertaining to a fixation to the intra-uterine phantasy and a failure to gain access to the phantasy of a common skin, which is understood as a symbiotic dependence between the two partners.

This confusion that Anzieu makes between adhesive identification, two-dimensionality and symbiosis reflects a quite generally widespread confusion between *adhesive identification* as a psychic process, and the *adhesive effect of projective identification*. A child stuck to the mothering object in physical reality is not necessarily in adhesive identification; but if the psychic organization is symbiosis, he is in projective identification, with the phantasy of sharing a common skin with the object. The adhesive identity does without the actual object; it denies every boundary with the other, since it denies otherness.

In adhesive identification, not only is the subject stuck to the surface of the object but the object is reduced to its surface; it is an object without an interior and most of the time an inanimate object. Now this does not seem to be the case in Anzieu's description of the phantasy of a common skin. We have given phenomenological examples of adhesive identification (see Chapter 5), as observed in autistic children, such as mimicry, echolalia and echopraxia, where the child sticks to the musicality of words or acts, and not to the meaning or content. One of the consequences of adhesive identification is an operation of unisensory reduction, where the object is entirely identified with its surface or with an aspect that serves as a surface. This does not seem to occur in the phantasy of the common skin, where the interior of the object to which the subject is stuck can be cathected: the subject can establish himself in the interior of the object, appropriate it, attack it and covet it through projective identifications.

The phantasy of a common skin refers not to the two- but to the three-dimensionality of psychic space. We can say that although the skin is shared it is no less a skin, a border giving access and representation to something beyond the border, that is to say, to an interior of the object which does not receive adhesive identifications but projective identifications, in a context of symbiotic dependence.[14]

Finally, the third stage, that of the constitution of a differentiated skin-ego, seems to us to correspond to the four-dimensionality of mental space (Meltzer), to the depressive position (Klein), to the phase of separation-individuation (Mahler) and to the prevalence of introjective identification marking the transition from a narcissistic relationship to an object relationship.

7.4.2 The skin-ego and the psychic skin

We will now discuss the relations between Didier Anzieu's notion of skin-ego and Esther Bick's (1968) notion of psychic skin, and look at the similarity that Anzieu establishes between these two notions.

Let us note, first of all, a conceptual difference: the skin-ego refers above all to a formation or a precise and delimited mental image that only gains access to the quality of skin-ego, or only corresponds to the characteristics of a skin-ego, after having been subject to a process of transformation or construction marked by a succession of stages; the psychic skin, on the other hand, denotes more of a state, a function independent of the specific qualities of the object or of the agency exercising this function. The momentary object and the optimal object thus both have a skin function and are experienced as a psychic skin, even if the characteristics of a real psychic skin, sufficiently well constituted and individuating, are subject to particular conditions belonging to a process of development.

Do the skin-ego and the psychic skin represent identical entities? If we can say that the skin-ego arises from the sense of integrity, of continuity of the tactile bodily surface, in a secure relationship of attachment, it seems to us that the notion of psychic skin as presented by Esther Bick is derived from a slightly different perspective (in the sense of an optical angle) with regard to the processes of the genesis and integration of the psychical apparatus. The psychic skin, according to Esther Bick, arises from the introjection of an external object (external from the observer's standpoint) providing a binding and containing force for the scattered elements of the infantile psyche. Although this external object seems to be of the same order as the one in question in the integration of the skin-ego, namely, the mothering environment, in the notion of the psychic skin the emphasis is placed on the feeling of being held, carried and nourished physically, but above all psychically (this split is always made from the observer's point of view). This feeling of being held together, contained in one's mental life, a bit like Didier Anzieu's descriptions of the maintenance and containing functions of the skin-ego, is presented as initial by Esther Bick, that is, if it arises from the sensory, multi-sensory, emotional and psychic experience of the feeding situation, it will allow the skin to be invested with its function of containing the parts of the self. Thus, when Didier Anzieu says that the functions of the skin-ego are based on the functions of the skin, could it not also be said that the functions of the skin are based on the functions of the skin-ego, in relations of mutual interdependence?

To put the same thing differently, Esther Bick insists more on the *relationship to the object* than on the sensory qualities of this relationship. We would like to put forward the hypothesis that the skin-ego represents a *psychic object* arising from the *bodily experience* of being contained or maintained by the subject's own skin, whereas the psychic skin is conceived as a *psychic object* arising from the *psychic experience* of being contained by an external skin, first felt to be interior.

The question that could be raised is that of a chronology in the integration of the bodily skin and of the psychic skin or skin-ego – is the ego *first and foremost* a *bodily* ego as Freud says (1923)? Indeed, is the sensation of bodily integrity created by tactile experiences a pre-condition of – and thus anterior to – the constitution of the skin-ego, as Anzieu seems to suggest, and, consequently of the possibility of real psychic exchanges, or is it these psychic exchanges, introjection and projection, and particularly the introjection of a containing external object, that permit the constitution of a psychic skin with which the bodily skin can be identified, as Bick seems to say?

Let us recall, for we have already made this point (see Chapter 1), that when one speaks of introjection at this stage of mental life, the existence of an interior and an exterior are not presupposed. Indeed, the introjection of the containing external object, on which the constitution of the internal world depends, is not equivalent to the passage in phantasy of an object from an *exterior* towards an *interior*, terms that imply the prior existence of a boundary; rather, it describes the very construction of this boundary, of this envelope, though the appropriation of the external containing function, which becomes interior insofar as it is elaborated as delimiting and defining the interior. At this stage, exteriority and interiority, and consequently introjection, only exist from the observer's point of view.

To the question of a possible succession between the integration of a bodily skin and the integration of a psychic skin, we would say that these two processes are contemporaneous, simultaneous and interdependent. The differentiation of the subject's bodily space – which, for Anzieu, has as its corollary the formation of the skin-ego, and for Bick is dependent on a delimitation of the internal psychic space – is already the very expression of a psychic differentiation with which it is contemporary. The baby who notices that his hand belongs to him is at the same time developing his capacity to link up sensations and perceptions and to form thoughts; he is constructing his bodily space and individuating his psychic space. *At the same time as the skin supports the construction of the psychic envelope* (psychogenesis of the skin-ego), *the psychic envelope, first exterior, and then introjected, supports the containing function of the bodily skin.* Psychic space and bodily space are not to be understood as a succession of processes ordered by a relationship of cause and effect, but as a state of undifferentiation leading to a progressive state of differentiation. The ego is not *first and foremost* a bodily ego, but an undifferentiated *psychosomatic ego* which gradually differentiates itself as a bodily ego and a psychic ego that are articulated, interlocking and mutually supportive.

We can find in the thought of Piera Aulagnier (1975) a model that makes it possible to merge, or envisage from the same angle, the notions of skin-ego and psychic skin. Piera Aulagnier describes psychic representation, or the representation of psychic activity, as being dependent on physical need:

> It is on the sensory vector that the instinctual "leans"; the perception of need itself opens up access to the psyche thanks to a representation that brings to the fore the absence of a sensitive object, a source of pleasure for the corresponding organ.
> (Aulagnier, 1975, p. 24)

She emphasizes the fact that it is *pleasure* (or unpleasure) that permits the association between the external object that is a source of satisfaction and the zone or bodily function that is a source of need due to the absence of this object. The psyche represents this sensory zone/exciting object duality to itself by means of an image: the image of the "complementary zone-object", where duality is unknown. This image is called a pictogram. We will borrow this description, insisting not on the affect of pleasure, but rather on the need for *security*. The need for a containing external object is based less on the flight from unpleasure and the search for pleasure than on the flight from anxiety and the search for security.

Let us now apply the model of the pictogram to the genesis of the psychic skin according to Esther Bick. When the baby has the experience of satisfaction and security arising from feeding and holding, the psyche employs pictographic activity to form a picture of the skin/containing object duality, in which the containing function of the introjected object will be identified with the skin, and duality denied. In this way the psychic skin will develop, which may be considered, initially, as a pictogram in which the psyche is reflected as an identical totality with the surrounding, enveloping world. Adhesive identification, and then the phantasy of a common skin can be approached in this way.

If we now consider the genesis of the skin-ego with the idea of the pictogram, we will see that the model of Piera Aulagnier allows for a total interweaving between the notions of psychic skin and skin-ego. Indeed, if the pictogram originating in satisfying sensory and secure experience offers the psyche the image of a skin and represents a "psychic skin", we can also say that the tactile experience of skin-to-skin containing or maintenance, provided, of course, that it is satisfying and secure, gains access to the psyche in the form of a complementary zone-object image – the object being the mothering object or the breast, and the zone being the skin – where duality is initially not recognized. The differentiation of the skin, under the influence of satisfying and secure sensory experiences, will lead to the individuation of the psyche and to the formation of a skin-ego which may have its origin in the pictographic representation of the sensory experience of a bodily skin that it unifies.

Piera Aulagnier's model applied to the skin-ego reintroduces the relationship to the object and makes it possible to envisage the identity between the notions of skin-ego and psychic skin, both of which account for the idea of an envelope for the psychic system, and of the fundamental functions of this envelope with regard to the integrity of the sense of identity.

7.5 Structural representation of the psychic envelope

We have seen, in connection with its function as a stimulus barrier, that the skin-ego, or psychic envelope, is represented as constituted of a two-layered structure. The descriptions that Didier Anzieu (1985) gives of this two-layered structure contain in substance the idea of an ontogenetic development from a first model, where the outer layer denotes the environmental envelope, the mothering entourage, and the inner layer the surface of the baby's body, the locus and instrument of the emission of messages, towards a second model, where the notions of outer and inner layers are applied to the skin-ego of the infantile psyche divided into these two elements. It is as though, at the beginning, the function of the stimulus barrier were assured by the mothering entourage (outer layer) that protects the baby, and above all his perceptual-sensory surface (inner layer), from destructive stimuli – this is the first model. If the outer layer sticks too much to the infant's skin, the development of the infant's ego will be impeded. On the other hand, if the outer layer is too loose, the ego will lack consistency. After the mothering entourage has exercised this stimulus barrier function, and if it takes place in good enough conditions, the infant introjects this function which becomes specific to his skin-ego, which then develops two layers: an outer layer guaranteeing the function of stimulus barrier and an inner layer representing a sensitive layer – this is the second model. In this schema, in the case of an excess or a deficit of the stimulus barrier, pathology offers various clinical pictures. Anzieu refers to the octopus-ego – which he was later to call (Anzieu, 1986b) the seaweed skin-ego – (the double layer is not outlined, the function of stimulus barrier is not organized), and the shell-ego (Anzieu, 1990) (a rigid shell replaces the absent container). These terms take up the images suggested by Tustin (1972). Likewise, in the absence of an epidermis (outer layer), the stimulus barrier can be sought in the dermis (inner layer).

In an article titled "Cadre psychanalytique et enveloppes psychiques", Anzieu (1986b) returns to this idea of the psychic envelope with a double structure: the *stimulus barrier* and the *surface of registration*. The stimulus barrier envelope interposes a protective screen between the external world and psychic reality and plays a role as a quantitative filter. The surface envelope of registration represents the sensitive membrane of the psychical apparatus; it deploys an optical screen which serves as a support for the projection of tactile, visual, sound and kinaesthetic images, and functions as a qualitative filter in the service of communication.

The development of the psychical apparatus entails the gradual differentiation of these two envelopes, and Anzieu highlights three stages in topographical development: non-differentiation, unsticking and the interlocking of the psychic envelopes. Various pathologies correspond to each stage:

- the non-differentiation between excitation and communication characterizes the hysterical envelope;
- the overdevelopment of the stimulus barrier envelope and the underdevelopment of the surface of registration envelope characterize the envelope of suffering where physical pain represents a substitutive bark guaranteeing the permanence of the sense of identity, or narcissistic depression linked to the fear of being emptied out, to instinctual drive haemorrhaging;
- the differentiation of two envelopes that remain stuck together, without an interval, characterizes psychosomatic states where the "operational (i.e. concrete, matter-of-fact) mode of thinking" (*pensée opératoire*) dominates psychic life;
- the excitation in the service of communication is a characteristic configuration of perversion;
- the absence of the two envelopes characterizes primary autism, whereas the absence of the communication envelope associated with the rigidification of the stimulus barrier envelope characterizes secondary autism (we would prefer to speak, where

secondary autism is concerned, of an absence of the stimulus barrier envelope and of rigidification of the inner envelope with the aim of ensuring the stimulus barrier function[15] – a scenario envisaged by Anzieu below);
- the alterations of the surface of registration layer can take the form of the "muscular second skin" of which Bick speaks (and which we link to secondary autistic states), or shameful and punitive superego registrations (redness, eczema, etc.), or memory gaps, an inability to fix memory traces, etc.;
- the juxtaposition – instead of superposition and interlocking – of the two envelopes is typical of borderline states, with difficulties in distinguishing between inside/outside, container/the contained, animate/inanimate, good/bad, and so on;
- the encircling of the two envelopes and the totality of the psychical apparatus by a third envelope, the superego envelope – usually the superego only represents a superposition in the form of a limited arc – characterizes the obsessional envelope which, in addition, features a pocket that is a "hiding place-dumping ground of affects";
- the interchangeability of the two envelopes, the presence of a tear that constantly has to be patched up, with, in addition, the duplication of the personal psychic envelope with a maternal envelope, like an "outer garment of skin", are characteristics of the narcissistic envelope.

The descriptive list of the pathologies of the envelope in connection with its two-layered structure is not exhaustive and could no doubt be completed.

Geneviève Haag also considers the psychic skin as a two-layered structure. In an article on the introjection of the psychic envelope and its division into two layers, Geneviève Haag (1986b), in the light of the elaborations proposed by Didier Anzieu, has put forward the hypothesis that the outer layer is formed by virtue of *normal adhesivity* on the model of the dead and exfoliating component of the epidermis; the space between the outer layer and the inner layer – a sensitive layer that registers "the most individualized representations of the inner theatre" (Haag, 1986b, p. 83, translated for this edition) – is the locus of functioning of the *identificatory projective system*.

Concerning the ontogenetic and structural development of this two-layered envelope, we situate *non-differentiation* in the auto-sensual or adhesive position organized in a two-dimensional mode by the intra-uterine phantasy; the *unsticking* of the layers characterizes the symbiotic position, with the phantasy of a common skin, where projective identification is operative – in the space between the two unstuck layers, according to Haag – thereby giving a third dimension to mental space; finally, the *interlocking* of the layers takes place with the elaboration of the depressive position giving primacy to introjective identification, organizing mental space in a four-dimensional mode, and guaranteeing the integrity of the sense of identity, and thus in particular of the psychic envelope.

7.6 Contributions of the model of the psychic envelope to metapsychology and to the representation of psychopathology

The model of the psychic envelope is unquestionably fruitful. Didier Anzieu constantly sought to cultivate and render fertile this notion of skin-ego, this concept of a psychic envelope which, with others, he developed with creativity (Anzieu et al., 1987, 1990, 1993; Anzieu, 1986bc, 1993b, 1994, 1995). For his part, Anzieu continued the work of identifying psychic envelopes and their alterations. He explored the notion of skin-ego in the history and pre-history of psychoanalytic concepts, in clinical work and in literature; with regard to the concept of psychic envelope, he established connections with the fields of philosophy, experimental psychology, biology, physics and mathematics. He also continued to clarify further and develop this model of psychic envelopes and of their deficiencies in the fields of psychic development and psychopathology. Didier Anzieu never ceased to confirm the interest, pertinence and impact of such a model.

The conceptualization of the psychic envelope in general, and of the skin-ego in particular, sheds decisive light both on metapsychology and on the psychoanalytic understanding of psychopathology. The point of view of the pathology of the envelope can elucidate individual pathologies, but also group, family and institutional pathologies.

We have seen, through the different modes of dysfunctioning of each function of the skin-ego, how all psychopathologies can be considered from the point of view of the pathology of the envelope. Autism, schizophrenia, borderline states, narcissistic states, psychosomatic states, perversion, hysteria and obsessional states are all forms of psychopathology that contain the alteration or undoing of one or several functions of the skin-ego. Anzieu (1985) sets out the main configurations of the skin-ego in connection with a singular pathology: sieve skin-ego, sound envelope deficit, a principally thermic, olfactory or muscular envelope, an envelope of agitation, an envelope of suffering. These configurations are neither fixed nor present in the pure state but capable, as Anzieu points out, of complex and varied telescopings.

We will now give an example in order to illustrate the possible and fruitful utilization in daily clinical work of the grid of the functions of the skin-ego.

> Jacqueline is a schizophrenic and epileptic patient I (A.C.) met in a day hospital for adults. Jacqueline went to this day hospital five days a week. The rest of the time, the patient was hospitalized in a classical psychiatric unit – where she had been for ten years, ever since the death of her mother, who had herself been hospitalized and was in a delusional state. Jacqueline was 30. Her father, an alcoholic, sometimes took her home for weekends, but was increasingly neglecting her. Jacqueline's discourse was logorrheic, very precious and rich, apparently dissociated and discordant, but its tenor and content fascinated many of the carers who had already witnessed several therapeutic failures with her. For our present purpose, we will insist above all on the bodily aspect of Jacqueline.
>
> She was quite a tall and waif-like woman who gave the impression of inhabiting a broken body, the trunk leaning to one side and the head to the other, with her neck jutted forward as if she were "offering" her head. Jacqueline's "bearing" was peculiar: seated in an armchair, she would put each hand inside the opposite sleeve of the garment she was wearing and push each hand up very high almost to the point of touching the shoulder; with the arc thus formed by her arms, she seemed to be leaning forward with her head almost resting in her arms, as if she were holding a baby. Jacqueline often spoke about meteorology and told me about her inner climatology. She always felt cold and "obliged" to keep her coat on. The sensation of "cold in her back" was associated with her epileptic attack and fall, and the sensation of "hot in her back" with life and

the capacity to remain upright. The epileptic attacks, which alerted the carers as soon as the first psychomotor manifestations appeared, were avoided most of the time by a significant amount of containing and restraining activity on the part of the carers around Jacqueline, holding her physically, speaking to her and asking her not to "go away" but to "stay" with them.

I noticed that very often the attacks were "triggered" by the evocation of an absence: the absence of a carer, the exceptional closure of the day hospital, the absence of her father who was not taking care of her and would not take her home with him at the weekend, or the inattention of a carer who wasn't listening to her any longer and was busy with another patient, and so on. Jacqueline said that one of the most unbearable and unavoidable mental pains connected with the epileptic attacks was due to the fact that they made a "hole": there was no registration, simply "absence". She wondered anxiously when she woke up from her attacks what had happened during her "absence". The registration and the memory were borne by others and she could only believe others, fill the hole with the memory of others, which made her painfully and doubly anxious: her anxiety to do with the hole was intensified by anxiety due to the dissociation that was thus reinforced. The only traces that were registered were the bruises on her body caused by her falling to the floor as a result of the attack. These bruises reassured her, she clung to them, displayed them, "treated" them. The registration on the body surface took the place of an impossible psychic registration.

I was able to make a link between the attack, the sensation of cold in her back, with her refrigerated experience (Resnik, 1985, 1986b, 1999). One day when Jacqueline associated the cold that she felt with the food that she had made for her father, which he had put in the freezer, I was able to understand her discourse as a way of speaking to me about the freezing of the feelings she had for her father, or towards me in the transference. The freezing was both a consequence of the absence and a defence against depression (the epileptic fall) due to absence, to being let down by her mother, her father, the institution, reifying no doubt a primal experience of being let down.

In Jacqueline, the skin-ego was essentially configured as a "thermal envelope of cold". The envelope of cold is understood by

Anzieu (1985) as having the aim of "creating or recreating a protective wrapping that is more hermetically sealed, more closed in on itself, more narcissistically protective, a shield that keeps other people at arm's length" (p. 194). Jacqueline's refrigerated envelope is both a consequence of, and a defence against, narcissistic collapse. If we try to envisage the state of the psychic envelope in Jacqueline, we will see that all the functions of the skin-ego are altered:

- the function of maintenance is deficient and Jacqueline resorts to self-clinging, to self-holding, as if she were carrying herself, as if she were carrying what in her is still an unmaintained baby. The epileptic fit appears to be a paroxystic dramatization of the experience of "being dropped", and can only be avoided by hyper-maintenance on the part of the mothering object-carers;
- the function of containing is lacking and Jacqueline has thoughts that leak; she is subject to the demands of others who "oblige her to". In addition, she has recourse to an external "second skin" (the coat) in order to feel united. One day she drew some flowers without a pot, without a vase, and manifested pain at feeling unable to complete her drawing. I was able to offer her an interpretation of her quest in me for something that could "hold things together" in her;
- the function of stimulus barrier or constancy is troubled and confusions between the inside and the outside are manifest; internal and external destructive attacks are not contained and trigger epileptic fits;
- the function of individuation is defective and Jacqueline tries to incorporate her maternal object (wearing her mother's clothes, acting "crazy" like her mother), as well as her paternal object (expressing the wish to be alcoholic);
- the function of intersensoriality or of correspondence, of concordance, is safeguarded but sorely tested by epileptic fits which provoke a suspension of the consensual capacity;
- the supporting function of sexual excitation or sexualization is disturbed and Jacqueline told me, in a pseudo-delirious discourse, that she didn't have any sexual organs, adding that these are "reserved for prostitutes" (her confusional state is reflected by, among other things, a confusion of genital-anal zones; she calls her genital organs "the buttocks in front"). Furthermore, when the question arose of her leaving the day hospital, she fell in

love with a nurse from whom she said she wanted a child (taking with her a part of the day hospital), and a sudden bout of bulimia led her to develop an increasingly prominent belly which made the whole institution think that she might be pregnant;
- the function of libidinal recharge or energization is not assured and Jacqueline is subject to acute fears of exploding during her epileptic fits;
- the function of registration or significance is deficient and Jacqueline presents psychic holes (following fits) which she tries to fill with registrations on the surface of her body (bruises);
- the self-destructive function or "anti-function", the toxic work of the skin-ego, is at work in Jacqueline's more or less controlled epilepsy.

In the same way, examples could be presented in connection with the pathologies of the psychic envelope in group psychic functioning. Didier Anzieu (1981) paved the way in his book on the group and the unconscious. Geneviève Haag, for example, offers us unique insight into the notion of "group skin" in therapeutic groups (see in particular Haag et al., 1989; Urwand and Haag, 1993). Research studies in psychoanalytic family therapy, which draw abundantly on the conceptions of Anzieu, also give a place to the function of the envelope in the family psychic apparatus, even if the envelope, considered as an organizer of the group in its own right – evolving in parallel with, and independently of, the "chronological organizers" in the form of group illusion, parental imagos and primal phantasies (see Ruffiot, 1981a) – is taken into account more at the level of its function of individuation and of exchanges with the outside than at the level of its functions of structuring the family psychic apparatus. Anzieu once again paved the way by proposing a study of the functions of the skin-ego in the couple (Anzieu, 1986b), as well as in the group and the family (Anzieu, 1993b). Evelyne Granjon (1986, 1987a, 1989), for example, suggested that genealogical issues should be understood as the foundational element of the family psychic envelope. Positive psychic transmission – or intergenerational transmission – organizes the envelope; negative psychic transmission – or transgenerational transmission – pathologizes the family psychic envelope.[16] Didier Houzel has also described the family envelope (Houzel and Catoire, 1989; Houzel, 1994), its relations of inclusion and tangentiality with individual psychic envelopes, its function as an organizer of interindividual and intergenerational relations, and its containing function linked to the integration of psychic bisexuality for each of the parental objects (the "maternal" qualities corresponding to intimacy, availability, the capacity to soothe, and the "paternal" qualities to force, consistency and orientability).

This theorization of the psychic envelope in the "group psychical apparatus", according to the terms of René Kaës (1976b, 1993, 1994) – or "psychical apparatus of grouping" (Kaës, 1987) – and in the "family psychical apparatus", as André Ruffiot (1981ab) calls it, was followed up by the application of the notion of psychic reality to institutions.[17] Didier Houzel (1992ab), in particular, has tried to conceptualize the notion of "institutional envelope". For example, he has defined the qualities that enable the institutional envelope to contain and shelter the individual and interindividual psychic processes in the institution: these concern "impermeability" (the institution must be able to keep within it what is happening, what is said, what is lived); "permeability" (exchanges with the outside world – patients' families, administration, other institutions – with which the institution is inevitably linked must be governed thanks to a selective permeability of the envelope); "consistency" (while the institution must be capable of evolution, of change, it must also be able to resist external and internal pressures); and "elasticity" (the institutional envelope must be able to allow itself to be deformed without rupturing). As for the family envelope mentioned above, these qualities are distributed and structured according to the model of psychic bisexuality: solidity and resistance are situated at the "paternal" pole, receptivity and flexibility at the "maternal" pole.

The theorization of psychic envelopes underpins the psychoanalytic understanding of institutional situations. Take, for instance, a number of situations that can currently be observed in psychiatric institutions. The recourse to the confinement and isolation of patients who are too greedy or too demanding, and who undermine the "institutional alpha function", may be understood as a rigidification of the stimulus barrier envelope which then assumes the form of an impermeable shell. The fugues of certain patients enacting phantasies of haemorrhaging can be understood as a dysfunction of the containing function of the institutional psychic envelope. A discontinuous, defective, "sieve" envelope (due to the absence of coherence and linkage in the team work, or to the excessive destructivity of the attacks) provokes, in the image of what José Bleger (1967) describes, a massive reintegration of the agglutinated nucleus, of the fragmented psychotic nucleus, that is responsible for catastrophic anxieties. This psychotic-symbiotic nucleus is first deposited in the frame which may be considered as the external layer of the institutional psychic envelope. The use of sleep treatments, electroshock treatment, all the agitation around drug experiments, neurobiological and neuropsychiatric models, or the "evaluation craze",[18] with the colonization of treatment by positivist, hyper-technical ideologies,[19] may be understood as a pathology of the envelope of which Anzieu (1986b) speaks, which consists in a dysfunctioning of the internal layer, the layer of communication, where excitation is put in the service of communication. True communication consists in being in contact with the inner world, with emotionality and thus with mental pain. The excitation that replaces communication only has the objective of "silencing", when what is being said is too painful and presents a threat for the one who is listening to his own inner security or identity.

Our aim in evoking these hypotheses, associated with the examples which we cannot develop further here, is simply to emphasize the fertility of this vast field of work and research.

Notes

1 Chapter written by Albert Ciccone alone.
2 On the genesis of the concept of psychic envelope, see Houzel (1987).
3 See Freud (1905). The mind is based on the body; it originates in the body. For Freud, "the ego is first and foremost a bodily ego" and is "ultimately derived from bodily sensations, chiefly those springing from the surface of the body" (Freud, 1923, p. 26, note 1). For Freud, "all presentations originate from perceptions and are repetitions of them" (Freud, 1925b, p. 137). For Winnicott, "the ego is based on a body ego but it is only when all goes well that the person of the baby starts to be linked with the body and the body-functions, with the skin as the limiting membrane […]. In other words, the psyche has come to live in the soma and an individual psycho-somatic life has been initiated" (1962a, p. 59 and 61).
4 According to Winnicott's (1960a, 1962a) term.
5 Idem.
6 Anzieu adds to this "dismantling anxiety", with reference to Meltzer (Meltzer et al., 1975). However, as we have seen (Chapter 5),

dismantling is not an anxiety, but a defence mechanism against catastrophic anxiety. The "consensuality" characteristic of the "common sense object" rests, according to Meltzer, on a mechanism contrary to dismantling.
7 These are Winnicott's (1960a, 1962a) terms.
8 Geneviève Haag (1987b, 1988b) has put forward the hypothesis that it is through the gaze – in the interpenetration of gazes – that the tactile is interiorized, integrated and "imprinted".
9 We understand the "intra-uterine" phantasy not as a reciprocal phantasy of "inclusion" between the newborn and the maternal womb – as Anzieu refers to it, borrowing the term from Sami-Ali (1974) –, which contains an idea of interiority, but as a phantasy annulling interiority and amounting to a *sensual and emotional feeling*, that of the intra-uterine condition.
10 Geneviève Haag (1987a, 1988b), in accord with the hypotheses of Didier Anzieu, developed a model of the process of *duplicating the symbiotic common skin* permitting a nondestructive individuating separation and an internalization of the individual psychic skin.
11 This is in keeping with what Frances Tustin says about the autistic child in whom all sensations are related to the primitive sensation which is tactile: "In elementary states, visual and auditory impressions are experienced in a touch-sensitive way" (Tustin 1985a, p. 96, translated from the French).
12 Anzieu (1990) describes the development of the self-organization of the psychical apparatus as following four stages: that of the constitution of the *self*, then of the *ego*, then of the *I*, and finally of the *subject*.
13 See Anzieu's (1994) book titled *Le Penser. Du moi-peau au moi-pensant*.
14 Didier Anzieu, to whom we submitted these reflections (see Ciccone, 1990), told us that he was in agreement with the idea that the phantasy of common skin is not linked to adhesive identification, but rather to projective identification and its adhesive effects.
15 We would say that *the failure of the stimulus barrier envelope – due to the failure of the introjection of an adequate container – rigidifies the sensitive envelope* which stands in for the external envelope ensuring structure, containing capacity and "verticality". This is in keeping with Bion's (1974–1977) remarks on the child in general and the autistic child in particular, when he says that as soon as the infant becomes aware of the absence of his parents, and so is free to do what he wants, he automatically reconstitutes the absent parent. But this reconstituted parent, who does not have the experience of a real parent, instead of

being wise and sensible as a parent imposing adequate "discipline" would be, will be so severe, so ferocious, that the child will be in danger of cracking under his own discipline. This will impede him from developing and put his life in danger. We understand the discipline of which Bion speaks as the stimulus barrier function which must first be provided by the mothering environment before it can be introjected by the ego to form the "stimulus barrier layer".

16 Since the prefix "inter" expresses the difference implied by the process of transformation inherent to the transmission between unconfused generations, intergenerational transmission concerns the "positive". As the prefix "trans" expresses the resolution of all difference, the way through all differentiation, transgenerational transmission concerns the "negative", the untransformable, the unthinkable (see Granjon, 1989)
17 See in particular Jaques, 1955; Fornari, 1971; Roussillon, 1977; Kaës, 1987, 1989b; Kaës et al., 1987, 1996.
18 According to the title of the book by Abelhauser, Gori, Sauret et al. (2011).
19 See the book *La Violence dans le soin* (Ciccone et al., 2014).

8

CONCLUSION

Psychic birth and psychopathological deviations

8.1 Recapitulation of the junctions between the different developmental hypothesis

Our reflection around this third postulate traces the ontogenetic development of the "psychic skin" and envisages the unfolding of the birth of psychic life, of the emergence of the internal world, and of the psychogenesis of the psychical apparatus. With reference to different models, we have described three stages in this process and three psychic positions. These stages are to be understood not as successive stages, but rather as successive levels of complexity, each stage consisting of a set of phenomena contained in the following stage where they continue to operate. The spatial representation of this would be that of the construction of an edifice where the foundational stage supports the structural stage which supports the stages of final touches.

Furthermore, as we have already pointed out, each position, combining a set of processes, is organized by the psyche during a particular phase of development in a privileged but nonexclusive way. Thus, for instance, the ego has experience very early on of object-related positions; but, and we will come back to this, when there is contact with catastrophic anxieties – essentially depressive anxiety – the ego regroups and gathers itself together in a particular position depending on its degree of complexity. Likewise, during later stages of normal development, if the ego is faced with depressive anxiety that is too catastrophic, it may have recourse to more archaic, more narcissistic positions than those it has the capacities to occupy.

Mental space, even when organized in four dimensions, may thus return to a two-dimensional organization; psychic processes, even when secondarized, may yield the central place to the primal process; identificatory projects, even if they utilize introjection, may have recourse to adhesiveness – and the same is true for the other characteristics.

The different developmental models are presented in a synoptic table in order to show the junctions between them, junctions that do not cancel out their differences (see Table 8.1).

We have developed most of the links contained in this table. It should be noted, with regard to Piera Aulagnier's thought, that it seems to us that the model of the construction of psychic space that she proposes can be likened to both the ontogenetic and structural model of the positions and of the multi-dimensional representations of psychic space. We know that the model of Piera Aulagnier (1975) consists of the articulation of three processes – primal, primary and secondary – operating in the three spaces of the same name. The primal process functions according to the postulate of self-engenderment, stating that "every existent is self-procreated by the activity of the system that represents it"; the primary process functions according to the postulate asserting that "every existent is an effect of the omnipotence of the Other's desire"; finally, the secondary process functions according to the postulate according to which "every existent has an intelligible cause of which discourse might provide knowledge" (Aulagnier, 1975, p. 6). Moreover, the activity of each process continues even during the deployment of the following process; the primal and primary processes are never reduced to silence. It seems to us that the primal space and process, with the pictogram and the unawareness of otherness, present the characteristics of the auto-sensual position, with the erasure of all differentiation, two-dimensionality and the adhesiveness of psychic functioning. Likewise, the primary space and process, with the phantasy and recognition of two psychic spaces subject to the omnipotence of one of them, can be likened to symbiotic, paranoid-schizoid processes and projective identification in three-dimensional space. Finally, the secondary space and process, with awareness of a dimension outside oneself, have the qualities of the depressive position, with the reinforcing of the skin-ego and the sense of identity, the prevalence of introjective identification, and four-dimensionality taking history into account.

Table 8.1 Envelope constituted as skin-ego

Approximate real age	Dominant positions	Dimensions of psychic space (Meltzer)	Phases of psychic development (Tustin, Mahler)	Organizing phantasies (Anzieu)	Privileged modes of psychic functioning (Aulagnier)	Structure of the psychic envelope (Anzieu)	Processes of identification and prevalent defensive mechanisms	Object relation
1st month	Auto-sensual position Adhesive position (Bick) "Autistic" position (Marcelli)	One- and two-dimensionality Surface	Phase of auto-sensuality (Tustin) "Normal autistic phase" (Mahler)	Intra-uterine phantasy	Primal process Pictogram Primal space	Undifferentiated double layer	Adhesive identification Dismantling	Narcissistic relation Primary narcissism Auto-sensuality Adhesive object
2nd month	Symbiotic position Paranoid-schizoid position (Klein)	Three-dimensionality Volume	Normal symbiotic phase (Mahler)	Phantasy of a common skin	Primary process Phantasy Primary space	Unsticking of the two layers	Projective identification Splitting	Narcissistic relation Secondary narcissism Autoerotism Symbiotic or syncretic object
5th to 8th month	Depressive position (Klein)	Four-dimensionality History	Phase of separation-individuation (Mahler)	[Envelope constitued as skin-ego]	Secondary process Statement Secondary space	Interlocking of the two layers	Introjective identification Repression	Object-related object relation Transitional object
2nd year								

Another point in this table calls for clarification. Didier Anzieu (1985) presents the intra-uterine phantasy as organizing the autistic envelopes. This phantasy thus belongs to the auto-sensual or adhesive position and operates in two-dimensional space, the space of the pictogram. This is why, as we have already suggested (Chapter 7), we picture this phantasy not as a phantasy of inclusion, as Anzieu proposes, but rather as a phantasy erasing interiority. We know that Piera Aulagnier only speaks of phantasy in connection with the primary space, but it seems to us that it is possible to envisage phantasmatic activity even in the primal space. As we shall see in the following chapter, the phantasy in the auto-sensual position, like the intra-uterine phantasy, does not concern objects – which imply three-dimensionality and the idea of interiority – but sensations, images of sensations. In our view this is how the idea of the intra-uterine phantasy put forward by Didier Anzieu should be understood, which we situate in the auto-sensual position and the primal space. In the auto-sensual position the infant does not seek to "return to the maternal womb", but rather the *experience of lost sensuality*, that of the intra-uterine condition.

Concerning the defence mechanisms, we have described the process of *dismantling* that is characteristic of the auto-sensual position and associated with adhesive identification, and we have evoked *splitting*, which is operative in the symbiotic position and coincides with projective identification. We will come back to this and will emphasize its relations with *repression*, a more complex and later process (Chapter 9).

We can back up this picture of psychic development, as summarized in our table, by submitting it to other perspectives. In fact, these three specific stages identified in the building up of the psychical apparatus can be found in different places.

Genetic psychology, for instance, proposes models of development whose different stages are superposed on the stages that we have described. We will simply mention the stages of development described by Henri Wallon (1941) and the developmental stages of the libidinal object described by René Spitz (1957, 1965):

- Wallon describes the *stage of motor impulsiveness* during the first month of life, with motor crises, explosive gestures and conditional reflexes linked to the two great needs (alimentary and postural); the *emotional stage*, from the second month onwards, with the expressive character of conditional reactions, the appearance of the smile, the clearly affective basis of the system of mutual understanding between the mother and the baby, the period of radical subjectivism or subjective syncretism, the period of affective symbiosis – see what we have described concerning symbiosis and the syncretic object (Chapter 6) –, and finally the *sensorimotor stage*, at the end of the first year, with reflexes of orientation or investigation, walking, speech, games of alternation (dialogue between several people), the incontinent sociability of the child: all this coincides with the three stages of our table;

- Spitz defines the *pre-object stage* in the first two months of life, when the baby only responds to external stimuli on the basis of interoceptive perception (only recognizes the breast if it is introduced into the mouth); the *stage of the precursor of the object* from the third month onwards, with the appearance of the smiling response (the first organizer of the mind according to Spitz); the first mother/infant communications; the *stage of the libidinal object* from the eighth month onwards (the second organizer of the mind – the third organizer will be the ability to say "no" at the beginning of the second year); the identification of the libidinal object: here again we find the three stages of our table.

Serge Lebovici (1961), in an essay systematizing the genetic evolution of the object-relation, based on the studies of psychoanalysts and psychogeneticists, also identified three stages in the first year of life that can be found in our table: the *narcissistic stage* (until the third month); the *anaclitic stage* (between the third and the sixth month approximately); and the *object stage* (from the sixth month to the end of the first year).

Group psychoanalysis proposes models of psychic organization in groups and particularly in family groups, where we can also find the three stages that we have described:

- Wilfred Bion (1961) analyzes the mentality of groups in the light of three basic assumptions: the pairing group, the fight–flight group and the dependent group. Certain points of the pairing group assumption recall adhesive phenomena: the response by pairing to psychotic anxieties, as well as the messianic hope invested in a leader who must never materialize, evoke a denial of the state of dependence that is characteristic of the adhesive position. The fight-flight group assumption, with the destructive struggle against a hated object or the flight from this object in order to mitigate the explosion of hate, recalls the paranoid-schizoid position. The dependent group assumption, finally, with its feelings of guilt and depression, may be likened to the "mentality" of the depressive position;

- José Bleger (1971) describes three types of groups, or rather three types of individuals in groups organized in a specific way. A first type is comprised of individuals who have never had a symbiotic relationship and who cannot establish it in groups (psychopathic, perverse, and "as if" personalities); these individuals will tend to form a "non-manifest syncretic group of sociability", which is reminiscent of autistic adhesiveness (which can do without the external object). A second type is formed by dependent or symbiotic individuals who will constitute a dependency group at the level of "syncretic" sociability, which is similar to the symbiotic organization we have described. Finally, a third group of individuals, neurotic or normal, function in terms of "interactional sociability" which, thanks to splitting, will guarantee the deposit and immobilization of syncretic sociability (or of the psychotic part of the group). The maturational level of this third type of group evokes the depressive position;
- Jean-Pierre Caillot and Gérard Decherf (1982) identify typical positions in the mental functioning of family groups: the paradoxical narcissistic position, the schizo-paranoid position and the phallic and genital positions. The paradoxical narcissistic position recalls what we have described in respect of the auto-sensual or adhesive position. It is characterized by an oscillation of the cathexes between a narcissistic pole where adhesive narcissistic identification dominates (prototype of the tendency of the psychical apparatus to binding) and an anti-narcissistic pole where adhesiveness is broken (prototype of the tendency of the psychical apparatus to unbinding). The phantasy of the ideal united family, which corresponds to the narcissistic pole, is responsible for fears of being submerged[1] and pushes the family group back towards the anti-narcissistic pole to which the phantasy of family dismembering corresponds, which pushes the group back towards the other pole, and so on. The paradoxical narcissistic position expresses an experience of soma-psyche and group non-differentiation; the container is two-dimensional. The second

position, namely the group schizo-paranoid position corresponds exactly to what we have described with respect to the symbiotic or paranoid-schizoid position: it is characterized by the prevalence of projective narcissistic identification, splitting of the breast into good and bad, and paranoid anxieties; psychic space is three-dimensional. The following positions, which Caillot and Decherf call the phallic and genital positions are characterized by the differentiation of psychic spaces, the decline of omnipotence, the predominance of introjective identification, access to four-dimensionality, generational and sexual differentiation, all qualities that can partly be found in the depressive position;

- André Ruffiot (1981b), finally, in his onto-eco-genetic hypothesis concerning psychic development in the family group, isolates stages that can be likened to those of our schema. A first stage, described as a stage of nondifferentiation, is organized by group illusion. The state of regression is reflected by a life in "pure psycheity", without bodily anchoring, based on a denial of bodies, of the sexes and generations, and on a cathexis of an undifferentiated family body. This archaic organization characterizes families with schizophrenic symptomatology. A second stage of ontogenetic development corresponds, according to Ruffiot, to the "inhabitation of the first psyche of the infant in the family body as a whole". The bodies of those around, perceived as a containing family body, shelter the psyche of the baby before he inhabits his own individual body – this coincides with what we have described in respect of the symbiotic phase and of the phantasy of a common skin. These experiences, reified in the family analytic process, are deemed to be prevalent in anorexic and psychosomatic families. André Ruffiot then distinguishes two other stages from the end of the first year onwards, corresponding to the two sub-anal stages (Abraham, 1924) separated by the "*dividing line*" (see Fliess, 1950) that marks the boundary between psychotic fixations and regressions on the one hand and neurotic fixations and regression on the other. These two stages are marked by a reinforcement of psyche-soma integration. The first is the locus of fixation of paranoiac and borderline structures, while the elaboration of the second guarantees neurosis.

Such comparisons are inevitably somewhat schematic and reductive, but we can nonetheless see a relative universality in the model that we have identified, based on the overlapping and grouping together of a certain number of hypotheses, both from the onto- and psychogenetic point of view and from that of psychopathological organizations.

8.2 Psychopathological deviations. A central position: the depressive position

Each of these three positions that we have explored contains a pathological potentiality inherent to the intensity of the anxieties specific to each state-stage of the psychic organization. If pathologization is understood as a fixation to this or that psychic constellation associated with an amplification of certain processes and with their distortion, under the effect of the working of destructiveness or of the death drive, we must insist on *the central place that is occupied by the depressive position in psychic destiny*. If the management of the anxiety characteristic of each position constitutes the dynamic element of psychic maturation, an intolerable and "unmanageable" intensity of anxiety puts a brake on all development and crystallizes the psyche. Now what makes the experience of anxiety – rather than the anxiety itself – excessively disturbing and harmful to development is always contact with the experience of *depressive pain*. The destiny of this depressive pain, and especially its transformation into autistic or paranoid anxiety, will be inherent to the mental state during the depressive experience. If the interior of the experience is occupied to a large extent by depressive anxiety, the recourse to psychopathological solutions will be increased. We have seen how the autistic child can be considered as psychologically premature, having experienced separation too early, well before his psychical apparatus can tolerate it. We have seen how the psychotic-symbiotic or schizophrenic child is struggling against the experience of separation that he experiences as being torn away, as an amputation.

Thus, just as we have envisaged relations to the world as oscillating from the outset between a state of narcissistic closedness and a state of openness to the object, one of the two states being prevalent depending on the mode of psychic organization, so we must consider subjectivity as oscillating from the genesis of mental life between the positions that we have explored (auto-sensual, then symbiotic) and the depressive position. *Pathologization will result from a failure of tolerance of the depressive position.* If depressive anxiety is experienced as nameless dread, the child will evacuate it by means of autistic rigidification, and the emotional evacuation will be guaranteed at the price of the dismantling of the psychic and perceptual apparatus, a dismantling that will not be able to transform catastrophic anxieties. If the depressive anxiety is experienced as a disintegration, the psyche will organize itself along paranoid-schizoid lines, evacuating emotion at the price of splitting, which in turn will nourish persecutory anxieties. In other words, the avoidance of depressive pain brings into play defences – specific to each stage of maturation – responsible for even more harmful anxieties. Real depressive anxiety is tolerated by the ego which, being sufficiently integrated, can experience depressive pain, that is to say, undergo the experience of loss. Depressive anxiety, proper, is experienced by the non-psychotic part of the personality. The experience of loss, in a personality more integrated than the autistic or psychotic personality, may lead to recourse to other positions than the auto-sensual or symbiotic position.

These considerations on psychopathology lead us to adhere to the remarks of Donald Meltzer (1984b, 1986; Meltzer and Williams, 1988) when he suggests that the depressive position precedes the paranoid-schizoid position. With his customary poetry, Meltzer sees the "aesthetic conflict" as one of the first emotional experiences attendant upon the arrival in the world of the baby; we have already alluded to this (Chapter 4). According to Meltzer, birth exposes the newborn infant to a bombardment of forms and sounds whose intensity makes an impression on its mind. The foetus has already had emotional experiences *in utero*: "proto-aesthetic" experiences such as those of being "rocked in the cradle of the deep of his mother's gracious walk" (Meltzer, 1986, p. 68; Meltzer et al., 1988, p. 17), experiences of anxiety and distress due to maternal anxiety which can be transmitted by heart beats, movements, postures and tonus, and also due to the claustrophobia which no doubt facilitates growth, for the latter is equivalent to the shrinking of the placental shelter. But birth is accompanied by particularly intense emotional experiences owing to the encounter with the aesthetic object – the "ordinarily beautiful and devoted mother" – who submerges the baby with an experience of a passionate nature.[2] Meltzer sees the "aesthetic impact" on the baby as the heart of the depressive position and suggests that the paranoid-schizoid position is secondary insofar as it corresponds to the closure of the perceptual orifices to protect the baby from the aesthetic impact, from the sparkle of the aesthetic object. Psychopathology as a whole derives its essence from "processes of avoiding the impact of the beauty of the world, and in particular of the passionate intensity of other human beings" (Meltzer, 1986, p. 80, translated from the French). Meltzer considers that the paranoid-schizoid position is always defensive against the pain of the depressive position.

An alternative to the paranoid-schizoid position, when faced with the violence of the aesthetic impact, might be to return in phantasy to the intra-uterine world; the "intra-uterine phantasy", as we have seen, organizes the auto-sensual position. It is worth recalling that, according to Meltzer's constructions, the attraction for the "beauty" of the object leads to questioning about the "interior beauty of the object", inaugurating the activity of thought (see Chapter 4). We have said that the intra-uterine phantasy should be understood not as the sign of a wish to return to uterine "interiority", but as a phantasy erasing interiority and the effect of an attempt to rediscover the sensory and sensual intra-uterine experience. The "questioning" about the "interior beauty" is thus a "questioning" about the sensual, sensorial and emotional qualities of the intra-uterine condition, for which the psyche may yearn as it clings to the auto-sensual or adhesive position when faced with the violence of the depressive position due to the aesthetic impact.

We totally share the idea that psychopathological deviations or the defensive organization result from contact with depressive pain. Meltzer (1984b) advises analysts, moreover, never to concern themselves too much with interpreting paranoid-schizoid mechanisms – otherwise they may even collude with them – but always to look for depressive anxiety.

However, what justifies retaining the generally accepted order of the positions is the fact that the depressive anxiety characteristic of the depressive position is *object-related* in nature; it essentially concerns the object and although it injures internal objects, it does not destroy them. On the other hand, the depressive anxiety that throws the subject back into auto-sensual and symbiotic positions is *narcissistic* in nature; it essentially concerns the ego and attacks the internal objects to the point of destroying them. This is why we feel justified in retaining the current picture of the ontogenesis of the different positions (auto-sensual or adhesive, symbiotic or paranoid-schizoid, and then depressive).

The depressive position thus occupies a central place in psychic development and in the potential for psychopathology. Melanie Klein discovered that what organizes mental life is first weaning, that is to say, the experience of losing the breast. The quality of this first work of mourning will impregnate all future experiences of separation.

It was in 1935 that Melanie Klein described the depressive position. The depressive state, which culminates at the moment of weaning, stems from the genetic point of view from the paranoid state. If paranoid anxiety is a form of persecutory anxiety pertaining to the protection of the ego, depressive anxiety is described by Melanie Klein as a form of persecutory anxiety relating to the protection of internalized good objects with which the ego identifies.[3] The depressive position, in which the transition from the introjection of part-objects to the introjection of whole love-objects occurs, faces the subject with the fear of losing the internalized object, each time he experiences the loss of the actual love-object. Melanie Klein (1940) thus regards the depressive position as "melancholia *in statu nascendi*". The infant cries over the loss of the breast and what it represents, that is to say love, goodness and security.

The depressive position is characterized by two series of feelings: persecution by bad objects (feelings arising from the paranoid-schizoid position) and nostalgia for the loved object, thus by defences linked to these feelings. These anxieties and these defences define the *infantile neurosis*. The infant overcomes the depressive position, in other words emerges from the infantile neurosis, thanks to real experiences with the objects of the external world. Creative experiences fortify the good internal objects which will come to the infant's help in situations of distress; they increase inner security and faith in reparative capacities. The need for reparation results from having access to the depressive position which integrates the good and bad aspects of internal and external objects and engenders feelings of ambivalence and guilt. In the depressive position the ego shows concern for its objects.

The depressive position is thus linked to the experience of loss, of lack. It is reached when this experience provokes feelings of guilt, of (ambivalent) love for the object, and mobilizes desires to make reparation. However, situations of loss of the object can always trigger various defensive reactions, and nothing can be taken for granted on approaching the depressive position: it is at this moment that the conditions necessary for mental health can be established or the conditions for pathology, in very varied registers. The failure to overcome the depressive position can lead to melancholia (or depressive illness), to mania, paranoia, schizophrenia or neurosis.

What are the defences mobilized on approaching the depressive position? They can be summarized as follows (Klein, 1935, 1940, 1946, 1952a):

- *flight towards the idealized internalized object*, which may result in the negation of reality and in schizophrenia;
- *paranoid-schizoid defences*: strengthening of splitting, denial and projective identification with the aim of destroying the persecuting object, which can lead to paranoia – the paranoiac transforms the object into a persecutor and is driven by the concern to annihilate it; his anxiety essentially concerns the ego and not the object (anxiety of a narcissistic nature);
- *manic defences*: idealization, omnipotence, triumph, negation of psychic reality and projective identification, with the aim of controlling and mastering the persecuting object; greedy and cannibalistic incorporation of good objects; and contempt for good objects through the negation of worry and anxiety about losing them – these defences constitute the manic position, the basis of manic-depressive illness; they are closely bound up with obsessional defences;
- *flight towards the good external object*, characteristic, according to Melanie Klein, of neurotic illness,[4] which can lead to servile dependency on objects and to ego-weakness.

Melanie Klein placed emphasis on the manic position. She regarded it as a normal position of psychic development, inherent to the need to make reparation for loved objects attacked in greedy and destructive phantasies. Hanna Segal (1964, 1981) has distinguished more clearly than Klein did omnipotent manic reparation from non-manic reparation. The reparation characteristic of the manic position is immediate and complete reparation, avoiding mourning and guilt by means of the omnipotent manoeuvre that consists in acting as if the object had been restored to a state prior to the damage. Manic reparation undoes the damage but does not deal with it. Non-manic reparation recognizes it and deals with it. Non-manic reparation is not a defence, for it is based on the recognition of psychic reality. It is this form of reparation that Klein speaks of when she says that the desire to make reparation marks the end of the infantile neurosis. Reparation – non-manic – assuages the ego which is experiencing guilt, and prepares the way for object-relations. The manic position, on the other hand, avoids guilt by transforming depressive pain into persecutory anxiety and by leading the ego to idealize the good object and to triumph over the persecuting object which is projected outside. The failure of manic reparation leads the ego to use obsessional defences in its attempt to make reparation. Manic defences thus operate in close collaboration with obsessional defences. While mania is a refuge from depressive anxiety, it can also serve as a refuge from a paranoid situation that the ego is unable to master. The manic position aims to control the persecuting object – contrary to the paranoid position that aims to destroy the persecuting object.

Concerning these "false reparations" (manic reparation and obsessional reparation), Anne Alvarez (1992) stresses the importance of not considering them only as defences against psychic pain, avoiding true reparation arising from the depressive position. They are also necessary means of recourse, stages of transition that are sometimes indispensable in the evolution towards authentic reparation. It is thus important to be able to recognize them as containing potentialities of developmental progress. While the manic state denies depression, it is also at certain moments a necessary respite from feelings that are too heavy and distressing, and it is important to discern such situations without discrediting them.[5]

Other than the manic position, we will describe another defensive position to which the ego can resort when it is prey to insurmountable depressive anxieties or uncontrollable paranoid anxieties: this is the *melancholic position*. To do this we will draw on the hypothesis put forward by Francisco Palacio Espasa (1977) on the subject of melancholic defences.

Francisco Palacio Espasa puts forward the hypothesis of a melancholic defence that is like an inverted double of the manic defence. While the manic defence consists for the ego in projecting the persecuting superego object into the external world and in introjecting the omnipotent idealized object with which it is identified, the melancholic defence consists in introjecting the persecuting object and in projecting the idealized object. Introjection of the persecuting object occurs both in the ego – in the form of persecuted-destroyed aspects – and in the superego, where the superego identification with this bad object attacks this same object introjected into the ego. The projection into the external world of idealized objects is aimed at preserving them from internal struggles. It is this projection – where the idealized object is lost – that is at the origin of the feelings of despair, desolation and helplessness characteristic of the melancholic state. When the melancholic defence struggles against paranoid anxieties, it is the persecutory aspects of introjection that dominate. When it struggles against depressive anxieties, it is the persecuted-destroyed aspects that are in the foreground. Faced with the triumph, control and contempt to which the manic defence leads, the melancholic defence has the effect of submission, expiation, as well as a certain form of seduction. Manic and melancholic defences operate alternately or simultaneously. Palacio Espasa gives several examples, where we can see in particular the recourse to melancholic defences (preserving a good object, even if it is situated outside) when manic defences fail (impossibility of projecting the persecuting superego and of identifying with an external object).

On the model of manic defences, melancholic defences can be grouped together as follows:

- denial of persecution and guilt;
- denial of the good aspects of oneself;
- projection of the good-idealized aspects of the self;
- negative omnipotence;
- identification with the persecuting object.

Francisco Palacio Espasa also speaks of "melancholic reparation" which, in suicide, for instance, functions analogously to manic reparation, but in reverse as it were.

We propose to go further than Palacio Espasa in his hypothesis, by advancing the idea of a *melancholic position*, grouping together the characteristics that have just been described. The basic process underlying this melancholic position can be found in what Melanie Klein describes as *projective identification concerning* not the bad parts but *the good parts of the subject*:

> The projection good feelings and good parts of the self into the mother is essential for the infant's ability to develop good

object-relations and to integrate his ego. However, if this projective process is carried out excessively, good parts of the personality are felt to be lost, and in this way the mother becomes the ego-ideal; this process too results in weakening and impoverishing the ego.

(Klein, 1946, p. 9)

Melancholic depression, as described by Bela Grunberger (1975), where the ego experiences a real state of slavery in total and crushing dependency on the ego-ideal projected into an individual by whom the subject seeks to be loved, is a good example of this pathologization of the melancholic position, which is a response to a failure to elaborate the depressive position and a failure of ego-integration. The greater the fear of loss is, the more the restoration of loved objects is distressing and the more the demands of the superego are severe. Thus, the melancholic position is characterized by an implacable cruelty of the superego, by intense feelings of shame and deep and inconsolable regrets. Melancholia represents a narcissistic megalomania, a triumph of narcissism over the devalued ego. Suicide may then be explained as a means of protecting the ideal object projected outside. The melancholic position avoids depressive pain due to sadistic attacks on the loved object by projecting the external ideal object and by destroying the introjected persecuting object.

To summarize, then, the depressive position is central in psychic development. Subsequent mental health depends on its working-through. The suffering linked to depressive pain can throw the subject back either into the *auto-sensual or adhesive or autistic position*, or into *the symbiotic or paranoid-schizoid position*, or alternatively project him either into the *manic position* or into *the melancholic position*. These positions are governed by dependence on a persecuting object, hostile to development, and dependence on an omnipotent, grandiose and triumphant ideal object, which is just as fearsome. This dependence is sterile and destructive. Mental health is based on overcoming the depressive position, thanks to reparation, based on the predominance of feelings of nostalgia towards the love object, nostalgia that is creative because it is governed by love for *external objects* and for *internal objects*. Mental health consists in not destroying external objects to protect one's internal objects, nor in destroying one's internal objects to preserve some external object.

Notes

1 Fears of being submerged correspond, in fact, more to a symbiotic organization than to an adhesive organization (see Chapter 6).
2 Didier Houzel (1988b, 1991) posits the coexistence of aesthetic emotions and feelings of "precipitation". During physical birth, but above all during psychic birth, the baby, he suggests, is subjected to the force of attraction of the aesthetic object so that he feels propelled on one side and sucked on the other into infinite space. The precipitation anxiety arising from this situation must be detoxified by the capacity for reverie or the alpha function of the containing maternal object.
3 In 1960, Melanie Klein would insist on the entanglement between the paranoid-schizoid and depressive positions: ego-related anxiety, that is, paranoid anxiety, necessarily includes a certain "concern for the object".
4 It seems to us that this defensive modality is closer to parasitism or to the "false-self" personality, where projective identification predominates.
5 On the manic defence, the reader may also consult Athanassiou (1996).

PART IV

FOURTH POSTULATE

> The introjection of a containing external object, giving the skin its function of a boundary, is prior to the activation of processes of splitting and idealization of the self and of the object.

This postulate will lead us, initially, to define and explore the processes of splitting and idealization, following the conceptions of Melanie Klein and her successors. To this end, we will consider the principle on which Melanie Klein's thinking on this subject is based: that of duality of the life drives and death drives.

Splitting produces persecutory objects and idealized objects, effects of the work of the life drives and death drives, objects that inaugurate phantasy life and, thereby, the activation of thought-processes. Thus, our reflection will subsequently focus on the development, starting from access to the paranoid-schizoid or symbiotic position, of the principal activity of this newly constituted subjective world, namely, the activity of thinking.

9

SPLITTING AND IDEALIZATION

The life drives/death drives duality

Access to the paranoid-schizoid position is characterized by the advent of a marked antithesis between a good object and a bad object. This antithesis is based, on the one hand, on successive experiences of gratification and frustration and, on the other, on internal processes. Successive experiences of gratification and frustration act as a powerful stimulation for both libidinal impulses, representatives of love, and destructive impulses, the matrix of hate. These experiences give the breast the power of being felt to be good and of being loved when it gratifies, and that of being experienced as bad and of being hated when it frustrates. In combination with external factors, which involve these experiences of gratification and frustration,

> a variety of endopsychic processes – primarily introjection projection – contribute to the twofold relation to the first object. The infant projects his love impulses and attributes them to the gratifying (good) breast, just as he projects his destructive impulses outwards and attributes them to the frustrating (bad) breast. Simultaneously, by introjection, a good breast and a bad breast are established inside.
>
> (Klein, 1952a, p. 200)

Although the notion of "ego-splitting" put forward by Freud (1927, 1940b) to account for the coexistence of two contrary psychic attitudes – one striving to satisfy above all the drive, the other striving to respect reality in spite of everything –, does not draw on the conflictual life drives/death drives duality, the splitting of the object and ego-splitting from Melanie Klein's perspective rest inescapably on this fundamental drive duality.[1]

9.1 The fundamental drive duality
9.1.1 A conflictual dialectic: life drives/death drives

The whole of Melanie Klein's thought concerning the good object/bad object dichotomy, the result of splitting, rests on the hypothesis of a drive duality, between the life drives and the death drives. Having elaborated a series of dualistic concepts – self-preservative drives or ego drives/sexual drives, ego-libido/object libido – Freud (1920) came to the conclusion that the psychic dynamic found its energy in the life drives/death drives polarity. But he left open the question as to whether this construction would prove to be useful (see Freud, 1925a).[2]

It was primarily Klein who used these concepts throughout her work; indeed, the life drive/death drives opposition played a much more functional role in her work than in Freud's. Klein situated the opposition between the drives at the very centre of her conception of early infantile conflicts and of their attendant anxieties, whereas Freud made little use of this drive duality to describe the various modalities of conflict.

From 1932 onwards, in *The Psychoanalysis of Children* (Klein, 1932), and especially in the part devoted to the Oedipus complex and the early superego, the life drives/death drives duality became very present in Klein's work. According to Klein, the death drive is present from the beginning of life and exacerbates sadism:

> To all appearances these phenomena of early development are already the expression of the polarity between the life-instincts[3] and the death-instincts. We may regard the force of the child's fixation at the oral-sucking level as an expression of the force of its libido, and, similarly, the early and powerful emergence of its oral sadism is a sign that its destructive instinctual components tip the balance.
>
> (Klein, 1932, p.124)

Melanie Klein (1932, 1946, 1948a) establishes a theoretical relationship between the death drive and anxiety: she considers the working of the death drives to be at the origin of anxiety. In this way she enriched the theory of anxiety with a new model of it. Indeed, to the ideas of Freud (1916–1917), who considered anxiety as the result of an automatic transformation of repressed libidinal impulses, and then as a signal preceding repression (Freud, 1926), and to the theory put forward by Ernest Jones (1929), who described an innate capacity for fear which he called the "instinct of fear", Melanie Klein added a third model in which anxiety stems directly from the destructive impulses. It is the danger produced by the death drives, which are expressed in the form of destructive impulses, which represents the primary cause of anxiety, even if the libidinal factor is present insofar as it can increase anxiety owing to libidinal frustration or, on the contrary, diminish anxiety owing to libidinal gratification. The primary anxiety generated by the death drives, she suggests, is the *fear of the annihilation of life*, in other words, the fear of death.[4] This fear of dying leads the subject to use projection onto an external object to get rid of destructiveness and then struggle against it. Paula Heimann (1952b) describes the vicious circle that is set up when the need to find an external object as a support for the projected destructive impulses meets with the presence of a real object that is itself destructive.

These considerations, which concern early intrapsychic conflicts, can be admitted on the condition of underlining both the place of the *relation to the object* and the role of the external object in the constitution and management of these conflicts, in the activation or transformation of these early anxieties – this is one of the aims of this book (particularly in Chapters 3 and 13).

Furthermore, these conceptions, which essentially concern the paranoid-schizoid or symbiotic position, can be extended to the auto-sensual or adhesive position. Following the hypotheses that we have put forward and developed in relation to the different propositions regarding the "autistic" position and early anxieties (Chapters 2 and 5), we would say that the work of the death drives, in the auto-sensual position, can be represented, for instance, by the image of a whirlwind movement dragging the psyche into a chasm, into a bottomless hole. This suction is reflected by a feeling of falling endlessly, of nameless dread. This primitive experience of anxiety brings into play defences such as the dismantling of the self and of the object, and adhesive identification. The same vicious circle mentioned above will set in if the environment arouses, confirms or reinforces this experience.

The drive polarity can thus be considered – from a descriptive rather than an explanatory point of view – as the source of psychic conflict, and the first psychic operations (adhesive sticking, projection, introjection) may be understood as responses to the menace of death inherent in this conflict. Melanie Klein's contribution with regard to the importance attributed to the death drive gives hate an equivalent role in psychic development to that of love and introduces the idea that the most fundamental human anxiety is not, as Freud thought, the fear of castration, but the fear of death.

9.1.2 The effects of the death drives

Freud had emphasized how the life drives have an effect of *binding*, and the death drives a contrary effect:

> The aim of Eros is to establish ever greater unities and to preserve them thus – in short, to bind together; the aim of the destructive instinct is, on the contrary, to undo connections and so to destroy things.
>
> (Freud, 1940a [1938], p. 148)

André Green (1986a, 1995) took up this notion and described an objectalizing function of the life drives and a de-objectalizing function of the death drives.

Thus, in addition to the production of death-anxiety, of which Melanie Klein speaks, we consider the effect of de-objectalization, as André Green describes it, to be a principal effect of the work of the death drives. If the life drives have the essential purpose of fulfilling an objectalizing function, the death drives have the aim, first and foremost, of fulfilling a *de-objectalizing function*, which is realized through *unbinding* and *decathexis*. The act of decathexis is described by Piera Aulagnier as the "only permanently successful murder" (Aulagnier, 1982, p. 314, translated for this edition). It is reflected by the inscription of a "hole", of a "nothing" in the representative and libidinal capital of the subject, from which any feelings of guilt or nostalgia are absent.[5] When cathexis is withdrawn from a psychic space and this space cannot be recathected, a state of "mental emptiness" sets in, in the words of André Green (1986a).

André Green (1986b, 1993) specified the activity of the death drives in the "work of the negative" – psychic work bringing together the different operations of repression, even to the point of rejection, including denial, negation, disavowal, and so on. Along the middle paths taken by this work of the negative – such as splitting and disavowal – the recognition and denial of the object or of reality, the "Yes" and the "No", coexist in a "conjunctive" manner, the work of the negative occurs under the primacy of the life drives (an example of this "conjunctive coexistence of the Yes and the No" is the transitional object). On the other hand, if this coexistence of recognition and denial is "disjunctive", if the work of the negative is reflected not by "Yes and No" but by "neither Yes nor No", this work of the negative then occurs under the primacy of the death drives; it prevents any form of cathexis and opts for the "refusal to live".

Hanna Segal (1993) formulates this conflict between the life drives and the death drives in relation to the experience of need, an experience the subject is confronted with at birth. Two reactions to this experience are possible:

> One, to seek satisfaction for the needs: that is life-promoting and leads to object-seeking, love, and eventually object concern. The other is the drive to annihilate the need, to annihilate the perceiving experiencing self, as well as anything that is perceived.
>
> (Segal, 1993, p. 55)

Destructiveness and the desire for annihilation are directed from the outset against the self and the perceived object. Hanna Segal asks herself, in the light of clinical observations, why the work of the death drive also provokes great pain, when this pain consists precisely in destroying the need and perception of need. Her answer is that "pain is experienced by the libidinal ego – originally threatened by death instinct" (ibid., p. 58). The libidinal ego, or "libidinal narcissism", can only be found, according to Segal, in secondary narcissism, for primary narcissism is entirely the expression of the death drive. Segal considers, moreover, narcissism as a whole as based on the death drive insofar as it is essentially de-objectalizing.[6]

The association between the terms primary narcissism and decathexis – decathexis implying that an object has first been cathected – is open to debate. We have already discussed the role played by objectality in the narcissistic state (Chapter 5). Primary narcissism must be considered, as Herbert Rosenfeld did very early on (see his article, "On the psychopathology of narcissism: A clinical approach" (Rosenfeld, 1964a)), not as an objectless state, but as a state in which the object is the locus of a primary object-cathexis and of narcissistic identification. This is the position we have adopted throughout our reflections in this book.

So the life drives and their derivatives (sexual impulses, self-preservative impulses) push towards cathexis, binding, creation and objectalization. The death drives and their derivatives (destructive impulses, hate, envy and cruelty) push towards decathexis, unbinding, annihilation and de-objectalization.

9.1.3 Death drives bound/unbound to the live drives, death drives and "fundamental violence": some hypotheses

The fusion of the life drive and the death drives had been postulated by Freud. He tackled this subject in the form of questioning in 1920 in *Beyond the Pleasure Principle* (Freud, 1920), and in a more affirmative form in 1924 in "The economic problem of masochism" (Freud, 1924) or in 1926 in *Inhibitions Symptoms and Anxiety*:

> What we are concerned with are scarcely ever pure instinctual impulses but mixtures in various proportions of the two groups of instincts.
>
> (Freud, 1926, p. 125)

Sadism and aggression are thus understood as a combination of the life and death drives. Nonetheless, notwithstanding this possible fusion, these two types of drives have opposing aims, the life drives tending towards union and binding and the death drives towards dislocation and unbinding.

Nathalie Zaltzman (1986), who shows how the reference to the death drives has an impact on practice, considers that certain death drives establish no association with the libido,[7] while others realize a fusion of the drives in the form either of an annexation of the death drives by the life drives or of a stranglehold of the death drives over the life drives. Herbert Rosenfeld (1971) postulates that even in the most severe states of defusion, clinical experience shows that we are dealing in fact with *pathological fusions* between the life drives and the death drives. This is the case, for instance, in the perversions, where erotization increases the power of the violence of the death drives, or in certain narcissistic states where a split-off and excluded psychotic part intoxicates the healthy parts and imprisons them in a delusional object. Hanna Segal (1993) explains that, in the fusions of the life and death drives, if the life drive predominates – as in aggression – the diverted death drive is in the service of life. In the contrary case, it is the libido that is in the service of death – as, for example, in the perversions. Melanie Klein always insisted, where the fusion of the life and death drives is concerned, on the compelling need for the balance to be in favour of the life drives.

Concerning this work of fusion, Florence Guignard (2015a) emphasizes its urgency, from the beginning of life. Drive fusion gives rise to "primary sadism", which allows for the realization of the movements of introjection/projection, of "taking-into-oneself/rejecting-outside-of-oneself", to use the terms of Piera Aulagnier (1975), movements that are, as we have seen, at the foundations of the construction of psychic life, of the emergence of subjectivity (Chapter 1). This is how Florence Guignard describes the experience of the baby in the first moments of life, and the urgency of the task of drive fusion:

> Catapulted into an air environment, deprived of the protection and warmth of its uterine container as well as of its nourishing capacities, the newborn infant needs rapidly, and even as a matter of urgency, to use not only its biological capacities for integrating the external environment but also its own skills which develop at a speed that will never again be equalled in its existence. This integration will confront it with the necessity to submit the different aspects of its instinctual drives to this sustained and constant work of fusion and defusion. The organization of this activity is referred to by the term *primary sadism*. This may be defined as a violent action aimed at taking possession of animate or inanimate objects in external reality, and then also in internal reality. This act of possession is matched by an equally violent movement of expulsion of everything that impedes this devouring [...]. Indispensable for survival, primary sadism is located, from the point of view of the genealogy of the drives, at the first level of fusion, that of the life drive with the death drive.[8]
>
> (Guignard, 2015a, p. 71–72)

Fourth postulate

For our part, and as regards the connection between the life and death drives, we would like to put forward the following hypotheses or considerations:

- we postulate, to begin with, that originally the activity of the death drives is dependent on the intensity of the emotional or proto-emotional experiences *in utero* – see what Donald Meltzer says about these first emotional experiences, of which we have spoken (Chapter 3) – which avoids or resolves in part the question of innateness;
- this activity of the destructive drives engenders experiences that may be described as beta elements, whose only destiny is to be evacuated and projected in order to undergo a transformation into alpha elements that can be psychically assimilated thanks to the alpha function of the mothering environment – a "binding" function, as André Green (1987) says;
- the destructive drives appear in the emerging psyche in a bound (thanks to the alpha function of the mothering environment) or libidinalized form, or in an unbound form destined for projection. The bound portion of the destructive drives is used by the ego to defend itself against the depositary objects of unbound destructiveness. This hypothesis is among others developed by Benno Rosenberg (1988) in an article titled "Pulsion de mort, negation et travail psychique: ou la pulsion de mort mise au service de la défense contre la pulsion de mort". It is clearly stated by Melanie Klein (1958) when she explains her opposition to Freud on the subject of the mechanism for deflecting the death drive. Freud (1924) envisaged this deflection solely as a transformation of the attack against the self into an aggression against the object. Klein distinguishes two processes in the mechanism of deflection:

    Part of the death instinct is projected into the object, the object thereby becoming a persecutor; while that part of the death instinct which is retained in the ego causes aggression to be turned against that persecutory object.

    (Klein, 1958, p. 238)

    Aggression is understood as resulting from the blend between the life drives and the death drives;

- the annexation or binding of a part of the destructive drives with the life drives is indispensable for the creative activity of the latter. A portion of destructiveness is necessary for every form of life or of survival: the act of nourishing oneself is, for instance, a clear example, owing to the necessity of using bound sadism, if only for biting or chewing. As Green says, "the life processes are only viable through integration with the forces of death. Taming death implies obliging it to link itself to life" (Green, 1982, p. 280, translated for this edition);
- consequently, the cathexis of an object as a container of an interior space that can evoke curiosity and desire – which develops symbolization, thinking (see Chapter 10) – implies the integration of the death drives with the life drives. The constitution of a three-dimensional space is dependent on drive binding;
- if the projection of the unbound destructive impulses is made impossible (due to the absence or failure of a container capable of receiving them, or due to the particularly destructive character of these unbound impulses), they poison the psyche which dies through self-destruction (this may be what happens in autism, for instance).

Based on these considerations, we will make a proposition on the subject of the concept of "*fundamental violence*" elaborated by Jean Bergeret in several texts and books (Bergeret, 1981, 1984, 1985, 1987ab) concerning the most archaic conflictual vicissitudes which the emerging psyche has to deal with. We propose to understand fundamental violence as covering the *part of the death drives linked to the life drives*. Although Bergeret seems to call into question the opportunity of taking into consideration the concept of the death drive and the early conflictuality between life and death drive impulses, we think it is possible to understand "fundamental violence" as follows.

Fundamental violence is presented by Jean Bergeret as a pre-ambivalent, animal-type instinct, that is, connoted neither with love nor hate, and whose aim is solely one of self-preservation.[9] This instinct gave rise to the phantasy of the possibility of the death of the other as a precondition of one's own survival. Fundamental violence stages an earlier conflict to that opposing the forces of binding and unbinding. Furthermore, it serves as a support for the libido and constitutes its reservoir of energy. Not all violence, however, is integrated by the libido: a part of this primary instinct of self-preservation recuperates for its own benefit a certain quantity of libidinal drive that is still free, paving the way for aggression, sadism and masochism.

This primitive conflict which envisages the possibility of the death of the other as a precondition of one's own survival, relating to issues of self-preservation, stages an "other". Even if Bergeret notes that this other is not an object with the status of a subject, but represents a "non-ego" rather than an "other", it seems to us that in this archaic conflict this "other", this "non-ego", is cathected with destructive power, with the power of self-annihilation. Understanding this necessity to kill, in phantasy, in order to survive, as the result of a projection of destructive impulses, as Melanie Klein spoke of it, seems to us compatible with the model of fundamental violence. Understanding survival by annihilating the other as based on the binding of the non-projected life and death drives, as we propose, seems coherent with the idea of a fundamental violence. Moreover, Bergeret, who likens fundamental violence on one occasion (Bergeret, 1985) to the objectalizing function described by Green as a function of the life drive, and on another (Bergeret, 1987b) to the de-objectalizing function described by Green as a function of the death drive,[10] is contradictory. But this contradiction can be resolved if we understand fundamental violence as we suggest, that is, as based on the synthesis of the life drives – and especially the self-preservative drives – with the non-projected death drives.

Furthermore, Bergeret wonders about the opportunity of resorting to a conception of the death drive in the metapsychological and psychopathological registers. Initially, having recognized the mechanisms of binding and unbinding, Bergeret (1985) situated them in the metapsychological register without attributing them with a character of an instinctual drive order, which made him doubt the necessity of introducing a death drive. Then, subsequently (Bergeret, 1987b), he called into question the very existence of a force of unbinding, explaining situations of unbinding by the absence alone of libido efficiency with respect to its binding function.

Now Bergeret points out that "the problem would present itself very differently if the 'death drive' were simply posited […] as a phantasy staging the idea that the survival of the subject risks imposing, out of *necessity* and not *pleasure*, the death of the object; and vice-versa" (Bergeret, 1987b, p. 174, our italics, translated for this edition).

Is it not precisely the *necessity* of destroying rather than the *pleasure* of destroying that is essentially involved in clinical situations where the work of the death drive is in evidence? The question of pleasure/unpleasure, and consequently of desire, is secondary, surely, to the problem of security/anxiety and, consequently, of need and necessity. Is it not by recognizing need, even if it is secondarily eroticized, that we can draw closer to the most archaic processes of mental life?

Jean Bégoin (1989) also called into question the clinical necessity of resorting to the concept of the death drive, arguing, among other things, that the countertransference effects produced by the idea of a constitutional death drive underlying destructive manifestations might be harmful. Jean Bégoin proposes the notion of "violence of despair", which, in his opinion, accounts better for the action and nature of the destructive impulses in the psyche than the notions of death drive or fundamental violence. The most violent defences (autistic, for instance) are always in the service of the struggle for survival. They protect against despair, which represents real psychic suffering, namely of not being able to develop oneself, of not being able to arouse sufficient love and attention in objects so that they foster this psychic development. Jean Bégoin suggests, for instance, that envy might be considered not as a direct expression of the death drive (see Chapter 14), but as the expression of a massive identification with the failure of the primary object to ensure the subject's development and capacities for autonomy.

These remarks by Jean Bégoin are valuable. However, they do not seem contradictory with the idea of a death drive, grouping together several destructive impulses, whose activation can very well be understood as resulting from a traumatic encounter between the infantile psyche and an object whose containing function is deficient. The violence of despair may be understood, it seems to us, as reflecting or expressing the activation of the death drives – in pathological fusion with the life drives – without considering these death drives as at the origin (because they are deemed "constitutional") of this violence, which avoids the possible harmful countertransference effects about which Jean Bégoin warns us. This recourse to the notion of the death drive must involve a *descriptive* and not *explanatory* vision of psychic functioning. This coincides, moreover, with what Donald Meltzer says about psychoanalysis itself, which he considers as a descriptive rather than explanatory science (Meltzer et al., 1975, Meltzer, 1984a).

Fourth postulate

So, to conclude on the question of the binding between the life drives and the death drives, or of *drive integration*, we wish once again to emphasize the *role of the object* in this work of integration – André Green (2000) also insists on this point. Here is a short sequence from the observation of a mother and her baby to lend weight to this idea.[11]

> The sequence occurs during a change of nappies; the baby is five months old. The baby is on the baby-changing table and he has a playful exchange with his mother whose face is very close to his. Suddenly, the baby attacks his mother's face with his hands. He scratches, catches hold of his mother's nose, grabs her hair. The mother takes hold of the baby's hands and says: "No, caress like this!", while caressing her cheeks with the baby's hands. The baby is astonished, looks at his mother intensely, and reproduces his attacks. His mother repeats her response. Then the baby caresses his mother's face and is jubilant. At a certain moment the mother moves away to grasp an object; the baby follows her movements with his eyes. Then we see the baby throwing one of his hands forwards and catching this hand with the other one, seeming to perform a movement in which one hand restrains the other that is thrown forwards. All this is accompanied by vocalizing.

What we see here is a mother who transforms the baby's attack into a tender contact, which helps the baby to bind aggression, to bind hate with love, in other words to achieve an element of instinctual drive integration. And the mother can do this because she is not destroyed by the baby's attack. Everything would have been different if the mother had been irritated, if she had said: "Stop scratching me like that!" or "How nasty you are being with Mummy!"

The mother transforms the destructiveness, because she resists the destructiveness, and the baby can then internalize or show the beginnings of an internalization of this transformative function which is first and foremost a limiting function. The restraining hand reflects the internalization of the parent who contains the bay, of the superego that contains instinctual drive activity. A superego that contains and limits is first and foremost a superego that restrains. It is then a superego that transforms.

The transformation of destructiveness, instinctual drive binding, is a task that is carried out first by the object and that implies the resistance of the object to destructiveness. Drive integration is thus dependent on the object's response to primary destructiveness.[12]

9.1.4 Manifestations of the death drives in psychopathology

Freud's (1940a) hypothesis that the death drive remains silent so long as it operates internally and only comes to our notice "when it is diverted outwards as an instinct of destruction" (p. 150), has long been refuted, first of all by Melanie Klein and her collaborators (Klein et al., 1952). Many observations reveal the multiple occasions on which the death drive is expressed by attacking the subject himself and not an external object.

We cannot enumerate all the psychopathologies in which the death drives are particularly operative. Many authors have analyzed the work of the death drives in more or less serious pathologies such as melancholia, "essential depression" (described by Marty, 1968, 1976), autism (see for example the conceptions of Manzano and Palacio Espasa, 1978), the psychoses, mental anorexia, hypochondria, psychosomatic manifestations (see, among others, the work of Joyce MacDougall, 1974, 1989), addictive behaviours, alcoholism, drug addictions (see, in particular, the articles of Rosenfeld, 1960, 1964c), etc.

Herbert Rosenfeld (1971, 1987) considers that the most virulent forms of manifestations of the death drive are met with in *severe narcissistic states*. He explains how, when certain narcissistic patients are faced in the transference with the reality of their dependence on the analyst representing the parents, the destructive aspects driven by envy nourish the wish to destroy the analyst, the source of what is living and good. At the same time, violent self-destructive impulses push them to want to destroy all progress, to abandon the analysis and to die – death being idealized as the only solution. In other narcissistic patients, displaying superiority and self-admiration, the defused, or rather, pathologically fused destructive impulses, dominate the whole of the personality and object relations. These patients keep very little of their libidinal self alive, which prevents them from experiencing any guilt. They try to get rid of their dependent part by atrophying it, by killing it in phantasy, and they identify almost entirely with their destructive narcissistic part which crushes the libidinal self that is unable to oppose the process of destruction, thereby procuring them with a sense of triumph.

All carers are faced on a daily basis in clinical work with psychotic or autistic pathologies, but also with less serious pathologies, with the triumph of destructiveness which may lead to psychic death, as in extreme autism, and even to physical death, as in suicide, or in any somatic decompensation which has an equivalent value to suicide.

Destructiveness does not only inhabit patients. It is taken over by the teams of carers who have different degrees of difficulty in receiving it and containing it. The work of the death drives in caregivers is manifested, for instance, by apathy, resistance to any change, the petrification of emotions and creativity, and the obsessionalization of controlling behaviours. While the last of these originally had the aim of protecting patients against their own destructiveness, they become obstacles or defences against any creative and living movement. The destructiveness of patients attacks the carers' desire to care and faces them with discouragement and despair. Destructiveness is taken over by the caregivers who destroy themselves by acting out their conflicts or by immobilizing exchanges. It can also be projected into the bodies of administrative power, who are accused (sometimes rightly, moreover) of killing any demands made on them by the strategy of slowness, whether it is a matter of not hearing or of making people wait too long. Finally, it can frequently be observed that, in teams of caregivers, the implacable work of the death drives results in the paralysis of all thought.[13]

Uncontained destructiveness that is taken over by the teams of caregivers, as is the case for any process of projective identification, is to be understood not only as the effect of a movement of externalization and projection on the part of the patient(s), but as a movement of contact and alliance between the destructive forces of the patient(s) and the destructive forces of the team of caregivers that are responsible for them.

Although the destructiveness spreads among the caregivers through projective identification, it needs to be pointed out that it is also – and this links up with the remarks by Jean Bégoin mentioned earlier – with the aim of *communication* that such contamination occurs. Projective identification also has the aim of communication. The despair, helplessness, immobilization produced by the patient's destructiveness are also to be understood as the effect of a communication by the patient about his emotional state. Such a patient is looking for a container to receive his emotional experiences. He is trying either to make the analyst feel his despair and helplessness which engender destructiveness or to protect himself against them by means of destructiveness, by the excitement of destructiveness. Even the most destructive patients, who undermine the therapeutic process, are seeking to communicate their ill-being and possess a capacity for cooperating with the therapeutic enterprise, *if we are able to recognize it*, as Herbert Rosenfeld (1987) says.

9.2 Splitting and idealization

9.2.1 Splitting, an integrating mechanism

The working of the death drive, according to Melanie Klein, gives rise from the beginning of life to anxiety which is experienced as a fear of annihilation. This fear takes the form of fear of persecution. The response of the self to this primary anxiety consists in falling to bits or splitting oneself. Splitting, which is a response to the need to master persecutory anxiety results in dispersing the death drive and in creating a "good" object separate from a "bad" object. The good object or good breast arises from gratifying experiences and the projection of libidinal impulses. The bad breast arises from frustrating experiences and the projection of destructive impulses. At the same time as being created outside, the good breast and bad breast are set up by means of introjection within the baby's mind. All subsequent relations are dependent on the goodness or ferocity of these first internalized objects.

The good internal breast is in the service of integration and is felt to be a whole object; it represents the nucleus of the ego. The bad breast, attacked by oral-sadistic and cannibalistic impulses, is felt to be a fragmented object and to be in the service of disintegration. Splitting thus results in a separation between love and hate: the good internal breast strengthens in the child the capacity to love his objects and is a source of consolation against anxiety. Oral-sadistic desires, aroused by frustration coming from internal or external sources, constantly give the infant the feeling that the good breast is destroyed and reduced to pieces within him. These phantasied attacks, influenced by what Melanie Klein (1952ab) calls greed, will fuel persecutory anxiety lest the bad breast (made bad by the infant's projections or external rivalry – this is from the observer's point of view, for there are grounds for assuming the infant is unable to distinguish the two sources of frustration) devour the infant with voracity equal to his own desires. This persecutory anxiety is counteracted thanks to experiences of gratification and love, and the infant's "physical nearness to his mother during feeding – essentially his relation to the good breast – recurrently helps him to overcome the longing for a former lost state, alleviates persecutory anxiety and increases the trust in the good object" (Klein, 1952a, p. 201).[14]

Ego-splitting and object-splitting coexist. Ego-splitting, which arises from the conflict caused within the ego by the polarity of the instinctual drives, is maintained by the processes of introjecting and projecting good and bad objects. The internalized good object constitutes the nucleus of the ego around which the latter grows and develops. We have seen that the libidinal impulses need the help of a portion of the death drives to struggle against the projected destructive impulses. It is this binding by the libido of the death drives working inside that will help to establish the internalized good object. This binding also concerns the superego which, when it is associated with the good object, is more helpful than severe, more protective than menacing.

Finally, splitting contributes to forming both persecutory and idealized figures. When they have the function of protecting the ego against terrifying figures arising from the bad breast, felt to be a terrifying persecutor, these figures arise from the good breast which tends to turn into an ideal breast, satisfying "the greedy desire for unlimited, immediate and everlasting satisfaction" (ibid., p. 64). The idealization, which corresponds to the exaggeration of the good aspects of the breast, is exacerbated when frustration, persecution or anxiety are increased. The infant can escape his persecutors by fleeing towards his idealized internal object.

To the notion of splitting may be added the idea that spatial splitting – which separates the good object and the bad object in space – is accompanied by temporal splitting – bound up with the rhythmicity of pleasant and unpleasant, reassuring and anxiety-producing experiences. As Donald Meltzer points out, "it is in the repeated rhythmic experience of destruction and restoration, of despair and hope, of mental pain and joy, that the experience of gratitude arises, from which the bond of love for, and concern about, the good objects are forged" (Meltzer, 1967, p. 40–41), in other words that the depressive position is approached. We will consider further this rhythmicity of experiences in its relations to the development of thought. Temporal splitting is both dependent on splitting in space (it is because good and bad objects have been discerned that their potential to succeed one another can be envisaged and sustain, as we shall see, the development of thought), and at the origin of splitting in space (it is because good and bad experiences have succeeded each other rhythmically that the perception of a good quality and a bad quality could occur and that the idealized figures and the persecutory figures could be separated in space – and in time, for there are grounds for assuming that these two notions cannot be distinguished at this stage).

Moreover, Donald Meltzer (1967) envisaged different axes and modalities of spatial splitting in the "geography" of unconscious phantasy. Apart from the spitting that separates the good-idealized figures from the bad-persecutory figures (part objects), Meltzer described the splitting that divides part-objects amongst themselves ("breast-that-nourishes" and toilet-breast), then the later splitting that separates in the body image the top from the bottom, the front and the rear, the interior and exterior, as well as the splitting that distributes the functions in these geographical zones (excretory functions below, in connection with the rear, and nourishing functions above, in connection with the breasts, eyes, mouth and mind).

9.2.2 Splitting, a disintegrating mechanism

Splitting and idealization represent, as we have seen, mechanisms of defence that are characteristic of the paranoid-schizoid or symbiotic position and that make it possible to take a step forward on the path of ego-integration. However, if they prove to be excessive, these processes can lead to severe disorders. The splitting of the ego and of internal objects leads to the feeling that the ego is in bits. At its height, this state is represented by *disintegration*. In normal development, disintegration is a transitory experience in the infant. If splitting and disintegration occur too frequently and for too long, they are considered by Melanie Klein (1946) as a sign of schizophrenia, and she detects certain indications of this illness in the very first months of life. She also understands states of schizophrenic dissociation and depersonalization in the adult as a regression to infantile states of disintegration.

However, for us, the link between splitting and disintegration is not clarified sufficiently by Melanie Klein. Sometimes, she considers excessive splitting as responsible for disintegration (Klein, 1946, 1952a), and at others, she considers disintegration, which is reflected in the ego's experience of "falling to pieces", as an alternative to splitting; anxiety, bound up with the activity of the death drive, induces the ego to respond through disintegration, by falling to pieces, or through splitting, by isolating and projecting on to the external object – the breast – persecutory or destructive elements. Both these conceptions of disintegration subsist in the later texts (see, for example, "Envy and gratitude", 1957).

Let us begin by examining the second model, *disintegration* representing here a *failure to gain access to the processes of splitting*. Melanie Klein, moreover, associates the process of disintegration with that of fragmentation described by Ferenczi (1949, 1932) as an expression of the death drive prompting the subject to react to disagreeable stimuli by falling to pieces. We liken this disintegration of which Klein speaks to the process of dismantling described by Meltzer, which constitutes an essential mechanism of defence in the auto-sensual position (see Chapter 5). The relation between this disintegration and splitting is therefore of an ontogenetic order; this disintegration as an alternative to splitting is, moreover, closer to unintegration than disintegration.

In the first model, disintegration owing to an excess of splitting gives rise to the experience of an inner catastrophe and corresponds to fragmentation, to the explosive disintegration of which Geneviève Haag (1985b) speaks. Excessive splitting does not always lead to disintegration; it can simply impede integration (Klein, 1958).

Other pathological consequences resulting from splitting are linked to its association with projective identification (see Klein, 1946). When splitting and projective identification are used excessively, they lead to a weakening and impoverishment of the ego, which becomes incapable of recovering the parts that it has projected outside. The exaggerated projection of the idealized good parts into the external object leads to the feeling that these good parts are lost and that the object represents the receptacle of the ego-ideal of the infant, which impoverishes and weakens the ego. When the exaggerated projection of persecutory experiences and the flight towards the idealized internal object is excessive, it disturbs the development of object relations and the ego feels entirely dependent on its internal object. The exaggerated projection of good and bad parts of the subject leads to an attitude of obsessional control: the need to control others corresponds to the need to control the parts of the subject that have been projected excessively.

The amplification of the paranoid-schizoid positions or the recourse to paranoid-schizoid positions corresponds, as we have already pointed out (see Chapter 8), to the compelling need to avoid depressive pain, but it can cause much more harmful damage:

> Schizo-paranoid phenomena are defensive attempts against atrocious depressive anxiety, but in fact they liberate persecutory anxieties that are even more terrifying. On many occasions we can see patients who are unable to bear the suffering of guilt associated with ambivalence regress to more primitive modes of splitting, with the attendant confusion and disorientation, with the aim of overcoming their suffering. However, persecutory anxiety, withdrawal from reality and the impoverishment of the ego are the price they have to pay.
> (Jaques, 1972, p. 11, translated from the French)

Donald Meltzer (1978) identified six forms of persecution or of persecutory object:

- persecution by a bad part of the self (which may be projected) which attacks the relation to the good object by means of tyranny, corruption, threats, seduction, propaganda to magnify jealousy and mistrust, etc.;
- persecution by bad objects (superego, puritanical and harsh) which are primarily bent on tyrannical control and imposing a relationship of enslavement;
- persecution by the damage done to good objects by sadistic attacks upon them (the pain due to this persecution is what is known as "persecutory depression");
- persecution by a particularly malignant bad object formed by the fusion between a malignant part of the self and a bad object;
- persecution by the paranoid object, formed by the projective identification of a malignant part of the self with a good object – the breast;

- persecution by dead objects at the origin of particular terrors (fear lest the dead come back to life, fear of ghosts, and so on).

Meltzer points out that when confusion is added to persecution, there is a tremendous tendency to act out.

9.2.3 Phenomenological approach

We will illustrate this conceptual approach concerning splitting by evoking the case of a child of seven, Dorothée, being treated in a day hospital and benefitting from therapeutic work in a small group, run by two carers including one of us (M.L.). This child presented a symbiotic psychosis. We will simply offer a few observations describing the child's frequent attitude and some anamnestic elements.

> Dorothée spent a lot of energy, during the small group sessions, trying to monopolize the "territory" around the sink, by making the tap run constantly, by annexing a number of the toys; she turned her back to the rest of the group, showing her behind, shouting, being turbulent, spitting ... as if she were inhabited by a character who was always severe, always angry, who told everyone what to do. Dorothée tried in such moments to annex one or several other children in the small group who had to join in her games, and to whom she granted more or less autonomy. A constant factor in these activities was the systematic eviction of one of the children or an adult, who was all-bad, and who was energetically rejected and denigrated, to whom Dorothée said: "Not you!" The child occupied the foreground and devoted a large part of her energy to establishing these alliances and formulating these rejections. She took in few good things and refused systematically what was given or proposed to her. The work of verbalization at the group level, the evocation of the "part of the group that says that they are always angry and unable to show that there is also a baby-part that needs help" sometimes allowed this idea to yield ... for a short while. At other moments, Dorothée would stand up in front of the blackboard and act as if she were the schoolmistress writing – scribbling – on the blackboard and then turn round to remonstrate one or the other of the children ... In all these moments we were therefore dealing with a Dorothée-character

who shouted, moaned, spat and uttered insults. Dorothée also showed a lot of anger and rage at times of separation; she sometimes managed to say, however, that it "hurts".

In those moments when it was impossible in the small group to put an end to Dorothée's omnipotent attitude, by suggesting that she should come and talk in the "group circle" about what was wrong, what was hurting, Dorothée allowed herself – it marked significant progress – to come and sit down right next to one of the therapists. She was clearly seeking a moment of symbiotic exchange, a moment of reparative symbiosis; Dorothée was then a very depressed child, on the edge of tears, saying frequently "hurt" (*bobo*) and showing her "holes" (in her body or on her clothes); she often sought to press her back against the therapist's body (often the female therapist), tried to get inside the other (in a form of intrusive penetration with her eyes), sought symbiotic complicity with the other, but also the complicity of the other in order to evince a third (often the male therapist or another child in the group), a third to whom she would say "not you", while pretending to be whispering secrets into the therapists "phagocyte" ear. Here again, one object was sought for its symbiotic capacity while another object was rejected, evinced: "That stinks", "Throw it in the dustbin", Dorothée said – the dustbin was a place to put bad-pooh things; it was also for Dorothée the place into which she threw her productions (drawings, cut-outs) as if she was unable to offer anything "good", as if there was nothing in her that made her worth loving.

Dorothée was a particularly good child during the first two years of her life. She was the daughter of a couple who were shopkeepers, for whom parenthood was extremely anxiety-producing and who devoted a great deal of energy to their shop in which they were very invested narcissistically. We can assume that Dorothée suffered from a lack of containing capacity and capacity for reverie on the part of her parents during her early childhood. She was a child who disturbed and made people feel insecure, who had to be looked after "on top of" professional obligations. Sometimes cherished and sometimes reprimanded because she asked for care, attention and, above all, to be cathected psychically, Dorothée manifested from the age of two worrying psychopathological signs. For reasons of convenience, always linked to the professional activity of her parents (the shop and the apartment being separate), Dorothée often found herself alone in the mornings (until the age of four approximately) when she woke up, the link with her parents being established by means of an interphone; the interphone was regularly switched on, making it possible to know from the noises or crying heard, if Dorothée was awake and if it was necessary to go and take care of her. This interphone perhaps reinforced persecutory feelings in the child, in addition to the worries linked to her impression of being alone, lost-forgotten, at the moment of waking up.

There are grounds for assuming that during early childhood, in the course of these first years when Dorothée was very good and her parents were very busy in the shop, that the infant had internalized the notion that being a dependent infant implies a hostile presence of the object. Indeed, the psychic cathexis of this child and their contact with the needs of an infant alarmed these parents and made them feel that they were bad parents. This was maintained by their inability to preserve an intimate space protected from the perpetual disturbances of the shop clients, to whom their devotion was total. Dorothée had integrated the fact that if she appealed to the parenting capacities of her objects, this appeal would provoke irritation and harsh relations that would be suddenly broken off. So she developed an omnipotent, pseudo-mature part of herself which entertained the illusion of independence, at the price of splitting, while rejecting and mistreating the baby-part: the remarks "it stinks", "thrown in the dustbin" denote the baby-part. This hypertrophied omnipotent aspect is dominated by the destructive impulses.

This scenario was played out on the external stage, on the group stage of therapy. If Dorothée got in touch with her baby-part, which led her to share a symbiotic experience with another child or with a therapist, she was obliged to distance the persecutory aspects representing the present hostile object so that the symbiotic object was protected and not suspected of having hostility in it. The baby that she showed was therefore a baby full of holes, bumps and bruises, in need of back-contact to feel gathered together and in security. The baby-part was so depressed that it sought help from the omnipotent parts in order to enter into total projective identification, in other words, in destructive symbiosis, with the object. Dorothée was then once again the rejecting object who threw the baby into the dustbin. The pooh-baby was expelled by the backside; Dorothée represented the anal sphincter of the group. She was both the parent who could only have a baby in her backside and could only expel it, and also the baby who could only enter into contact with the parent through the backside, which led her to feel either imprisoned in the backside or expelled and thus abandoned (the ego is thus trapped in the anal compartment of the "claustrum", as Meltzer (1992)[15] would say).

This example shows the association between the mechanisms of splitting and projective identification in the externalization of internal conflicts. It also shows the associations between the mechanisms of splitting, incorporation and projective identification with the incorporated object (see Chapter 1). When Dorothée was identified with the persecuting parent who controlled objects and was contemptuous towards the baby, she was in projective identification with her internal persecuting parent who was sadistic towards her baby-part. Experiences of shared symbiosis do not nourish the baby enough, for they are taken over by the omnipotent part that takes advantage of the situation to incorporate the external object and to enlarge itself.

9.2.4 Splitting, between dismantling and repression

We have already described dismantling (Chapter 5), which may be considered as the lower limit of splitting.[16] We will now try to represent its higher limit, namely, repression.

Melanie Klein (1952a, 1957, 1958) distinguishes splitting from repression insofar as while splitting can lead to a disintegration of the self, when there is a fusion of the drives the death drive prevails over the life drive. On the other hand, repression, even when excessive, does not expose the subject to states of disintegration, for when the subject is capable of using repression – Klein situates the onset of repression towards the second year of life – the integration of the mind is sufficiently strong. In repression, splitting produces above all a division between the conscious and unconscious.

Thus, although splitting is distinct from repression, it determines and influences its utilization:

> If early schizoid mechanisms and anxieties have not been sufficiently overcome, the result may be that instead of a fluid

> boundary between the conscious and unconscious, a rigid barrier between them arises; this indicates that repression is excessive and that, in consequence, development is disturbed.
>
> (Klein, 1952a, p. 87)

A greater synthesis in the ego, and a good assimilation of the superego by the ego, in other words, a sufficiently moderate use of the mechanisms of splitting in order to overcome, in spite of everything, paranoid anxieties, will facilitate a moderate use of the process of repression, which in turn will make the conscious and unconscious more "porous" for each other.

Splitting, used to combat internal and external persecutors, modifies anxiety very little, for it is accomplished by an ego that is not well organized. Thus, persecutory images continue to intoxicate the ego even if they are split-off and projected. On the other hand, in repression the more organized ego is able to separate itself from unconscious ideas and terrifying figures more efficiently.

Wilfred Bion (1956, 1957) explains that, in the personality, where the nonpsychotic part has recourse to repression to dissociate certain tendencies of the conscious mind, the psychotic part uses splitting and projective identification as a substitute for repression. With the mechanisms of splitting and projective identification, the psychotic part of the personality attempts to rid itself of the apparatus which the psyche needs to carry out repressions. If repression is constitutive of a division between unconscious and conscious, splitting and projective identification lead to replacing the unconscious, in the psychotic part of the personality, by the world of dream material.

Splitting, which is an active process with regard to internal objects, separates the persecuting figures from the idealized figures. It is thus a primary mechanism aimed at reducing confusion. Between dismantling, which suspends all mental activity and fragments, autisticizes, internal objects, and repression, a more elaborate and organized mechanism which guarantees the integrity of the object, splitting, as an integrating mechanism, is first and foremost constitutive of internal objects, even if they remain part-objects. Splitting distinguishes, isolates, "manufactures" objects identified as antagonistic but whose dialectic may be understood as inaugurating the initiation of the activity of phantasies and thought-processes. This point will be the subject of the following chapter.

Splitting and idealization

It may be added that, just as we tried to do with regard to the evolution of the different modes of identification as well as the structuring of the different dimensions of psychic space (Chapters 4 and 5), so we will need to study the paths of transition from a predominant mechanism of defence to another more complex one (dismantling, splitting, repression).

Notes

1 For a synthetic overview of Melanie Klein's ideas concerning the death drive and splitting and their role in the processes of integration and disintegration, see her late texts: "Envy and Gratitude" (1957), "On the development of mental functioning" (1958) and "Our adult world and its roots in infancy" (1959).
2 On the necessity that forced itself on Freud of resorting to the notion of the death drive, with regard to his clinical work, the context of his private life, the historical context, the history of the group of the first psychoanalysts and his work of theorization at that time, see the analyses of Jean Guillaumin (1987, 2000) and René Kaës (2000). On the genesis, history and significance of the notion of the death drive, see, also, Green (2007).
3 We will not enter into the epistemological biases that have led certain translators or authors themselves to use the term instinct rather than drive.
4 On this point Klein deviates from the opinion of Freud (1923, 1926), who did not regard the fear of death as a primary anxiety and amalgamated death-anxiety and castration-anxiety.
5 Piera Aulagnier stresses the difference between the act of decathexis, a sign of the working of the death drives, and the act of repression in the service of the realization and preservation of desires and cathexes. Repression is only possible towards an idea or image that cannot be decathected.
6 Note that Green (1983) distinguished between a "positive primary narcissism" striving towards unity and identity, and a "negative primary narcissism" attached to the destructive drives, striving towards unbinding and manifesting themselves through the feeling of emptiness.
7 The libido denotes the energy of the life drives; no similar term is used to denote the energy specific to the death drives. Freud (1940a [1938]) pointed out that he did not possess one. The terms *destrudo* (Weiss, 1935) or *mortido* (Federn, 1952) have apparently not had success.

Fourth postulate

8 Florence Guignard sees a genealogical dimension in the organization of the drives: the first generation, she suggests, is constituted by the life and death drives; their fusion gives rise to the second generation formed of the sexual drives, which in turn gives rise to the third, consisting of the ego-drives (self-preservation, master and other drives relating to the ego).

9 Bergeret (1987a) evokes the "forgotten" text of Freud, *A Phylogenetic Fantasy: Overview of the Transference Neuroses* (Freud, 1915c) in which Freud postulates the existence of a violent primitive instinct centred on self-preservation and which is not yet cathected by the libido (a primitive instinct that Freud situates in phylogenesis).

10 Green's propositions here date back to 1984: the article "Pulsion de mort, narcissisme négatif, fonction désobjectalisante" (1986a) is the publication of a paper read in 1984; the book *Propédeutique* (1995) contains a chapter on this subject that takes up again a conference of 1985 ("L'objet et la fonction objectalisante").

11 This observation can be found in Ciccone (2003a) and Ciccone and Ferrant (2015).

12 On the question of object's resistance to destructiveness, see Winnicott's elaborations on what he calls the "anti-social tendency" (1956b, 1958b). On the function of the object's transformation of the baby's destructiveness, see, for instance, Haag (1999); Ciccone (2003a, 2014).

13 On the work of death, destructivity, unbinding and violence in institutions, see Kaës et al., 1996; Ciccone et al., 2014.

14 Note that Melanie Klein brings together under the same term, that of persecution, primitive anxieties which exist from birth and are the direct expression of the death instinct, reflected in the feeling of being annihilated from the inside, and anxieties that could be described as secondary arising from fears that the attacked, split and projected object will seek retaliation for the attacks that it has suffered, on the other.

15 See Chapter 4 and, further on, Chapter 12.

16 We would like to draw attention to the concept of "parcellization" put forward by Daniel Marcelli (1981), even though we do not adhere to his ontogenetic representation. In fact, Marcelli situates parcellization in the psychotic levels and splitting in the pre-psychotic levels. We understand what Marcelli says about parcellization as describing the dismantling characteristic of the auto-sensual position. The split object seems to us to belong more to the register of symbiotic and schizophrenic psychotic processes, as we have shown with the case of Dorothée

10

THE GENESIS AND DEVELOPMENT OF THOUGHT-ACTIVITY

At the same time as the psychic skin is forming, the main activity of the psychical apparatus, namely thought-activity, is developing. With access to the symbiotic or paranoid-schizoid position and the operation of the processes of splitting and idealization that we have just described, differentiated objects appear, of antagonistic character and nature, which are organized in terms of an essentially conflictual dialectic. There is also the perception of a boundary between the self and the outside world. This still tenuous perception is subject to the symbiotic organization and to the phantasy of a common skin that characterize the symbiotic position. Projective processes begin to operate predominantly and mental space is gradually structured in a three-dimensional fashion. Let us endeavour now to picture the development of thought-activity.

We have already described or pointed out certain metaphors accounting for the primitive, primordial psychic elements and the first forms of thought which emerge from them (Chapter 2): pictogram (Aulagnier, 1975), agglutinated object or nucleus (Bleger, 1967), agglomerate (Marcelli, 1985), ideogram (Bion, 1957), audiogram (Maiello, 2000), beta element transformed into alpha element (Bion 1962ab), demarcation signifier (Rosolato, 1985), formal signifier (Anzieu, 1987a), formal container (Nathan, 1990), and prenarrative envelope (Stern, 1993,). All these notions imply a link between different elements: sensory and perceptual elements, emotional elements, present and past elements, inside and outside elements. Thought-activity is an activity of "linking".

Furthermore, all these figures of emerging thought assume a source that contains a double pole: a perceptual (or sensory, sensual) pole, and an intersubjective pole (the link to the object). Perception and intersubjectivity are at the foundations of thought; they are located at the two poles of the emergence of psychic life.[1]

To describe the first forms of thought-activity, we will summarize in this chapter Freud's conception of the infant hallucinating the object of the satisfaction of need, and point out some later developments. We will then see, with Melanie Klein and Hanna Segal, how symbolization unfolds, in its relation to paranoid anxieties and depressive pain. Bion's proposals will make it possible to clarify and link these points of view by articulating them with a more "cognitive" dimension.[2] Finally, we will emphasize with Daniel Marcelli the role of the time factor and the rhythmicity of experiences in the development of thinking.

But let us first clarify once again how perceptual experiences and intersubjective experiences are at the origins of thought.

10.1 Perception and intersubjectivity at the origins of thought[3]

10.1.1 The perceptual, the sensory, the sensual

Perception represents one of the poles of the "fabrication" of psychic reality, of psychic substance, and therefore one of the sources of the emergence of thoughts. We have seen the role played by sensoriality, sensuality (which concerns the "sensitive" sphere in general, beyond the five senses of sensoriality), and the perception of bodily impressions in the constitution of the first objects to which the nascent psyche "adheres", as well as in the constitution of the primitive psychic elements themselves. Everything that is found in the mind (nascent, emerging) has previously been found in perceptions, as was suggested by Freud (1923, 1925b),[4] who underlined how the mind arises from the body, derived from bodily sensations, and how perception is the nucleus of the ego, all presentations being repetitions of perceptions. Even hallucination, to which we will return, and which Freud (1895, 1900, 1911a) considered as a first form of thought, an idea that is open to criticism, implies a prior perception. The hallucination by the baby of the object or of the satisfaction of need presupposes one or more previous experiences of perception of this object or this satisfaction.

Sensoriality was placed at the origin of thought by Bion (1957, 1962ab, 1963) as well as by Piera Aulagnier (1975) and others. One of the first psychic functions is to connect sensory impressions to each other. To construct an objective object, to make it exist, to recognize it, that is to say to construct at the same time a subjective object, it is first necessary to gather together, to link the sensory impressions coming from this object: what we feel, see, hear and touch comes from the same object. The object is thus constructed. It is a "consensual" object. The perception of the world presupposes the presence of consensuality, which we have already discussed (Chapter 5). This operation is based on a capacity for attention. Both Bion and Meltzer (Meltzer et al., 1975) have described this process very well.

The first psychic activity or thought-activity is therefore an activity of linking. The reverse of this process corresponds to the operation of dismantling described by Meltzer (Meltzer et al., 1975), which we have also discussed, and which consists in a movement of disconnecting sensory impressions: what we feel about the object does not come from the same place as that which we see, hear or touch. Thus, the object no longer exists. Such a dismantling operation implies a suspension of attention which produces a suspension of the ego: the object no longer exists, nor the ego. This is an autistic process, an anti-thinking activity.

Perception makes it possible to grasp the external world, the outside world, but also the internal world, the subjective world, and the corporeal world of one's own body, which is situated between the external world and the internal world. The perception of the external world and of the corporeal world calls upon external sensoriality (that of the five senses) and internal sensitivity (kinaesthesia, proprioception, interoception). The perception of the corporeal world, and even more that of the subjective world, merges with sensation; perceiving and feeling are equivalent.[5] The perception of the subjective world concerns affects, emotions. The "primitive thought" of which Bion speaks (1957, 1962ab) – we will come back to this – includes both sensory impressions and emotions, which are also "objects of the senses". The "sense-impressions", according to Bion's formula, specific to emotional experiences, are analogous to the sense-impressions produced by concrete objects. These sense-impressions as a whole – which define what is sensual – represent beta elements whose destiny consists in being transformed into alpha elements available for thought.

At the foundation of psychic life is drive activity, as we have recalled (Chapter 2) – psychoanalysis has made it one of its basic statements –, but also, and first and foremost, that which is sensory or sensual, sensitive and perceptual. The drives play a role insofar as they cathect sensations, sensory and emotional perceptions, and influence their destiny. The infant's psychic skills, like his cognitive, intellectual skills, develop from sensoriality, sensations and perceptions.

For example, in his sensory play the infant deploys capacities for abstraction very early on. Indeed, when he receives information through a sensory channel, he can transfer it and process it with relevance in another sensory channel. This defines amodal perception, or perceptual amodality. Experiments show, for example, that if, without him seeing it, we give the infant a pacifier or a teat to suck, of a particular shape (more or less round, thin or wide), and if we present him with series of drawings or distinct forms of teats, he will preferentially direct his gaze towards the design of this teat, or towards a similar form, and he will do this from the age of three weeks (Meltzoff and Moore, 1979). In other words, the infant is able at a very early stage to transfer to the visual channel, to recognize, visually, information first received via the tactile channel, forms first explored by the mouth. The infant relates one meaning to another, and this early skill is considered by some to be the source of the adult's intellectual capacity to metaphorize, to use metaphors (Sibton and Mazet, 1991). The infant's sensory and perceptual activity leads him to construct a representation of the perceived object from which he extracts an invariant. This fixed structure is a kind of prototype that he can transfer from one sense to another. In other words, the infant "theorizes", as Bernard Golse (1998) also says, he builds a generalizable model of his experience; he's a real scientist.

Moreover, when we observe infants, we see them behaving like real researchers, seeking to solve problems. Very early on, the infant takes pleasure in solving problems and cathects psychic work for himself. The infant does not only seek drive satisfaction or the satisfaction of somatic need. He also has a need for knowledge, he enjoys solving problems. Melanie Klein (1932) spoke of the "epistemophilic impulse"; Bion (1962b) described the "knowledge link" which, alongside and jointly with the "love link" and "hate link", connects the infant to his objects (any subject is, moreover, connected in the same way to the world).

These sensory and perceptual capacities of the infant are present very early on. Such capacities are even described in the foetus, as we have already pointed out (Chapter 3).[6] Studies on foetal sensory and perceptual skills support the hypothesis of a "prenatal culture", of familiarization with the cultural environment from foetal life onwards, and of "transnatal continuity" in perceptual experience.

10.1.2 The intersubjective experiences

Intersubjectivity, intersubjective experiences, represent the other pole of the construction of psychic life. Thoughts are first thought by another before being thought and appropriated by the infant; we emphasized this when we described the alpha function (Chapter 3). The infant thinks first with the thinking apparatus of another before he can internalize his own thinking apparatus. In other words, it is in intersubjectivity that subjectivity is founded.

The notion of intersubjectivity has a double meaning. It designates both what separates, what creates a gap, and what is common, what articulates two or more subjectivities. Intersubjectivity is both what holds together and what conflictualizes the psychic spaces of related subjects.

We can say that Bion, who provided an eminently relevant model of the genesis of thought-activity, was a particularly intersubjectivist psychoanalyst. The "alpha function" he described accounts for the intersubjective interaction between the object and the subject, the parent and the infant, as well as between the analyst and the patient. Bion also insisted on the encounter, on contact, as the place where analysis takes place.

> Investigate the caesura; not the analyst; not the analysand; not the unconscious; not the conscious not sanity; not insanity. But the caesura, the link, the synapse.
>
> (Bion, 1971, p. 57)

> The relationship between the two people is a two-way affair, and insofar as one is concerned with demonstrating that relationship it is not a matter of talking about the analyst and analysand; it is talking about something *between* the two of them.
>
> (Bion, 1978, p. 18)

Attention is always paid to this point of contact, of encounter, and analysis concerns the encounter itself: "There is no semiology and psychoanalysis of the patient; there is a semiology and a psychanalysis of the encounter", as Salomon Resnik (1999, p. 87, translated for this edition), a pupil of Bion, also says, – indeed, one of his books is called *Semiologia dell'incontro* [*Semiology of the Encounter*] (Resnik et al., 1982). Psychoanalytic work is thus a co-work, a co-construction carried out as much by the analyst as by the patient. Psychoanalytic treatment is based on a model of the sharing of experience, the sharing of affect,[7] from an intersubjective perspective.

Intersubjectivity is a central notion in a number of works on infant development, related or outside psychoanalysis, but which feed the models of certain psychoanalysts, and in different epistemologies – even if the definitions of intersubjectivity cannot be superimposed from one epistemology to another. We talk about "joint attention" (Bruner, 1975), "emotional sharing" (Trevarthen, 1979, 1989a), "affective tuning" (Stern, 1985), "interpersonal self" (Hobson, 1993), "dyadic ego" (Emde and Oppenheim, 1995), "shared consciousness" (Trevarthen and Aitken, 1996), "mutual emotional regulation" (Tronick and Weinberg, 1997; Gergely, 1998), etc.; all notions – we have already mentioned some of them (Chapter 2) –, often used in modern psychoanalysis, which endeavour to account for the intersubjective processes at work in psychic growth. All the studies which develop these notions explore, in a more or less explicit way, how subjectivation or thought originates, takes its source in intersubjective experiences.

If subjectivity and thought develop from intersubjective experiences, this growth process will require and be determined by the psychic work of the object.

This point of view could coincide with the hypothesis that thoughts pre-exist thinking. We should thus speak not of the birth or the emergence *of* thought, but of birth *to* thought – to use the formulation of the very title of this book. Bion (1962b), as we shall see, said that thoughts were epistemologically prior to thinking. But if thoughts, in some of their forms – because the term "thought" is complex and covers a set of different elements –, pre-exist thinking, it is less in the sense that raw thoughts are there in rudimentary form, close to bodily or sensory experiences, waiting to be thought, as Bion says, but rather in the sense that thoughts are first *thought by another* before being appropriated by the subject in the early stages of life by the infant. This dimension is of course present in Bion's model, which highlighted the psychic work of the object on which the subject is dependent, psychic work that is necessary for the mental growth of the subject, of the infant.

Bion's conceptions, with his deeply intersubjective model, but also those of Winnicott on the mirror role of the mother (1967, 1971), have led the *"reflexive function"* of the object to be considered as one of the fundamental intersubjective processes. Such a notion is used in psychoanalytic discourse but has mainly been developed in the field of developmental psychology, attachment theories, and even cognitive psychology (see Fonagy and Target, 1997; Gergely, 1998; Fonagy, 1999, 2001; and others). The reflexive function consists in a subject being able to perceive and understand the mental states of another (like his own) and to reflect them. The studies which use this notion have sought, among other things, to examine in detail the effects on the child of specific disorders of this function in the parent.

It should be noted that this reflexive function is not limited to reflecting the moods, affects and emotions of the infant, in order to allow him to recognize himself in a mirror reflection process. The reflexive function consists in *actively* participating in transforming the projected emotions, the infant's communications, which are similar to what Bion called "sense data" or "sense impressions", that is to say, fragments of distinct sensations, sorts of chaos in which the bodily and the psychic, the sensory and the emotional, the self and the other are barely differentiated. The infant needs a primary experience of being actively contained by the mind of the object in order to transform the perceptual data of sensory and emotional experience into his own thinking mind.

Margot Waddell, for example, in a book entitled *Inside Lives: Psychoanalysis and the Growth of Personality* illustrates this idea very well with a short passage from *Peter Pan* (Barrie, 1911), where it is a question of a mother who strives to put order in the minds of her children:

> It is the nightly custom of every good mother, after her children are asleep, to rummage in their minds and put things straight for the next morning, repacking into their proper places the many articles that have wandered during the day. If you could keep awake (but of course you can't), you would see your mother doing this, and you would find it very interesting to watch her. It is quite like tidying up drawers. You would see

her on her knees, I expect, lingering humorously over some of your contents, wondering where on earth you had picked this thing up, making discoveries sweet and not so sweet, pressing this to her cheek as if it were as nice as a kitten, and hurriedly stowing that out of sight. When you wake in the morning, the naughtiness and evil passions with which you went to bed have been folded up small and placed at the bottom of your mind and on the top, beautifully aired, are spread out your prettier thoughts ready for you to put on.

(Barrie, 1911, p. 12 cited by Waddell, 1998, p. 35)

Bion (1962ab, 1965) envisages this function by considering how the breast is a "thinking breast". Its function is to transform and make more tolerable for the infant's mind the emotions and feelings that the infant projects into it. It supplies the infant with meaning, understanding as well as love. While for Melanie Klein the breast is a metaphor for primary maternal functions, such as feeding, gratifying and satisfying, for Bion it is a metaphor for the mind. When the parent brings her mothering and loving abilities to the infant, she brings her thinking self, her mental and emotional states which, by embracing the chaos of the infant's mental life, support the infant's processes of self-integration.[8]

While the object is active in achieving this reflexive function, it should be emphasized how active the infant is as well in this intersubjective process. Infant observation shows their extraordinary ability to reach for their object, to reach for the parent, to bring the parent into existence, to create the parent or the feeling of parenthood, to animate or revive their object. We can see, for example, all the work that an infant does when his mother has her mind elsewhere, is not in contact with him, to bring the mother back to him. For instance, he will be interested in what interests the mother, in an attitude of joint attention, then he will reproduce, between the mother and himself, what he has grasped from the scene which kept the mother away from him; he will try to catch her eye until the mother makes contact with him, etc.

It is indeed such early quests for the object, among others, which oblige us to reconsider the notion of primary narcissism, and to think of it otherwise than as simply describing a state of nondifferentiation, which is partly the aim of this book.[9]

Infant observation shows their ability to adapt to the environment. Infants are relatively competent at adapting and transforming their object. Obviously, not all babies are equally competent, and not all environments, objects and parents are as easy to revive psychically. But interactionists who do microanalysis have shown that three-quarters of the interactions are adjustment interactions (Tronick and Cohn, 1989). Only a quarter of the interactions with an infant produce contact, communication, communion, you could say. In other words, it is normal to fail in this respect. The object does psychic work, adjusts, and the infant also makes an effort; he is forced to make an effort to meet the object, to be in contact with it – even if the two partners are obviously not in a symmetrical, equivalent position.

Interactionists, like developmental psychologists, have in particular studied and created models, in their own way, of intersubjective experiences. Daniel Stern (1985), for example, proposed the very central notion of "affective tuning", which we have discussed (Chapter 3). Others had spoken long before of "interactive synchrony" (Brazelton et al., 1974; Condon and Sandler, 1974; Bower, 1977). Affective tuning describes the fact, for the mother or for the adult interacting with the infant, to translate an emotional state of the infant by a behaviour, by an expression whose form, including intonation, will reproduce the form, intensity and rhythm of the expression the infant has produced in the interaction. Affective tuning results from an adult's intimate understanding of the infant's subjective experience. And Stern shows well how the more the infant experiences affective tuning, the more he has the feeling that emotional life, subjective life, subjectivity is shareable. The less the baby benefits from affective tuning behaviours, the more he will have the feeling that the subjectivity is not shareable. Daniel Stern (1997, 2003) has also described in detail the "moments of encounter"; he has explored and modelled the conditions and the intersubjective modifications relating to the experiences of encounter between an infant and his partner, or between a patient and his therapist. One could say that these experiences produce intersubjectivity and have an effect on the growth of each of the partners.

There are a number of indicators that point to an experience of intersubjectivity in the infant. Colwyn Trevarthen, for example, has described very well the "proto-conversations" between the infant and his partner from the first months, the behaviours of "intersubjective control" after six months, where the infant acts and observes, in order to see the effect produced, performing an "emotional and shareable assessment of reality", developing a "shared consciousness" (Trevarthen, 1979, 1989ab; Trevarthen and Aitken, 1996). He has demonstrated the early nature of these experiences of intersubjective sharing, during which the infant displays immediately, in the very first months, sensitivity to the feelings, interests and intentions of those around him.

An index of intersubjectivity is represented by the "referential gaze", the "social reference", terms which describe the way in which the infant refers to the expression on his partner's face and the affect that it communicates (contentment, anger, fear) before taking action or in order to understand the meaning of an enigmatic situation (see Sorce and Emde, 1981; Klinnert, 1985; Sameroff and Emde, 1989). Faced with an unknown, enigmatic or uncertain situation, the infant will read the meaning of the situation on the face of the other, of the adult present, and will regulate his behaviour according to the emotional signal that this adult is giving. The infant is thus seeking a common experience, a shared subjective experience. When the adult encourages his activity, approves his intention to act, the infant will experience a "dyadic ego" (Emde and Oppenheim, 1995); he will feel supported in his undertaking and experience.

Other indicators of intersubjectivity in the infant are given by the behaviours of "joint attention" (Bruner, 1975) – sharing an event with others, achieving shared contemplation –, by the behaviours of "proto-declarative pointing" (Bretherton and Bates, 1979) – showing others where an event occurs – behaviours and conduct that bear witness to the constitution of what cognitivists call a "theory of mind" (see Baron-Cohen et al., 1985; Leslie, 1987; Frith, 1989, Frith et al., 1991), an expression which reflects the recognition of a thought in oneself and in others, a singular thought specific to each. We have discussed these notions in connection with the neuropsychological and neurodevelopmental theories of autism (Chapter 2), and a certain number of studies in the cognitive field have shown that the absence of these behaviours, of these indicators of intersubjectivity, heralds autistic development. Indeed, an infant who at 18 months has never had a behaviour of joint attention, who has never had a gesture of proto-declarative pointing, who has never shown a referential glance and who, moreover, has never had a game of make-believe, is a baby who has a very high probability of becoming autistic (see Baron-Cohen et al., 1992, 1996). The absence of these signs attests to a failure of intersubjectivity, characteristic of autism.

What developmental psychologists call "reflexive consciousness" appears from the age of 18 months onwards (see Emde, 1999), which can be considered as the effect of the outcome of repeated experiences of affective sharing. The child is capable, for example, not only of getting in contact with a feeling of disarray experienced by another person, but also of getting involved in this situation by acts addressed to the other: from 18 months onwards the child can take care of another child in distress, comfort him and help him.

In all these situations of intersubjectivity, briefly outlined above, we can say that intersubjective sharing leads the child to three types of experience, which can overlap:

- the first is learning, understanding, forming a mental image of another person's affects, another person's emotions, thereby gaining an understanding of his mental states;
- the second is the infant's understanding of his own affects and emotions reflected or indicated by the other person, by the object – indicated or even transmitted and imposed by the object;
- the third is the infant's exploration of his own affects or emotions inside the object, inside another mental space (this is a definition of projective identification, or a form of projective identification – we will come back to this).

Thus the infant's thinking is set in motion, his own thoughts are "fabricated" and developed.

10.1.3 A junction point between perception and intersubjectivity: the mutual gaze

The experience connecting the two poles, perceptual and intersubjective, of the constitution of thoughts, resides in exchanges or perceptual sharing, and particularly in the exchanges of gazes, in the mutual gazes which allow and support the sharing and transmission of psychic elements, and in particular affects.

What happens in the exchange of gazes between the infant and his partner?

Daniel Marcelli (2006), referring to certain ethological studies,[10] recalls that exchanging gazes is characteristic of the human world. In the animal world, looking into the eyes of another animal is a sign of a conflict, a threat, and such an exchange between two members of the same species is extremely rare and particularly brief. Even in monkeys, the animals closest to humans, there is hardly ever a shared gaze, nor joint attention between a mother and her cub. Even if the little chimpanzee is seeking his mother's gaze, she does not return the look. Exchanging gazes almost immediately leads to avoidance.

The ability to share gazes over the long term seems very specific to the human race. Through exchanging gazes, human beings have gained an inter-relational dimension that is fundamental to their human condition.

How does it start in the infant? How and why do parents and infants look at each other?

Looking at the other person is a way for the infant to see the other person but also to see himself. It is the same in any intimate bond, as in the state of love, for example. Each person sees himself in the partner's gaze, in the interest the latter shows in them, making them feel they exist and reflecting an image of them.

Although we continue to speak, ever since Winnicott (1967), of the mother's face as a mirror for the infant – the infant sees himself in the gaze of his mother looking at him –, it should be added that the same thing can be said of the infant's face: it is also a mirror for the parent.

What does the parent see in the infant's gaze? He sees himself, he feels he exists as a parent, as a good parent when the infant gratifies him with an intense look and a broad smile. He sees his narcissism comforted, confirmed and repaired. But we can also wonder what the parent sees when the infant looks away, avoids his look, refuses to look at him. He will see himself as a bad parent, and he will also possibly see the face of his own parent, if he was devaluing, unloving and abusive.

The way the parent interprets the manifestations of the infant's gaze, his turning away, for instance, will of course be decisive for the infant's ability to see himself in the parent's eyes. The more the parent interprets the infant's withdrawal as an abandonment, as a repetition of the withdrawals, avoidances, and coldness of the objects that the parent himself may have known, the more the development of parenting will be stunted, and thus the development of the infant himself, who will not be able to find in the parent's gaze the support needed for his narcissistic construction. How the infant sees himself in the parental gaze is dependent on the reaction of the parent to the movements of the infant's gaze, on the projections that the parental gaze conveys to the infant, and on the quality and nature of the parental gaze towards him.

The parental gaze carries projections relating to the experience of parenthood and the phantasied place in which the infant is put. Daniel Marcelli (2006) distinguishes, in a very evocative way, three types of maternal gaze – but one can say parental – directed at infant, at his birth:

- the first is *"envisagement"*: the mother, serene, because everything has gone well, looks at the baby's gaze, thinks of him, dreams, imagines what he will become. She *en*-visages all the possibilities for the baby;
- the second is *"de-visagement"*: it characterizes the look of a worried mother, for whom the prenatal or perinatal conditions were anxiogenic. The mother scrutinizes the baby, wonders if everything is going well, if everything is normal. She *de*-visages the baby;
- the third, finally, is *"inenvisagement"*: the mother experienced a trauma, a bereavement, for example, during pregnancy; her gaze is then absent. Or else it engulfs the infant's: it does not accommodate the infant's eyes, but searches for its lost object, beyond the infant's gaze. She *in*-envisages the infant.

These different qualities of the gaze – if they persist and qualify the bond durably – will of course have effects on the way in which the infant himself cathects the object and the world, and is involved in mutual gazing.

It can be said that mutual gazing is at the source of intersubjectivity. It is its witness and the condition of its emergence – or one of the conditions. Through mutual gazing, the infant and his partner seek a sharing of affect, emotion, and as a corollary, a sharing of intention, as Marcelli emphasizes. The purpose of making eye contact is to establish contact with the other, to better perceive his affective state or his emotional intimacy when he is an interlocutor, to better grasp the depth of his thoughts, as well as his intention. Each seeks the affective state of the other, and each seeks or attributes an intention to the gaze of the other. The exchange of gazes is thus a witness to the activity of intersubjective processes.

The place of the gaze, of exchanging gazes, is obviously central in the realization of the behaviours of affective tuning and moments of encounter described by Stern, of which we have spoken, as well as in all the experiences of affective interactions, of transmissions of affects.

The exchange of gazes is also at the source of imitation, of social cohesion, as Marcelli again emphasizes, of the recognition of the other and of oneself as a human being and a relational being. Note that in the exchange of looks, it is obviously not only the look that is seen by the infant, as by any subject; it is the whole face.

Let us recall with Marcelli that the infant's ability to imitate appears very early on – in other words, his ability to establish social ties, and to maintain a mutual gaze. We are familiar with Meltzoff's experiments (Meltzoff and Moore, 1977, 1983, 1994; Meltzoff, 2002), which show that as early as 12 days old, an infant can imitate certain behaviours, such as protruding the tongue and opening the mouth. He can even imitate a few minutes later (for example, if he has a dummy that prevents him from sticking out his tongue, he will do it a few minutes later, even if he is in front of a still face). At six weeks, an infant can even reproduce the next day an imitation made the day before with a partner, when he meets this person again, as if to verify that it is indeed the same person, waiting for the latter to produce the same gesture and to respond to his call. These imitations are, moreover, transmodal: for instance, a three-month-old infant will look at the eyes and mouth of his interlocutor and react by effecting movements of his face and hands or by vocalizing in response to the changes in vocal expression of the adult; furthermore, he will do all this in rhythmic coordination with him (Trevarthen and Aitken, 1997) – in other words, it is the rhythm which he imitates.

Human imitation is not simply the reproduction of perceived behaviour. It supposes an attentive gaze, and an attribution of affect, emotion or intention that the infant, by imitating, will try to share, or that the adult, by supporting the movement of the infant and by imitating him too, will also try to transmit.

Furthermore, in experiences of mutual attention, it is the infant who controls the exchange. We know, in fact, that the average duration of moments of mutual visual attention of the infant at three or four months is five seconds, while that of the adult is 20 seconds (Stern, 1974). It is therefore inevitably the infant who controls mutual attention. And there will be a problem if the parent retains control: there will be an impingement, an effect of overexcitation. The difficulty can of course come from the fact that the parent, as indicated above, sees in the infant's look a devaluation of his parenthood and experiences the infant's withdrawal as a rejection of himself, a rejection of his proposition of linking link: exchange and interaction will then be interrupted.

The gaze can thus be an attractor but also a persecutor. The adult's gaze is a powerful attractor and stimulator for the infant, as is the infant's gaze for the adult. Eye contact and sharing will stabilize the behaviours of the infant, like those of his partner. But while the gaze is an attractor, it can also be very much a persecutor. The mutual gaze and sharing by means of the gaze can be weakening; they can give rise to persecuting and terrifying anxieties and, if these are not contained, recognized and dealt with, the diversion or avoidance of the gaze will become a defensive measure in the infant as with any other subject. We know the extent to which the gaze of the other can be avoided when it is experienced as penetrating, as is the case for the psychotic or autistic child, and how much his own gaze can similarly be used as an intrusive, attacking and penetrating weapon in turn.

We know that certain beliefs, moreover, attribute to the gaze an evil potentiality, and to eye contact a capacity to transmit the "evil eye", the evil. Thus, in certain traditional societies, for example, one should never look directly into the eyes of an infant or subject it to any face-to-face stimulation (Héritier-Augé,1987, cited by Marcelli, 2006).

10.2 The hallucination of the object of satisfaction of the need

Let us now look at the first forms of thought-activity in the infant, starting with the question of hallucination, a figure of primitive thinking according to Freud.

Freud advanced the hypothesis that the baby hallucinates the object of satisfaction of the need in its absence, provided that a primary and primordial experience of satisfaction of need has already taken place. The development of thought is based, for Freud, on the hallucination of the absent object which itself is based on memory traces of the experience of satisfaction of need. How does the transition occur from the primary experience of satisfaction to the hallucination of the object?

In the "Project for a scientific psychology", Freud (1895) explains that when a state of *urgency* and *wishing* reappears, the "mnemic image of the object" is reactivated, and that "in the first instance this wishful activation will produce the same thing as a perception – namely a *hallucination*" (p. 319). In *The Interpretation of Dreams*, Freud (1900) describes how an essential component of the experience of satisfaction of an internal need (for example hunger) is "a particular perception (nourishment, in the example chosen) the mnemic image of which remains associated thenceforward with the memory trace associated with the memory trace of the excitation produced by the need" (p. 565). It is therefore necessary to dissociate in this first experience of satisfaction the "mnemic image", which is the image of the object – Freud specifies that it is food in the example of hunger and by metonymic association we can say that it is the breast in the Kleinian sense of the term –, and the "memory trace" which designates the memory of the need, the memory of psychophysiological tension. Freud underlines the association between the mnemic image of the object and the memory trace of the need:

> As a result of the link that has been established, next time this need arises a psychical impulse will at once emerge which will seek to recathect the mnemic image of the perception, and to re-evoke the perception itself, that is to say, to re-establish the situation of the original satisfaction.
> (Freud, 1900, p. 565–566)

In other words, the experience of satisfaction establishes in the psyche a link between the experience of need and the object of satisfaction, which – the experience and the need – are impressed on memory.[11] When the felt need arises again, the psyche, thanks to the work of linking carried out in the first experience, will recathect the image of the object, that is to say, will hallucinate the object of satisfaction. This hallucination will make it possible to tolerate waiting and frustration. Thus, when satisfaction is hallucinated, perception is actualized, and a "perceptual identity" is produced (Freud, 1900, p. 566). As the hallucination is not satisfactory, the hallucinatory "regression" must be brought to a halt before it proceeds beyond the mnemic image of the object, beyond its perceptual trace; it will then seek out other paths so that the perceptual identity can be established with objects from the outside world. It is this activity which corresponds to thought proper, which Freud defines as a "substitute for a hallucinatory wish" (p. 567). Hallucination is therefore very much at the foundation of thought. And yet this proposition is questionable.

This hallucination process of the object of satisfaction, as Freud conceives it, is equivalent to that which we have described with regard to projective identification with the internal object (Chapter 1). It is based on the meeting between a capacity for linking and introjection on the part of the psyche, and the presence on the external stage of an adequate nourishing object. The first introjections can thus be understood as the activation of the first thoughts, which contribute to psychic separation-individuation and to the development of the internal world.

In addition, hallucination of the object, to use Freud's terms, is a temporary remedy, and must not replace the perception of lack for too long. The pathologization resulting from an excessive use of such a process will lead, as we have seen, to the development of the autarchic world of psychosis, where the subject turns away from any object relationship and abuses the delusion that we understand, and as we have already pointed out (Chapter 1), as an extreme state of projective identification with internal objects. If the world of the psychotic subject – in a state of "psychosis proper" – is composed of hallucinations of objects, that of the autistic subject – in a state of "proper autism" – will be composed of hallucinations of sensations. The psychotic subject deprives himself of the objectalizing capacities of his *perceptual apparatus* in order not to experience separation; he clings to his "perceptions of internal objects", lives within his ideal and idiosyncratic picture of the world, in projective identification with his objects. The autistic subject, for his part, deprives himself of the objectalizing capacities of his *sensory apparatus* and escapes the experience of separation by means of the hallucinatory search not for the object but for the sensation that the object would produce. His identification with objects, as we have seen (Chapter 5), is an adhesive identification. Frances Tustin (1987) considers that autistic objects and forms represent "idiosyncratic hallucinations" that prevent the child from coming into contact with common sense facts and prevent him from experiencing the absent object.

The hallucination of the object, as an act of psychic cathexis distant from perceptions, that is to say as a primary thought process, is in itself unconscious and only acquires the possibility of becoming conscious when, according to Freud, it links the perceptual traces of objects to the residues of verbal perceptions. This idea is present already in the "Project for of a scientific psychology" (1895) and is set out in *The Interpretation of Dreams* (1900). Freud returns to it in "Formulations on the two principles of mental functioning" (1911a). He specifies there the principle to which conscious thought is subject, namely the reality principle: the state of need calls for the hallucination of the object; the persistence of the need prompts the psychical apparatus to represent the real state of the outside world and to seek an actual modification. The representation of what is pleasant (pleasure principle) gives way to the representation of what is real, even if unpleasant (reality principle). With the introduction of the reality principle, a form of thought-activity remains split off and subject only to the pleasure principle: it is at the origin of the creation of phantasies. Freud returns, in "The unconscious" (1915b), as if he had rediscovered it with more clarity, to the idea that conscious thought is determined by the links between perceptions/thing-presentations and perceptions/word-presentations. The former remain unconscious; only their links with the second can give them the possibility of acquiring conscious status.

A major difficulty stems from the use of the term "hallucination" by Freud (1900) to designate different experiences: the primary experience of an original thought resulting from the quest for "perceptual identity", that is, a repetition of the perception of the object of satisfaction of the need; the psychotic experience in which satisfaction has not appeased the need, the internal cathexis equivalent to the perception being maintained in a permanent, continuous manner, while psychic activity exhausts itself in retaining the desired object; the experience of the dream, finally, fulfilling the wish by means of regression to a primary psychic activity exempt from any consideration of concrete reality. How far can these contexts be considered similar? Thought, as a "substitute for a hallucinatory wish", as Freud calls it, cannot arise with the same consistency from these three types of experience. It is paradoxical to conceive that a thought can arise from a hallucination, which may be defined rather as an "anti-thought", an alternative or a dead end to the work of thought.

René Roussillon (1995), with his conception of "primary symbolization", extends and adds complexity to Freud's propositions,

The development of thought-activity

clarifying more precisely these primary processes. René Roussillon takes up Winnicott's conceptions (1951, 1952a, 1960b, 1971), relating to transitionality and the object's inherent work of adaptation, and builds the model of primary symbolization. Primary symbolization refers to the process of creating thing-presentations from primary hallucination. Primary symbolization is a linking activity between a mnemic trace and a thing-presentation; it transforms perceptual traces into thing-presentations (secondary symbolization consisting in establishing a link between thing- and word-presentations). The thing-presentation results from the conjunction of a hallucination with an analogous perception, which produces a transformation of the hallucination: the hallucination is transformed into an *illusion*, in the Winnicottian sense. This is in the context of the "found-created" described by Winnicott, which assumes that the object, if sufficiently adapted, satisfies the infant at the moment when the latter feels the need for satisfaction. As Winnicott (1960b) puts it, the "good enough" mother responds and adapts to the infant's spontaneous gesture and sensory hallucination. In doing so, she attunes to the "true self", and the infant can begin to enjoy the *illusion* of omnipotently creating and controlling the object. This is the foundation of symbol formation according to Winnicott. Illusion, the transformation of a hallucination due to its coincidence with an analogous perception, opens up the field to the production of primary symbols.[12] Primary symbolization thus presupposes a *transitional* stage, between hallucination and the thing-presentation.

Mnemic traces, of experiences of satisfaction as well as of dissatisfaction, are reactivated by the *compulsion to repeat* (Freud, 1920); they require symbolization, a work of primary symbolization, along with the creation of primary symbols and thing-presentations. And this, as René Roussillon emphasizes, requires the intervention of the object, an externalization in the thing. The role of the object is thus fundamental for primary symbolization. If the object satisfies, it offers a coincidence between hallucination and perception, which produces an illusion. The Winnicottian term "found-created" describes this coincidence between a hallucination of satisfaction and a similar perception, and René Roussillon proposes another expression, that of "destroyed-found", or "destroyed-(re) found" (see Roussillon, 1991, 1995, 1999) to designate the meeting between the activation of a toxic perceptual trace and an experience of real satisfaction. The "destroyed-found" corresponds to the perceptual denial of primary destructiveness, of primary dissatisfaction (the subject destroys, the object survives). If the object fails in this function of producing coincidence, or "presenting objects", as Winnicott (1962a) says, if the object fails to belie the primary hallucination of dissatisfaction, of destruction, a "primary narcissistic encystment of earlier experiences may occur which are then condemned to be hallucinatorily activated and to harass the psychic apparatus in a persecutory fashion" (Roussillon, 1995, p. 1439, translated for this edition).[13]

For a primary symbol, a thing-presentation, to occur, the hallucination must therefore coincide with a "perception", and the object must in reality carry out the work that is necessary for the subject to experience this coincidence. However, continuing to call this primitive state of thinking "hallucination" is questionable. Bion (1962a), for example, as we shall see, already used this same model but without resorting to hallucination: he spoke of "preconception" (empty thought, waiting for the object) which, combined with a "realization" (satisfaction, meeting the object), produces a "conception" (which he differentiated from "thought" proper – we will come back to this). He described the first matrix from which thoughts arise, as we have seen (Chapters 2 and 3) in terms of "beta elements" (Bion, 1962ab, 1963), raw impressions arising from the senses – hallucination corresponding to one of the vicissitudes of beta elements when they become what Bion called "bizarre objects" (Bion, 1956, 1957, 1958, 1962b).

To return now to the primary hallucination, the hallucination of the object of satisfaction. This is not only at the origin of thought – under the conditions that we have just described –, but also translates the emergence of phantasy, which underlies thought-activity. This takes us back to the line of continuity between need/wish/phantasy in Freud's words. The psychic impulse of which Freud speaks (1900), arising from the re-presentation of the need, which leads to the cathexis of the mnemic image of the object of satisfaction, is defined by Freud as the wish. Hallucinatory satisfaction corresponds to wish-fulfilment. In other words, the movement that tends to produce the hallucination is called the wish, while the hallucination itself realizes the wish-fulfilment. Phantasy is nothing other than the staging of this hallucinatory fulfilment of the experience of satisfaction.

Susan Isaacs (1952) links phantasies to the instinctual drive impulses in which they find their source. She defines phantasy as "the mental corollary, the psychical representative, of instinct" (Isaacs, 1952, p. 83). She considers the very first phantasies, whose imaginary or hallucinatory fulfilment is not distinguished from actual fulfilment, as "affective interpretations of bodily sensations" (ibid., p. 96). Laplanche and Pontalis (1964), for their part, insist on the link which unites phantasy more specifically with wish than with need or drive. It is in the gap between wish and need, in the disjunction between the reduction of need by real experience and wish-fulfilment through hallucinatory reliving that phantasy emerges. The origin of phantasy is thus linked by Laplanche and Pontalis to the appearance of autoerotism, that is to say, at the time when the vital functions are detached from the world of needs to join and create that of sexuality.

If we followed these authors, and if we remember that autoerotism, in the sense that we defined it (Chapter 2), that is to say, as the narcissistic recathexis of an object relationship following the loss of the real object – and this is how Laplanche and Pontalis understand it –, is absent in the purely autistic states, for lack of introjective capacity, and is replaced by auto-sensuality, we would be led to postulate the absence of phantasy life in the autistic mental state. It is true that Meltzer considers the autistic state proper to be essentially without mental activity (Meltzer et al., 1975). But the clinical observation of children and adults with autism bears witness to hallucinatory states, even at the most dismantled moments in these patients, whose behaviour sometimes seems to correspond to purely internal excitations which are part of a process that suggests the presence of phantasy activity. Since purely autistic states are only virtual, it is possible that these manifestations are attributable to the symbiotic part which developed in spite of the autistic nucleus. However, as we said before, we consider "phantasy" activity of a purely autistic nature as staging not objects, but rather bodily sensations or *images of bodily sensations*. Autistic thought-activity is not non-existent but could be defined as an "activity of no-thought", as a movement activating hallucinations of dismantled bodily sensations, that is to say, non-thoughts. We will see with Bion the nature of the elements that can be considered to have reached the status of thought.

10.3 The formation of symbols

We have mentioned primary symbolization, as described by René Roussillon. We will now return to the symbol-formation as envisaged by Melanie Klein and Hanna Segal.

Symbol-formation, and its role in the development of the ego, are explained by Melanie Klein in a 1930 article based on the analysis of a four-year-old child, Dick, presenting an exceptional early inhibition of development. Dick's analysis allowed Melanie Klein to observe in this child a total and apparently constitutional incapacity to tolerate anxiety, as well as a premature defence against sadism, due to an exaggerated identification with the object treated sadistically. This premature and exaggerated defence against sadistic tendencies directed against the maternal body and its contents resulted in a paralysis of all phantasy life and all activity of symbol-formation. Melanie Klein was thus led to conclude that symbolism originates in sadism, driven by the interest shown in the mother's body and its contents. Oral and muscular sadism (biting, tearing, grinding) and urethral and anal sadism (cutting, stabbing, burning, drowning) transform the functions of the body into destructive actions and the contents of the body into dangerous weapons.

Sadism thus gives rise to anxiety because it becomes a source of danger and because the ego feels threatened by the weapons it has used to destroy the object from which it now fears reprisals. It is therefore anxiety, more than libidinal interest, that drives the child to liken the organs (penis, vagina, breast, mouth) with other objects, which in turn will become a source of anxiety, thus leading the child to constantly establish new equations, which is the basis of symbolism and interest in new objects. Excessive intolerance to anxiety will prevent the establishment of a relationship with reality, inhibit the epistemophilic impulse and halt the development of phantasy life. Symbolism, thus interrupted, will give way to the characteristic withdrawal of early psychoses, one of the symptoms of which is a lack of affect and anxiety.

In a 1957 article, Hanna Segal locates the starting point of the process of symbol-formation in the first projections and identifications of the infant, in other words in the projective identification processes, processes prevalent during the paranoid-schizoid or symbiotic phase or position. In projective identification, the infant projects in phantasy large parts of himself into the object, and this object is then identified with the parts of the self that are felt to be contained within it. The parts of the outside world into which internal objects are projected are identified with these objects which they come to represent.

These early symbols, says Segal, are felt by the ego not to be symbols or substitutes but to be the original object itself, and she suggests designating them by the term "symbolic equations". Segal sees the symbolic equation as the basis of the schizophrenic's concrete thought.[14] Substitutes are felt and treated as if they were *identical* to, or barely different from, the original object. This is mainly due to the fact that in massive projective identification the ego returns to a state of confusion with the object; the symbol merges with the thing symbolized and therefore becomes a symbolic equation.[15]

However, in a 1979 postscript to this article (in Segal, 1981), Segal specifies that it is not projective identification in itself that leads to concretization, but the particular relationship between the projected part and the object into which it is projected. This coincides with our point that pathologization is not just an amplification of early phenomena but also corresponds to a distortion of these same phenomena, in particular due to the work of destructiveness.

The absence of symbol-formation, as in the case of Dick – on the subject of which Segal (1957) suggests that it could be a formation of many symbolic equations rather than an absence of formation of symbolic relations with the outside world – as well as the formation of symbolic equations, produce the same result, namely a poverty of thought, an inhibition of intellectual development and an inadequacy of the functioning of cognitive processes. But the formation of symbolic equations is part of the normal development of thought during the paranoid-schizoid phase: the function of the symbolic equation is to deny the absence of the ideal object or to control the persecuting object; the symbolic substitute is felt to *be* the original object. On the other hand, the symbol proper, whose formation is located in the depressive position, is felt to be a *representative* of the original object; the symbol is not intended to deny the loss, it is used to overcome it. If depressive anxiety becomes insurmountable and projective identification is used again as a defence, symbols can return to the state of symbolic equations.

Symbolic equations therefore characterize the paranoid-schizoid position, and symbols the depressive position. The symbol becomes a representative of the object, rather than an equivalent of the object, only when separation is accepted, only when the symbiosis is resolved. This is how the symbol is seen by Segal (1981) as a "precipitate of a process of mourning" (p. 90):

> Only what can be adequately mourned can be adequately symbolized.
>
> (Segal, 1981, p. 91)

The approach to the depressive position is a powerful stimulant to the creation of symbols, because the ego is more and more concerned with protecting the object which it perceives as whole and unified from its aggressiveness and possessiveness. The symbol, no longer identified with the original object, helps to displace the aggressiveness and thus reduce guilt and the fear of loss. In addition, the symbol, created in the internal world, helps to restore and take possession again of the original object injured in sadistic phantasies. Another function of the symbol lies in communication, not only communication with the outside world but also internal communication: the ability to communicate with oneself, to be "in touch" with one's unconscious phantasies, with one's internal world, is based on the ability to form symbols. This capacity for symbolization makes it possible to deal not only with depressive anxieties, situations of mourning, but also unresolved early conflicts, anxieties that could not be faced because of the overly concrete aspect of experience with the object and the substitutes of the object in symbolic equations.

Hanna Segal (1957) says that the process of symbol-formation is "a continuous process of bringing together and integrating the internal with the external, the subject with the object and earlier experiences with the later ones" (p. 397). This consideration, which introduces the temporality of experience, speaks of access to the fourth dimension of psychic space (Meltzer et al., 1975) revealing the creation of an internalized historicity which is achieved in the depressive position.[16]

10.4 Development of thoughts and thought-activity

In his articles from 1954 to 1958, Bion explains how the acquisition of verbal thought depends on gaining access to the depressive position, whilst at the same time determining it. Verbal thought synthesizes and articulates sense-impressions. It thus plays an essential role in awareness of internal and external reality, and is therefore subject to attacks aimed at denying the reality of separation and the pain of depression.

The development of thought-activity

Verbal thought develops from "primitive thought", of the preverbal type, the foundations of which are established in the paranoid-schizoid phase – or position –, provided that splitting and projective identification are not too marked. Primitive thought is formed from the connections between sense-impressions on the one hand, and between sense-impressions and consciousness on the other, that is to say, from awareness of sensory information. It consists of a "primitive matrix of ideographs [which] contains within itself links between one ideograph and another" (Bion, 1957, p. 269). These ideographs are essentially composed of visual images – which seem to be of the same order as the "thing-presentations" of which Freud speaks and which we have mentioned above. Primitive thinking, based on the activity of linking, comes from the non-psychotic part of the personality.

If splitting and projective identification are exaggerated, the attacks on linking, due to the psychotic part of the personality, will lead to the creation of "bizarre objects" (see Chapter 3). These are "prototype ideas" that can, for example, produce hallucinations. Excessive attacks on linking by means of splitting and projection rid the psyche of what unites, of what binds, so that the psychotic subject, or the psychotic part of his personality, can "compress" but cannot unite, can "merge" or "agglomerate" but cannot articulate. In psychosis, the processes of compression or agglomeration replace the processes of linking.

In 1962 Bion (1962a) proposed his theory of thinking. He classifies thoughts chronologically into preconceptions, conceptions or thoughts and concepts. He also adds beta elements, alpha elements and dream thoughts (see Chapter 3), but it was in 1963 that he was to classify more precisely these three primitive thought-objects in the development of thought, the beta element representing "the first matrix from which thoughts can be supposed to arise" (1963, p. 22).

The *preconception* is defined as an "empty thought". Bion gives as an example the "innate disposition corresponding to the expectation of the breast", the "*a priori* knowledge of the breast". The *conception* differs from the thought. The conception results from a conjunction between a preconception (expectation of the breast) and a realization (meeting with the real breast). The conception is therefore the result of an emotional experience of satisfaction. *Thought*, on the other hand, is generated by the mating of a preconception with frustration.

How does thought develop? A preconception (expectation of the breast) combined with frustration (absence of the breast) is experienced as a "no-breast", a bad internal "no-breast". If *the capacity to bear frustration* is sufficient, this bad internal "no-breast" becomes a thought which makes the tolerated frustration even more tolerable. This is how an apparatus for thinking thoughts is developed. If the capacity to bear frustration is insufficient, instead of modifying the experience of frustration, the mind can only evade it. Instead of a thought, a bad object then presents itself, the only fate of which is to be evacuated, evacuation merging with the actual realization of satisfaction. In this case, the only purpose of breastfeeding is to avoid awareness of separation, which may explain greed, for example. Everything that could become a thought is dealt with by evacuation, and instead of a thinking apparatus, an "apparatus for projective identification" develops to rid the psyche of bad internal objects.

To return now to the conception (conjunction of a preconception with a realization). As experiences of satisfaction are repeated, the conception can itself be treated as a preconception. If the realization that unites with the conception turns out to be negative or unsatisfactory, the consequences will differ depending, once again, on *tolerance of frustration*. Insufficient capacity to tolerate frustration will lead to *omnipotence* and *omniscience*. Sufficient capacity to tolerate frustration will support the development of *learning from experience*. Bion instances as an example the apprehension of what is true and what is false. Omniscience, which is based on an intolerance of frustration, that is to say, an intolerance of the necessary doubt accompanying any activity of knowledge, leads to the dictatorial assertion that a thing is true or false, good or bad. Learning from experience, on the other hand, fosters discrimination between what is true and false.[17]

Let us dwell on the distinction that Bion offers between conception and thought in order to try to understand this better – although in his later texts dealing with the development of thoughts and thought-activity, Bion (1962b, 1963, 1965, 1970) does not seem to come back to this distinction, which seems essential to us (see, nonetheless, *Learning from Experience*, where Bion (1962b) postulates that the bad breast, that is to say, the desired but absent breast, is much more likely to be recognized as an idea than the good breast, that is to say, the breast that gives itself).

In order to picture the difference between a conception and a thought, imagine the following situation: a researcher is confronted with a problem that he has to solve, and he has the feeling that there is a mathematical formula which can bring him the solution. We can say that this feeling represents a preconception. If a mentor who knows this formula reveals and explains it to him, we are in the situation where a preconception coincides with a realization. The conception will emerge in the mind of the researcher when he can say to himself: "That's it, I've understood". Now suppose that the researcher, wishing to grow in the image of his mentor, remains or is left in his solitude and by dint of tenacity discovers for himself the formula allowing him to solve his problem. When the researcher can say to himself: "That's it, I've found it", we will be in the situation where thought appears. However, if this researcher cannot tolerate the pain inherent in his ignorance combined with his desire to know, then rather than looking for the formula using his experience, and referring to his mentor, he may be tempted to invent a formula and nourish the illusion that he has solved his problem, which corresponds to omnipotence and omniscience.

We would say that for the non-psychotic personality, or for the non-psychotic part of the personality, the situation by which the desired breast is absent presents itself to the psyche in the following form: "I miss the breast, I think of it, that is to say I imagine it satisfying me, but I still miss it because the hallucinatory satisfaction does not satisfy me". On the other hand, for the psychotic part of the personality, the idea that the breast is not there is unthinkable and its absence is reflected in the mind by "the breast is there". The need and the pain related to waiting are evacuated by identification projection, and omnipotent hallucinatory satisfaction is ensured by projective identification with the internal object which leads to the certainty that: "I cannot feel any need for the breast, for I am the omnipotent breast".

We have considered the preconception, the conception and thought. What about the concept? Bion defines the concept as a conception or a named thought, that is to say, fixed. In *Elements of Psychoanalysis*, Bion (1963) explains that "the concept is derived from conception by a process designed to render it free of those elements that would unfit it to be a tool in the elucidation or expression of truth" (p. 24). Let us underline the example he offers in *Learning from Experience* (1962b) to illustrate what the concept represents: an infant sees a man he feels loved by and he hears his mother repeating the phrase, "That's Daddy"; the infant says "Da-da-da" and his mother answers "That's right, Daddy". From this emotional experience the infant abstracts certain elements which, when they appear to be conjoined in other situations, are given the name "Daddy". The hypothesis called "Daddy" therefore corresponds to a "statement that certain elements are constantly conjoined" (p. 67). This statement is a concept. So the concept is derived from an abstraction.

Bion (1962a) proposes the idea that all of these "thoughts" require an apparatus to play the same role as the alpha function, namely of transforming sense-data. Thoughts must be transformed before they can be communicated. Thoughts are thus prior, epistemologically, to thinking.[18] These primitive thoughts, these "proto-thoughts" are nothing but beta elements that the mind must deal with either by evasion or by modification. Evasion, which consists in getting rid of the proto-thought, will produce a new beta element, an exciting element that will again have to be evacuated. Modification, on the other hand, corresponds to the activity of thinking and produces alpha elements.[19]

Thought-activity is based on the existence of alpha elements available for thought, and on the existence of an apparatus for processing thoughts. Alpha elements are provided by the alpha function (see Chapter 3). The thinking apparatus is formed by the internalization of the "container-contained apparatus" resulting from the infant's experience of his emotions being understood by his environment (see Chapter 3). The infant's thought-activity is thus dependent on the exercise of the alpha function of the container (mothering object), in which the projected contents (raw experiences of the infant) have been deposited, which is capable of transforming them. Mental growth is based on the internalization of this container-contained apparatus formed from the process of projective identification (Bion was to develop and expand this model in 1970 in *Attention and Interpretation*).

Finally, it is in *Elements of Psycho-Analysis* (1963) that the Bionian theory of thinking finds its completion with the famous "Grid" through which Bion offers a repertoire of thoughts according to their nature, structure and function. The Grid has a certain number of columns corresponding to a systematic categorization of the use that can be made of thoughts, and a certain number of lines representing a genetic classification of thoughts. The conjunction between the nature of a thought (beta element, alpha element, dream thought, preconception, conception, concept, etc.) and its use (definition, notation, investigation, action, etc.) will determine the quality of the statement. The somewhat "objectifying" and "instrumental" nature of the grid should not obscure the fundamental importance that Bion attached to emotional and subjective experience. As he himself pointed out (Bion, 1974–1977), while it may be possible to use the Grid retrospectively, it should not distract the psychoanalyst during his work inside the sessions; it is only a tool and should not replace observation or psychoanalysis.

Bion's model of thinking places a fundamental emphasis on the experience of absence and the capacity to tolerate pain caused by frustration. The quality of mental development is inherent in the meeting between a capacity if not innate, then at least constitutional, – perhaps linked to genetic inheritance but above all to the vicissitudes of foetal emotional life – in the infant to tolerate frustration[20] and a capacity in the parent or mothering object to welcome, contain and transform the raw experiences of the infant dealt with by projective identification. This aptitude of the mothering object corresponds to the "capacity for reverie". The representation of a double condition, constitutional and environmental, for satisfactory psychic development is found for example in Frances Tustin who, as we have seen (Chapter 2), considers the emergence of autistic states as based on the conjunction between constitutional hypersensitivity in infants and failure in the containing function of the mothering environment. However, in this double constraint, it seems that Bion gives a primordial place to the capacity to tolerate frustration:

> An infant endowed with a marked capacity for toleration of frustration might survive the ordeal of a mother incapable of reverie and therefore incapable of supplying its mental needs. At the other extreme, an infant markedly incapable of tolerating frustration cannot survive without breakdown even the experience of projective identification with a mother capable of reverie; nothing less than unceasing breastfeeding would serve, and that is not possible through lack of appetite if for no other reason.
> (Bion, 1962b, p. 37)

10.5 The rhythmicity of experiences, a condition of the development of the capacity for thought

We have stressed the need for a rhythmicity of exchanges between the baby and his mothering environment for the containing function to operate adequately, and we have pointed out the way in which such rhythmicity supports the development of thoughts (Chapter 3). If the original experiences of satisfaction and frustration form the basis of future psychic development, it is above all the *rhythmic repetition* – sufficiently rhythmic and at a sufficiently supportive rhythm – of experiences which determine the quality of this development. Daniel Marcelli (1985) has envisaged the role of this rhythmicity in the development of thoughts – starting from "agglomerates", a notion which represents psychic elements in their most primitive form (see Chapter 2).

We have already discussed the epistemological problem posed by the use of the concept of hallucination in considering the processes that initiate thought-activity. Daniel Marcelli, working on the question of the transition from perceptual-sensory activity to the activity of symbolic representation, refutes the idea that the hallucination of the absent object could bring about the junction between these two registers of activity, thought based on hallucination. Indeed, clinical experience revealing that the subject who is prey to hallucinations is never able to "think" and to be creative on the psychic level, leads Marcelli (1985) to say that "the hallucinatory process extinguishes more than it stimulates the activity of thinking " (p. 419, translated for this edition). How then does the symbolic function, the function of thinking, fit into the perceptual-sensory functioning of the infant?

According to Marcelli, the element providing the link between the register of perceptual-sensory activity and the register of symbolic thought-activity is the "time" factor. It is the repetition, the rhythmicity of the experiences, of the exchanges between the infant and the parent, which allows him to organize these experiences according to a time frame, based on ritualization, and to link together the different agglomerates. This link will essentially relate to the succession between an unpleasant or exciting agglomeration and a pleasant or soothing agglomeration. And Marcelli hypothesizes that the first activity of thought independent of perceptual-sensory activation concerns a thought about time which could be formulated as follows: "After that, there will be something else". The infant, he suggests, is only capable subsequently of depicting his experiences.

What are the necessary conditions for these thoughts about succession to arise and for symbolic thought to develop? The repetition and rhythmicity of experiences, conditions of their predictability, must be combined with a very early capacity in the infant, namely the *capacity for attention*. Attention, the reverse of dismantling, creates links, bridges between experiences. The capacity for attention is considered by Marcelli to be the first outline of the ego. Predictability and attentiveness, when combined, determine the *anticipatory capacity* which allows the infant to match two emotional states, two agglomerates and, by searching for clues of a future agglomerate, to develop thinking about time, about succession.

To illustrate anticipation, Daniel Marcelli gives as an example the feeding situation where the infant, who at first does not know that he is screaming because he is hungry, soon begins to look for clues of a second state of satisfaction, because he knows that after an emotional state of tension an emotional state of relaxation and satisfaction will follow. Based on the observations of Jérôme Bruner (1973), Marcelli also instances as an example the motor schema of prehension. During the first attempts to grasp an object, the infant extends a closed hand towards it, and opens it only on contact with the object, but suddenly an unexpected change occurs in that the infant then extends and presents an open hand towards the object. This is a sudden reorganization of the gestural components explained by an "increase in the anticipatory organization of the act" (Bruner, 1973). Suddenly the infant knows that prehension follows the thrust of the arm and it no longer needs skin contact, activation, to achieve it (opening of the hand). Prehension is anticipated and Marcelli comments with this reflection:

> The "function of thinking" frees the infant from perceptual-sensory dependence.
> (Marcelli, 1985, p. 425, translated for this edition)

How does the thought of an absence, in other words the activity of symbolic representation, fit into these thoughts on succession? According to Marcelli, symbolic representation brings together two functions. The first is a function of "figuration" or "presentation" which has the role of depicting or presenting the object. The second is a function of "temporization", "deferment" or "remanence", which has the role of delaying, deferring the activity of figuration. Hallucination, which amounts to a figurative operation, makes the object present, following the activation of neuro and perceptual-sensory functioning. It is therefore not equivalent to the perception of an absent object. The mental representation of the absent object results from the association between the operation of figuration and the operation of deferment, which releases the image of perceptual-sensory activity.

How does one pass over from an operation of figuration, which characterizes perceptual-sensory activity and applies to the perception of the object, whether hallucinatory or not, to the association between this operation of figuration and the operation of deferment, an association that characterizes the function of symbolic representation, and is thus linked to temporality? It is once again the rhythmicity of the experiences which, for Marcelli, if it is associated with a sufficient capacity for attention on the part of the infant, will make it possible to establish this correlation leading to the distinction between perceptual-sensory activity and the activity of symbolic thinking.

Thanks to the internal and external rhythmicity of the exchanges and the infant's capacity for attention, the *capacity for deferment*, which Marcelli defines as the ability to delay and keep, even for a minimal amount of time, information just received, may emerge. This capacity for deferment allows the baby to link together different successive agglomerates and to lay the foundations of the symbolic function. From this capacity for deferment, the first thought can arise, which is a thought of the type "one succeeds the other".

All these "capacities" required of the infant (attention, anticipation, deferment) seem to us to be based on just one capacity, namely the *capacity to tolerate the pain due to frustration, separation and anxiety.* We do not follow Marcelli when he seems to consider affect as a secondary element to perceptual-sensory activity or as an element that is only agglomerated with this activity (see Chapter 2). It is the struggle against pain and anxiety that organizes psychic development, as we have reiterated throughout this book. The *development of thought* is based not so much on a representation of absence as on *a representation of the emotional experience around this experience of* absence.[21] On the other hand, we support the importance given in Marcelli's theorization to ritualization and the rhythmicity of experiences. This rhythmicity concerns the function of "presenting objects" (Winnicott, 1962a) devolved to the environment.

The fundamental role of the rhythmicity of experiences in psychic development gives an overview of one of the functions of the frame and the importance of its permanence, or the illusion of its permanence – rhythmicity giving an illusion of permanence, an illusion of continuity –, in psychoanalytic care as in all care metaphorizing the feeding situation.[22]

Notes

1 One of us has developed this point at length (Ciccone, 2004, 2014).
2 We use the term used by Jean Bégoin (1985) – with reference to Roger Money-Kyrle's (1968) article "On cognitive development" – which defines the Bionian model of psychic functioning as a "cognitive" model, where development proceeds from ignorance to knowledge. This model follows, in its Kleinian filiation, the Freudian model (a psychosexual model where development proceeds from orality to genitality), and the Kleinian model (a structural model).
3 Excerpts from Chapter 6 of the book *La Psychanalyse à l'épreuve du bébé. Fondements de la position clinique* (Ciccone, 2014).
4 Which eighteenth-century sensualism had already said (Condillac, 1754).
5 On this question, see for example Despinoy and Pinol-Douriez, 2002.
6 See Mehler et al., 1978, 1988; De Casper and Fifer, 1980; De Casper and Spence, 1986, De Casper and Granier-Deferre,1994; Herbinet and Busnel, 1981; Lecanuet et al., 1989, 1995; Busnel et al., 1989; Busnel, 1997.
7 See Parat, 1995; Ciccone and Ferrant, 2015.
8 On the relationships between intersubjectivity and containing function, see also Mellier, 2005; Ciccone, 2012.
9 See on this subject Ciccone, 2018; Roussillon, 2018.
10 In particular Vauclair and Deputte, 2002; Premack and Premack, 2003.
11 The model of Piera Aulagnier's pictogram explores these processes, the pictogram inseparably linking areas of excitement and object of satisfaction.
12 See also the conceptions of Marion Milner (1955) on the role of illusion in the formation of symbols, which René Roussillon takes up again.
13 See Winnicott and the "antisocial tendency", an effect of the failure of such a denial on more secondary levels (1956b, 1958b).
14 This idea was already stated in a 1950 article: "Some aspects of the analysis of a schizophrenic", although the term "symbolic equations" is not used.
15 Such concrete thinking can very often be observed in adult schizophrenic patients who take words "literally", do not have access to metaphor, and with whom interpretive work is very difficult. We could give

many illustrations of this, such as, for example, the case of a patient followed by one of us (A.C.) in a day hospital who, following associative material arising in a group setting, responded to an interpretation that she feared that the food she received from the "mother-day hospital" would be stolen from her, by questioning each patient in the group to find out who had really eaten off her plate. See also the examples given by Harold Searles (1962) in his article "The differentiation between concrete and metaphorical thinking in the recovering schizophrenic".
16 See Chapters 4 and 8.
17 It is through learning from experience that what Bion (1962b) called the "knowledge link" or K link develops. We know that Bion distinguished three basic relationships uniting two objects: the "love link" or L link, the "hate link" or H link and the "knowledge link" or K link. The K link by means of which "x knows y" is not just "x is in possession of knowledge named y", but means that "x is concerned with knowing the truth about y". The K link is therefore an active link. xKy represents a painful emotional experience, as it involves a feeling of doubt and a depressive experience. If this pain is not tolerated, the psyche will evade the experience and the xKy link will boil down to "x has knowledge named y", which represents omnipotent knowledge apparently devoid of pain more than real knowledge gained from experience.
18 In 1963, Bion distinguished the "primitive thought-activity" at work in the development or creation of thoughts, from the thought-activity involved in the use or processing of thoughts, which is considered to be subsequent to the existence of thoughts.
19 Speech can thus be an activity which consists either in communicating thoughts, in which case words will have the value of alpha elements designating the representation of things, or in using the musculature of spoken language to rid the psyche of thoughts, in which case words will have the value of beta elements designating things in themselves and not their representation.
20 Melanie Klein also considered the child's capacity to tolerate anxiety and frustration to be largely based on constitutional factors (see Klein, 1930, 1932, 1945, 1952a).
21 Piera Aulagnier (1982), for example, explains clearly how the thought, that is to say, the thought about an experience, arises from an experience of suffering jeopardizing cathexes and consists in operating a link between this suffering, the presence and effects of which cannot be denied, and a cause which can remain a support for cathexis.
22 See Ciccone, 2005, 2012d, 2014.

PART V

FIFTH POSTULATE

> In the absence of introjection of the containing functions, projective identification continues unabated, with all the confusions of identity that result from it.

Let us recall that the absence of introjection of a containing object promotes, first of all, further adhesive identification. Projective identification operates in three-dimensional space, three-dimensionality determining the development of the sense of interiority and the potentiality for activating thought.

We will begin by studying the process of projective identification, its normal and pathological aspects, its different variations in ordinary development as in psychopathology, and its relationships to internal and external objects.

Then we will focus on the reasons for, and the consequences of, resorting to pathological projective identification, including identity confusion, as well as the phenomenology of this intra- and intersubjective psychic process.

11

PROJECTIVE IDENTIFICATION

Definition and description[1]

We owe the notion of projective identification to Melanie Klein.

We can find precursors to this notion in the models built by Freud. For example, it could be said that the models of *identification* in Freud's work are based in part on processes of projective identification. This is true with regard to Freud's (1900) description of "hysterical identification", where the subject aims to enjoy what another person enjoys by appropriating part of the other person's identity. This is equally true of the process that Freud calls "narcissistic identification", which we have already discussed (Chapters 1 and 5), and which he describes for example in the Leonardo da Vinci type of homosexuality (Freud, 1910): the male homosexual was once a child who had a close bond with his mother and who, as an adult, commemorates this bond by identifying with the mother and by seeking sexual partners who represent him as a child. It is thus a question of depositing in another person an infantile part of oneself and of dramatizing, theatralizing, the bond with this infantile part by identifying (projectively) with the parent (with the mother) who is the co-subject of the singular bond with this infantile part. There is a double projective identification here. We can also evoke the *reversal* of which Freud speaks (1915a), which consists in subjecting another person to what the subject has himself undergone: the object is put in the place of the subject, the subject is identified with the persecuting or traumatizing object; this is a process of projective identification. Similarly, *idealization*, which consists in transferring ego-cathexes on to an ideal object, in putting an object (the leader of a crowd, the object of love, the hypnotist) in place of the ego-ideal

(Freud, 1921), implies processes of projective identification. We can also mention *telepathy*, a transmission of unconscious thought, which Freud studies in texts that remained taboo for a long time (Freud, 1922a, 1941a). *Projection, transference*, in fact all these phenomena which imply a transit of psychic contents, contain processes of projective identification.[2]

If we can identify precursors in Freud's thought for projective identification, and in particular in his way of thinking about identification, it must be stressed that for Freud, identification rests on an oral model: it is a question of taking something from the object and putting it in oneself. It was Melanie Klein who would explore and highlight the *anal* perspective of identification: putting something of oneself inside the object.

The notion of projective identification was therefore proposed by Melanie Klein. The term was introduced in 1946 to designate a process, the modelling of which would be one of the most fruitful for the entire post-Kleinian current. We will look at the successive contributions of its main representatives.

11.1 Definition of projective identification

The notion of projective identification derives from Melanie Klein's conceptions of the phantasied relationships that the child has with the interior of his mother's body, sadistic relationships underpinned by greed and envy and also driven by epistemophilic impulses (see Klein, 1927, 1928, 1930, 1931, 1932, 1945), and from her conceptions which we have spoken about concerning the death drive and persecutory anxieties (Chapter 9).

Melanie Klein describes the process of projective identification by taking as her starting point the phantasied attacks resulting from sadism, which develop in the paranoid-schizoid position and culminate on approaching the depressive position. The phantasied assaults by the child on the mother's body follow two main lines: one is "the predominantly oral impulse to suck dry, bite up, scoop out, and rob the mother's body of its good contents"; the other line derives from "the anal and urethral impulses expelling dangerous substances (excrements) out of the self and into the mother" (Klein, 1946, p. 8). The expulsion in hatred of these harmful excrements is accompanied by the projection into the mother of split-off and bad parts of the ego, and "much of the hatred against parts of the self is now directed against the mother. This leads to a particular form of identification, which establishes the prototype of an aggressive object-relation" (ibid.). Melanie Klein (1946) suggested the term "projective identification" for these processes.

Projective identification concerns not only the bad parts, although Klein gives a clear primacy to the projection into the mother of destructive impulses, but also the good parts, the good inner breast. "The projection of good feelings and good parts of the self into the mother is essential for the infant's ability to develop good object-relations and to integrate his ego", notes Melanie Klein (1946, p. 9).

Projective identification consists for the ego in taking possession of an external object which becomes an extension of the ego. Projection operates in interaction with the introjection. The reintrojection of a persecuting object reinforces the fear of internal and external persecutors. On the other hand the reintrojection of the good object develops the feeling of love and protects the child against the persecutory anxiety which is thereby mitigated. The introjection-projection-reintrojection of good feelings improves the relationship with the internal world and with the external world and strengthens the self which becomes more integrated (see Klein, 1952a).

As early as 1947 and 1949, Herbert Rosenfeld described the process of projective identification in schizophrenic depersonalization, in paranoia, and in homosexuality. But above all, he saw projective identification at work between the patient and the analyst, and interpreted it in the transference. In 1952, he specified that if projective identification represents a defence mechanism to rid the ego of unbearable impulses, it also represents the most primitive form of object-relation (Rosenfeld, 1952ab).

Hanna Segal, in her 1967 article "Melanie Klein's technique", saw projective identification as the clearest illustration of the link between impulses, phantasies and defence mechanisms: projective identification is a very elaborate phantasy; it is also an instinctual drive expression, an omnipotent satisfaction of libidinal and aggressive impulses; finally it is a defence mechanism by which the ego gets rid of unwanted parts. It is worth noting the difference that Segal makes explicit, instancing an example, between the interpretation of projection and the interpretation of projective identification. Her example is that of a patient reporting, on the eve of a holiday break, how her children were quarrelling and jealous of her. When the analyst interpreted that the children represented her and that she felt jealous of the analyst because of the holiday interruption, the patient accepted the interpretation without being really touched by it. The interpretation that would have been more judicious – considering the material of the other sessions – concerns not projection alone, but projective identification, and would have consisted in showing her how, by subtle manipulations, she actually *forced her children to take charge of parts of herself*, jealous and wrathful parts which she got rid of and which she controlled by controlling her children. We understand very well, through this example, what projective identification is, with its concrete effects in the relationship – we will come back to this later on.

Hanna Segal understood many transference (and countertransference) situations in terms of projective identification, as did Rosenfeld. For example, a patient who projects his infant part into the analyst, with all the emotions related to it, may find himself silent and withdrawn, and participate in making the analyst himself feel helpless, rejected and lacking in understanding, that is to say in the image of the patient's infant ego.

Projective identification, or identificatory projection as some prefer to call it,[3] is therefore conceived from an ontogenetic point of view: it is a necessary process for the development of personality, for the establishment of the first object-relations (in a world of part-objects), and which unfolds in the paranoid-schizoid or symbiotic position. It is also at work in the defensive positions of the manic position and the melancholic position as we have described them (Chapter 8). If, in the paranoid-schizoid position, projective identification aims essentially at the destruction of the persecuting object, in the manic position it aims rather at controlling it, in collaboration with obsessional defences. On the other hand, in the melancholic position, projective identification is more directly in the service of protecting the idealized object, by installing it outside the mind and inside an external object. Furthermore, the activity of projective identification continues even in the depressive position, with regard to libidinal and aggressive impulses, but the identificatory project leans in this case in favour of introjection.

Despite this ontogenetic status, Melanie Klein (1946) regarded projective identification as having a highly pathogenic potential. If it is used excessively, or if the ego cannot elaborate the depressive position and consequently regresses and becomes attached to schizoid mechanisms, such as splitting and projective identification, then the foundations of schizophrenia or paranoia will be laid. Concerning the excessive nature of which Klein spoke, Bion (1962a) emphasizes that it must be understood as qualifying not only the frequency of use of the mechanism, but also and above all the *belief in its omnipotence* which, if it is excessive, pathologizes projective identification.

11.2 Normal projective identification and pathological projective identification

It was Bion who, as early as 1959, postulated that there is a normal degree of projective identification, and that projective identification associated with introjective identification provides the basis on which normal development rests. Projective identification allows the infant to get rid of feelings of terror into the mother (or mothering object). If she accepts them, she can detoxify them and return them to the infant in a tolerable form. If she refuses them, if she does not understand the infant's distress and cannot contain it, the latter will reintroject a "nameless dread" (Bion, 1962a, p. 96). His feelings will not have been modified and soothed but will have become even more painful.

The bond between mother and infant rests, according to Bion, on "realistic" projective identification and on the mother's capacity to introject the infant's projective identifications. It is by means of projective identification that the infant can communicate his feelings, that he can explore what, in the interior space of his object, excites his curiosity, and that he can finally experience his own feelings within a personality capable of containing them.

We have already described the "container-contained" and "alpha function" model developed by Bion (Chapters 3 and 10). It is worth recalling that this is based on projective identification in the service of communication. When an emotional experience puts the infant in a state of confusion and an inability to think, the infant splits off and projects this part of himself, which is in a state of distress, into the mothering object. She contains this projection and, in her "reverie", transforms the elements that are intolerable for the infant into more tolerable feelings that the latter can reintegrate, which fosters the development of thought. Bion (1962b) supposes that "projective identification is an early form of that which later is called a capacity for thinking" (p. 37). Projective identification also gives the child the possibility of exploring the environment, the surrounding psychic world, and therefore of developing his capacities for symbolization – Segal (1957) had already described this link between projective identification and symbol-formation (see Chapter 10). Bion writes:

> Denial of the use of this mechanism, either by the refusal of the mother to serve as a repository for the infant's feelings, or by the hatred and envy of the patient who cannot allow the mother to exercise this function, leads to a destruction of the link between infant and breast and consequently to a severe disorder of the impulse to be curious on which all learning depends.
>
> (Bion, 1959, p. 106–107)

These operations in play between an infant and his mothering object are also found in the psychic mobilizations between a patient and his analyst.

We are indebted to Bion for the idea of normal projective identification, but we are also indebted to him for elaborating a differentiation between normal projective identification and pathological projective identification, which is qualitative and not only quantitative. Indeed, the pathology of projective identification is no longer envisaged only in terms of its massive or excessive aspect, but also in terms of the qualities of the projected parts of the self.

In normal development, the projected parts remain relatively unaltered and can be reintrojected into the ego. On the other hand, when hostile and envious impulses are intense, things happen differently. The projected part disintegrates into tiny fragments which, when expelled from the personality, force their way into objects and encyst them. These will in turn be disintegrated into tiny particles. Objects will then be perceived as fragmented into pieces, each containing a hostile part of the ego. These pieces or particles are called by Bion (1956, 1957, 1958, 1962b) "bizarre objects". The purpose of this dispersion of the ego is to free it from all perception, because the perception of reality – external reality and psychic reality – is felt to be a violent persecution by the psychotic part of the personality, due in particular to the depressive anxiety that it implies. This is why it is first of all the perceptual apparatus which is attacked with the aim of destroying it. The object responsible for this perception is attacked and reduced to pieces at the same time as the perceptual apparatus. This type of projective identification is aimed at both the persecuting object and the ideal object, which becomes persecuting in that it arouses unbearable feelings of envy.

"Bizarre objects" are charged with persecutory hostility. The particles expelled by projective identification are infinitely worse after their expulsion than they were before. Thus, when the subject wishes to reintegrate them, he feels he is the victim of an intrusion; he feels assailed and tortured. The mutilation of the perceptual apparatus only increases the suffering due to painful perceptions. Likewise, the persecuting nature of "bizarre objects" reinforces the anxieties of the ego. A vicious circle is thus established.

So, while we can consider the psychopathology of the defence mechanism of projective identification in terms of its excesses, Bion shows how it can be pathological in its very form. This is the case with psychotic personalities, or in the psychotic part of the personality, dominated by envy and hostility. Remember that Bion locates the origin of the disturbance of normal projective identification, and therefore the origin of psychotic processes, in the conjunction between an innate disposition in the child for excessive destructiveness, and a failure of the environment concerning its containing function (or "container" function, according to Kaës, 1976a, 1979).[4] As soon as this conjunction is realized, everything that promotes awareness of reality or emotions – and first of all thought, the activation of which links sense-impressions to consciousness – will be attacked and treated by projective pathological identification which rids the psyche of fragments of the ego, products of its destructiveness (see Bion, 1957, 1959).

Normal projective identification is therefore in the service of *communication*. It can become pathological if it is used excessively or exclusively, because it impoverishes the ego. Projective pathological identification in itself – because of its excessively destructive and omnipotent quality – is in the service of *evacuation*. Rosenfeld (1970, 1987) underlines the absolute necessity, in analytical treatment with psychotic patients, of distinguishing pathological projective identification used to communicate – which represents an intensified or distorted form of normal projective identification – from pathological projective identification used for the denial of psychic reality. In the first case, the patient is receptive to the analyst's understanding of him. On the other hand, in the second case, the patient splits and projects into the analyst a disturbing mental content in order to get rid of it permanently. The analyst's interpretations are then experienced as an attempt to reject and reintroduce the intolerable and frightening content into the patient. The processes of communication and evacuation, as well as the processes of projective identification which consist in trying to control the analyst's body and mind, can coexist, and it is essential to distinguish and interpret them correctly.

The differentiation between normal projective identification and pathological projective identification is linked to the differentiation between the healthy and the ill parts of the personality. This idea is fundamental in the psychoanalytic investigation of the post-Kleinians. Rosenfeld insists on the imperative need to distinguish between the parts of the ego that exist almost exclusively in a state of projective identification with external objects or internal objects, and those parts of the ego that are less dominated by projective identification and have an existence separate from objects. It is these parts which, because they try to form a relationship of dependence on the analyst representing the feeding object from which they are separated, are able to use processes of introjection uncontaminated by the concretization caused by omnipotent projective identification.

Donald Meltzer (Meltzer, 1967; Meltzer et al., 1980, 1982) suggested we should distinguish between normal projective identification in the service of communication and thought, and pathological projective identification in the service of the evacuation, destruction and denial of psychic reality, by referring to them with different terms. He suggests reserving the term projective identification for the normal process, and designating the pathological process, corresponding to the omnipotent unconscious phantasy that Melanie Klein described, by the term *"intrusive identification"*. The distinction between projective identification and intrusive identification leads Meltzer to differentiate what he calls the "container", which represents the "interior of the object", from what he calls the "claustrum", which designates the "interior of the object penetrated by intrusive identification". As he points out, this modification makes it possible to raise to a qualitative level (following in this way the concern that Bion already had) distinctions of a quantitative nature, which consist in the juxtaposition of adjectives such as "normal", "excessive", "massive", etc., with terms of projective identification.

11.3 Projective identification with external objects and with internal objects

Based on the remarks of Rosenfeld (1970, 1987) and a discussion of Meltzer (1989a), we can make the following statements:

- the normal form of projective identification, in the service of communication, takes place with external objects. It is based on non-verbal communication (between the infant and the mothering object, or between the patient and the analyst);
- the pathological form of projective identification (intrusive identification) which consists in penetrating the object in phantasy in order to control it or to borrow its identity, as well as the pathological form which consists in getting rid of a disturbing mental content, takes place first with internal objects and secondarily with external objects. External objects are concerned in the various ways the subject *acts* towards them, for example pushing external objects, by more or less subtle perverse manoeuvres; taking charge of unwanted parts or emotions; or else, working to reduce external objects to a host function hosting the parasitic parts of the subject; or controlling external objects in order to control the internal objects of which they are the depositories, or of sticking to external objects, which produces, in the symbiotic relationship, what we have called the adhesive effect of projective identification, etc.[5]

Melanie Klein described projective identification in the phantasied relationship between the ego and external objects (the breast – the mother as a partial object). However, the idea that the process of projective identification functions with internal objects is still present in Melanie Klein, even if it is not clearly stated. We find it, in a fairly obvious way, for example in her 1955 article "On identification" where she explains, during her interpretation of the novel by Julien Green (1947) *If I Were You*, the changes in the identity of the subject operated by projective identification. We find it again in her analysis of the case of Richard, a posthumous work published in 1961, during her reflections on the close relationship between internalization and projective identification.

Nevertheless, it was Donald Meltzer, it seems, who was the first to propose and clarify this notion of projective identification with internal objects, in a 1966 article entitled "The relation of anal masturbation to projective identification". This process is based, according to Meltzer, on anal masturbation. Meltzer draws on the link established by Klein (1946) between projective identification and the processes of anality, to highlight the intimate relationship that exists between projective identification with the internal object and anal masturbation.

Projective identification with the internal object is based on anal masturbation, as this induces the phantasy of penetrating the object. The prototypical sequence would be as follows: after a meal and in the absence of the mother, the baby, assimilating in a hostile way the breasts with the mother's buttocks, explores its own behind and idealizes its roundness and its softness equated with those of the breast; the penetration of his anus gives shape to a phantasy of secret intrusion into the mother's anus, in order to rob its contents which are imagined to be retained to nourish the father and the other internal babies. Two consequences result from this process: on the one hand there is an idealization of the rectum and faecal contents based on the confusion between the rear of the baby and of the mother, both equated with the breasts, and on the other hand there is projective identification with the internal mother, which invalidates the differentiation between the baby and the mother.

Projective identification with internal objects gives a "pseudo" aspect to the personality and nourishes a feeling of being fraudulently adult. It is revealed, for example, in analysis, through pseudo-cooperation or concern for the analyst instead of adult-type cooperation, through submissive behaviour or a desire to convince the analyst and to have his approval and admiration instead of a desire to understand the interpretation. It manifests itself in dreams depicting the idealization of faeces as food, the idealization of the rectum and the idealization of the act of going to the toilet. It is observed in the pseudo-mature character, which is only a counterfeit of maturity, and which creates docility, helpfulness, and a preference in children for the company of adults, high verbal capacity, conformism and snobbery. All of these traits mask a deep intolerance of the frustration and anxiety that are responsible for violent outbursts of anger, suicide attempts, vicious attacks on others, cruelty to animals, recourse to lies, etc.[6]

We have already developed the hypothesis we put forward that projective identification with the internal object underlies the phantasy of incorporation, which is its dynamic expression (see

Chapter 1). We have suggested that this process can be applied to delusions, hallucinatory states, and even dreams.

The modification of the sense of identity caused by projective identification is explained by the "gathering up" of the ego inside an unintegrated internal object, or rather imago (see Chapter 1), that is to say dissociated from the nucleus of the ego, a nucleus constituted as a "centre of attraction", as an "attractor" at the centre of the psyche. The occupation by the ego of a "territory" or an unintegrated zone gives the personality this false, pseudo aspect that is characteristic of states of projective identification, schizoid states. It is as if the "centre of attraction", the true nucleus of identity, were not powerful enough to agglutinate the ego (without however imprisoning it), which wanders from dissociated spaces into dislocated spaces, far removed from the centre.

The attraction of internal objects by the central nucleus of the ego, which is *enriched* and *unmodified* by them, characterizes successful introjection, the introjective identification with an integrated object. The ego can embark on this venture without leaving its attracting nucleus; it can move about without getting lost.

It is imperative to determine in processes of identification – as Melanie Klein (1955) also pointed out – whether introjection prevails over projection, that is to say whether the ego widens its identificatory experience without changing profoundly, or whether projection prevails over introjection, that is to say whether the ego separates from its authentic sense of identity to borrow the identity of the internal, penetrated object.

We have already proposed and developed the idea that, in the process of identification, projective identification with the internal object, in other words the incorporation of the object, precedes and determines its introjection (see Chapter 1). Projective identification with the internal object is a feature of the paranoid-schizoid position, the manic position or the melancholic position, depending on the nature of this object. Introjective identification is the mark of the successful elaboration of the depressive position. Projective identification is part of the normal work of all mourning; it precedes and paves the way, necessarily, for every introjective identification. But if it does not yield, it prevents introjection and weakens the sense of identity.

Thus, these processes are described as operating inside the mind, and not from one mind to another, even if the presence of the real object on the external stage is sometimes essential for the realization of projective identification in some of its forms (communication or evacuation of affects, parasitism, etc.). This point is important because the concept of projective identification is often misinterpreted. The "victim" of projective identification claims, for example, to have been "acted on" by the other, as if parts of the other had actually penetrated or controlled him. In this case, the "victim" is in fact speaking of his own projective identification, and not that of the other, a projective identification which leads him to "feel acted on by another".

In this connection we would like to clarify what the term "deposit" means, which is so frequently used to account for an aspect of projective identification. This term may suggest that we could really get rid of a part of ourselves – it is true that all these phantasied processes are experienced very concretely. "To deposit in the other" means *to put the other person in contact with what is similar in himself*. The relationship that the other person will have with this "deposit" (feeling acted upon, manipulated) will depend on the relationship he has with that part of him that is similar to what has been "deposited" in him. We will not develop this idea any further, but simply recall that Melanie Klein (1955) insisted on the fact that the choice of real objects, as a support of identificatory images, that the subject will penetrate – in projective identification –, is motivated by *evidence that the object has something in common with the subject*, even if he is unaware of it. The external object – which the subject will incorporate in order to penetrate it intrusively and divest it of its identity – is already the representative of an internal part of the subject.[7] This is why we insist on the fact that projective identification concerns above all the subject and his internal world. The external world is only concerned by the acts that it will suffer due to the state of mind of the subject in projective identification. But the object is only a "victim" if he participates, from his place as a real object, in the phantasy scenario of the subject. In this case, the role he plays is supported by a projective identification in him with one of his own internal objects with which he has been brought into contact, because it is sufficiently similar to that which motivated the recourse to projective identification in the subject. This is how we should understand, for example, the concept of "common phantasy".[8]

The question of the place of the object in the situation of projective identification also makes it possible to differentiate projective identification from simple projection. In simple projection, the subject gets rid of what is projected, without maintaining a link with this content, while in projective identification the subject maintains a close link with the content or the part of him that is projected, or even with the object that is the recipient and receptacle of the projection, an object that the subject will control in order to control the aspects projected into him (Kernberg, 1975, 1987; Ogden, 1982). We will see in the next chapter the effects of induction, of influence, generated by projective identification in the link with the external object. This notion of a link maintained with the projected part, an "empathic" link, says Kernberg (1987), corresponds well to the idea that projective identification produces a *symbiotic link* with the object, as we have emphasized several times (see, in particular, Chapters 6 and 7), its phenomenology embracing all the figures of the symbiotic link, from the most normal symbiosis, the most creative "psychic substance", to the most destructive symbiosis.[9]

Concerning the link to the internal object and its effects on the link to the external object, and also concerning the distinction between the normal and pathological aspects of projective identification, let us note the way in which Meltzer (1992), reflecting on the intrusive penetration of the internal object, distinguishes two different conceptions in the subject of the internal world of the object (of his mind, and of his subjectivity): the first conception is the product of the imagination and corresponds to the reconstruction of the interior world of the object, respecting the privacy of its interior space; the second conception is the product of omniscience and corresponds to the intrusive penetration of the object. Imagination is on the side of mental health, omniscience on the side of pathology.

If these projective/introjective processes are at work in the psychic space of the subject, with effects in the intersubjective and concrete interactions of the subjects concerned, it is worth noting that Salomon Resnik (1973, 1986a, 1999) has proposed the idea of "internal projection in the body", outside the psyche, to describe a process based on a dissociation between body and thought, occurring in the phenomena of "somatopsychosis" and hypochondria.[10] The zones or bodily organs represent "autistic archipelagos" where "the psyche can be projected without coming into the world".

> The *internal projection* [...] means that the ego is trying to get rid of a mental pain into the body, through a split, a categorical body/mind dualism.
> (Resnik, 1986a, p. 215–216, translated for this edition)

Resnik (1985) also speaks of "claustrophobic sympathy" in relation to the body, based on an agoraphobic anxiety that pushes the ego, in an "autistic" tendency, to escape into the body to "convert" psychic anxieties into physical symptoms and thus avoid mental pain. The soma, in the context of "internal projection", has a function similar to that of the external object in the context of projective identification.

Let us now consider the motives, consequences and phenomenology of pathological projective identification.

Notes

1 Chapter written by Albert Ciccone alone.
2 For a detailed study of the precursors of the concept of projective identification, in Freud's models, see the part devoted to this question in the book *La Transmission psychique inconsciente. Identification projective et fantasme de transmission* (Ciccone, 2012a).
3 Geneviève Haag, for example (Haag, 1987b). Florence Guignard makes the same choice, in French, and explains this choice in a note to the chapter entitled "Introduction à la projection identificatoire" in her book *Quelle psychoanalyse pour le XXIe siècle?* (2015b): "Drawing on a long experience as a translator in psychoanalysis, I adopted this more accurate translation of the English term 'projective identification'. In fact, the difference in structure between the Saxon and French means that, in most cases, it is more correct to nominalize the adjective in French and to adjectivize the noun" (Guignard, 2015b, p. 73, translated for this edition).
4 Along with the inadequacies of the environment, that is to say, of the psychic functioning of the mothering object, four essential traits must be found in the personality, according to Bion (1957), for it to develop according to the model of schizophrenia, where projective pathological identification is prevalent, namely: "A preponderance of destructive impulses so great that even the impulse to love is suffused by them and turned to sadism; a hatred of reality, internal and external, which is extended to all that makes for awareness of it; a dread of imminent annihilation and, finally, a premature and precipitate formation of object relations" (Bion, 1957, p. 44).
5 The relationship between external object and internal object, in the particular context of projective identification aimed at appropriating the identity of the object, may be considered as follows: "Viewed through the projective glasses of a part of the ego, part of

the real external object becomes both the external object of desire and the internal object of identification [...]. The statement 'I desire the object' corresponds exactly to the statement 'I am the desirable object'" (Guignard, 1985, p. 174, translated for this edition). Florence Guignard underlines the schizoid aspect of this mechanism: "There is therefore a denial of the two remnants, namely the remnant of the ego and the remnant of the person that is the object of desire and projective identification in external reality" (ibid.).

6 Developmental progress leads to an obsessional organization, where internal objects are no longer penetrated but controlled and separated from each other omnipotently.

7 Concerning jealous and persecutory paranoiacs, Freud writes: "They do not project into the blue, so to speak, where there is nothing of the sort already. They let themselves be guided by their knowledge of the unconscious, and displace to the unconscious minds of others the attention which they have withdrawn from their own" (Freud, 1922b, p. 226).

8 It is such a situation, a real intersubjective interaction, that James Grotstein (2005) proposes to call "projective transidentification". He reserves the term "projective identification" for phantasy and the internal situation, and applies that of "projective transidentification" as soon as two real subjects are concerned and affected by this process.

9 On the distinction between projection and projective identification, see also Grotstein, 2005; Ciccone, 2012a.

10 Rosenfeld (1964b) previously considered the role of projection and introjection in hypochondria. The hypochondriac, after having projected his internal objects into external objects, immediately reintrojects these external objects which he splits and rejects into the body and the bodily organs.

12

PROJECTIVE IDENTIFICATION

Motives, consequences, phenomenology[1]

We have distinguished three kinds of process designated by the term projective identification: *communication, evacuation, intrusive penetration.* A first form of projective identification consists in communicating emotional states, in experiencing emotions with the help of the alpha function of an external object. This is normal projective identification. It requires the presence of the external object. The other two forms of projective identification are pathological forms – intrusive identification. They consist in getting rid of a disturbing mental content by projecting it into an object, or in penetrating inside an object to degrade, control or take possession of it.

Pathological projective identification, as a psychic process, is carried out with internal objects and produces a mental state whose characteristics define what can be called *projective identity*. External objects are affected by the effects produced by projective identification with regard to the subject's relation to them, insofar as external objects are understood as representatives of internal objects, just as internal objects represent external objects (they constitute themselves as private replicas of external objects). For example, the process of projecting a mental content into an object (second form of projective identification, between communication and appropriation of identity) should be understood as follows: the projective aspect consists in getting rid of the mental content, the identificatory aspect consists in persuading oneself, by a delusion of clairvoyance, that the object is responsible for this mental content. The subject will seek in the world of external objects a replica of his internal scenario and will "act" to put the external object in the place assigned to it in his omnipotent phantasy.

What are the reasons for pathological projective identification?

12.1 The motives underlying pathological projective identification

As the final words by Salomon Resnik, quoted in the previous chapter, make clear, it is obviously always *mental pain* that ultimately brings into play the defensive mechanisms of whatever kind they may be, and, in particular, projective identification. We have seen that projective identification is a response to persecutory anxiety, greed, envy, and intolerance to frustration.

Herbert Rosenfeld (1970, 1987) described projective identification in the transference, particularly in psychotic patients, in its relation to *psychic separation* and the *envy* that this mobilizes. The patient who begins to feel that he is separate from the analyst is subject to aggressive reactions, feelings of humiliation, at the origin of which is envious anger. Any progress in the analytical treatment of psychotic patients provokes very violent reactions where the patient spoils and devalues all that he has received that is good, and is then in a dangerous situation where the risk of suicide is maximal. Faced with this violent desire directed against the qualities of the analysis and the analyst, the healthiest part of the patient has recourse to an array of defences, in particular projective identification, where the envious part of the self is split off and projected onto an external object which is then identified with the envious part of the patient. Another aspect of projective identification as a defence against envy lies in the phantasy that the patient may develop of penetrating the envied and admired object. If the projective identification is total, the relationship will take the form of an early narcissistic relationship, where separation between the self and the object is denied. According to Rosenfeld, projective identification in the psychotic subject is a defence against excessive *envy*, more than against separation anxiety.

Donald Meltzer (1967) summarizes under six main headings the motives underlying the tendency to massive and pathological projective identification:

1. *intolerance of separation*, the constant need for physical or verbal contact revealing the absence of a psychic equivalent of the skin;

Fifth postulate

2. *need for omnipotent control*, deriving from confusional states whose origin lies in an inadequate or faulty splitting-and-idealization of self and objects;
3. *envy* – we will come back to this later (Chapter 14);
4. *jealousy* towards the breast ("delusional" jealousy or "possessive" jealousy);
5. *deficiency of trust*, the result of excessively destructive projection which provokes an access to projective identification not through violence but through deception or ruse, which results in an attitude of distrust or trickery (cf. paranoia or perversion);
6. *excessive persecutory anxiety* (excess in the amount of anxiety or in its terrifying qualities).

We will add to this list a seventh motive, which concerns the external object and combines with the other six, namely *the failure of the external object to ensure its function of containing normal projections*. If the mothering object cannot contain the infant's projections, if it fails to *transform* these projections – and if it is itself transformed by them (see Rosenfeld, 1987) – the tendency to projective pathological identification will be exacerbated. The same is true in the analytic situation, and in particular in the psychotic transference where projective identification dominates.

After this overview of the motives underlying pathological projective identification, we will now try to identify the consequences related to the use of such a procedure, first with regard to the ego, then with regard to the relationship with the object.

11.2 The internal consequences of projective identification. Projective identity

Melanie Klein (1946) mentioned the *weakening* and the *impoverishment* of the ego for which excessive projective identification is responsible, and in particular the excessive projection of good parts. The excess of projective identification leads, moreover, to a *difficulty in assimilating internal objects*, with, for example, the feeling of being controlled by them, the feeling of intruding into objects, or of often being intruded by hostile external objects. These disorders are the basis of schizophrenia.

Projective identification is responsible for intense *anxieties*, as Klein pointed out. For example, the phantasy of breaking into the object to control it can trigger the fear of being controlled and persecuted from within the object. The reintrojection of a dangerous object invaded by violence exacerbates situations of internal and external persecution. These different disorders are at the basis of paranoia. We may add that if projective identification is responsible for anxieties, it can also be used as a defence against these same anxieties, as a way of getting rid of them.

Melanie Klein also elaborated the *claustrophobic consequences* of projective identification. She reaffirms them in her article "On identification" (1955). But in this article, she describes above all, as we saw in the previous chapter, the *changes in the identity* of the subject that projective identification brings about.

Herbert Rosenfeld, who explored the clinical features of projective identification in a remarkable way, clearly described the consequences of this process for the sense of identity, especially in schizophrenic subjects. Projective identification leads to the loss of parts of oneself, the loss of certain emotions, a loss which results in feelings of *depersonalization* (1947, 1952a, 1987). Omnipotent projective identification is responsible for feelings of *confusion*: confusion between ego and object whenever, for example, the subject approaches an object with love or hate (1952ab, 1987); between reality and phantasy or between real objects and symbolic representation, which is manifested, for example, by a disturbance of verbal contact and concrete thinking because the subject in projective identification loses part of his ability to understand symbols and therefore words (1952a, 1963, 1970, 1987). In schizophrenia, projective identification leads, as Rosenfeld (1963) explains, either to a *psychotic identification*, where the patient assumes an identity different from his own, or to *confusional states*. Besides schizophrenia, it was also in homosexuality and paranoia (1949), drug addiction (1960) and hypochondria (1964b) that Rosenfeld identified and described the process and consequences of projective identification.

Since the 1950s, Hanna Segal has described the psychic states in which projective identification predominates. These states alter the perception of the object and can give the subject the impression of being emptied, of being persecuted or of being merged with the object (see, for example, Segal, 1956, 1967). Like Rosenfeld, she highlighted the concrete experience of the transference in the patient in projective identification (Segal, 1975). This concrete experience of the transference means the patient is likely to experience the analyst's interpretations as a projective identification in return, that is to say as an attempt by the analyst to get rid of his unwanted parts and to drive the patient mad. This is why, Segal (1975) writes, "it is essential for the analyst to understand that, when he interprets anxiety, the patient may feel that he is in fact attacking him, or if he interprets the patient's sexual feelings, the patient may experience it concretely as the analyst's sexual advances towards him or her" (Segal, 1975, p. 134), and, Segal adds, taking into account the bankruptcy of the symbolic function in the patient in projective identification, "it is useless to interpret to the psychotic as if he were a neurotic. Ordinary interpretations of the Oedipus complex for instance could well be experienced as a sexual assault and in fact make the patient worse" (ibid.).[2]

It is with Donald Meltzer (Meltzer, 1984a, 1988, 1989a, 1992; Meltzer and Sabatini Scolmati, 1985) that we will summarize the consequences of pathological projective identification. Donald Meltzer distinguishes, in the process of projective identification, between the projective pole and the identificatory pole. The consequences are twofold:

- the consequences of projection and intrusion into the object are reflected in *claustrophobic feelings*;
- the consequences relating to the identificatory aspect are reflected in an *alteration of identity*, as a result of which the subject may even behave in an exaggerated manner like the (internal) object into which he has intruded.

The *identificatory consequences* of this process are of three kinds, depending on the degree of destruction that has been caused in the (internal) object:

- if the object is not too damaged, a *pseudo-maturity* will be observed in the subject in projective identification;
- if the object is damaged, identification with this object "in poor health" may result in *hypochondriacal states*;
- finally, if the object is very damaged, "mentally ill", the observable consequences of projective identification are *manic-depressive states*.

The claustrophobic consequences are different depending on the "compartment" into which the subject has intruded:

- intrusion into the breast or the head of the object will give a *grandiose* aspect to the personality in projective identification;
- intrusion into the genitals will result in an *erotomanic* aspect;
- intrusion into the rectum, finally, will give a *persecutory, violent, perverse, sadomasochistic, or tyrannical* aspect to the claustrophobic experiences.

Meltzer (1988) specifies that analytical work must first focus on the identificatory aspect, which represents the manic side of the process and offers very strong resistance. Once the identificatory phenomena have been overcome, claustrophobic anxieties appear, and the subject may feel the desire to leave the state of projective identification, which we designate by the term "projective identity". But, at that moment, the manic aspects again put up a lot of resistance (especially grandiosity and erotomania). It is only persecutory feelings that can really induce the subject to want to withdraw from projective identity. The persecutory aspect must first replace the erotomaniac aspect characterizing the intrusion into the genitals, this erotomaniac aspect having itself taken the place of the delusional aspect characteristic of the intrusion into the head or the breast.

There is therefore a progression in projective identification, from the point of view of the space occupied in phantasy in the object (the head or the breast, then the genitals, then the rectum), with a transition, for the subject, from a grandiose manic aspect to a more hypochondriacal and more depressive aspect, as the occupation of the object becomes increasingly uncomfortable. Only the persecutory claustrophobic anxieties resulting from intrusion into the rectum, which gives rise to feelings of imprisonment, can motivate the subject to leave the projective identity. But the withdrawal from projective identity summons depressive anxieties (being dropped) which reactivate the projective identification used to flee dependence on the object, and the fear of being dropped. Claustrophobic anxieties "push", separation anxieties "pull" (Meltzer, 1989a). This anxiety about separation, about being dropped, which corresponds to the projective situation of intruding into the rectum of the object, is not anxiety about death or falling endlessly,[3] but anxiety about "being defecated, expelled outside and finding oneself in the toilet, that is to say about becoming one of the wrecks of society, a tramp or mentally ill" (Meltzer, 1988, p. 110, translated from the French).

It is also important to underline the immense loneliness generated by projective identity. If the subject who uses (or abuses) projective identification develops a false identity, if he is an intruder, an impostor, a "poseur", a "fraud", says Meltzer (1992), if he suffers from (claustrophobic) anxiety, he also suffers from loneliness. The intruder is in fact also "an exile from the world of intimacy, from the beauty of the world, which at best he can see, hear, smell and taste only second-hand through the medium of the object" (Meltzer, 1992, p. 72).

In conclusion, we would say that leaving the projective identity ultimately means *assuming one's own identity*, being oneself, living inside oneself. Only this state is compatible with mental health.

12.3 Phenomenology of projective identification

How is projective identification reflected in the relation to the object?

The link that projective identification establishes and maintains is of a *symbiotic* nature, as we have emphasized on several occasions. Normal projective identification characterizes normal symbiosis, and pathological projective identification characterizes destructive symbiosis.

The characterology of the projective identity gives us phenomenological insight into this identificatory process. Melanie Klein (1946) describes the following character traits as specific to projective identification:

- *obsessionality*, which demonstrates the need to control others in order to control the parts of the self projected into others;
- *compulsive attachment and interest* in others;
- *artificiality* in relating to objects and to oneself;
- *excessive withdrawal* from object relations.

We have already traced, with Meltzer (Meltzer et al., 1975), some characterological features of the projective identity, in opposition to the adhesive identity (see Chapter 5). We will now recall them: they concern addiction, the struggle against separation, delusional clarity of insight and caricatural behaviour – Meltzer is talking about children here:

- the *dependence* is reflected, in projective identification, by a delusional sense of independence due to the loss of differentiation between adult and infantile capacities;
- the *struggle against separation* is due to the fact that the child experiences the rejection of his tyranny as a profound threat to his omnipotence;
- the *delusion of clarity of insight* is manifested by the delusional illusion of knowing and seeing clearly inside the object, which often leads the observer to overestimate the intelligence of the pseudo-mature child;
- the *caricature of objects* presented by the projectively identified child is an aggressive caricature (of which the dress of the transvestite is an extreme example) with a pompous, pretentious, crude appearance.

Meltzer (1967, 1992) also describes some typical manifestations of projective identification observed in the treatment of psychotic children:

a) utilization of the body of the analyst as a part of the self;
b) utilization of the room as the inside of an object; in such situations, the analyst tends to represent a part-object inside this object, while also being equated with the object;
c) reversal of the adult-child relationship, where the analyst is made to contain and represent an alienated part of the infantile self;
d) exertion of omnipotent control over the analyst.

(Meltzer, 1967, p. 16; 1992, p. 35)

The subject in projective identification shows little depressive anxiety. The object is used as a "toilet-breast"; it is a valued object, considered necessary, but not loved. It arises from splitting and the partial nature of the object relation.

Rosenfeld (1970, 1987) presents two types of object relations underpinned by the process of projective identification: the parasitic relationship and the delusional relationship. He describes these two relationships in the transference. In the *parasitic relationship*, the analyst must function for the patient like his own ego. The patient maintains the belief that he lives entirely from the analyst and acts as a parasite. Severe parasitism may describe a state of total projective identification.[4] In the *delusional* relationship, the schizophrenic feels like he is living completely inside the object, probably the mother, who represents a delusional unreal world. The healthy parts of the ego are then trapped in the object and cause mental and physical paralysis which can include catatonia. Rosenfeld describes object-relations affected by projective identification as marked by manipulation, control, seduction (possibly even including hypnotic or telepathic influences). Resnik (1973) has described the bodily and behavioural aspects of *induction* and *influence*, which are the interactive and intersubjective correlates of projective identification.

We will illustrate this concrete aspect of projective identification in the relation to the object with the example of a particular intersubjective relationship in a mother–child couple that I (A.C.) had in treatment.

> This mother, Mrs E., and her child, Dimitri, are not psychotic, but pathological projective identification plays a singular role in their relationship. Dimitri is five years old. He comes across as a very precocious child, intellectually and psychologically. This couple is characterized by the fact that the child occupies in phantasy the place of an adult; he "takes charge" of his mother, sometimes becoming the mother of his own mother-child, sometimes her husband, mother-wife. But this situation is spoken, conscious, and Mrs E. suffers from it. She suffers from the fact that her child does not behave like a child. I will only focus here on one particular aspect of this relationship, in order to shed light on the question at hand, and we shall see, among other things, how the management of the Oedipus complex can make abundant use of projective identification.
>
> Mrs. E. is surprised, sometimes very troubled, by Dimitri's precociousness, and especially by his "intralucidity". She is surprised by certain thoughts and certain words of her child in which she notes a premonitory aspect. She is disconcerted by the faculty he shows for understanding "life situations" (love, death, mourning …), and by the impression he gives of knowing about certain events before he is told about them. She reports the following example: Dimitri looks at her and tells her that her eyes are not normal, that she wants to cry; she is then brought into contact with a feeling of sadness that she had not really perceived; troubled by her son's intuition, she begins by denying it; but he insists; she ends up crying; her son then

wraps his arms around her and cuddles her like an adult would comfort a child. Mrs. E. interprets this sequence in the following way: "He sees into me ... he knows what I think before I even think it ... I have the impression that our brains are not separated".

We will see, through this singular sequence, but also through many other elements that I cannot relate here, that the mother gets the child to take charge of part of her own faculty of experiencing her emotions – first projective identification. The child, who is hypersensitive and very much on the lookout for the slightest indications concerning his mother's mood, takes advantage of his perception of sadness to "interpret" his mother's depression and, through his insistence, makes her take upon herself his own depressive infantile experience at the same time – second projective identification – depressive pain that he will be able to console by becoming the mothering object of his mother, that is to say, by assuming the adult identity – third projective identification.

This mother, whose mental health is not otherwise worrying – any more than the child's is – experiences projective identification not as a confusing loss of identity or as a destructive intrusion, but as a permeability of her psychic space facilitating the other person's (the child's) direct contact with her own internal objects or her own unconscious affects. She does not have the persecutory feeling that thoughts or emotions are transmitted to her against her will; rather, she has the feeling that *her* thoughts or emotions are interpreted to her by her child, brought into consciousness before she herself has recognized or experienced them. The child uses his shared symbiotic needs to carry out his oedipal desires, while getting rid of his own depressive and dependent infantile experiences. This particular oedipal situation can thus be read in terms of *mutual projective identification*.

We will end this overview of the process of projective identification by emphasizing once again, with Donald Meltzer, the place it occupies in the psychoanalytic process and in developmental dynamics, as a necessary psychic mechanism but one whose relinquishment alone ensures the future potential of mental health:

> It seems clear that, since massive projective identification can function to counter any configuration producing psychic pain at

infantile levels, no other problem can be really worked through until this mechanism to some considerable degree been abandoned. In the neurotic patient this may be accomplished in a matter of months or a year of analysis, but in borderline and psychotic patients it is the major work, taking years – and its accomplishment represents an analytical achievement of the first order. In fact, as I have said it would probably be called the crucial step in establishing fundamental health and removing the danger of psychotic deterioration.

(Meltzer, 1967, p. 23)[5]

Notes

1 Chapter written by Albert Ciccone alone.
2 Rosenfeld (1987) also emphasizes the concrete nature of the countertransference experiences that the analyst can have when the patient abuses powerful projective processes.
3 See the primitive anxieties that we described in Chapter 2, with Klein, Winnicott and Tustin.
4 Margaret Mahler (1968) has also described the "parasitic symbiotic relationship".
5 For more developments on projective identification, in particular for a description of its effects of psychic transmission and its effects on the work of subjectivation, see Ciccone, 2012a.

PART VI

SIXTH POSTULATE

> Disturbances of introjection, resulting either from the inadequacy of the real object, or from phantasied attacks against it, lead to the development of a "second skin" formation.

We will first consider the problem of the inadequacies of the real mothering object (parental object, family object), and its consequences for the infant's psychic birth.

We will then look at the baby's phantasied attacks on the containing object.

Finally, we will explore the ways in which a "second skin" is formed when there is a failure to introject an adequate containing object. In so doing, we will provide an overview of the semiology of early mental disorders in the infant.

13

THE INADEQUACIES OF THE CONTAINING OBJECT

13.1 Aetiological point of view

We have mentioned the essential qualities of the mothering object in ensuring its function as a container (Chapter 3). In this chapter, we will consider pathologization from the point of view of object dysfunctioning. More than the object itself, the dysfunctioning or inadequacy will concern the relationship between the object and the nascent psyche. To paraphrase Winnicott, who said that a baby alone does not exist (Winnicott, 1947, 1952b, 1960a) – there is always a parent to hold it, watch it, love it … –, we would like to say that a parent alone does not exist: there is always a child to cathect the parent and make him or her a parent, to introduce the parent to parenthood.

This is why the pathology of the mothering object, like the presence of a traumatic event in the history of the subject, is not a sufficient condition for compromising the future of the nascent psyche. We adhere to the thesis that the *psychic danger stems from the interaction between an inadequate mothering environment and a constitutional fragility in the child*. We have underlined this point in the thinking of different authors (Bion, Meltzer, Tustin – see Chapters 2 and 10). The pathologizing effect of the psychic alterations in the object will be confirmed in coincidence with a particular constitutional sensitivity of the child, with a greater or lesser degree of difficulty in the child to tolerate frustration, with a vulnerability of constitution that prevents the child from taking advantage of the nourishing qualities of its object. It should be recalled that this "constitutional equipment" with which the infant is born is shaped by the proto-emotional experiences of intra-uterine life (see Chapters 2 and 3).

Psychopathology has its sources in what is constitutional and congenital, in the history of the subject – the history of his encounter with the world and the vagaries of his future history –, and in the parental or environmental projections of which he is the object. Obviously, the more the parental inadequacies are massive, toxic or radical, the more the role played by the constitutional factor will be reduced, until it is zero, in the emergence and evolution of a psychopathology in the child. And it is the same in the other direction.

Although we talk about the infant's particular sensitivity, or even hypersensitivity, to the affective states of his object, and in particular to its more or less temporary decathexis, we must also consider the hypersensitivity of the parent or mothering object to the infant's withdrawals. In the last century, Rosenfeld (1963) had already envisaged, both for the aetiology of schizophrenia and the disorders of the mother–infant relationship, not only the mother's influence on the infant, but also the mother's reaction to a particularly difficult schizoid infant.[1] The observation of infants going through transient states of autistic withdrawal, and of their parents, has shown us – we have already discussed this (Chapter 3) – how intensely wounded some parents feel when their child looks away from them, making them temporarily unable to come to his assistance, whereas more narcissistically integrated parents can go and find their baby in the depths of his autistic withdrawal and bring him back to "psychic life".

To support this idea of a double precondition for the pathological development of the nascent psyche, let us add that the intensity of its alteration is never proportional to the intensity of the inadequacy of the real object or to the intensity of the traumatic event that can impact the growth process. Piera Aulagnier (1985b), for example, notes that equally disturbing-disturbed psychic environments can be found in subjects with very varied psychopathologies. Leon Kreisler and Bertrand Cramer (1981), in another example, emphasize the phantasy activity of the child who may interpret in a completely variable way the emotional states of the parent: for example, a depressive withdrawal may be experienced by the child as a sadistic seduction, as an abandonment, as a state of preoccupation with a third party, etc. Let us emphasize, then, along with Paula Heimann (1952b), Piera Aulagnier (1975) and others, the pathologizing impact of the telescoping between the phantasy scenario elaborated by the child and the story actually experienced on the family-social stage, which serves to confirm the phantasy.

Furthermore, when the child's history includes early traumatic events, more than the particular traumatic event itself, it is the defensive system set up by the psyche, with the precarious means at its disposal, to fight against traumatic experiences, which constitutes an impediment to its development. Hanna Segal (1972) demonstrates this well. She presents, for example, the case of a borderline patient who has built a delusional, self-sufficient and omnipotent system to protect himself against the re-emergence of an early catastrophic situation (abrupt and traumatic weaning, followed by the consecutive loss of two parents). Hanna Segal shows that it was not so much the actual initial catastrophe as the defensive system put in place to avoid its re-emergence which stifled the patient's capacity for maturation and prevented him from living, "erasing" his infantile part and his object relations. Here again, as we have pointed out with regard to the relationship between external factors and constitutional factors, even if the subject has the capacity to use effective or adequate defences, the intensity of the trauma, its violence and its duration, can prevent or destroy that possibility.[2]

This deep entanglement between the reality of the object and the phantasies of the child about it, or between the reality of the child and the phantasies of the parent about it, as well as the singularity of each protagonist's defensive response to the weight of external reality, along with the combination of external reality and constitutionality, make the question of causality particularly complex. This is why Donald Meltzer (1984a) says of psychoanalysis that it is a "purely descriptive" science and limited by the "essential mystery of the processes of symbol-formation" (Meltzer, 1984a, p. 549, translated from the French). Meltzer thinks that modern science, even if its causal explanations are only approximations, deals with a universe in which causal relationships exist; and that science believes in their existence even when it cannot define them. On the other hand, psychoanalysis is concerned with a universe in which causal relationships do not exist, which makes any explanatory theory inadequate. Physiological processes are concerned with causal relationships, but as soon as one moves on to psychic processes, consideration of such relationships is no longer relevant.[3]

13.2 The children of depression

The first configuration that we will examine concerning the inadequacy of the mothering environment is that characterized by depression. Even though the child may escape psychopathology, for the reasons we have mentioned previously, a depressive context will certainly have an impact. We would like to say a few words, for example, concerning the "dead mother complex" (Green, 1983).

Depression is present in all nascent parenting experiences, in both the mother and the father. Maternity and paternity imply a change of identity. This produces a more or less intense crisis, a disorganization which is followed by a neo-organization of identity. Such an experience is inevitably accompanied by depressive affects, due to the experience of loss which accompanies such a transformation. In the post-partum period every mother, like any father, presents more or less manifest depressive tendencies. Her emotional detachment from her baby is such that her capacity to understand and recognize his needs is relatively limited; so she counts on the baby to use her breasts, her hands, her voice, and to awaken in her a good feeling of motherhood, so that he can "cure" her of her depression. It is the same for the father.

Post-partum depression is nourished by the current experience of motherhood and by past experiences modulating the history of the subject and the history of the development of her personality, in other words by those aspects of the past that are transferred to the current situation.[4] Traces of these past experiences can envelop the ordinary process of post-partum depression. We can thus say that everything that endangers the mental state of the mother (family and emotional isolation, childbirth in a foreign country, traumatic history such as, for example, the loss of a baby, etc.) should be considered as a risk factor. When maternal depression sets in, it increases if the mother does not find support from her own objects, both internal and external objects: the child's father, but also her own parents, her own mother (due to conflict, separation, bereavement). It is likely to be amplified if the perinatal circumstances have been dramatic (accidents or incidents experienced as catastrophic, an unexpected caesarean, etc.). Maternity and the context of the baby's birth can therefore precipitate a cyclical depressive process, or reveal or repeat an already existing depression. The father may also be affected by depression because of the psychic neo-organization implied by the experience of fatherhood, to which all the above-mentioned circumstances can apply. These depressive contexts will compromise the ability of the environment to make itself available to the baby's psychological needs. Note that parental depression, when it has no troublesome symptoms, can easily go unnoticed.

If parental depression is too intense, too invasive, it can have important consequences for the development of the baby. It will produce avoidances and withdrawals which may take the form of autistic withdrawals or even involve manifest withdrawals.[5] This is the case, for example, when, as Tustin (1985a) puts it, a mother experiences the child she is carrying as a "guarantee against the hidden feeling of an unbearable loss": the birth of the child will then be felt as the "loss of the reassuring part of her body" (Tustin, 1985a, p. 23). If the foetus represents for the mother an "auto-sensual consolation for her loneliness and her despair at the centre of her being" (Tustin, 1984b, p. 115, translated from the French), birth will then be experienced as a frightening experience of unbearable loss. This can make the mother so depressed and lacking in self-confidence that she is no longer able to protect the baby from an experience that resembles her own, an experience of premature separation, an experience of narcissistic loss.

The characteristic of any depressive experience, says Piera Aulagnier (1985b), is to "abolish the bonus of pleasure that one should encounter in acting, thinking and contact: it is to this absence of pleasure that the *infans* reacts" (Aulagnier, 1985b, p. 270, translated for this edition). The *lack of sharing of an erogenous pleasure* will have destructive consequences for the nascent psyche which needs the "food" that is pleasure, the shared experience of pleasure, in order to experience fully its own experiences of pleasure (see Aulagnier, 1986).

In addition to abolishing the bonus of pleasure, depression in the mother can lead to what Francisco Palacio Espasa (1980) calls a "de-emotionalization of the mother-child relationship", which transforms primary maternal preoccupation into technical and social preoccupation involving huge distortions of empathy. And the same is true for the father.

This technical concern of which Palacio Espasa speaks links up with what André Carel (1981) describes as a "dissociation in the maintenance situation", where "somatic *holding* continues while psychic *holding* is atrophied" (Carel, 1981, p. 131, translated for this edition). The child is then the object of what Carel calls "*disregard*" on the part of his parents: he is excluded from parental psychic cathexes; he is "raised and protected as regards his body, but with disregard for his psyche" (ibid.). The psychic outcome for the child will be threefold: first, a relative well-being thanks to the persistence of a healthy part of the baby in relation to the healthy parts of the parents;

second, a state of intense distress; third, an autistic-looking withdrawal. These three states can coexist.

As André Carel demonstrates, if the parents' *anti-depressive struggle* is combined with a counter-cathexis of parental hostility towards the child, hostility due to the fact that the child has actually, or in phantasy, exposed the parents to the danger of death or madness, the child will be the object of disregard as a psychic being. The coincidence of this disregard with a constitutional hypersensitivity in the child can generate autistic states.

> André Carel illustrates these considerations by studying, among other things, two pairs of twins, one twin child in each pair presenting an autistic-type development, in such a context of disregard. Note that in the two cases reported, the attitude of disregard towards one twin corresponded to a psychic hyper-cathexis of the other by the parents, the second twin being physically ill and monopolizing the entire narcissistic and libidinal capital. Being in good physical health, it was felt on the one hand that the first twin, who was to present autistic symptoms, could be excluded from psychic cathexes, and on the other hand that he was responsible for the damage suffered by the second, which caused him to be reproached for being alive while the other was dying.

The abolition of pleasure, de-emotionalization, technical preoccupation and disregard are reflected in the behavioural register, among other things, by inadequate holding of the child, an absence of words addressed to the child, a poverty of interactions and a scarcity of exchanges of happy and smiling facial expressions. Depressed parents have difficulty in holding the child, communicating with him, but also in comforting him, in "cushioning the baby against shocks", in the words of Tustin (1985b, p. 15, translated from the French). They show little reaction to the baby's expressions, as well as to his lack of expression. They are often far removed from him, psychically but also spatially. They "drop" their child, in the clearest sense of the popular expression.

This depressive picture combined with hypersensitivity in the child can have the consequence, as we have already seen (Chapter 2), and this is essential, of a sudden awareness in the child of separation – psychical and bodily – well before his psychical apparatus is ready to endure such an ordeal. In ordinary development, the disillusionment caused by the experience of bodily separation is bearable and stimulating – because the establishment of a relationship with others is developed contemporaneously with the emergence of the self. If, on the other hand, the child cannot be helped to bear the shock of the awareness of separation, due to the psychic unavailability of the environment and his particular sensitivity to this lack, autistic encapsulation as a solution will be more likely.

Didier Houzel (1988b, 1991), drawing on the notions of "aesthetic object" and "aesthetic conflict" proposed by Donald Meltzer (1984b, 1986; Meltzer and Harris Williams, 1988), suggests that the parental depressive state leads the baby to experience this absence of psychic life directed towards him not as if it were a *loss*, but as an *excessively violent attraction*. In the event of maternal depression, the normal aesthetic shock, the

> fascination, enticing to the point of dizziness, due to the seduction of the aesthetic qualities of the surface of the object, [...] is no longer restrained and cushioned by physical communication, by the gradual discovery of its internal psychic qualities, by its alpha function, by the child's mechanisms of introjection and by the development of his thinking.
> (Houzel, 1988b, p. 101, translated for this edition)

More than the loss of the object, it is its violent force of aesthetic attraction, uncushioned, unrestrained, which is harmful to the development of the baby. The object is moreover all the more painfully and violently enticing because it is absent (psychically).

Avoidance, withdrawal – including withdrawal of the autistic type – is not the only reaction to a depressive environment. This is especially true if the environmental disturbance is not intense, or if the child has been able to build a healthy part of his personality that is sufficiently strong and saves him from having to resort to withdrawal or absence from himself and the world.

In this regard, let us consider the "dead mother" syndrome, described by André Green (1983). This is the consequence not of a real death of the mother but of a "psychic death" following a depression that suddenly transforms the mother, the source of vitality for the child, into a distant, almost inanimate, figure. The picture is the same as the one we have just described, but in this case the mother's mental absence is abrupt and traumatic. The causes of the mother's depression can be various: sudden loss of a loved one, a disappointment in love or in the professional sphere, the death of an infant, miscarriage, etc. Whatever the case, the traumatic event produces a sudden decrease in the mother's interest in the child, a sudden and mutative change in the maternal imago. This transformation is experienced by the child as a catastrophe, because love is suddenly lost and nothing in the way of explanation can account for the situation. Loss of love is therefore associated with a loss of meaning. The "dead mother" is an object that is present but absorbed by mourning.

We could – and we should – describe the same processes and consequences when faced with the experience of a father's "psychic death". Whether the child is confronted by a "dead mother", in Green's sense of the term, or a "dead father", the catastrophic experience will be of the same order. We should therefore speak of the syndrome not of the "dead mother" but of the "dead parent".

A series of defence mechanisms will be set up in children, in this situation of the "dead mother", as described by Green:

- the *decathexis of the maternal object* and *unconscious identification with the "dead mother"* – a phantasy of incorporation underpinned by a process of projective identification is recognizable here (see Chapters 1 and 11);
- the *early oedipal triangulation*, where the child is obliged to find someone responsible (the father) for the mother's breakdown;
- the *triggering of secondary hatred*, the aim of which is to dominate and defile the object, to take revenge on it;
- the *autoerotic excitation* marked by a reluctance to love the object ("the basis of future hysterical identifications");
- the *early development of the phantasy-based and intellectual capacities of the ego*, where the child devotes his efforts to guessing or anticipating his mother's variations of mood and is subject to a "compulsion to imagine", a "compulsion to think".

All these defences are organized with a triple aim: to keep the ego alive, to revive the mother, and to compete with the object of mourning in an early triangulation.

The recathexis of the relationship with the mother is always marked by what is ephemeral and threatened with a catastrophic experience. Once the child has become an adult he will be perpetually in search of an object that cannot be introjected, without

The inadequacies of the containing object

being able either to renounce it or accept its introjection in the ego cathected by the "dead mother". He will develop what André Green calls the "dead mother complex", where the failure of individuating separation leads the subject to recurrently relive the loss of the primary object which he perpetually strives to retain. The subject will show an inability to love, a deep loneliness, feelings of emptiness, attesting to a depression with libidinal loss. This depression gives rise to manifestations belonging to the "blank" series which characterizes the "clinical experience of emptiness" or the "clinical experience of the negative": negative hallucinations (see Green, 1977),[6] blank psychosis (see Donnet and Green, 1973), blank mourning, etc., all resulting from massive decathexis which leaves traces in the unconscious in the form of "psychic holes".

Didier Anzieu (1987b) describes a maternal imago akin to the "dead mother", yet different in that the psychic absence comes in this case not from depression but from impassiveness in the face of the feelings, expectations and need in the child for manifestations of attachment. The mother is cold, distant and rejecting, and any attempt by the child to move her fails. Anzieu identifies this imago, not of the dead mother but rather of "death in the guise of the mother, a mother from whom annihilation rather than life emanates" (Anzieu, 1987b, p. 125, translated for this edition), in all his patients who suffer from the "pains of loneliness". Again, when the paternal imago is marked by such impassiveness and coldness the same effects are present.

We will now make a digression concerning the psychopathologies to which the complex of the dead mother refers. This "blank mourning", this failure of the experience of individuating separation (Mahler, 1968), can be explained, according to Green (1983), by a maternal decathexis that is sufficiently noticeable by the child to wound his narcissism and disturb the "resolution of the depressive phase" while complicating it in the process. However, Green's conceptualization of the dead mother complex seems to extend the range of its effects, in some cases, to psychosis. What level of ego-integration must this configuration of the dead mother complex have for it to escape psychosis? Or can this internal "dead mother" be understood as a *psychotic enclave* in a personality which may not be psychotic? Thus, depending on the degree of "encystment" of the "dead mother", depending on the intensity of the processes of projective identification with this incorporated object, the psychotic aspects will be more or less contained or brimming over.

If maternal or parental depression can be linked to events that are more or less foreign to the child – as we have considered so far – it can also occur through the very fact of meeting the child, when this newborn child is too much of a disappointment. Every birth is accompanied by a necessary gap between the real child and his pre-cathected image, but when this gap presents itself as an abyss, when the encounter is traumatic – think, for example, of children with a malformation or disability – catastrophic consequences may arise.

As Piera Aulagnier (1986) reveals, the "trauma of the encounter" between a mother – or rather a parent – and her newborn, the failure of the anchoring of the child's body in the "psychic body" present in the parental psyche before the child's birth and which anticipated his image, deprive the child of the psychic representative that should have welcomed him. To survive, the child may resort to three types of psychic response:

- a first type of response will lie in withdrawal, possibly autistic;
- a second type of response will consist in the child always trying to stay as close as possible to what he assumes is expected by the parent, in order to get closer to his pre-cathected psychic representative (this reaction, based on an early "understanding", anticipates the consideration of separation and represents an experience of reality-testing that comes "too early" and at the expense of psychic autonomy);
- a third type of response, finally, will lie in cathecting a body in a state of need, rather than cathecting a body relating through pleasure (the link to the object will also be preserved, but it will present itself as a conflictual link based on the power to demand or refuse the contribution that the body needs – food, sleep, etc. – a contribution for which the object is cathected solely because it possesses the desire and power to grant or refuse it).

These three types of response represent solutions, one could say, when faced with the impossibility of taking advantage of the psychic qualities of the external object, an absent, unavailable, disappointed object, and probably full of hate, preoccupied about an unbearable difference between the anticipated image of the child and the reality of this newcomer. The first solution corresponds to all forms of narcissistic withdrawal. The second solution is the organization of a false self, the pseudo-identity trying to reduce or do away with the separation from the object — we will return to this in the next chapter. Finally, the third solution consists in cathecting and maintaining a tie with the object based on conflict, hatred and excitation.

13.3 The children of mourning

Let us now consider what we will call the case of *children of mourning*. By this we mean not only children whose conception or birth is linked to the loss of a loved one — this case is linked to what we have described in connection with children of depression —, but especially children whose function, which is unconsciously assigned to them, is intended to avoid the pain of mourning through the *commemoration of the deceased* that they bring about.

This configuration is sometimes found in psychotic children. Jean Guyotat (1980, 1982), drawing on his clinical experience and statistical research, has pointed out the high frequency, in a given generation of families of psychotics, of the death of a family member, especially a child, over several generations. Often the birth of the future psychotic child coincides with, or is linked to, a death. Genevieve Haag (1984b) has made the same observation. Our experience of psychotic children has brought us abundant examples confirming this.[7] Jean Guyotat has suggested that these death/birth coincidences strengthen in a given individual the narcissistic organization of his ties of filiation. In addition, Guyotat noted in many of his patients, psychotic but also depressive or psychosomatic, the hypercathexis they made of these coincidences. He explained this hypercathexis by the necessity for the patient to defend himself from death by controlling it by thought.

The child of mourning, as we understand it, that is to say, a child who serves as a replacement, stands in for an impossible mourning, hinders the work of mourning by making the deceased present. To paraphrase Freud (1917), the shadow of the deceased has fallen on the child.

Monique Bydlowski (1978) has described how the newborn serves as a barrier to the work of mourning when he takes the place of the deceased. She linked the question of the desire for a child associated with death or mourning to manic celebration (the resurgence of sexual need after the loss of a loved object, the bringing to the boil of the incestuous sexual drive as a result of death or the announcement of a danger of death) on the one hand and to the denial of the loss of the object (the newborn satisfies a fetishist desire by creating a fantasy of immortality, a narcissistic negation of the loss of a part of oneself) on the other. Finally, Monique Bydlowski considered that the unborn child identified with a deceased person is caught up in a recurrent staging of a death wish — the death of the other is all the more unbearable since it fulfils intensely repressed death wishes towards him or her; the newborn then participates in the inability to mourn the lost object.

To illustrate this theme of the child of mourning, we could cite cases we have come across where the conception of a child who became psychotic followed a series of miscarriages or the death of a previous child whom the newborn was expected to replace[8] — remember that such an event is not a sufficient condition, by itself, to jeopardize the psychic evolution of the unborn child. Nevertheless, we have chosen to present the case of a child who is not psychotic and whose conception did not coincide with the death of a family member, but whose family and individual histories present what we might call "character traits" of a child of mourning.

> Julien is an 11-year-old child, the oldest of three siblings, whom his parents brought, on the advice of their paediatrician, first for a consultation and then for a few days' hospitalization in an infant psychiatric ward. In his letter, the paediatrician described Julien as a child who had difficulties at school (repeating a grade, "dysorthography", "probable dyslexia") and who currently had psychomotor instability. Julien was restless and nervous, and had tics. On top of this there were depressive tendencies: the child suffered from the fact that he sometimes had bad marks at school (although his educational level was quite satisfactory at the present time) and "one day he had even pretended to commit suicide". The paediatrician, having found no remedy other than prescribing drugs, deferred to the opinion of the child psychiatric service for further investigations.
>
> It was in this context that one of us (M.L.) met Julien. Very quickly difficulties of separation appeared between Julien and his mother. Julien was a lively and intelligent child, who expressed himself easily even though this involved a lot of writhing. He evoked a sports activity at which he was very good: wrestling. Julien spoke easily about his difficulties; he himself said he had tics: clearing his throat, hitting his buttocks with his feet while

The inadequacies of the containing object

walking, and swinging his legs back; and above all a fairly spectacular movement which Julien demonstrated: it involved bending forward, putting his elbows on his knees with arms bent, hands clenched near the throat while raising his elbows upwards but always leaving them in contact with the body. Julien also talked about his difficulty in accepting bad grades at school. He was then on the verge of tears, as he was when he spoke of the separations from his mother and his family. Concerning the famous mock suicide, Julien at first did not want to talk about it, but finally he spoke quite freely on this subject: he said that he had had a very bad grade at school that day and had "put a string around his teddy bear's neck as if to hang it".

In another meeting, this time in the presence of his mother, we talked about tics. In fact, the theme of the difficult separation between Julien and his mother soon became mixed up with this discussion of tics. Mrs. R. described herself as a "mother hen", who felt very anxious as soon as she was separated from Julien and her two other children. She was "afraid that something would happen to them". Mr. R. was then mentioned, a father whose presence was said to be important. Mrs. R. said she was demanding about academic results, because "it is important for them to succeed in life". The episode of the mock suicide then came up, followed by Mrs. R's childhood history. She related, in front of Julien, who was a little embarrassed but very present, her "version" of this event. It had happened on returning from school. Julien had had a very bad grade and Mrs. R. said she had got angry, raising her voice. Following this, alone in his room, Julien went on to hang a string on the curtain rod, made a slip knot on this string, climbed onto a stool with his teddy bear in his arms and put the string around his neck. Mrs. R., entering the room at that time, was very upset at this spectacle of Julien on the stool. In this version of the facts, Julien was much more involved in the mock hanging than he himself had suggested.

Mrs. R. became increasingly emotional and it was from that moment that she began to speak about her own history. She did it in tears. Julien heard for the first time certain episodes concerning his mother's childhood. She belonged to a family of eight children. She had lost her father at the age of six, and this death had led to the dispersion of the family. The children were separated from their mother and scattered about in institutions, in foster families. Mrs. R. was upset as she spoke of her disarray at losing all her bearings, her parents and brothers and sisters. Added to this was a sense of shame: she was ashamed to have experienced it and ashamed to speak about it. Julien listened very attentively. "I have never told him", she said. This painful childhood past had driven her ever since becoming a mother to pamper her children to the point of being overprotective. The death of Julien's grandfather remained unexplained.

Mrs. R. went on to say that having remarried, her mother had sought, many years after this family breakdown, to find and reunite all her children, which happened when Mrs. R. was 14 years old. There had been the joy of reunion and the pleasure of reforming a family. Unfortunately, this happy reunion did not last since Mrs. R.'s stepfather had died in a car accident in the six months that followed. Mrs. R. was very insistent then on one point, namely she had predicted that a serious accident was going to happen … the very day her stepfather died, as if in thought she had foreseen or predicted the catastrophe. Finally, three years after this tragedy (Mrs. R. was then 17 years old), the family once again suffered a bereavement: Mrs. R. lost her favourite brother in a motorcycle accident, a death which she said she had, yet again, predicted that very morning. Mrs. R. was in tears. She said that she had thought a lot, on the birth of Julien (her first child), about her dead brother, as if Julien was identified with this brother, and she added: "When Julien was born, I reproached myself for being joyful; why was he the one who died and not me? Whenever I felt joy with Julien, for his baptism for example, I reproached myself for being happy".

Then Mrs. R. mentioned her father's death. She ended up saying, in dribs and drabs and almost hidden from Julien who heard nevertheless, that he had committed suicide, that she was sure of it even if nobody ever actually admitted to her that that was really the cause of his death. Mrs. R. made a gesture evoking the hanging, after which Julien left the office. He had heard enough and let his mother continue.

This material could be commented on at length, but we will only make a few comments to illustrate our point about the "child of mourning":

- the death occupies an important place in this family, starting with the shared unspoken story concerning the hanging of Mrs. R.'s father;
- the shock produced by such an event in a child's psyche leads the child to try to master this impact and manage guilt by organizing a scenario in which the disaster is predicted;
- the repetition of similar disasters confirms the phantasy; the latter takes centre stage and mobilizes all cathexes; much of the energy is spent waiting for the disaster;
- the unborn child, identified with the deceased, attracts these cathexes; he must, from his position, participate in the repetition; the repetition of the scenario testifies to the desperate attempt to gain mastery over what presents itself to the psyche as unthinkable, unrepresentable.

It is noteworthy that Julien staged the hanging. His mother, who "saw her brother" during Julien's birth, could not help but "see her father" during this episode which was very shocking and violent for her. These acts may be considered as having a commemorative value.

In addition, we would like to suggest a hypothesis with regard to Julien's spectacular tic: Julien wrestled; the posture he adopted while having an irrepressible tic corresponded, on close observation, to a combat posture by means of which the wrestler protects himself from the risk of ... strangulation. It could be said that this tic dramatized the morbid scenario that was foreign to the child but which nevertheless haunted him.

13.4 The children of hatred and perversion

Let us now consider the consequences of a psychic organization of the mothering environment, or of the relationship between the external mothering object and the child, where hatred or perversion is to the fore. Hate-filled or perverse relationships in the parent–child couple, or within family exchanges, are generally considered as having the potential to foster the emergence of psychotic potential (schizophrenia, paranoia) in the child.

The first pathogenic relationship we will consider is the one described by Paul-Claude Racamier (1980ab, 1986, 1987, 1992, 1995) under the term of *"narcissistic perversion"*. This is based on a "denial of the object's own *value*"[9] aimed at reducing it to a tool/

object. This process is considered by Paul-Claude Racamier as a perversity with particularly harmful effects for the one who falls prey to this "moral predation". Narcissistic perverts are frequently more or less lastingly scarred psychotics and are often found among the parents of psychotic subjects.

The sources of narcissistic perversion are fundamentally antidepressive, and the pervert is driven by the twofold need to avoid mourning and plug psychotic anxieties. This double constraint pushes him to get rid of the disillusionments and the situations of mourning that are hurtful to him by exporting them onto close objects (spouse, children, friends, etc.). The object into which the conflict is exported, which Racamier calls a "non-object object", is an object of utility which will receive the heavy burden of having to take responsibility for the psychic conflicts of the perverse narcissist, in a relationship of dependence that is all the more alienating in that his own narcissism is actively discredited. To achieve this, it is important that the state of dependence of the object of utility, of the "puppet", is absolute; any move towards autonomy by the prey will be vigorously combated, mainly by discrediting it. It is therefore a question for the narcissistic pervert of narcissistically valuing himself by attacking the self of the other and by enjoying his rout.

The narcissistic pervert feeds on the narcissism of others. In addition, his favourite fields are language, words and the social sphere onto which cathexes are transferred. More than the truth, being or having, what matters to him is appearances, seeming, which gives him a "profound stamp of inauthenticity".

Paul-Claude Racamier says he has identified two versions of narcissistic perversion. One, the most "poisonous", can be observed especially in women called "phalloid":

> The phalloid narcissistic mother is of course a castrating woman, utterly full of hate, who constantly avoids the depression that is menacing here, who is eager to take possession of her victims even if they are dead, and who is even capable of using her own children as hostages, as instruments of revenge and guided missiles.
> (Racamier, 1987, p. 14, translated for this edition)

The other, more advantageous version, closer to "glorious narcissism", is found more in men.

What is the origin of narcissistic perversion? Racamier locates its sources in a *"narcissistic seduction"* suffered by the future pervert. The aim of narcissistic seduction is to constitute between the very young child and his mother "a unique and omnipotent symbiotic being, sheltered from instinctual drive vicissitudes, ambivalence and Oedipal conflicts, and even more so, from separation and mourning" (Racamier, 1987, p. 15, translated for this edition). Thus the narcissistic pervert develops "the active illusion of actually, and with impunity, replacing the father in the mother's life, the father being ousted in thought and in fact" (ibid.). We could reasonably reverse the roles attributed by Racamier to the father and the mother, and describe the same toxic effects in a father who jealously guards the narcissistic benefits of a symbiotic relationship with a child cathected as an anti-mourning object. It is the maintenance by a parent of an infantile and primitive megalomania which is the basis of narcissistic perversion. So what we see is a transgenerational process: the narcissistic pervert, who is himself a former object of narcissistic seduction, will establish psychoticizing relationships. Transmission concerns a narcissistic lack, which is no doubt increasingly difficult to fill.

In this description of narcissistic perversion, we recognize the workings of the process of *projective identification*. It is through projective identification that destructive symbiotic ties are welded, that anxieties and conflicts are exported or transmitted into an object that has the task of sheltering them (see Chapters 6, 11 and 12).

Racamier's conceptions can shed light on many clinical situations concerning dual relationships, but also groups, families and institutions. Narcissistic perversion is seen in the intimacy of inter-individual relationships as in the social sphere. We could give many illustrations.

> For example, in families whose members are linked by a *destructive symbiosis*, we frequently observe the need to guarantee the conflictual immunity, of which Racamier speaks, of a member or of the whole family group by maintaining the pathology of another member, the depositary of madness and object of contempt. Psychotic children can, in a way, sometimes be considered as sacrificed children. Getting rid of the child – by decathecting its infantile needs, or by a real separation – then amounts to the family group getting rid of the sick part of each

of its members. We can also witness somatic or psychic decompensations of a parent when the psychotic child shows signs of well-being, that is to say of better capacity for individuation.

Other easily identifiable situations, which can be decoded as the staging of a narcissistic perversion, concern the institutional life of a team of caregivers – Racamier himself gives several illustrations in this connection. Take the example of a situation in which a team of caregivers is given the impossible role of managing a conflict that is imposed on it. Decomposed (first discrediting manoeuvre) and stumbling, it is not uncommon for it to be decomposed or discredited a second time (the "double barrelled" and "reduplicative" nature of narcissistic perversion, according to Racamier) by a brutal and savage "interpretation" formulated by the same person who treated the caregiving team as prey, aimed at designating the latter as the source of the conflict and criticizing it for its inability to find a solution or for its destructive impulses. The narcissistic pervert, in these cases, is often someone who occupies a high hierarchical position in the institutional organization or at the level of imagined or supposed skills, medical or psychological. The caregiving team is then a place for externalizing his own internal conflicts.

A team of caregivers can itself be an agent of narcissistic perversion towards patients. It is, in fact, sometimes difficult for them to put certain patients in any other place than that of the mentally ill. We can observe, for example, situations where, in a caregiver-patient group, a heavy and distressing silence induces a secret desire on the part of the caregivers for a patient to express himself noisily. When a patient then starts "acting crazily", the tension subsides, the group laughs, while looking distressed by the intensity of this madness. The narcissistic completeness of the group that was attacked by the agonizing silence is re-welded by the pathological representation (in both senses of the term) of the patient, who is discreetly or slyly treated sadistically and who is unconsciously expected to play the role assigned to him.

We would now like to link this notion of narcissistic perversion[10] to that of *"tyranny-and-submission"* as described by Donald Meltzer (1987b).[11] Tyranny consists in producing a slave by destroying an internal object in a person, in particular his superego, in order to take its place and to subjugate this person. Meltzer differentiates tyranny-and-submission from sadomasochism. While sadomasochism is a "game" that repeats an infantile phantasy and stages the "murder of a baby inside the mother", tyranny-and-submission is a "serious matter" that involves much more primitive survival processes linked to extreme persecutory anxiety which drives the tyrant to find a slave into whom he can project this anxiety. If sadomasochism belongs to the domain of intimate sexual relations, tyranny-and-submission is found very naturally and continuously in the social sphere.

This evocation of the techniques of narcissistic perversion and tyranny-and-submission leads us to recall the schizophrenogenic modes of communication described by Harold Searles (1959) as testifying to a relentless *"effort to drive the other person crazy"*. The word "crazy" is equivalent in Searles's writings to "schizophrenic", and he considers the continuous effort, largely or totally unconscious, of the important person or persons around a subject to drive him crazy as an element in the aetiology of schizophrenia. Searles distinguishes different modes and different motives, all essentially unconscious, which account for the pathogenic relationship staging this effort to drive the other person crazy.

Regarding the modes of communication, Searles defines six, all of which tend to foster an emotional conflict in the other person in order to make different parts of the latter's personality act against each other:

- the *sadistic interpretation*: whether it is the work of a close relative or an analyst, this aims to constantly question adaptation, to constantly draw attention to areas of the personality that are contradictory and repressed, reinforcing conflict and anxiety;
- the *excessively seductive behaviour*: this creates an intense conflict in children between their desire to develop their individuality and their desire to remain in a situation of infantile symbiosis;
- the *simultaneous, or rapidly alternating, stimulation and frustration*: whatever needs are involved, these produce an effect of disintegration;
- the *double bind*: this form of communication, particularly rich in pathogenic effects, was highlighted by Gregory Bateson (1956), who shows how the schizophrenic suffers from being

in a situation where he is exposed to a double discourse, both of whose antagonistic contents nullify any possibility of taking on meaning, and how the discourse of the schizophrenic himself conveys a meaning oscillating between contradictory and incompatible propositions without any possibility of choice, meaning torn between mutually exclusive messages;[12]
- the *multi-level relationship*: this consists of relating to the other person on several levels that have no relationship between them, which tends to force him to dissociate himself; such an interrelationship with a parent causes significant trauma to the child if it is frequently repeated;
- the *sudden switching of emotional wavelengths*: this technique, similar to the previous one, which consists in sudden and unpredictable changes in mood, recalls what we said about the "dead mother", but the sudden change in mood is frequently repeated here, with catastrophic consequences for the child.

All of these modes or techniques have a common purpose: they aim to "undermine the other person's confidence in his own emotional reactions and his own perception of reality" (Searles, 1959, p. 260). However, as Racamier says (1980a), "the child whose perception is invalidated is faced with the alternative of believing in the testimony of his senses or of believing his object; [...] he is torn between his ego and his object" (Racamier, 1980a, p. 149, translated for this edition).

Harold Searles enumerates several reasons underlying this effort to drive the other person crazy – we have already mentioned, in one way or another, most of them –: "psychosis wishes" (the psychological equivalent of murder), the wish to externalize one's own madness, the perception of a discreet craziness in the other, an aborted love relationship, blackmail with madness (the parent of the schizophrenic threatens the child with going crazy and drives him to experience any wish for individuation as a monstrous wish to drive him crazy), etc. The most powerful motive of all concerns the *wish to perpetuate the gratifications offered by a mode of symbiotic relationship*.

These conceptions support the picture Searles (1965, 1979) had of schizophrenia: the schizophrenic, according to Searles, suffers from the incompleteness of the ego of his mother, or of any other parental figure whose functioning demands that the child should not achieve his own individual identity but should remain totally devoted to him.

All these considerations concerning pathological symbiosis, in which the relationship between the schizophrenic and his object has its place, can also apply to the therapeutic relationship between a caregiver and a schizophrenic patient. Searles emphasizes, in this regard, and this point seems essential to us, the importance of recognizing the *gratifying aspect of the symbiotic relationship*, of recognizing the powerful attraction that this type of relationship exerts, so as not to perpetuate its unconscious benefits and, under the cover of conscious therapeutic intentions, not to be unconsciously driven by an effort to *keep* the other person crazy.

Let us now consider, with Piera Aulagnier, hatred and violence, and the pathological effects of this destructive symbiosis, in the different registers of psychic functioning (originary, primary, secondary). Piera Aulagnier (1985b) illustrates the hateful atmosphere in which the future psychotic evolves by describing the four most frequent scenarios in parents linked by hate. She specifies that, for her, *the child is less a symptom than a revealer of parental pathology.* These four types of parental couple are described as follows: a couple gives the impression of "pretending", not showing open hatred but an obvious distancing of all affect; a couple where the father is actively absent and where the mother makes the child, whom she holds responsible for this absence, the father's mouth-absence, with the latter's psychic complicity; a couple who have the particularity of being complementary in the register of their symptomatology, where neither of them wanted children but mutually reproach each other for having imposed the birth of a child on them; and finally, a couple in which hatred serves as cement, the two partners remaining together until death ensues, the death of one causing, despite mutual death wishes, a decompensation in the other. This fourth scenario is particularly present in paranoia, but is also present in schizophrenia. In any case, it is "the most likely to make the subject topple over into psychosis" (Aulagnier, 1985b, p. 274, translated for this edition).

The emotion and excitement arising from the explosive scenes that erupt between the parents far exceed the capacities of the child's stimulus barrier. The emotional intensity caused by the violence will make these scenes the equivalent of a primal scene. The erotization of violence by the parental couple will confirm this phantasied organization. The child will experience the violent intrusion of a conflictual environment "tearing itself apart".

What are the effects of this hateful atmosphere in the register of the originary? The originary register is the space of pictograms, and Piera Aulagnier extends her model of the pictogram, which we have spoken about several times, to the psyche-world relationship. The pictogram of "the subject's own psychic space–ambient psychic space" defines the self-representation that the psyche forges of its links with the space of the world, a space complementary to its own and generated by it.

When the ambient psychic space is dominated by hatred and violence, the pictogram of the junction of the "subject's own psychic space–ambient psychic space" will depict an intrusive experience imposed by the complementary object. The image will be comparable to that of a fire igniting the flesh: "We are just one 'burning' entity [...], flesh and fire become inseparable" (Aulagnier, 1985b, p. 277, translated for this edition) – a fine image with which to describe destructive symbiosis.

The nascent psychic space will only be safe from violence and the experience of catastrophe when its complement is absent. The complementary object, whose very presence is a source of suffering, becomes the target of the death drives that it mobilizes. Instead of "desire for the object", the "wish not to have to desire it any more" sets in. The first phase of drive fusion – satisfaction of both the life drives (by the presentation of the breast) and the death drives (by the appeasement of the state of tension) – fails; the death drives are exacerbated and the life drives push the psyche to continue to demand, in a forever unsatisfied quest, the encounter with a complement to which it can be joined.

If violence and hatred continue to occupy the foreground, in both the primary and secondary registers, this violence of affects will be compounded by the "commentary" of the parental discourse on the existence and origin of these affects. The child will hear this commentary and be confronted with a statement about origins from which any idea that the origin of the child is founded on desire and love will be absent.

To describe the effects of the hate-filled parental relationship in the primary and secondary registers, we must return to the conceptions of Piera Aulagnier set out in 1975. The psychotic potentiality, in this psychic climate of hate, will flow, as far as the primary and secondary registers are concerned, from the confrontation with a statement on the senseless or missing origin in the discourse outside the psyche. The senseless statement is an alien statement and in contradiction with the logic according to which the overall discourse works. As a result, the child will find himself needing to develop "primary delusional thinking" to create meaning and to preserve access to the field of representation and signification.

Three possible vicissitudes will be available to this primary delusional thinking: first, the encystment of this theory in a part of the psyche, which preserves psychotic potentiality as a possibility and gives the appearance of relative normality; second, the establishment of a more or less complete system of significations conforming to primary delusional thinking, which gives a paranoid picture; and third, the systematic recourse to a single and exhaustive interpretation of any meaningful experience, with a decathexis of everything that escapes this single interpretation, which characterizes schizophrenia. Primary delusional thinking plugs a hole in the other's discourse, or takes on the task of demonstrating the truth of a false premise regarding origins.

Schizophrenic potential derives from three conditions. The first concerns the absence of a "wish to have a child", the "non-desire of a desire" which manifests itself in the impossibility of finding any pleasure in anything that testifies to the singularity of the child. The desire for life directed towards the child is replaced by the fear of his death, the "pleasure of having the child" is replaced by the "unpleasure of always having to run the risk of losing him" (Aulagnier, 1975, p. 141). The second condition concerns an experience of unpleasure for which the parental physical and mental space is responsible, an experience which confirms the atmosphere of hostility and menace. The third condition concerns a discourse which either refuses to recognize the unpleasure that the child has experienced, or imposes a senseless commentary on this experience and on all possible suffering. Primary delusional thinking will then have to forge an interpretation that reshapes this threefold experience. Moreover, it will have to find a voice guaranteeing the authenticity of its delusional theory; this voice will first be that of the mothering object itself, then that of substitutes.

The paranoid potentiality results, for its part, from the situation of need in which the child has been placed to recognize himself as the fruit of hate. Desire and hate are indistinguishable or equivalent:

> If the origin of existence, of oneself as well as of the world, which can never be separated, refers to a state of hate, one will be able to preserve oneself as a living being, and preserve the

> world as existing in its own right, only as long as there is something left to "hate" and someone whom you "hate".
>
> (Aulagnier, 1975, p. 196)

The paranoid exists "neither *for,* nor *by,* nor *with* others, but *against* them" (Aulagnier, 1975, p. 200). The hate and persecution to which the paranoid is subjected result, according to him, from the envy that others feel towards knowledge, a power which he has supposedly inherited, in a phantasy of exclusive parentage. The paranoid projects onto the social scene the parental conflict from which he originated, and must find a founding referent of a law in relation to which he will place himself in the position of exclusive heir. This referent will be the substitute for one of the two idealized parents while the other has become the enemy to be fought.

The transition from psychotic potentiality to psychotic realization results on the one hand from the repetition of traumatic experiences, and on the other from the loss in reality of the idealized voice, a voice that is necessarily marginal compared to the overall discourse which gave a point of anchorage to primary delusional thinking, confirmed the position of exclusive heir, and guaranteed the admissibility of the subject's discourse, and therefore his non-psychoticization. This voice, originally that of the mothering object, must be carried by a real, living being who can be found each time a false verdict threatens the subject's discourse, in order to continually confirm to him, in the face of the prevailing discourse, that his delusional thinking is sensible.

Although, in her book *L'Apprenti-historien et le Maître-sorcier*, Piera Aulagnier (1984) also insists on the idea that an environment imposing traumatic experiences and dramatic psychic ordeals too early on the *infans* exercises a psychoticizing function, she affirms or reaffirms that while certain events can facilitate the toppling over into psychosis, the fact remains that the infantile psyche itself has the power to interpret events in such a way that endows them with a psychoticizing effect that in themselves they did not have, or else to link them to causal interpretations allowing it to defuse the psychoticizing potentiality that they possessed. Furthermore, Piera Aulagnier envisages other events – in addition to the loss in reality of a voice guaranteeing the subject the authenticity of his speech – that are likely to trigger the transition from potentiality to psychotic realization: these include, in particular, meeting another person who reveals an identificatory flaw that the subject was unaware of and of which he could have continued to remain unaware. Piera Aulagnier adds that this revealing-triggering function can be held by an analyst who is not aware of it or who is not vigilant with regard to the risks involved in interpretation – that is to say, disclosure – and to the conditions that need to be respected in order to protect the subject from it.

We will conclude these reflections concerning the configuration of an environment of hate, or one motivated by hate, by evoking the proposals of Juliet Hopkins (1987, 1990) on the effects of parental rejection on the attachment of the child and on his internal experience. Juliet Hopkins takes up the studies on attachment, inaugurated by Bowlby (Bowlby, 1969, 1973, 1980; Bowlby, 1988), and more particularly those studying, among other things, infants rejected by their mothers (Ainsworth et al., 1978; Main and Stadtman, 1981; Parkes, Stevenson-Hinde et al., 1982), and describes the characteristics of the "avoidant attachment" that a "rejecting mother"[13] produces on her baby. The baby of a rejecting mother develops an avoidant attachment, and is caught in an insoluble and interminable conflict, characterized by the following paradox: the baby cannot approach the mother because of her rejection, and cannot withdraw from the bond because of his attachment; the mother who pushes the baby away attracts him at the same time; rejection also has an effect of attraction. Juliet Hopkins thus describes the particular psychic constellation that is organized in the child: the child sees his desire to be held in moments of distress associated with a terror of rejection, a terror of physical contact (from fear lest contact degenerates into mutual aggression), which produces intense pain. In such a child, the representation of an "untouchable or repugnant self" develops.[14]

We could continue and consider the effects of mistreatment and violence, but we will reserve them for the section devoted to "emotional deficiencies".

13.5 The children of psychosis

The failing mental state, even the proven psychopathology of the mothering object, of the mother or the father or of the parental couple, at the time of the conception and birth of a child, present the characteristics of a potentially risky situation for the future of this child, even if, as Winnicott (1961) states, "parental psychosis does not produce childhood psychosis" (p. 72), as well as for the precarious psychic balance of the parent or parents who have to raise him.

Some studies on the psychic evolution of children of schizophrenic mothers[15] reveal that ten to fifteen per cent of these children develop psychosis (twenty to thirty per cent if the psychopathology affects both parents), thirty to fifty per cent develop serious behavioural and personality disorders, ten per cent present a brilliant intellectual "false-self" development, whilst twenty-five to thirty per cent do not present any disorder. Juan Manzano and his collaborators (Manzano and Lalive, 1983; Manzano, Palacio Espasa and Knauer, 1984), carrying out observations in a group studying and caring for young schizophrenic mothers, noted the absence in the children of a serious psychic or early developmental psychopathology, but in some cases identified signs of hyper-maturity or hyper-adaptation which they considered to be indicative of "as if" or "false self" personalities, capable of splitting themselves in a schizophrenic decompensation during a later phase of development. Pierre Bourdier (1972) has described the "hypermaturation" of the children of psychotic parents, which he explained on the one hand by the existence of parental substitutes, recourse to which is all the easier when the parents are "officially psychotic", and on the other by the hypothesis of an early maternal function preserved or even reinforced in the psychotic mother, whose madness can coincide, as long as the baby's dependence is absolute, with the "normal illness" of the mother as described by Winnicott (1956a, p. 302). On this view the psychotic mother thus protects the child from primitive anxieties, but does not allow the establishment of a depressive position, being herself too threatened by the experiences of separation and therefore by the individuation of the child. Removing the child from the mother's care in favour of a substitute (spouse, grandparent, etc.) appears to be an attempt to restore a maternal function to someone who did not fulfil that function at the proper time, and whom the substitute represents, if necessary. The child, on the other hand, will be able to identify with the substitute, that is to say, with the caring function, and thus contribute to caring for the parent, to restoring the threatened object, which Bourdier considers as being at the origin of many caring vocations.

The observation of interactions between a psychotic mother and her baby (see David, 1981; Lamour, 1989; Lamour and Barraco,

1988, 1995) highlights severe disturbances: avoidance of gaze, absence of shared gaze, unpredictability of maternal commitments or responses, alternating fusional movements and rejecting movements, absence of speech addressed to the child, no exchange of vocalizations, no reinforcement or even no perception of motor progress and autonomization, disturbance or poverty of "affective tuning" (Stern, 1985), reversal of adjustments (it is the baby who adjusts to the mother), hyper-adaptation of the baby to its mother and her inadequate responses, state of permanent alert in the baby, "bombardment" by maternal phantasies, high level of "psychic excitation" maintained by the mother, aggressive or even erotic stimulation, etc. And the same mismatch could be observed between a psychotic father and his baby.

Let us note the work of Micheline Enriquez (1986, 1988) who, drawing on the conceptions of Piera Aulagnier (1975, 1984), studied, on the basis of analyses of patients who had psychotic parents, the impact on the child of parental delusions, delusions concerning origins. She explains how the child negotiates the violence of the parent's delusional discourse, a discourse which forces him to mutilate himself by renouncing any position that would lead him to be confronted again, during his adult life, with the primary delusional theory.

Clinical experience regularly confronts us with the legitimate panic effect produced within psychiatric care teams (adult or infant–child) by the announcement of a pregnancy or a planned child in psychotic subjects, or even subjects with no serious psychopathology but who have already had a psychotic child. Concerning psychotic parents, the frequent belief in an inevitable transmission of psychopathology can be observed in healthcare teams. It can be said that, whatever the reality of the reproduction of psychosis, such a belief, possibly reinforced by the idea of the participation of hereditary genetic factors, has a function. Belief in the transmission of psychosis has a defensive function; it reassures caregivers, and society in general, who are faced with the mystery, the scandal and the tragedy of madness, as to the existence of mental pathology.[16] One might also think that too much expectation of repetition leaves little room for a potential outcome other than repetition.

Myriam David (David, 1981) discusses the difficulty that a team of carers treating a psychotic woman who has become a mother has in making a decision on whether to keep the baby close to its mother or to separate them. It is clinical work on a case-by-case basis which makes it possible to assess the risk to the child of maintaining an early relationship with his mother, father and family. Let us point out the usefulness of observation at home, or in a reception centre, of the parent–baby couple or the family group not only for evaluation but also for prevention: the observer, in the sense of the method of Esther Bick (1964), represents a prop for the parent and provides valuable support for the development of the particularly fragile and vulnerable relationship between parent and baby. Let us also insist on the need to identify the projections to which the parents are subjected by the caregiving and socio-educational teams – and to which the teams are themselves subjected by the parents – projections which lead the teams to devalue or invalidate these parents, considering them from the outset as incapable of being parents, as parents who, in themselves, are not good enough. In this "wish for failure" concerning the parent–child relationship, certain aspects of the psychoticizing relationship that these parents experienced with their own mothering environment are repeated with the healthcare or socio-educational teams. The panic, if it is not contained and elaborated, that a so-called psychotic parent deposits in the healthcare teams, in the social services, is violently returned to the sender, confirming him/her in their conviction that they are only able to generate madness, thereby confirming the potentially psychoticizing movement triggered. This process is in the service of repetition, and also of the illusion that madness is a remote threat, outside, always transmitted by someone else who is the bearer of "evil".

13.6 The lack of stimulation. The affective deprivation

Although our purpose is mainly concerned with the psychic qualities of the immediate environment, it is possible to approach the question of the inadequacy of the object in terms of the lack or excess of stimulation offered to the child. This dysfunctioning relates to the third role played by the environment according to Winnicott (1962a), namely, after "holding" and "handling", the "presentation of objects". The environment must not only present the world, the objects (the breast and others), but present them at the right time, just when the baby is ready to "create" them. The "good enough" environment maintains the baby in the omnipotent illusion of creating the object, before helping him to negotiate the process of disillusionment (see Winnicott, 1947, 1951).

The psychopathology of massive frustration refers on the one hand to the ideas of Spitz (1965), with his description of "hospitalism", that is to say, the harmful effects of institutionalization in the first year of life (more than the placement itself, it was the emotional and relational context that was harmful), and his description of the clinical picture of "anaclitic depression", and on the other to those of Bowlby (1951), with his considerations on the consequences of frustrating separations, which are damaging for character and psychological maturity. We should also mention Racamier (1953, 1954) who spoke of deficiency disorders in the context of "frustration pathology".

Studies of deficiencies in mothering and maternal care tend to group together deficiencies in sensorimotor stimulation, stimulation in the first modes of communication, "social" stimulation and "affective" deficiency (see for example Ajuriaguerra, 1977). Concerning the emotional pole, the term "affective deficiency", that is to say, lack of love for the child, lack of satisfactory responses to the attachment needs of the child, should be understood as a "failure of libidinal cathexis" on the part of the parent(s). However, this cathexis of the child is relatively independent "quantitatively" from the amount of stimulation given to the child. A poorly cathected child can be very stimulated – for example, out of a desire for manic reparation, or out of phobic avoidance of real communication – and vice versa. Sensorimotor stimuli in parent–child interactions represent a behavioural aspect which tells us little about the intersubjective relationship.

Deficiencies in "affective" and sensorimotor stimulation, studied for example by Spitz or Bowlby or others[17] in situations where the child is separated both physically and early from his mothering environment and is placed in a frustrating substitute environment, can also be described, in terms of their harmful effects, in cases where the child is not physically separated from the mothering object, but where this object is frustrating in terms of what it can or wants to give to the child, not so much at the level of affective or sensory stimulation as at the level of psychical cathexis. The mothering object can be frustrating because it is psychically absent, which relates to the problem of depression mentioned above, or because it is hostile to the child, which relates to the problem of hate and perversion also considered previously, or because it itself is deficient at the level of its own affective infantile experiences and identifications with a sufficiently good parental imago, that is to say, sufficiently in contact with infantile needs: "We cannot give what we have not received" (as Salomon Resnik says, 1986a, p. 45, translated for this edition).

Affective and sensory deficiencies, while they have a definite impact on the development of the personality, must be considered in their association with disorders in children of what Ajuriaguerra (1977) calls the "appetite for stimuli", the "appetite for affects". Furthermore, as Ajuriaguerra points out, pathology stems more from the inadequacy rather than deficiency of stimuli.

Léon Kreisler and Bertrand Cramer (1981) see this inadequacy in, for example, the lack of continuity in the safe-guarding of the child, the multiplicity of solicitations from different people, irregular behaviour, etc. They point out, moreover, that to the pathology of lack it is necessary to add the pathology of excess. Overstimulation, an overload of excitation, results in "submerging the possibilities of mental integration" (Kreisler and Cramer, 1981, p. 248, translated for this edition), with a significant discharge in the soma (colic, insomnia, vomiting of the infant); hence the fundamental importance of the containing object's function as a stimulus barrier. Anne Decerf (1987) describes very well how, in early parent–baby interactions, the parent must adapt to the interactional capacities of the baby and in particular respect his cyclical withdrawals from the interaction; failure to do this risks overexciting his child, by asking him to be continually present in the relationship. The infant responds to overexcitement, which overloads his capacities for mental resistance, with an abnormally long withdrawal. During repeated pathological relationships and harmful interactions, the evolution of the overstimulated baby can range from psychosomatic disorder to withdrawal of the autistic type.

Concerning the effects on the baby of emotional deprivation, let us note the contribution of Selma Fraiberg (1982), inspired among others by Spitz's studies on the deficiencies of the mothering environment. Selma Fraiberg reports on observations of a group of babies (3–18 months) who have lived in situations of danger and extreme emotional deprivation: these infants were victims of neglect and ill-treatment, with seriously depressed or even schizophrenic mothers who were psychologically absent for a very large part of the inter-relations, thus exposing the baby to unpredictable fits of fury or rage which burst through the walls of depression and terrorized the baby. Here, we are in the context of gross abuse and neglect. Fraiberg describes different "early defence behaviours" in babies: avoidance, freezing, fighting, affect transformations and attitudes of reversal.

Avoidance is observed from three months. It is selective and discriminating: the baby may avoid only his mother. Avoidance is effective against "external" dangers, but cannot protect the baby against urgent somatic needs, and we then observe a major disorganization (fury, screaming, howling). When the suffering becomes intolerable, a mechanism of rupture obliterates this sensation, a mechanism which can be understood as an early form of splitting.

Freezing reaction is also observed from the first months: freezing of posture, motility, voice and gaze; clinging to the mother with mute terror. When the toxic and traumatic situation is permanent, the effectiveness of freezing and withdrawal reactions is exhausted; the cost of maintaining immobility will be pain, the defences collapse, and the infant sinks into a state of total disorganization, as if he were disintegrating.

Fighting is used by the slightly older baby to protect himself from the dangers of disintegration. One can see the traces of fear on the face of a terrified, intensely anxious child, disappear as soon as he starts fighting with his mother. When the battle is lost, anger arises and with it reappear the signs of the state of disintegration.

Affect transformation is observed in babies from nine months, and consists for example in replacing the reactions of howling with terror when faced with a threatening or sadistic mother by reactions of excited laughter, silly laughter, grating and theatrical laughter. Laughter is a defence against intolerable anxiety. The changes in affect and anxiety are part of a sadomasochistic relationship, and the child becomes, as it were, a willing and enthusiastic partner in a sadomasochistic game with the mother.

Reversal of attitudes is observed at the end of the first year and consists in turning aggression against oneself. The child experiences such fear with regard to his parents and their reprisals that he cannot attack them and then he turns aggression against himself, with a pain threshold so high that he does not feel the pain of the blows he inflicts on himself.

All of these early defences in infants who are victims of extremely serious dangers and deprivation, reveal, when they fail, states of total disintegration in which the child loses all contact with those around him. When help is given to the child and his parents, these pathological defence mechanisms may be seen to disappear, and if no help is given, a serious pathological organization (or disorganization) of the personality in the child when he is older is to be feared. Certain studies on violence, for example, and in particular on extreme violence, highlight the way in which the subjects in question were the object of mistreatment and serious neglect in their childhood and from their infancy (Berger et al., 2007; Berger, 2008, 2012, 2016; Bonneville, 2010, 2015).

To conclude, on this point, it should be emphasized that, more than the inadequacies resulting from an excess or a lack of stimulation, it is always the nature of the *affects* – and *phantasies* – characterizing the relationships underlying these dysfunctions and giving them meaning, which determines the possible pathologization of early development.

13.7 The family universe. The family psyche

We have considered the inadequacies of the mothering object essentially in the here-and-now of its relation to the child. The function of the mothering object can be ensured by the mother as much as by the father, the parental couple or the family group. In addition, the containing quality of the object is dependent on the feeling it itself has of being contained by another or a group which recognizes it and confirms it in its parental function. In other words, the disorders of "parenthood" (*parentalité*), of "motherhood" (*maternalité*), of "fatherhood (*paternalité*)",[18] result to a large extent from a defect of "internal parenthood", from a lack of internalization of a parental object, in the form of "psychic biparenthood" (Ciccone, 2012bc, 2014, 2016a) as we have envisaged it (Chapter 3), which gives support and internal security. Disorders of parenthood also concern relationships between couples, when one parent cannot support the other, when one is envious of the relationship between the baby and the other parent and sees the baby as a narcissistic rival, etc. Parenthood can be contaminated by marital disorders, and also by the oedipal conflicts which one or both of the parents have not sufficiently decathected.

Let us now look at the function of the mothering environment relating to *psychic transmission*, to the psychic registration of the child in the group chain and in the chain of filiation. Long before birth, as soon as phantasies about the child exist in the family psyche, the child becomes a locus of projection of the representative capital of the parents which he will inherit in one way or another.

The filial registration of the unborn child begins with the choice of partner by the future parents. Alberto Eiguer (1983, 1984, 1986b) has studied the nature of the investments presiding over the formation of the parental couple. Isidoro Berenstein and Janine Puget (1984) have explored the bonds uniting the two members of a couple, with their unconscious pacts and agreements. The notion of "negative pact" proposed by René Kaës (1987, 1989ab, 1992, 1993), on the subject of the psychic processes of grouping, is particularly enlightening regarding the transactions characteristic of the bonds uniting the couple, even the family group.[19]

The question of filial and genealogical registration is present in the thought of Freud who, for example in *Totem and Taboo* (1912–1913), raises questions, not about the family but about human groups, on the transmission of psychic processes and states from one generation to another, on the continuity of the psychic life of successive generations. Faced with the observation that we cannot avoid transmission – "we may safely assume that no generation is able to conceal any of its more important mental processes from its successor" (Freud, 1912–1913, p. 159) –, Freud postulates the existence of a "collective mind". In 1914, in "On narcissism: an introduction", Freud (1914) notes that the individual leads a twofold existence, "one to serve his own purposes and the other as a link in a chain which he serves against his will, or at least involuntarily" (p. 78). He also sets out one of the functions incumbent on the child: he is a refuge for parental narcissism and must participate in the illusion of the ego's immortality. This heralds the representation of the "narcissistic contract" developed by Piera Aulagnier (1975), to describe this mission which the newborn infant has of ensuring the continuity of the generations. The group recognizes the newcomer as the subject of the group and, in return, asks him to take upon himself the group's founding statements in order to ensure the immortality of the group.

Whilst the question of psychic transmission and filial ties has interested several authors (see in particular Guyotat, 1980, 1991), a certain number of works concerning psychic transmission have focused on the processes of filiation more particularly from the angle of negative transmission (Kaës, 1984, 1985, 1988b, 1989ab, 1992, 1993; Granjon, 1985, 1986, 1987ab, 1989; Baranes, 1987, 1989,

1991). The prevailing idea in this research is that stated by René Kaës according to which all affiliation is based on the flaws of filiation. The links between groups, like those of couples, are woven essentially from the negative inheritance, that is to say, what, in the current transmission and/or previous transmissions, could not be transformed and integrated psychically, and on the need to make an elaborative repetition of it. What is transmitted in inter- or rather trans-generational transmission, in the trans-subjectivity of couples and groups, is not only the positive (history, novels, family myths, conscious objects and fantasies favouring identifications, etc.), but also and above all the negative, that is to say what is lacking, what is missing, what has not been registered, what has been denied, disavowed, repressed or projected. The status of this negative (repressed or extrajected, projected, externalized) and the topographical location of its psychic "place of lodgement" will be related to the individual, group or family psychic structure.

Haydée Faimberg (1987, 1988) has studied psychic transmission in connection with *unconscious identifications* based on what she calls the "telescoping of generations": mute, inaudible identifications, identified through a secret history of the patient and condensing a history which does not belong to the patient's generation (you will recall the case of Julien, cited above). Faimberg characterizes the "narcissistic object regulation" belonging to these identifications by two functions: a "function of appropriation" and a "function of intrusion". Through the function of appropriation, the *internal* parents[20] identify with what belongs to the child and appropriate his "positive identity". Through the function of intrusion, they expel everything they reject into the child and they define him by his "negative identity". The child is the victim of an "identificatory capture", a prisoner of the alienating power of the narcissism of his internal parents which hinders the development of a psychic space specific to his identity. This alienating function produces a splitting of the ego in the child which is the source of a feeling of strangeness. These unconscious identifications arise when the internal parents function within the framework of the narcissistic organization as a result of which "they cannot love the child without taking possession of him, and cannot recognize his independence without hating him" (Faimberg, 1987, p. 190, translated for this edition). The child, a captive of the parents' narcissistic organization, becomes what each of them has not accepted in their own story. The internal parents are registered in the psyche as parents who regard the child as part of themselves.[21] The whole psyche is organized around this identificatory process. Jean-José Baranes (1989) speaks of *alienating identification*, in children, *with the denied and split-off internal objects of the parents.*

Thus we would say that the *repetitive tendency of the unconscious can be understood as responding to a necessary affiliation through a negative inheritance.* The repetition is not only the work of the death drive and the processes of resistance, but stages the imperious and sometimes desperate attempt to master what escapes, what cannot be represented or given psychic status, and which always remains there as it is, omnipresent and haunting the psychic space: the negative heritage[22] is a genuine culture of untransformed beta elements, albeit perhaps still transformable; in any case, that is the challenge of psychoanalysis, and in particular of psychoanalytic family therapy.

Very mindful about the clinical experience of the earliest mother–baby relationships, Selma Fraiberg, Edna Adelson and Vivian Shapiro (1975) have looked into the repetition of a morbid past, concerning the history of certain parents, in their present relationship with their child, and on the help that might be possible to save the parent–child couple from this repetition. These authors developed the hypothesis that, in cases where history repeats itself and the parent identifies with pathological figures from his or her past (figures at the origin of violence, abandonment, seduction, etc.), the parent's memory of his or her childhood history, even if it is intact, was accompanied by a *repression of affects* linked to the traumatic events. Identification with the terrifying figure, and therefore repetition of the morbid history, then seems to be the only solution. Fraiberg, Adelson and Shapiro note that as soon as the parent is able to access his or her repressed affects and emotions, and therefore identify with the injured child, the risk of repetition is mitigated, and the baby's future is less threatened.

One of us has particularly developed the question of transmission, and proposed a model of the processes of psychic transmission, especially in traumatic contexts, highlighting, on the one hand, how transmission uses processes of *projective identification* in a privileged way, in their different versions, and, on the other, how traumatic transmissions are treated and reorganized by the construction of *transmission phantasies* (Ciccone, 1996ab, 1997ac, 1998d, 2000, 2012a, 2016b, 2017). The transmission phantasy is a scenario, conscious or unconscious, a myth constructed by the subject, featuring the idea that an event or a traumatic experience is the result of an inheritance, of a transmission. The transmission phantasy has a triple function: a function of *exoneration* (what happens to the subject comes from an ancestor); a function of *reregistering the subject in the genealogy*, suturing the break in the ties of filiation (the idea of inheritance confirms filiation, restores a filiation when it is threatened by a disorganizing traumatic element); and a function of *appropriation*, of *subjectivation* (the subject becomes the subject of the traumatic experience, in the same movement that leads him to relinquish it or to withdraw from it). The transmission phantasy thus reorganizes a traumatic transmission.

There is a singular intersubjective process that represents both a modality of traumatic transmission and a mechanism that accounts for and supports the deployment of a phantasy of transmission: this is *imagoic encroachment* (Ciccone, 1997a, 2000, 2012a). Imagoic encroachment describes the process by which a parental imago is imposed as an object of identification *of* the child (the parent identifies the child with the imago) and as an object of identification *for* the child (the parent uses interactive manoeuvres forcing the child to identify with the imago). This intersubjective process, which is carried out by means of an alienating form of projective identification, has its place among other processes of the same order such as those supporting the phantasy of "the reversal of the order of generations" (Jones, 1913), the toxic work of "trans-generational objects" (Eiguer, 1986c, 1987, 1989, 1991, 1997), alienating identifications through "identificatory capture" and "the telescoping of generations" (Faimberg, 1987, 1988), the transmissions of "crypts" and "ghosts" (Abraham and Torok, 1987; Tisseron et al., 1995).

All these considerations lead us to evoke the interest of a family approach to individual psychopathology. The development of psychoanalytic family therapy essentially concerns the families of psychotics, or those with psychotic functioning. It undoubtedly partly stems from the difficulties, even failures, in the individual analytical treatments of psychotic patients, children or adults.[23] With a psychotic child – especially in the register of symbiotic psychoses – who is unable to achieve psychic individuation, it is understandable that an exclusive individual treatment of such a child can be compromised until the family has somehow given its authorization for the development of a psychic space specific to the child. In addition, the particular position that the psychotic child occupies in the family, the result of complex unconscious cathexes and pacts, often leads the family, as experience shows, to attack the treatment of the child as soon as there is progress.

Psychoanalytic family therapy, in its theory and technique, is essentially inspired by the work of Didier Anzieu and René Kaës on psychoanalytic work in groups (Anzieu et al., 1972; Kaës, 1976b; Anzieu, 1981). André Ruffiot (1981ab, 1988) proposed the notion of family group psychical apparatus – following Kaës' conception of the group psychical apparatus – and laid the theoretical and technical foundations for psychoanalytic family therapy. The theoretical contributions of Alberto Eiguer (1983, 1986a, 1987; Eiguer and Litovsky, 1981), Jean-Pierre Caillot and Gérard Decherf (1982) and others, have led to a semiological systematization of the psychic functioning of the family – we have gone from the notion of a *psychotic* or *psychosomatic* family, etc., to the notion of a family with psychotic or psychosomatic *functioning,* etc. – depending on its anxieties, its defence mechanisms, its object relationships, its level and complexity of psychic development (with the notion of psychic organizers).

Finally, more than the family itself, it is the process of individuation that is the object of psychoanalytic family therapy. Belonging to the group and developing an autonomous psychic space constitute, for each member of the family, the twofold aim of family therapy.

When the theory of care practice takes into account or even favours the option of family psychic care, the question of the relevance of individual treatment for the patient with symptoms, simultaneously with family treatment or after family treatment, still arises.

Two points should be emphasized here: the need to offer the family a place of listening and speaking does not exclusively concern families with psychotic functioning, nor does it exclusively concern child psychopathology. All psychopathology, whatever the age of the subject, involves intrafamilial relationships, and is in part the effect of dysfunctioning or suffering in these relationships, and is itself the cause of suffering. Any treatment of a subject, whatever their age, can threaten those around them and can itself be threatened by the feelings of rivalry or envy that it may mobilize in them.

Three main reasons thus plead in favour of a family listening to psychopathology, whatever it is, whatever the age of the patient, and without it necessarily taking the form of psychoanalytic family therapy:

- making an alliance with the "adult" aspects of parenting to protect the treatment, especially when the patient is a child, but not only then, a treatment that will be threatened when elements of negative transference come to the fore. It is therefore essential to be able to count on parents, for example, when a child does not want to go to a session, when a teenager decides to break off all treatment, as soon as a central aspect of subjective and reality has been approached, mobilizing significant resistance;

- witnessing real intersubjective interactions, painful relationships, possible toxic inductions, in the reality of their manifestations and not only in their remote narration, if we want to understand the context and the emotional atmosphere. It is difficult, in fact, to really understand what a subject is going through (whether a child, a teenager, or indeed an adult) if one is never a witness to what is happening "for real" in toxic, painful relationships, which may be at the origin, partly in any case, of his sense of ill-being, distress and psychopathology;
- taking into account the family suffering generated by psychopathology itself. The suffering of one of its members causes the whole family and those around them to suffer, and it is essential to be attentive to this suffering.

While caring for children generally goes hand in hand with listening to parents (more rarely to the family, including siblings), the teams of caregivers who take care of adolescents are sometimes more timid when it comes to working with families. As for adult caregivers and adult psychiatric services, it is very rare for the latter to develop the conviction that they need to listen to the patient's spouse, parents, children and family. And yet the entourage is just as involved in the psychopathology of an adult subject as in that of a child, and suffers as much from this psychopathology.

Notes

1 See also the article by Michel Soulé (1978) on the "child who came from the cold".
2 To further this debate on the toxic effects of a traumatic environment and on the conditions of a psychopathological development of the subject or subjects subjected to such an environment, one could turn to the studies on "resilience", that is to say the capacity to resist a traumatic context (Rutter, 1981b; Rolf, Master et al., 1990; Cyrulnik, 1999; etc.).

3 In 1910, at the end of his text on Leonardo da Vinci, Freud realized that psychoanalysis was not explanatory and stated that the prediction of events (linked by causal relationships) was not conceivable from the psychoanalytic point of view. He reaffirmed this idea at the end of his work (Freud, 1933).
4 See also Ciccone, 1995b, 1997b, 1998b.
5 Brazelton's team developed the experimental situation of the "still face" and highlighted its effects (Tronick et al., 1978; Gianino and Tronick, 1988): when a mother presents herself to her three-week-old baby (at the request of the examiner) with an intentionally immobile and expressionless face, the baby reacts by becoming visibly worried, by making jerky movements, by turning his face away and then trying to catch his mother's eye. Faced with the failure of his repeated efforts, the baby withdraws into an attitude of helplessness, his face turned away, his body curled up and motionless.
6 In Green's work negative hallucination does not refer to a pathological process in itself: negative hallucination, as a "representation of the absence of representation" (Green, 1977, p. 652, translated for this edition), as Green says, is necessary for thought, it "structures" representation. If it is constitutive of thought, it can also be positivized, producing a positive hallucination. We would say that toxic negative hallucination not only makes reality absent, but produces "psychic holes".
7 Odile Bourguignon (1984), in her research on the death of children and family structures, observed a higher proportion of family members suffering from psychiatric disorders in families with dead children than in families without dead children. She put forward the idea that in some families death and psychosis would present themselves as equivalent individual solutions: death as an alternative to psychosis.
8 Such a context marked, for example, the history of the painter Vincent van Gogh, born a year to the day after the birth and death of a child named Vincent Wilhelm. The future painter found himself burdened with the impossible role of resuscitating a deceased child, with the untenable role of a dead/living child. Everyone knows the intense mental troubles and suffering that marked the existence and the end of Vincent van Gogh's life. It was in a similar situation that the conception and then the birth of Didier Anzieu's mother took place, as the latter recounts in a very moving way (Anzieu, 1986a). The story repeated itself when she became a mother, which plunged her into a deep depression.

9 Denial of value is a denial among the various "organized denials" that Racamier (1986) describes: denial of meaning, denial of significance, denial of existence, denial of autonomy and individuality and finally denial of self-worth.
10 On narcissistic perversion, see also Eiguer, 1989.
11 See Ciccone, 2003b.
12 The notion of "paradoxical communication", proposed by the school of Palo-Alto under the influence of Bateson in a systemic model, was taken up by Anzieu in 1975. He applied it to psychoanalytic treatment and demonstrated its full fruitfulness, in particular with regard to the analysis of narcissistic personalities and the understanding of negative therapeutic reactions.
13 Let us recall the three types of attachment described by Mary Ainsworth (Ainsworth et al., 1978), Bowlby's collaborator, on the basis of her test of the "strange situation" (Ainsworth and Wittig, 1969) – the child is left alone for a short while in an unknown room, then brought back to the mother; the observation of his reactions at the time of the reunion makes it possible to identify three types of attachment, since his reactions are considered to reveal the nature of his sense of security, of the expectation he has concerning the physical and emotional availability of his mother: "secure" attachment, "insecure avoidant" attachment and "ambivalent or resistant" insecure attachment. Mary Main, another Bowlby collaborator, described a fourth style of attachment: insecure "disorganized-disoriented" attachment (Main and Solomon, 1986).
14 Such a self-image is characterized by a feeling of primary guilt, as discussed by René Roussillon (1991).
15 For a review of the literature, see for example Duchesne and Roy, 1991.
16 This ties in with the notion of a "transmission phantasy" which is discussed below.
17 See the study by Myriam David and Geneviève Appell (1961) on the factors of emotional deprivation, carried out in a nursery.
18 Terms that we owe, among others, to Benedeck (Benedeck, 1959; Benedeck and Anthony, 1970) and Racamier (Racamier et al., 1961; Racamier, 1978).
19 The negative pact is a contract of linking, an intermediate, trans-subjective psychic formation, constituting an unconscious alliance. Alongside and bound up with the other intermediate formations such as the contract of instinctual renunciation (Freud, 1908, 1930), the

The inadequacies of the containing object

shared fulfilment of wishes (Anzieu, 1966) and the narcissistic contract (Aulagnier, 1975), the negative pact "condemns to repression, denial or disavowal, or even maintains unrepresented and imperceptible, that which would jeopardize the formation and maintenance of this link and the cathexes of which it is the object"(Kaës, 1987, p. 32, translated for this edition). The negative pact is a pact that relates to the negative, and its aim is to deal with it (fighting against, denying it, circumscribing it, etc.) with the aim of preserving the link or the activity of linking and of reinforcing its positivity; "negative pacts are pacts concluded both on the basis of, and against, the negative" (Kaës, 1989a, p. 135, translated for this edition). The negative pact ranges from the negating alliance (Couchoud, 1986) to shared denial (Fain, 1981).

20 Faimberg puts forward these propositions only in relation to psychoanalytic treatment, and her conceptions cannot be extrapolated to the psychoanalytic approach of the real family group. Faimberg speaks of "internal parents" and not of real parents. The internal parents are the parents registered in psychic reality, internal objects with which the subject identifies and which appear *between* what the patient says and what the analyst hears, or *between* what the analyst says and what the patient hears.

21 We would say that in the case of these alienating identifications, the internal parents have the status of an *incorporated object* (see Chapter 1).

22 To illustrate these points, we once again refer the reader to the case of Julien cited above, as well as to trans-generational considerations regarding the origin and transmission of certain psychopathologies such as narcissistic perversion.

23 Gisela Pankow (1983), who worked extensively with psychotic patients, noted that "treating mental illness without concern for the family structures is doomed to failure" (p. 121, translated for this edition). In 1956 already, far in advance of all the conceptual considerations concerning the family approach to mental illness and family therapies, Georges Devereux (1970) said: "The psychotic child has the vicarious role of the 'one who is crazy' within the family that suffers from a latent neurosis. It is the family that is ill: the fever from which the child is suffering is not his, but that of his family. Furthermore, the 'vicariously crazy' child is so 'useful' to his family that it literally tears him away from the hands of the psychiatrist as soon as his condition begins to improve. Indeed, if the psychological scapegoat got better, it would not be long before his family became openly neurotic" (p. 28, translated for this edition).

14
PHANTASIED ATTACKS ON THE OBJECT

14.1 Greed and envy

We have discussed the fundamental instinctual drive conflict between tendencies towards integration and tendencies towards disintegration, which, according to Melanie Klein, is operative from the beginning of life, brings into play the processes of splitting and projective identification, justifies sadistic attacks against the object and engenders persecutory anxieties (see Chapter 9). We have evoked the essentially sadistic nature of part of the phantasied relationships that the baby maintains with his mothering object (see Chapter 11).

The attacks made by the baby in phantasy, due to the instinctual drive activity that is active in him and to the dissatisfaction that he may experience when faced with a poorly adjusted or even inadequate nourishing object, derive from greed, of which one of the observable expressions is voracity, and from envy (Klein, 1952ab).

Voracity is a manifestation of cannibalistic oral impulses. It constitutes one of the two main forms of sadistic phantasies (the second is underpinned by anal sadistic phantasies, the basis of projective identification): oral sadistic phantasies aim to empty the body of the object of everything that is good and desirable. The phantasied attacks, arising from *voracity*, result in the development of fear of the voracity of the object, and therefore of persecutory anxiety. This leads to increased splitting, with narcissistic withdrawal towards the internal ideal object, which is increasingly threatened because it risks being destroyed with the same voracity as that shown by the baby.

If persecutory anxiety and the destructive impulses are excessively predominant, the intense greed can result in a lack of manifest voracity and one will see, for example, that the baby takes no pleasure in eating, or refuses food. This state may lead, as Melanie Klein (1952b) shows, to a subsequent inhibition about ingesting sublimated food, that is to say a disorder of intellectual development. Furthermore, the greed manifested by exaggerated voracity, where food becomes the only source of gratification and where interest in people is not developed, indicates an excessive predominance of paranoid-schizoid mechanisms, based on increased intolerance to frustration. This comes either from the child, who, from a constitutional point of view, has greater difficulty in tolerating frustration, or who presents an ego that is still far too feeble, or from external reality which imposes exaggerated experiences of frustration on the child. This state can lead to eating and developmental disorders but also to a narcissistic withdrawal, and Klein gives the example of the baby who, when the breast has been absent for too long, despite his crying, refuses to take it when it is offered and only wants to suck his fingers, which are more trustworthy than the breast. The baby then needs to recover the relationship with the internal breast and regain sufficient security to re-establish a good relationship with the external breast and with the mother. Still, the internal breast must be well established. During his experiences of the continual and repeated failures of adjustment by the external object, the infant does not acquire the capacity to establish inside himself a good object which he can idealize and with which he can take refuge during episodes of frustration.

The other feeling that justifies the subject's need to carry out sadistic attacks in phantasy on the object is *envy*. Envy is distinguished from greed in that it is linked to projection and is derived from urethral and anal sadistic impulses. If greed leads to emptying, exhausting and devouring the maternal breast (destructive incorporation), envy aims at the deterioration of the maternal breast through projective identification: penetrating in phantasy inside the object in order to take possession of it or to damage it (Klein, 1957).

Karl Abraham, one of Klein's analysts, briefly described envy, around the 1920s (Abraham, 1919, 1920, 1921), as the expression of an entanglement between feelings of hate towards someone who has a coveted possession, and an urge to snatch it from him. Whilst Melanie Klein referred to envy in 1928 in connection with early oedipal wishes (Klein, 1928, 1932, 1945), and again in 1952 in connection with voracity (Klein, 1952a), it was in 1957, in *Envy and*

Gratitude, that her conception of envy found its full development. Envy is the most powerful manifestation of the destructive impulses. It corresponds to the "angry feeling that another person possesses and enjoys something desirable" (1975, p. 181). It prompts the individual to take possession of the object, to spoil it or to spoil what it contains that is desirable and which arouses envy.

The baby develops the desire for an inexhaustible and omnipresent breast, following the experiences of satisfaction that he has had with the "good breast". The breast is good not only because it nourishes, but also because it keeps destructive impulses and persecutory anxiety at bay. The infant attributes omnipotent qualities to this good breast and it is the good breast that arouses envy. The envied good breast is transformed into the bad breast. The envious impulse aims to strip the good breast of what it possesses.

Jean-Michel Petot (1982) points out that, in the case of envy, the good object is transformed into a bad object without any sadistic attack having been carried out beforehand by the baby. He sees this as a counter-example to the classical Kleinian schema where the object becomes bad following the destructive projections of which it is the target. In the case of envy, it is after the transformation of the good object into a bad object that it is attacked in phantasy. Jean-Michel Petot proposes to resolve this apparent contradiction by envisaging a projective dimension of envious anger, based on the conviction that the breast keeps for itself the milk and the love from which it deprives the baby in an avid and malicious manner.

We would like to add that in our opinion the phantasied attack does not follow the transformation of the good object into a bad object; rather, the envious impulse constitutes in itself an attack against the good object, as Melanie Klein said (and especially the internal object), which then loses its goodness. The feeling of envy corresponds to a transformation of the good object into an object which refuses to distribute its goodness.

It is intolerance to frustration that develops the feeling of envy. But, as Herbert Rosenfeld (1964a) points out, envy in turn increases the difficulty of accepting dependence and frustration. The strength of the infant's envy helps maintain the omnipotence of narcissistic object relationships.

The envious impulse leads the ego to devalue and degrade the object, or else the food and the aid that the object brings, at the very moment when this aid is felt, that is to say at the very moment when the ego gets in touch with depressive feelings. These depressive feelings are confused with feelings of persecution, and this *confusion between depressive anxiety and persecutory anxiety* is reflected by precocious and premature guilt. A second consequence of envy is the *confusion between the good and the bad object*. The ordinary good/bad split is replaced, in situations of envy, by excessive splitting between a very idealized object and a very bad object, a split which itself fuels envy.

The envious attack is an attack on linking, as described by Bion (1959), that is to say an attack on the object's capacity (the mothering object originally) to introject the projective identifications of the subject (first, those of the baby). The envious attack is aimed at destroying alpha function.

What defences can the subject use against envy? Melanie Klein lists several:

- *idealization*, which is also a consequence of envy;
- *confusion*, which too is both a consequence of and a defence against envy;
- *flight from the original object* and cathexis of other objects, which corresponds more to a dispersion of object relations than to the establishment of stable object relations uncoloured by persistent hostility;
- *devaluation* of the object or devaluation of the self;
- *greedy internalization*;
- *activation of envy in others*;
- *repression of feelings of love* and therefore intensification of hatred.

Finally, *feelings of envy* are dependent, according to Melanie Klein, both on the constitutional strength or weakness of the ego from the start of postnatal life, and on the impact of actual life experiences. This will be proportional to the intensity of the paranoid anxieties which arise in part from the work of the destructive impulses.

14.2 Attacks in the auto-sensual position

The voracious and envious attacks we have just described take place in a paranoid-schizoid context. What about possible phantasied attacks on the object in the auto-sensual position? Is the autistic child, in the autistic state proper, or the baby going through the auto-sensual phase, free from sadism, or can they experience impulses or make greedy or envious attacks?

Donald Meltzer (Meltzer et al., 1975) considers autism proper to be devoid of sadism or characterized by minimal sadism and therefore minimal feelings of persecution. The triumph that the autistic child displays in his relation to objects corresponds more to a "joyful possessiveness" than to a sadistic attack, as long as the processes of splitting and idealization remain largely ineffective. We have seen (Chapter 5) that the process of dismantling the perceptual apparatus, specific to the auto-sensual position (ex-"autistic position"), is a "passive" process – unlike splitting which is the product of active attacks by the ego. In addition, adhesive identification, a mode of identification specific to the auto-sensual position, caricatures objects, but without aggressiveness, unlike projective identification.[1]

Didier Houzel (1988b) recognizes in the autistic child envious impulses towards the aesthetic object. However, the attacks he describes, which seem to be part of destructive impulses of penetration, seem to us to be more attributable to a symbiotic part than to the autistic nucleus proper.

Do specifically autistic terrors (see Chapter 2) impel the child to make attacks? Autistic anxieties, inherent in the premature awareness of separation, are reflected in autistic children, as Frances Tustin often describes, by an experience of bodily amputation and particularly amputation of the mouth. This experience leads these children to develop a fear of predators of which they might be the innocent victims, predators which might invade them and take from their mouths the object which gives sensations. This fear is not always linked, according to Tustin, to the projection of their own predatory impulses; the autistic child is not a predator (see Tustin, 1986).

However, Tustin describes an early "sadistic urge to bite" in children with autism, an urge that has supplanted that of sucking and makes the child scared, hence his reluctance, for example, to latch onto and then to bite into food. Tustin also considers that autistic capsules can conceal tendencies to cruelty, to "primitive savagery". All of this nuances the idea of "autistic innocence". In addition, it seems important to us to keep in mind that the use of autistic defences, autistic encapsulation, the annihilation of thought, just like the refusal of human relationships, represent the most murderous psychic attacks that exist, because their aim is psychic death.

So what about destructiveness in the auto-sensual or autistic position (see also Chapter 9)? The autistic position, in the autistic subject, deprives the psyche of any possibility of finding refuge inside an object, insofar as it flattens the perceptual world and the internal world. As a result, any inclination to carry out attacks, linked to the longing for psychic shelter, is itself destroyed or evacuated. The autistic position thus separates the life drives from the death drives. However, as we have already said (Chapter 9), only the binding of the drives allows for the cathexis of an object with an interior space. The binding of the life and death drives determines the creation of three-dimensional space. The two-dimensional flattening, accompanied by a drive unbinding, represents a triumph of the death drive which destroys any feeling of need, of desire, and any space for thought.

In addition, the countertransference experience of caregivers trying to enter into contact with an autistic subject frequently includes, alongside violent destructive drive impulses, a sometimes intense feeling of intrusive penetration (of being penetrated by the patient or of penetrating him if communication is attempted). It may be supposed that the autistic subject has evacuated into unbinding or non-binding, not only instinctual but also emotional,[2] any capacity to experience feelings of penetration, feelings that are particularly annihilating for him. These feelings are experienced at that time by the caregiver, and sometimes with murderous hostility in phantasy.

The attempt to make contact with an autistic subject, that is to say the attempt to open a space, causes him to experience the risk of the two layers (stuck together) of two-dimensional space being torn apart and of the tearing of psychic skin. The absence of sadism, the non-binding or unbinding of the life and death drives, can only offer the life drives the solution of clinging auto-sensually to the first sensory modality that presents itself. It is a clinging for survival, before the destruction of any possibility of finding refuge in and through the cathexis of an object.

Notes

1 This absence of sadism in the autistic state proper leads some authors to emphasize the importance in the treatment of an autistic subject of the experience of reappropriating primary sadism (see for example Suarez-Labat, 2013).
2 Emotion reflects how the ego *is affected by* the drive and the object, or by the drive-cathected object.

15

"SECOND SKIN" FORMATION

15.1 A "psycho-bodily" second skin

The "psychic skin" is formed by introjecting the containing function of the external object, and by introjecting the relationship to the external object in the containing experience. The internalized containing object is felt to be a skin and the skin is experienced as a boundary, holding together the sense of self. If this introjection is faulty, as a result of the inadequacy of the containing function of the external object and/or the incapacity of the nascent psyche to take advantage of environmental psychic qualities, a "second skin" phenomenon will appear on both the bodily scene and the psychic scene. The "psychic skin" will be based on a substitute for the skin container instead of being based on the containing function of the skin. We can then speak of "pseudo-containing" through the "second skin" effect.

Esther Bick (1968) illustrates this hypothesis with examples that show the infant's responses to states of non-integration or disintegration in the bodily mode of aggressive hyperactivity (the case of the baby Alice), of postural and motor hypercathexis (the case of the little girl Mary), and according to the psychic modalities of projective identification and adhesive identification (Bick, 1986).

While Esther Bick insisted above all on the notion of "a muscular second skin", we would say that the "second skin" concerns or groups together different modes of pseudo-containing (see Chapter 2):

- a sensory and sensual mode (clinging to autistic objects and forms);
- an intero- and proprioceptive mode (kinaesthetic clinging and clinging to the hypertonicity of the musculature[1]);

- a mental mode (clinging to pseudo-thinking, cognition or psychic excitation);
- an intellectual mode (clinging to knowledge).

All these "second skins" – *sensory second skin, muscular second skin, mental second skin and intellectual second skin* – replace dependence on the object with pseudo-independence thanks to the pathological use of primitive modes of identification (adhesive identification, projective identification). This pseudo-independence is the other side of absolute dependence on an external object. The function at the level of the internal world of these psychic "second skins", based on sensory, muscular, mental or intellectual modalities, consists in maintaining a sense of identity, a sense of going on being.

15.2 The effects of the "second skin"

The "second skin" pseudo-containing mode can therefore give rise to effects of *encapsulation* that are consequences of adhesive identification: turning away from object relations, narcissistic withdrawal into an auto-sensual world by clinging to objects, forms and auto-sensual or autistic manoeuvres.[2] But the constitution of a "second skin" can also sustain openness to the outside world, communication, and therefore psychic development, by giving a sense of closure and impermeability to the internal space, a closure that contains and neutralizes archaic anxieties, which can be provoked precisely by certain experiences of communication. This support is obviously a fragile support, albeit one which comes to the rescue of a defective psychic skin.

The main effect that we are going to discuss concerns the processes of projective identification rather than adhesive processes: it is the *"pseudo" effect* which we have already spoken about several times (Chapters 11 and 12).

The "pseudo" aspect of personality covers the phenomena described by Donald Winnicott (1949, 1952a, 1954, 1955, 1956a, 1959, 1960b, 1963) under the term of "false self", and Helene Deutsch (1934, 1942) under the term of "'as if' personality".

Helene Deutsch defines the "as if" personality type as being characterized by a lack of authenticity. The "as if" subject presents a real loss of object-cathexis and functions in the register of mimicry which results in a seemingly good adaptation to reality. His attitude towards the environment is passive, and he has a strong ability to mould himself on it. This passivity and this capacity for adaptation are reflected by great suggestibility, "negative goodness", "mild amiability". The "as if" development of the personality is based on a lack of introjection, a sense of inner emptiness justifying a "readiness for identification" which means that any object will serve as a bridge for mimetic identification. In this description of the "as if" character of personality, we recognize the work of projective identification, with its adhesive, mimetic aspects, which predominate when the aim is to *borrow the identity of the other*, not in order to control it or to triumph over it but to fill an inner void.

The notion of "false self" was developed by Winnicott to describe an organization in the subject that responds to a failure in the active adaptation of the environment consisting of an impingement of the environment on the baby, or rather his psychic life. This impingement disturbs the continuity of existence and impels the baby to *react*. Continuity of existence supports the development of the true self, while the reaction to impingement is constitutive of the false self. If the parent knows how to identify with the child's needs, the child begins to exist and a real self develops. If the parent is not "good enough",[3] the child begins to react rather than exist. The parent who is "good enough" responds to the baby's spontaneous gestures and adapts in such a way as to protect his illusion of omnipotence. The parent who is not good enough does not make the baby's omnipotence real, does not respond to his spontaneous gestures but replaces them with his own, which places the baby in a position of submission, the first stage of the false self. The false self therefore develops on the basis of submission to a seductive environment.

The false self is brought to the fore by primitive defence mechanisms aimed at protecting the true self from the threat of annihilation. The false self is an aspect of the true self, hiding and protecting it by reacting to the failures of environmental adaptation. The hidden authentic self will suffer from impoverishment due to lack of experience.

The false self cannot achieve the independence of maturity. This gives way to a pseudo-maturity, a false force based on a model provided by the environment, generating a sense of futility. This false development based on submission and obedience goes hand in hand with great dependence on the object. If obedience, a manifestation of the false self, is taken as a sign of growth, it is the "success" of a false and unreal life that will be favoured.

The "normal" false self corresponds to the polite, courteous, adapted social attitude, to the internalization of the rules decreed by the environment. The false self is "abnormal" when it takes the place of the authentic self. In this case, the true self is threatened with annihilation, and a feeling of inanity and hopelessness develops. The affirmation of the true self can then lead to suicide.

Winnicott (1949, 1960b) finds that the false self often resides in the "mind". It is a pathological formation of the dissociated intellect that we are trying to describe through what we call the "intellectual 'second skin'". Winnicott describes how the psyche is "seduced by the mind" and breaks off its relationship with the soma to establish a pathological psyche–mind relationship. In this artificial self, intellectual functioning becomes a thing-in-itself, where the psyche is falsely localized, replacing the good primary object by developing the illusion of independence.

Pseudo-maturity is based, as we have seen with Donald Meltzer (1966), on the process of projective identification with internal objects (see Chapter 11). But we can see at work, in the false self, more archaic processes of identification. Geneviève Haag (1984b) considers the false self, and this endorses the notion of the "second skin" of which Esther Bick spoke, as resulting from a kind of surface identification, that is to say adhesive identification, whose characteristic is pure imitation and which includes pathological autistic elements:

> In the false self, the possibility of an interpenetrating relationship has not been built ("getting inside another person's head", in phantasy). We find something of the failure of the interplay, back and forth, between projection and introjection, both in "false-self" personalities and in structures where this element of surface identification is found whose effect, for the subject, is to be able to live only in strict imitation.
> (Haag, 1984b, p. 174–175, translated for this edition)

This idea echoes Searles (1971) suggestion that the ego-functioning of "as if" personalities is cracked at its foundation by autism. This autism remains masked in everyday life, but emerges with clarity in the evolution of the transference in an analytical situation. Frances

Tustin (1980, 1981ab) links the false self to the experience of early psychic separation which characterizes the psychotic child and especially the autistic child, always with the idea that the latter is "psychologically premature". In this connection, she points out the need in psychotherapy with psychotic children to speak with them about their panic, their rage and their "predatory rivalry" before interpreting feelings such as love, aggression, envy or jealousy. If these feelings, which the child experienced in a compact and precocious manner, are interpreted too early, before he can distinguish and tolerate them, then the precocity will be reinforced and the development of a false self favoured.

The false self is therefore conceived as constituted both passively and actively. The passive aspect characterizes the dimension of alienation to the desire of the other, of reaction to his impingement, of submission to his seduction. The active aspect corresponds to the defensive function of the false self erected to stand in as a substitute skin. Let us recall what Piera Aulagnier (1986) describes as a possible response in the child to a traumatic encounter for the parent (see Chapter 13): the child may try to conform as much as possible to what is assumed to be desired by the parent in order to match the psychic representative pre-cathected by him or her. Let us also recall what André Green (1983) describes as a possible consequence of introjecting a "dead mother" – we prefer the term "dead parent" – (see Chapter 13): the child may develop intense intellectual activity based on the attempt to master the traumatic situation by guessing and anticipating the mood variations of the parent. This intellectual hyperactivity is at the origin of brilliant professional successes, but is accompanied by an erotic delibidinalization which is responsible for deep emotional difficulties. These scenarios envisaged by Aulagnier and Green can occur in the context of a defensive false-self organization of the personality. The false self takes up all the space and prevents the development of the true self which, abandoned, forgotten, is at mortal risk. The assertion or even the rebellion of the true self is also expressed by various symptoms which, as we have said, can ultimately lead to suicide.

It may be added that while intellectualization can be evidence of a false-self organization, it can also take the form of an intellectual deficiency: pseudo-deficiency, in psychotic children for example, can be understood as a defensive false-self organization that suffocates the authentic intellectual capacities which could allow them to understand what must not be understood, to perceive what must remain denied, to become aware of what, to preserve family balance or parental health, must remain hidden.

15.3 Phenomenology of the "second skin" in the baby. Semiology of early psychic disorders

The phenomenological and psychopathological aspects of the "second skin" in the baby have been illustrated through several clinical cases discussed in this work (see in particular, Chapters 2 and 5). We will present here a synthetic overview of the semiology of early psychic disorders in the baby, while emphasizing the function of the "second skin" covered by these pathological manifestations (the auto-sensual manoeuvres – autistic or confusional – which we will enumerate are described and their logics explained in detail in Chapters 2 and 5).

We will group the autistic and very early psychotic signs in a third series of symptoms (as André Carel (1981) does), among the series evidencing *psychic distress* in the baby.

The first series of symptoms concerns the *major vital functions*: sleep, alertness, eating, tonic motor skills, psychomotor skills. These functions can be disorganized or unorganized. Their disorders are common to all forms of psychic distress and serve as warning symptoms.

A second group of symptoms concerns the quality of *mentalization* and *psychic organizers*:

- rare or absent smile even after three months;
- phobic stranger anxiety that is exaggerated or even absent after 12 months;
- lack of recognition of the specular image, even after 18 months, or a rejection of mirror images;
- poverty of transitional phenomena, games;
- disorganized or absent pre-language;
- expression of depressive affects, or else the coexistence of excessive calm and range in an anxious tone;
- rarity of exchanges, interactive solicitations, "joint attention" behaviours (Bruner, 1975) and "protodeclarative pointing" (pointing to attract attention (Bretherton and Bates, 1979).

A third series of symptoms, finally, groups together the *more specifically autistic and confusional manoeuvres or signs of "relational avoidance"*[4] which can be found in the contexts of transient autistic disorders, the onset of an autistic state, or even an early psychotic state with autistic signs:

- absence of joint attention, protodeclarative pointing and make-believe behaviours at 18 months (the absence of these behaviours accounts for a defect in "theory of mind"[5] and is considered in itself as an indicator or precursor of autism[6]);
- avoidance of the attachment object (Fraiberg, 1982): observed from three months in situations of gross neglect or mistreatment, of a severely defective environment; avoidance is selective and discriminatory; it protects from external danger, but when there is too much (somatic) need, the distress is too great and results in a disorganization, and then a rupture which obviates the experience of distress (this corresponds to a form of splitting or absence from oneself);
- immobilization or "freezing" (Fraiberg, 1982): a defence which also collapses after a certain time, followed by ego-disintegration;
- perpetual motion (Ciccone, 1995a), agitation: a defence in itself, or a reflection of the collapse of earlier defences, of panic and disintegration;
- "hallucinatory denial of perception" (Mahler, 1968), "withdrawal of cathexis from the *sensorium*" (Mahler, 1968), "sensory deafferentation" (Carel, 1981);
  - gaze avoidance, peripheral gaze, penetrating gaze, intermittent strabismus;
  - suspended, fixed gaze as if gripped by or fascinated in a "quasi hypnotizing quest" (Haag, 1984a), hallucinated gaze;
  - "cyclops effect" (Haag, 1984a);
  - indifference to the voice, contrasting with an early fascination with music or mechanical noises;
- auto-sensual clinging to external sources of excitation:
  - use of objects or parts of the body as "autistic objects" or "confusional objects" (Tustin, 1972, 1980, 1990) (exaggerated or even exclusive interest in objects or parts of the body, hard or soft and interchangeable – clinging to any small object, tongue-sucking, faecal retention, drooling saliva, etc.);
  - frequent and intense fixation of attention on a sensory source (light, sound, etc.);

- proprioceptive auto-sensual clinging:
  - stereotypies (excessive interest in hand games with or without manipulation of objects, "arm flapping", spinning, scratching, tapping, smelling, licking, swaying, rhythmic movements while falling asleep, verbal stereotypies), creation of "autistic forms" (Tustin, 1984a, 1990) or "confusional forms";
  - posturomotor withdrawals (arms bent at the elbow), with at the level of the upper limbs a non-use of the parachute functions and at the level of the lower limbs a withdrawal by avoiding support positions and locomotor rejection; stiffness;
- prehensive mannerisms and locomotor mannerisms:
  - starting to walk on tiptoe, with arms waving;
  - "sign of the burning object" (see Marcelli, 1983, or Haag, 1984a);
  - delicate pincer grasp formed not by the pad of the index and thumb but by the edge of these fingers;
- rejection of humans, struggle against all requests for human contact; lack of interest in people, especially in faces (possible interest in parts such as hands or clothing); phobia of body contact, lack of anticipatory attitude when taken in the arms and of postural adjustment during carrying; absence of interactive vocalizations and pre-language exchanges;
- undifferentiated attitude towards animate or inanimate objects, towards human or non-human objects; undifferentiated relational behaviour regardless of the interlocutor;
- use of humans as an instrument, as an extension of the body ("getting someone else to do something" – see Marcelli, 1983, or Haag, 1984a);
- compulsive interest in certain objects, in particular small objects, with an abandonment of the object once it is out of sight ("sign of oblivion" – Carel and Michel, 1985); captivating fascination with the specular image; abnormal concern for an inanimate, fetish object;
- fits of rage at the slightest change in the environment, tyrannical demands for immutability, coexisting with excessive calm, lack of reaction to separation; early phobic fear of certain noises or certain familiar objects;
- absence of any transitional phenomenon (absence of games, of autoerotic activities);

- self-destructive activities in place of autoerotic activities, with apparent insensitivity to pain; turning of aggression against the self, observed at the end of the first year (Fraiberg, 1982);
- almost total refusal of any initiative, of any spontaneity (Manzano and Palacio Espasa, 1978);
- language or behavioural disorders:
  - echolalia;
  - monologues, logorrhoea or mutism;
  - use of the pronoun "you" or "he" instead of "I";
- mimicry, echopraxia;
- obsessions, rites, ceremonials (especially during meals, defecation, etc.);
- magical gestures (such as wiping after being touched);
- anxiety that is little developed or developed in the form of phobias and terrors; lack of expression of affects or expression of affects of explosive rage, of noisy or mute terror; changes in affect, observed from nine months (Fraiberg, 1982) (the baby who screamed in terror during exciting, traumatic situations, begins to react to the same situations with a grin, a silly laugh or a theatrical laugh, which is a defence against intolerable anxiety).

All these early autistic or psychotic manoeuvres or effects are underpinned by the processes of adhesive identification and dismantling, and consist of creating or accounting for the creation of a "substitute psychic skin" capable of protecting the scattered elements of the self from a catastrophic experience. The absence of an adequate psychic skin which can hold the baby together in his mental life, forces him to resort to auto-sensual, autistic or confusional manoeuvres, revealing that the containing function, first assured by the external object and gradually introjected by the baby, cannot be sustained, in a more or less momentary way. This results either from the *inadequacy of the external object*, whose alpha function is ineffective, the absence of the "capacity for reverie", the unavailability of a capacity for understanding and psychic holding, or from the *inability of the baby to take advantage of the psychic qualities of the maternal environment* as a result of excessive intolerance to frustration, exaggerated envious attacks on the external object, constitutional hypersensitivity exposing the baby too much or too early to depressive experiences, neurophysiological equipment that is altered or defective, etc., or from the interaction of these two types of pathogenic situation, which is particularly damaging for the psychic evolution of the newborn.

Early autistic or psychotic symptoms can be more or less intense and more or less numerous. The quantity of autistic and confusional manifestations, their duration and their intensity compared to periods of "normal" psychic functioning that is open to the world, will determine the onset of autism, and even of early psychosis, or the gradual overcoming of transient autistic withdrawals. Clinging to, and by means of, auto-sensual, autistic or confusing manoeuvres ensures temporary psychic survival but hinders the process of birth to psychic life.

Notes

1 Concerning the muscular and kinaesthetic mode of "second skin" containing, let us recall the studies of Wilhelm Reich (1927, 1933) which may be considered as precursors in the reading of tonic muscle phenomena favouring their conjunction with psychic phenomena. Reich considered "muscular armour" to be related to "character armour", muscular stiffness representing the somatic effect of psychic inhibition. He described the relations between anxiety and muscular stiffness or muscular agitation (anxiety is avoided by muscular tension, softening of the muscular armour causes anxiety, the more "libidinal motility" develops, the more the musculature relaxes, etc.).
2 See the image of the "empty fortress" given by Bruno Bettelheim (1967).
3 Winnicott speaks of "a good enough mother", but as we have tried to do since the beginning of this book, we stress the idea of "parenthood" rather than "motherhood". The father is indeed just as concerned – as is the whole entourage that takes care of a baby – by the requirement to be "good enough".
4 Terminology proposed by André Carel (1998), in particular because it is difficult to pronounce before 18 months on the autistic nature or otherwise of a symptom or a group of symptoms.
5 Term coined by Premack and Woodruff (1978). See Baron-Cohen, Leslie and Frith, 1985; Frith, 1989; Frith, Morton and Leslie, 1991. See Chapters 2 and 10.
6 See Baron-Cohen et al., 1992, 1996. See Chapters 2 and 10.

EPILOGUE

We set out to explore the birth of subjectivity, its conditions, its modalities, and to give an account of psychic life in its initial states. We have modeled the processes of structuring and complexification of the psychic apparatus, with particular focus on the modes of transition from one degree of complexification to another. We have underlined the fruitfulness, both for metapsychology and the understanding of psychopathologies, of the model of psychic envelopes and of the container, whose conditions of constitution as psychic objects we have studied.

Many questions have simply been opened up and put into perspective, and merit further investigation or development (some have already been researched or explored in other books). This is the case, for example, with the question of the history of object relations and the transition from one aspect of object relations to another; or the question of psychic transmission and its modalities, and the modalities of appropriation or subjectivation of the transmitted contents.[1] This is also the case with regard to the constitution of the first images of the body, and the complexification of the psychic integration of the bodily zones, according to their function and their place within intersubjective relations.

We have discussed the early alterations in psychic development, the different types of suffering they produce or the psychopathological figures they generate. Outside the context of the onset of a serious psychopathology, many babies go through, in particular circumstances, transient and resolving psychopathological states (we have mentioned, for example, situations of transient autistic withdrawal). An in-depth study on the healing modalities of these early and transient psychopathological states needs to be carried out.[2]

Our contribution to research concerning this vast field represented by the early states of psychic life is based on an approach combining observation of normal development and observation of psychopathology. The study of psychopathology provides information on normal development, and vice versa. There is no solution of continuity between the normal and the pathological (and the line separating the two is always a partly arbitrary and provisional construction). All psychopathological processes can be found in normal psychic development, in the vagaries of this development or in disturbing contexts. It can be said that pathologization results partly from an amplification of certain normal processes, but also and above all, for the most part, from the amplification of the destructive aspects of these processes. Pathology distorts normal processes. We have studied the conditions underlying the realization of this distortion.

The picture of any psychic state as the effect of an oscillation between several positions, one of which predominantly attracts the psyche, can account for – and seems to us to be congruent with – the complexity of each singular psychic situation (normal or pathological). Any approach to subjectivity, any clinical approach, must take this complexity into account and the coexistence of different, even contradictory, states and processes, operating according to sometimes antagonistic logics within the same psychic situation. The narcissist-related dimension contains the object-related dimension and vice versa. The psychotic dimension contains the neurotic dimension and vice versa.

Our discussion has given an essential place to the containing object – external then internal – and to the intersubjective links with this object, in the construction of subjectivity and the sense of identity. At a time of "à la carte maternity", of the hypertechnicization of perinatality as well as of most nursing practices and even social practices, at a time of *"homo economicus"*,[3] where managerial and economic logics are invading hospitals and places of care and colonizing the whole of the social sphere, and where the processes of "desubjectivation" which they generate and promote produce the "disquiet" characteristic of postmodernity,[4] it is important to emphasize the fundamental importance of taking into account and listening to the subjectivity of the baby, as well as that of his parents, of protecting the intimate, emotional exchanges between the baby and his first object relations, his first containing objects. We might also wonder if the fascination that the non-human animated world has for many children, and their keen interest in virtual worlds featuring mechanical, robotic, all-powerful characters, in beauty that is ideal but cold, etc., could not be understood as an attempt to control a cold and dehumanized universe, encountered not only in the first mothering environment, but also in the social sphere containing this environment.

Donald Meltzer (1984b, 1986) has emphasized the importance for a baby of experiencing the emotional impact of the beauty of the world. This experience can generate suffering, but it is from this experience that thought can emerge and the question of meaning can open up, as soon as the baby begins to wonder about the "inner" beauty of its object. And the environment – family, social – can, at any age, encourage or hinder this emotional impact and this openness to thinking. It can at any age help a subject locked into his "claustrum" to get out of it, to escape from it in order to open up to the world and develop his emotional life.

> We can [...] imagine escaping from the simplicity of a computer-dominated life, escaping from a two-dimensional life, from a life where things are only what they seem to be and nothing else, from a life of causality and automaticity; in other words, escaping towards a life in another world of experiences where the essence of life is constituted by emotions awakened in the subject by the beauty of the world.
> (Meltzer, 1984b, p. 28, translated from the French)

Let us emphasize, finally, the optimistic aspect, as regards psychic care, of the conception according to which a containing object can help and support growth, whatever the context. Psychic care, of which feeding is a metaphor, consists first of all in welcoming and accommodating the infantile part of the patient who is suffering or in distress. It is a question of accepting the primitive identifications and the possible destructiveness which they convey, and of keeping alive the concern to think about (*penser*) – and to heal (*panser*) – the singular experience of the encounter in order to facilitate the development in the other of his own thinking and therefore of his own psychic container. The container must be firm enough and flexible enough, thanks to the harmonious blend of maternal and paternal functions, to contain the shared emotional experience in the care situation, which often presents itself as a tormented experience. Psychic development is only possible if the mind finds a containing object. Every unborn psyche, every child, is waiting for psyche to welcome it.

Notes

1. On this subject, see Ciccone, 2012a.
2. Part of this question is examined, among others, in a book called *Les Traces des experiences infantiles* (Ciccone et al., 2018).
3. See Cohen, 2012.
4. See Kaës, 2012.

BIBLIOGRAPHY

Abelhauser, A., Gori, A., Sauret, M.-J. (eds.) (2011). *La Folie évaluation. Les nouvelles fabriques de la servitude*. Paris: Mille et une nuits.
Abraham, K. (1919). A particular form of neurotic resistance against the psychoanalytic method. In: Jones, E. (ed.), *Selected Papers of Karl Abraham*, trans. Douglas Bryan and Alix Strachey. London: Routledge, 2018, p. 303–311.
Abraham, K. (1920). Manifestations of the female castration complex. In: Jones, E. (ed.), *Selected Papers of Karl Abraham*, trans. Douglas Bryan, Alix Strachey. London: Routledge, 2018, p. 338–369.
Abraham, K. (1921). Contributions to the theory of the anal character. In: Jones, E. (ed.), *Selected Papers of Karl Abraham*, trans. Douglas Bryan, Alix Strachey. London: Routledge, 2018, p. 370–392.
Abraham, K. (1924). A short study of the development of the libido, viewed in the light of mental disorders. In: Jones, E. (ed.), *Selected Papers of Karl Abraham*, trans. Douglas Bryan, Alix Strachey. London: Routledge, 2018, p. 418–501.
Abraham, N. (1987). Le "crime" de l'introjection. In: Abraham, N., Torok, M. (eds.), *L'Écorce et Le Noyau*. Paris: Flammarion, p. 123–131.
Abraham, N., Torok, M. (1972). Mourning or melancholia: Introjection *versus* incorporation. In: Rand, N. (ed.), *The Shell and the Kernel, Vol. 1*, trans. N. Rand. Chicago: Chicago University Press, 1994, p. 125–138.
Abraham, N., Torok, M. (1987). *The Shell and the Kernel*, edited and translated by N. Rand. Chicago: Chicago University Press, 1994.
Adamo, S., Rustin, M.E. (eds.) (2014). *Young Child Observation. A Development in the Method and Theory of Infant Observation*. London: Karnac.
Adrien, J.-L. (1996). *Autisme du jeune enfant*. Paris: Expansion Scientifique Française.

Aguayo, J. (2002). Reassessing the clinical affinity between Melanie Klein and D.W. Winnicott (1935–51): Klein's unpublished 'Notes on baby' in historical context. *The International Journal of Psychoanalysis*, 83(5): 1133–1152.

Ainsworth, M.D., Blehar, M., Waters, E., Walls, S. (1978). *Patterns of Attachment: A Psychological Study of the Strange Situation*. Hillsdale, N.J.: Lawrence Erlbaum Associates Publishers.

Ainsworth, M.D., Wittig, B.A. (1969). Attachment and exploratory behavior of one-year-olds in a strange situation. In: Foss, B.M. (ed.), *Determinants of Infant Behavior, IV*. London: Methuen, p. 111–136.

Ajuriaguerra, J. de (1977). *Manuel de psychiatrie de l'enfant*. Paris: Masson (new revised edition).

Alvarez, A. (1992). *Live Company: Psychoanalytic Therapy with Autistic, Borderline, Deprived and Abused Children*. London: Routledge.

Alvarez, A., Reid, S. (eds.) (1999). *Autism and Personality*. London: Routledge.

American Psychiatric Association. (2013). *Diagnostic and Statistical Manual of Mental Disorders*, Fifth Edition (DSM-5).

Amy, M.D. (ed.). (2014). *Autismes et Psychanalyses. Évolution des pratiques, recherches et articulations*. Toulouse: Érès.

Amy, M.D. (ed.). (2016). *Autismes: spécificités des pratiques psychanalytiques*. Toulouse: Érès.

Anzieu, D. (1966). Étude psychanalytique des groupes réels. *Les Temps modernes*, 242: 56–73.

Anzieu, D. (1971). L'illusion groupale. *Nouvelle Revue de psychanalyse*, 4: 73–93.

Anzieu, D. (1974a). Le moi-peau. *Nouvelle Revue de psychanalyse*, 9: 195–208.

Anzieu, D. (1974b). La peau: du plaisir à la pensée. In: Zazzo, R. (ed.), *L'Attachement*. Paris-Neuchâtel: Delachaux et Niestlé, p. 140–154.

Anzieu, D. (1975). Le transfert paradoxal. De la communication paradoxale à la réaction thérapeutique négative. *Nouvelle Revue de psychanalyse*, 12: 49–72.

Anzieu, D. (1981). *Le Groupe et l'Inconscient. L'imaginaire groupal*. Paris: Dunod.

Anzieu, D. (1985). *The Skin-Ego*. new revised trans. Neomi Segal. London: Routledge, 2018.

Anzieu, D. (1986a). *Une peau pour les pensées. Entretiens avec G. Tarrab*. Paris: Clancier-Guénaud.

Anzieu, D. (1986b). Cadre psychanalytique et enveloppes psychiques. *Journal de la psychanalyse de l'enfant*, 2: 12–24.
Anzieu, D. (1986c). Introduction à l'étude des fonctions du moi-peau dans le couple. *Gruppo*, 2: 75–81.
Anzieu, D. (1987a). Les signifiants formels et le moi-peau. In: Anzieu, D. (ed.), *Les Enveloppes psychiques*. Paris: Dunod, p. 1–22.
Anzieu, D. (1987b). Antinomies de la solitude. *Nouvelle Revue de psychanalyse*, 36: 123–127.
Anzieu, D. (1990). La peau psychique. In: Anzieu, D. (ed.), *L'Épiderme nomade et la Peau psychique*. Paris: Apsygée, p. 27–129.
Anzieu, D. (1993a). La fonction contenante de la peau, du moi et de la pensée: contenant, conteneur, contenir. In: Anzieu, D. (ed.), *Les Contenants de pensée*. Paris: Dunod, p. 15–39.
Anzieu, D. (1993b). Le moi-peau familial et groupal. *Gruppo*, 9: 9–18.
Anzieu, D. (1994). *Le Penser. Du moi-peau au moi-pensant*. Paris: Dunod.
Anzieu, D. (1995). *Le Moi-peau*. Paris: Dunod (new revised and enlarged edition).
Anzieu, D. (ed.). (1972). *Le Travail psychanalytique dans les groupes*, Vol. 1. Paris: Dunod (new edition), 1978.
Anzieu, D. (ed.). (1987). *Les Enveloppes psychiques*. Paris: Dunod.
Anzieu, D. (ed.) (1990). *L'Épiderme nomade et la Peau psychique*. Paris: Apsygée.
Anzieu, D. (ed.) (1993). *Les Contenants de pensée*. Paris: Dunod.
Athanassiou, C. (1982). La constitution et l'évolution des premières identifications. *Revue française de psychanalyse*, 46(6): 1187–1209.
Athanassiou, C. (1988). Le remaniement des souvenirs. *Revue française de psychanalyse*, 52(1): 67–90.
Athanassiou, C. (1996). *La Défense maniaque*. Paris: Presses Universitaires de France.
Aulagnier, P. (1975). *The Violence of Interpretation: From Pictogram to Statement*, trans. Alan Sheridan. London: Routledge, 2001.
Aulagnier, P. (1982). Condamné à investir. *Nouvelle Revue de psychanalyse*, 25: 309–330.
Aulagnier, P. (1984). *L'Apprenti-historien et le Maître-sorcier. Du discours identifiant au discours délirant*. Paris: Presses Universitaires de France.
Aulagnier, P. (1985a). Le retrait dans l'hallucination, un équivalent du retrait autistique? *Lieux de l'enfance*, 3: 149–164.
Aulagnier, P. (1985b). Quelqu'un a tué quelque chose. *Topique*, 35–36: 265–295.

Aulagnier, P. (1986). Naissance d'un corps, origine d'une histoire. In: McDougall, J. (ed.), *Corps et Histoire*. Paris: Les Belles Lettres, p. 99–141.

Bailey, A., Phillips, W., Rutter, M. (1996). Autism: Toward an integration of clinical, genetic, neuropsychological and neurobiological perspectives. *Journal of Child Psychology and Psychiatry*, 37(1): 89–126.

Baranes, J.-J. (1987). Vers une métapsychologie transgénérationnelle. *Adolescence*, 5(1): 79–93.

Baranes, J.-J. (1989). Déni, identifications aliénantes, temps de la génération. In: Missenard, A. (ed.), *Le Négatif, figures et modalités*. Paris: Dunod, p. 78–100.

Baranes, J.-J. (1991). Des répétitions plurielles: vers une métapsychologie transgénérationnelle? In: Baranes, J.-J. (ed.), *La Question psychotique à l'adolescence*. Paris: Dunod, p. 47–94.

Baron-Cohen, S. (1989). Perceptual role-taking and protodeclarative pointing in autism. *British Journal of Developmental Psychology*, 7: 113–127.

Baron-Cohen, S. (1991). The theory of mind deficit in autism: how specific is it? *British Journal of Developmental Psychology*, 9: 301–314.

Baron-Cohen, S., Allen, J., Gillberg, C. (1992). Can autism be detected at the age of 18 months? The needle, the haystack and the CHAT. *British Journal of Psychiatry*, 161: 839–843.

Baron-Cohen, S., Cox, A., Baird, G., Swettenham, J., Nightingale, N., Morgan, K. Drew, A., Charman, T. (1996). Psychological markers in the detection of autism in infancy in a large population. *British Journal of Psychiatry*, 168: 158–163.

Baron-Cohen, S., Leslie, A.M., Frith, U. (1985). Does the autistic child have a theory of mind? *Cognition*, 21: 37–46.

Barrie, J.M. (1911). *Peter Pan*. London: Everyman.

Bateson, G., Jackson, D., Haley, J., Weakland, J. (1956). Toward a theory of schizophrenia. *Behavioural Science*, 1: 251–264.

Bégoin, J. (1984). Présentation: quelques repères sur l'évolution du concept d'identification. *Revue française de psychanalyse*, 48(2): 483–490.

Bégoin, J. (1985). Du fantasme à la pensée. Directions du mouvement kleinien et postkleinien. In: Gammil, J. (ed.), *Mélanie Klein aujourd'hui*. Lyon: Césura Lyon Édition, p. 105–121.

Bégoin, J. (1989). La violence du désespoir, ou le contresens d'une "pulsion de mort", en psychanalyse. *Revue française de psychanalyse*, 53(2): 619–640.

Benedeck, T. (1959). Parenthood as a developmental phase: a contribution to libido theory. *Journal of American Psychoanalytic Association*, 7(1–4): 389–417.

Benedeck, T., Anthony, E.J. (eds.) (1970). *Parenthood: Its Psychology and Psychopathology*. Boston: Little Brown and Company.

Berenstein, I., Pujet, J. (1984). Le socle inconscient du couple (trad. fr.). *Gruppo*, 1986(2): 83–98 and *Gruppo*, 1987(3): 83–102.

Berger, M. (2008). *Voulons-nous des enfants barbares?* Paris: Dunod.

Berger, M. (2012). *Soigner les enfants violents*. Paris: Dunod.

Berger, M. (2016). *De l'incivilité au terrorisme*. Paris: Dunod.

Berger, M., Bonneville, E., André, P., Rigaux, C. (2007). L'enfant très violent: origine, devenir, prise en charge. *Neuropsychiatrie de l'enfance et de l'adolescence*, 55(7): 353–361.

Bergeret, J. (1981). La violence fondamentale. L'étayage instinctuel de la pulsion libidinale. *Revue française de psychanalyse*, 45(6): 1335–1350.

Bergeret, J. (1984). *La Violence fondamentale*. Paris: Dunod.

Bergeret, J. (1985). Les pulsions dans la métapsychologie d'aujourd'hui. *Revue française de psychanalyse*, 49(6): 1461–1478.

Bergeret, J. (1987a). *Le « Petit Hans » et la Réalité ou Freud face à son passé*. Paris: Payot.

Bergeret, J. (1987b). *Les Interrogations du psychanalyste*. Paris: Presses Universitaires de France.

Bettelheim B. (1967). *The Empty Fortress: Infantile Autism and the Birth of the Self*. New York: Free Press.

Bick, E. (1964). Notes on infant observation in psycho-analytic training. In: Harris, M. (ed.), *Collected Papers of Martha Harris and Esther Bick*. Perthshire: Clunie Press, p. 240–256.

Bick, E. (1968). The experience of the skin in early object-relations. In: Harris, M. (ed.),*Collected Papers of Martha Harris and Esther Bick*. Perthshire: Clunie Press, p. 114–118.

Bick, E. (1986). Further considerations on the function of the skin in early object relations. *British Journal of Psychotherapy*, 2(4): 292–299.

Bion, W.R. (1954). Notes on the theory of schizophrenia. In: Bion, W.R. (ed.), *Second Thoughts*. London: Heinemann, 1967, p. 86–92.

Bion, W.R. (1956). Development of schizophrenic thought. In: Bion, W.R. (ed.), *Second Thoughts*. London: Heinemann, 1967, p. 36–42.

Bion, W.R. (1957). Differentiation of the psychotic from the non-psychotic personalities. In: Bion, W.R. (ed.), *Second Thoughts*. London: Heinemann, 1967, p. 43–64.

Bion, W.R. (1958). On hallucination. In: Bion, W.R. (ed.), *Second Thoughts*. London: Heinemann, 1967, p. 65–85.

Bion, W.R. (1959). Attacks on linking. In: Bion, W.R. (ed.), *Second Thoughts*. London: Heinemann, 1967, p. 93–109.

Bion, W.R. (1961). *Experiences in Groups and Other Papers.* London: Tavistock.
Bion, W.R. (1962a). A theory of thinking. In: Bion, W.R. (ed.), *Second Thoughts.* London: Heinemann, 1967, p. 110–119.
Bion, W.R. (1962b). *Learning from Experience.* London: Heinemann.
Bion, W.R. (1963). *Elements of Psycho-Analysis.* London: Heinemann.
Bion, W.R. (1965). *Transformations: Change from Learning to Growth.* London: Heinemann.
Bion, W.R. (1966). Catastrophic change. *Scientific Bulletin of the British Psycho-Analytical Society*, 5: 13–26.
Bion, W.R. (1967a). *Second Thoughts.* London: Heinemann.
Bion, W.R. (1967b). Notes on memory and desire. *The Psychoanalytic Forum*, 2: 272–273 and 279–280.
Bion, W.R. (1970). *Attention and Interpretation.* London: Tavistock.
Bion, W.R. (1971). *Two Papers: The Grid and Ceasura.* Rio de Janeiro: Imago Editora, 1977.
Bion, W.R. (1974–1977). *Brazilian Lectures.* Rio de Janeiro. Imago Editora.
Bion, W.R. (1977a). Emotional turbulence. In: Bion, F. (ed.), *Clinical Seminars: Brasilia and Sao Paulo and Four Papers.* Abingdon: Fleetwood Press, 1987, p. 223–233.
Bion, W.R. (1977b). On a quotation from Freud. In: Hartocollis, P. (ed.), *Borderline Personality Disorders.* New York: International Universities Press, p. 511–518.
Bion, W.R. (1978). *Four Discussions with Bion.* Strathclyde: Clunie Press.
Bion, W.R. (1979). *The Dawn of Oblivion*, Stathclyde, Clunie Press; also in Bion, W.R. (ed.), *A Memoir of the Future, Vol. 3*, London: Karnac, 1991, p. 427–578.
Bion, W.R. (1991). *A Memoir of the Future, Vols. 1–3.* London: Karnac.
Bion, W.R. (1997). *Taming Wild Thoughts.* London: Karnac.
Bleger, J. (1967). *Symbiosis and Ambiguity: A Psychoanalytic Study.* London: Routledge, 2012.
Bleger, J. (1971). The group as institution and within institutions. *International Journal of Therapeutic Communities*, 1989, 10(2): 109–115.
Bonneville, E. (2010). Effets des traumatismes relationnels précoces chez l'enfant. *La Psychiatrie de l'enfant*, 53(1): 31–70.
Bonneville, E. (2015). *Les Traumatismes relationnels précoces.* Toulouse: Érès.
Bourdier, P. (1972). L'hypermaturation des enfants de parents malades mentaux. Problèmes cliniques et théoriques. *Revue française de psychanalyse*, 36(1): 19–42.
Bourguignon, O. (1984). *Mort des enfants et Structures familiales.* Paris: Presses Universitaires de France.

Bibliography

Bower, T.G.R. (1977). *Le Développement psychologique de la première enfance* (trad. fr.). Brussels: Pierre Mardaga, 1978.

Bowlby, J. (1951). Maternal care and mental health. *Bulletin of the World Health Organization*, 3: 355–533.

Bowlby, J. (1969). *Attachment and Loss, Attachment, 1*. New York: Basic Books.

Bowlby, J. (1973). *Attachment and Loss, Vol. 2, Separation: Anxiety and Anger*. New York: Basic Books.

Bowlby, J. (1980). *Attachment and Loss, Vol. 3, Loss: Sadness and Depression*. New York: Basic Books.

Bowlby, J. (1988). *A Secure Base: Clinical Applications of Attachment Theory*. London: Routledge.

Brazelton, T.B. (1973). *Neonatal Behavioural Assessment Scale*. London: Heinemann Medical Books.

Brazelton, T.B. (1979). Behavioural competence of the newborn infant. *Semin Perinatol.*, 3(1): 35–44.

Brazelton, T.B. (1982). Le bébé: partenaire dans l'interaction (trad. fr.). In: Brazelton, T., Cramer, B., Kreisler, L., Schappi, R., Soulé, M. (eds.), *La Dynamique du nourrisson*. Paris: ESF, p. 11–27.

Brazelton, T.B., Koslowsky, B., Main, M. (1974). The origins of reciprocity: The early mother-infant interaction. In: Lewis, M., Rosenblum, L.A. (eds.), *The Effect of the Infant on Its Caregiver*. New York: John Wiley Interscience, p. 49–76.

Bremner, J., Meltzer, D. (1975). Autism proper, Timmy. In: Meltzer, D., Bremner, J., Hoxter, S., Weddell, D., Wittenberg, I. (eds.), *Explorations in Autism: A Psycho-Analytical Study*. Perthshire: Clunie Press, p. 35–55.

Bretherton I., Bates, E. (1979). The emergence of intentional communication. In: Uzgiris, I. (ed.), *New Directions for Child Development*, Vol. 4. San Francisco: Jossey-Bass, p. 81–100.

Bruner, J.S. (1973). Organization of early skilled action. *Child Development*, 44: 1–11.

Bruner, J.S. (1975). From communication to language. A psychological perspective. *Cognition*, 3: 255–287.

Brusset, B. (1988). *Psychanalyse du lien*. Paris: Le Centurion.

Bullinger, A. (2015). *Le Développement sensori-moteur de l'enfant et ses avatars*, Vol. 2. Toulouse: Érès.

Busnel, M.-C. (1997). Audition fœtale et réactivité prénatale à la voix maternelle "adressée". In: Busnel, M.-C., Daffos, F., Dolto-Tolitch, C., Lecanuet, J.-P., Negri, R. (eds.), *Que savent les fœtus?* Toulouse: Érès, p. 35–49.

Busnel, M.-C., Granier-Deferre, C. (1989). La sensorialité fœtale. In: Lebovici, S., Weill-Halpern, F. (eds.), *Psychopathologie du bébé*. Paris: Presses Universitaires de France, p. 157–164.

Butterworth, G., Cochran, E. (1980). Towards a mechanism of joint visual attention in infancy. *International Journal of Behavioral Development*, 4: 253–272.

Bydlowsky, M. (1978). Les enfants du désir. Le désir d'enfant dans sa relation à l'inconscient. *Psychanalyse à l'université*, 4(13): 59–92.

Caillot, J.-P., Decherf, G. (1982). *Thérapie familiale psychanalytique et Paradoxalité*. Paris: Clancier-Guénaud.

Carel, A. (1981). Processus psychotiques chez le nourrisson. In: Resnik, S. (ed.), *Autismo infantile e Educazione*. Rome: Ministero delle pubblica istruzione, Istituto della enciclopedia italiana, p. 117–138.

Carel, A. (1988). Transfert et périnatalité psychique, la fonction alpha à l'épreuve de la naissance. *Gruppo*, 4: 49–66.

Carel, A. (1998). Les signes précoces de l'autisme et de l'évitement relationnel du nourrisson. In: Delion, P. (ed.), *Les Bébés à risque autistique*. Toulouse: Érès, p. 27–46.

Carel A., Michel, E. (1985). Thérapie familiale psychanalytique des nourrissons autistes. *Entrevues*, 10. Lyon: CHS St Jean de Dieu, p. 21–33.

Ciccone, A. (1990). Questions épistémologiques à la notion de moi-peau. In: Anzieu, D. (ed.), *L'Épiderme nomade et la Peau psychique*. Paris: Apsygée, p. 133–136.

Ciccone, A. (1995a). Le nourrisson et la douleur psychique. *Dialogue*, 128: 6–15.

Ciccone, A. (1995b). Manque et répétition. *Cahiers de psychologie clinique*, 5: 29–50.

Ciccone, A. (1996a). La filiation à l'épreuve du handicap: fantasme de culpabilité et fantasme de transmission. *Contraste*, 4: 61–70.

Ciccone, A. (1996b). Trasmissione e nascita alla vita psichica. *Psicoanalisi e Metodo*, 1: 16–31.

Ciccone, A. (1997a). Empiétement imagoïque et fantasme de transmission. In: Eiguer, A. (ed.), *Le Générationnel. Approche en thérapie familiale psychanalytique*. Paris: Dunod, p. 151–185.

Ciccone, A. (1997b). L'éclosion de la vie psychique. In Ciccone, A., Gauthier, Y., Golse, B., Stern, D.N. (eds.), *Naissance et Développement de la vie psychique*. Toulouse: Érès, p. 11–37.

Ciccone, A. (1997c). Répétition d'échecs et rencontre traumatique avec le handicap, dans la perspective de la transmission psychique. *Dialogue*, 137: 25–30.

Ciccone, A. (1998a). Intérêts et limites de l'observation de bébés. In: Ciccone, A., Cresti-Scacciati, L., Druon, C., Lafforgue, P., Sandri, R., Williams, G. (eds.), *L'Observation du nourrisson et ses applications*. Toulouse: Érès, p. 39–48.

Ciccone, A. (1998b). Observation d'un groupe mères-bébés en service hospitalier de maternité: maternité et prévention. *Revue de psychothérapie psychanalytique de groupe*, 29: 43–64.

Ciccone, A. (1998c). *L'Observation clinique*. Paris: Dunod.

Ciccone, A. (1998d). Troubles du sommeil sévères chez un très jeune enfant: traitement dans un dispositif de consultations thérapeutiques familiales. *La Psychiatrie de l'enfant*, 41(2): 403–441.

Ciccone, A. (2000). Travail du traumatisme et fantasme de transmission dans la rencontre avec le handicap. *Le Divan familial*, 5: 177–186.

Ciccone, A. (2001). Enveloppe psychique et fonction contenante: modèles et pratiques. *Cahiers de psychologie clinique*, 17(2): 81–102.

Ciccone, A. (2003a). Les enfants qui "poussent à bout": logiques du lien tyrannique. In: Ciccone, A. (ed.), *Psychanalyse du lien tyrannique*. Paris: Dunod, p. 11–45.

Ciccone, A. (2003b). La "tyrannie-et-soumission": apports de Donald Meltzer. In: Ciccone, A.(ed) *Psychanalyse du lien tyrannique*. Paris: Dunod, p. 167–177.

Ciccone, A. (2003c). La place du père. Clinique de la fonction paternelle. In: Anzieu-Premmereur, C., Pollak-Cornillot, M. (eds.), *Pratiques psychanalytiques auprès des bébés*. Paris: Dunod, p. 125–152.

Ciccone, A. (2004). Naissance de la pensée. *Groupal*, 15: 21–40.

Ciccone, A. (2005). L'expérience du rythme chez le bébé et dans le soin psychique. *Neuropsychiatrie de l'enfance et de l'adolescence*, 53(1–2): 24–31.

Ciccone, A. (2007). Rythmicité et discontinuité des expériences chez le bébé. In: Ciccone, A., Mellier, D. (eds.), *Le Bébé et le Temps*. Paris: Dunod, p. 13–38.

Ciccone, A. (2011). Pour une nouvelle représentation de la fonction paternelle. *Revue belge de psychanalyse*, 58: 63–84.

Ciccone, A. (2012a). *La Transmission psychique inconsciente. Identification projective et Fantasme de transmission* (revised, updated and enlarged edition). Paris: Dunod.

Ciccone, A. (2012b). Contenance, enveloppe psychique et parentalité interne soignante. *Journal de la psychanalyse de l'enfant*, new series, 2(2): 397–433.

Ciccone, A. (2012c). Introduction. La part bébé du soi. In: Ciccone, A. (ed.), *La Part bébé du soi. Approche clinique*. Paris: Dunod, p. 1–22.

Ciccone, A. (2012d). Rythmes et harmonies dans le soin psychique. In: Korff-Sausse, S. (ed.), *Art et Handicap*. Toulouse: Érès, p. 207–219.

Ciccone, A. (2013a). Rhythmicity in infants' experiences and their development. *Journal of Physiology-Paris – "An International Review Journal for the Neurosciences"*, 107(4): 286–290.

Ciccone, A. (2013b). Apprentissage, douleur psychique et rythmicité des expériences. *Journal de la psychanalyse de l'enfant*, new series, 3(1): 41–57.

Ciccone, A. (2014). *La Psychanalyse à l'épreuve du bébé. Fondements de la position clinique* (new enlarged edition). Paris: Dunod.

Ciccone, A. (2015). Rôle de la rythmicité dans le développement du bébé. *L'Encéphale*, 41: 15–21.

Ciccone, A. (2016a). La parentalité soignante. In: Ciccone, A. (ed.), *Violences dans la parentalité*. Paris: Dunod, p. 9–25.

Ciccone, A. (2016b). Effets sur la parentalité d'une anomalie, un handicap ou une psychopathologie précoce chez un enfant. In: Ciccone, A. (ed.), *Violences dans la parentalité*. Paris: Dunod, p. 91–106.

Ciccone, A. (2016c). Rythme et bisensualité psychique. In: Amy, M.-D. (ed.), *Autismes: spécificités des pratiques psychanalytiques. Autismes et psychanalyses – II*. Toulouse: Érès, p. 75–95.

Ciccone, A. (2017). The traumatic effects of encountering disability. The bond and psychic transmission put to the test. In: Korff-Sausse, S., Scelles, R. (eds.), *The Clinic of Disability. Psychoanalytical Approaches*. London: Karnac, p. 17–47.

Ciccone, A. (2018). Psychopathologie du bébé, de l'enfant et de l'adolescent. In: Roussillon, R. (ed.), *Manuel de psychologie et de psychopathologie clinique générale*, 3rd enlarged edition. Paris: Elsevier-Masson, p. 173–249.

Ciccone, A., Cresti-Scacciati, L., Druon, C., Lafforgue, P., Sandri, R., Williams, G. (1998). *L'Observation du nourrisson et ses applications*. Toulouse: Érès.

Ciccone, A., Ferrant, A. (2015). *Honte, Culpabilité et Traumatisme*, new enlarged edition. Paris: Dunod.

Ciccone, A. (ed.) (2012). *La Part bébé du soi*. Paris: Dunod.

Ciccone, A. (ed.) (2014). *La Violence dans le soin*. Paris: Dunod.

Ciccone, A. (ed.) (2018). *Les Traces des expériences infantiles*. Paris: Dunod.

Cohen, D. (2012). *Homo Economicus, prophète (égaré) des temps nouveaux*. Paris: Albin Michel.

Condillac É.B. de (1754). *Traité des sensations, followed by Traité des animaux, Corpus des Œuvres Philosophiques en Langue Française*. Paris: Fayard, 1984.

Condon, W.S., Sander, L.W. (1974). Neonate movement is synchronised with adult speech: interactional participation and language acquisition. *Science*, 183: 99–101.
Cosnier, J. (1970). À propos de l'équilibre des investissements narcissiques et objectaux dans la cure analytique. *Revue française de psychanalyse*, 34(4): 575–598.
Couchoud, M.-T. (1986). Du refoulement à la fonction dénégatrice. *Topique*, 37: 93–133.
Cyrulnik, B. (1999). *Un merveilleux malheur*. Paris: Odile Jacob.
Damasio, A.R., Maurer, R.G. (1978). A neurological model for childhood autism. *Archives of Neurology and Psychiatry*, 35: 778–786.
David, M. (1981). Danger de la relation précoce entre le nourrisson et sa mère psychotique. *La Psychiatrie de l'enfant*, 24(1): 151–196.
David, M., Appell, G. (1961). Étude des facteurs de carence affective dans une pouponnière. *La Psychiatrie de l'enfant*, 4(2): 407–442.
David, M., Appell, G. (1966). La relation mère-enfant. Étude de cinq patterns d'interaction entre mère et enfant à l'âge de un an. *La Psychiatrie de l'enfant*, 9(2): 445–531.
De Casper, A.J., Fifer, W.P. (1980). Of human bonding: newborns prefer their mother's voice. *Science*, 208: 1174–1176.
De Casper, A.J., Granier-Deferre, C. (1994). Fetal reactions to recurrent maternal speech. *Infant Behavior and Development*, 17(2): 159–164
De Casper, A.J., Spence, M.J. (1986). Prenatal maternal speech influences newborn's perception of speech sounds. *Infant Behavior and Development*, 9: 133–150.
Decerf, A. (1987). Les interactions précoces de la mère et de l'enfant et la naissance de la vie psychique. *La Psychiatrie de l'enfant*, 30(2): 501–517.
Delion, P. (ed.) (2004). *L'Observation du bébé selon Esther Bick. Son intérêt dans la pédopsychiatrie aujourd'hui*. Toulouse: Érès.
Delion, P. (ed.) (2008). *La Méthode d'observation des bébés selon Esther Bick. La formation et les applications préventives et thérapeutiques*. Toulouse: Érès.
De Myer, M.K., Alpern, G.D., Barton, S., De Myer, W.E., Churchill, D.W., Bryson, C.Q., Pontius, W., Kimberlin, C. (1972). Imitation in autistic, early schizophrenic and non-psychotic subnormal children. *Journal of Autism and Childhood Schizophrenia*, 2: 264–287.
Despinoy M., Pinol-Douriez, M. (2002). Sensations et perceptions dans la clinique psychanalytique. In: Boubli, M., Konicheckis, A. (eds.), *Clinique psychanalytique de la sensorialité*. Paris: Dunod, p. 5–26.
Deutsch, H. (1934). Über einen Typus der Pseudoaffektivität ("als ob"). *Internationale Zeitschrift für Psychoanalyse*, 20: 232–335.

Deutsch, H. (1942). Some forms of emotional disturbance and their relationship to schizophrenia. *Psychoanalytic Quarterly*, 11: 301–321.

Devereux, G. (1970). *Essais d'ethnopsychiatrie générale*. Paris: Gallimard.

Donnet, J.-L., Green, A. (1973). *L'Enfant de ça. Psychanalyse d'un entretien: la psychose blanche*. Paris: Éditions de Minuit.

Duchesne, N., Roy, J. (1991). Enfants de mère psychotique: risques développementaux et interactions précoces. Revue de la littérature. *Neuropsychiatrie de l'enfance et de l'adolescence*, 7: 291–299.

Eiguer, A. (1983). *Un divan pour la famille. Du modèle groupal à la thérapie familiale psychanalytique*. Paris: Le Centurion.

Eiguer, A. (1984). Le lien d'alliance, la psychanalyse et la thérapie du couple. In: Eiguer, A. (ed.), *La Thérapie psychanalytique du couple*. Paris: Dunod, p. 1–83.

Eiguer, A. (1986a). La famille du psychotique: nouvelles hypothèses. *Revue française de psychanalyse*, 50(6): 1607–1627.

Eiguer, A. (1986b). L'organisation inconsciente du couple. In: Eiguer, A. (ed.), *Le Couple: organisation fantasmatique et crises d'identité*. Toulouse: GRECE, p. 2–31.

Eiguer, A. (1986c). Les représentations transgénérationnelles et leurs effets sur le transfert dans la thérapie familiale psychanalytique. *Gruppo*, 2: 55–74.

Eiguer, A. (1987). *La Parenté fantasmatique*. Paris: Dunod.

Eiguer, A. (1989). *Le Pervers narcissique et son complice*. Paris: Dunod.

Eiguer, A. (1991). L'identification à l'objet transgénérationnel. *Journal de la psychanalyse de l'enfant*, 10: 93–108.

Eiguer, A. (1997). La part maudite de l'héritage. In: Eiguer, A. (ed.), *Le Générationnel. Approche en thérapie familiale psychanalytique*. Paris: Dunod, p. 13–68.

Eiguer, A., Litovsky, D. (1981). Contribution psychanalytique à la théorie et à la pratique de la psychothérapie familiale. In: Ruffiot, A. (ed.), *La Thérapie familiale psychanalytique*. Paris: Dunod, p. 99–148.

Emde, R. (1999). Une progression: les influences intégratrices des processus affectifs sur le développement et en psychanalyse (trad. fr.). *Revue française de psychanalyse*, 63(1): 189–216.

Emde, R., Oppenheim, D. (1995). La honte, la culpabilité et le drame œdipien: considérations développementales à propos de la moralité et de la référence aux autres (trad. fr.). *Devenir*, 2002, 14(4): 335–361.

Enriquez, M. (1986). Le délire en héritage. *Topique*, 38: 41–67.

Enriquez, M. (1988). Incidence du délire parental sur la mémoire des descendants. *Topique*, 42: 167–183.

Faimberg, H. (1987). Le télescopage des générations. À propos de la généalogie de certaines identifications. *Psychanalyse à l'université*, 12(46):181–200.
Faimberg, H. (1988). À l'écoute du télescopage des générations: pertinence psychanalytique du concept. *Topique*, 42: 223–238.
Fain M. (1981). Diachronie, structure, conflit œdipien, quelques réflexions. *Revue française de psychanalyse*, 45(4): 985–997.
Falzeder, E. (ed.) (2002). *The Complete Correspondence of Sigmund Freud and Karl Abraham, 1907–1925*, trans. Caroline Scharzacher. London: Routledge.
Federn, P. (1952). *Ego-Psychology and the Psychoses*. New York: Basic Books, Inc.
Ferenczi, S. (1909). Introjection and transference. In: Balint, M. (ed.), *First Contributions to the Problems and Methods of Psychoanalysis*, trans. E. Mosbacher. London: Hogarth, 1952, p. 35–93.
Ferenczi, S. (1912). On the definition of introjection. In: Balint, M. (ed.), *Final Contributions to the Problems and Methods of Psychoanalysis*, trans. E. Mosbacher. London: Hogarth, 1955, p. 316–318.
Ferenczi, S. (1932). *The Clinical Diary of Sandor Ferenczi*, ed. J. Dupont, trans. M. Balint, N.Z. Jackson. Cambridge, MA: Harvard University Press, 1995.
Ferenczi, S. (1949). Notes et fragments (1930–1932). In: Balint, M. (ed.), *Final Contributions to the Problems and Methods of Psychoanalysis*, trans. E. Mosbacher. London: Hogarth, 1955, p. 219–279.
Field, T.M., Fox, N.A. (eds.) (1985) *Social Perception in Infants*. Norwood: Ablex.
Fischer, S., Cleveland, S.E. (1958). *Body Images and Personality*. Princeton, NY: Van Nostrand.
Fliess, R. (1950). *The Psycho-Analytic Reader*. London: Hogarth.
Florence, J. (1978). *L'Identification dans la théorie freudienne*. Brussels: Facultés Universitaires St-Louis.
Fonagy, P. (1999). Understanding of mental states, mother–child interaction and the development of the self. In: Maldonado Duran, J.M. (2008) (ed.), *Infant and Toddler Mental Health: Clinical Models of Intervention with Infants and their Families*. Washington: American Psychiatric Publishing, p. 50–70.
Fonagy, P. (2001). *Attachment Theory and Psychoanalysis*. London: Karnac.
Fonagy, P., Target M. (1997). Attachment and reflective function: Their role in self-organization. *Development and Psychopathology*, 9: 679–700.

Fornari, F. (1971). Pour une psychanalyse des institutions (trad. fr.). *Connexions*, 1973, 8: 90–122.

Fraiberg, S. (1982). Pathological defenses in infancy. *The Psychoanalytic Quarterly*, 51(4): 612–635.

Fraiberg, S., Adelson, E., Shapiro, V. (1975). Ghosts in the nursery: A psychoanalytic approach to the problems of impaired infant-mother relationships. *Journal of American Academy of Psychiatry*, 14(3): 387–421.

Freud, A. (1965). *Normality and Pathology in Childhood*. London: Karnac and the Institute of Psychoanalysis.

Freud, S. (1895). *Project for a Scientific Psychology*. S.E., 1. London: Hogarth, p. 281–397.

Freud, S. (1900). *The Interpretation of Dreams*. S.E., 4 and 5. London: Hogarth, p. 1–621.

Freud, S. (1905). *Three Essays on the Theory of Sexuality*. S.E., 7. London: Hogarth, p.123–143.

Freud, S. (1908). "Civilised" sexual morality and modern nervous illness. S.E., 9. London: Hogarth, p. 181–204.

Freud, S. (1909). Analysis of a phobia in a five-year-old boy. S.E., 10. London: Hogarth, p. 5–149.

Freud, S. (1910). *Leonardo da Vinci and a Memory of his Childhood*. S.E., 11. London: Hogarth, p. 57–137.

Freud, S. (1911a). Formulations on the two principles of mental functioning. S.E., 12. London: Hogarth, p. 218–226.

Freud, S. (1911b). *Psycho-analytic Notes on an Autobiographical Account of a Case of paranoia' (Dementia Paranoides)*. S.E., 12. London: Hogarth, p. 1–82.

Freud, S. (1912–1913). *Totem and Taboo*. S.E., London: Hogarth, p. 13, 1–161.

Freud, S. (1914a). *On the History of the Psycho-analytic Movement*. S.E., 14. London: Hogarth, p. 7–65.

Freud, S. (1914b). *Narcissism: An Introduction*. S.E., 14. London: Hogarth, p. 69–102.

Freud, S. (1915a). *Instincts and Their Vicissitudes*. S.E., 14. London: Hogarth, p. 109–140.

Freud, S. (1915b). *The Unconscious*. S.E., 14. London: Hogarth, p. 166–215.

Freud, S. (1915c). *A Phylogenetic Fantasy: Overview of the Transference Neuroses*. Cambridge, MA: Harvard University Press, 1987.

Freud, S. (1916–1917). *Introductory Lectures on Psychoanalysis*, S.E., 15–16. London: Hogarth.

Freud, S. (1917). *Mourning and Melancholia*, S.E., 14. London: Hogarth, p. 237–60.
Freud, S. (1920). *Beyond the Pleasure Principle*, S.E., 18. London: Hogarth, p. 1–64.
Freud, S. (1921). *Group Psychology and the Analysis of the Ego*, S.E., 18. London: Hogarth, p. 65–143.
Freud, S. (1922a). *Dreams and Telepathy*. S.E., 18. London: Hogarth, p. 197–220.
Freud, S. (1922b). *Some Neurotic Mechanisms in Jealousy, Paranoia and Homosexuality*. S.E. 18. London: Hogarth, p. 223–232.
Freud, S. (1923). *The Ego and the Id*. S.E., 19. London: Hogarth, p. 3–66.
Freud, S. (1924). *The Economic Problem of Masochism*. S.E., 19. London: Hogarth, p. 155–170.
Freud, S. (1925a). *An Autobiographical Study*. S.E., 20. London: Hogarth, p. 7–70.
Freud, S. (1925b). *Negation*. S.E., 19. London: Hogarth, p. 233–239.
Freud, S. (1926). *Inhibitions, Symptoms and Anxiety*. S.E., 20. London: Hogarth, p. 87–174.
Freud, S. (1927). *Fetishism*. S.E., 21. London: Hogarth, p. 147–158.
Freud, S. (1930). *Civilization and its Discontents*. S.E., 21. London: Hogarth, p. 59–145.
Freud, S. (1933). *New Introductory Lectures on Psychoanalysis*. S.E., 22. London: Hogarth, p. 1–182.
Freud, S. (1940a [1938]). *An Outline of Psycho-Analysis*. S.E., 23. London: Hogarth, p. 144–207.
Freud, S. (1940b[1938]). *Splitting of the Ego in the Process of Defence*. S.E., 23. London: Hogarth, p. 275–278.
Freud, S. (1941a [1921]). *Psychoanalysis and Telepathy*. S.E., 18. London: Hogarth, p. 177–193.
Freud, S. (1941b [1938]). *Findings, Ideas, Problems*. S.E., 23. London: Hogarth, p. 299–300.
Freud, S. (1950 [1887-1902]). *The Origins of Psychoanalysis*. New York: Basic Books, Inc. 1954.
Frith, U. (1989). *Autism: Explaining the Enigma*. Oxford: Wiley: Blackwell.
Frith, U., Morton, J., Leslie, A.M. (1991). The cognitive basis of a biological disorder – autism. *Trends Neuroscience*, 14(10): 433–438.
Gaddini, E. (1969). De l'imitation (trad. fr.). *Revue française de psychanalyse*, 1988, 52(4): 969–987.
Gaddini, R. (1981). Il cambiamento catastrofico di Bion e il "breakdown" di Winnicott. *Rivista di psicoanalisi*, 27(3–4): 599–609.

Gampel, Y. (1983). I was a holocaust child: Now I am fifty. In: Wilson, J. (ed.), *Holocaust Survivor and the Family*. New York: Praeger Special Studies / Praeger Scientific.

Gampel, Y. (1988). Facing war, murder, torture, and death in latency. *Psychoanalytic Review*, 65: 499–509.

Gergely, G. (1998). Naissance de la capacité de régulation des affects. In: Appell, G., Tardos, A. (eds.), *Prendre soin d'un jeune enfant*. Toulouse: Érès, p. 63–74.

Gianino, A., Tronick, E.Z. (1988). The mutual regulation model: the infant's self and interactive regulation and coping and defensive capacities. In: Field, T. McCabe, F. Schneiderman, N. (eds.), *Stress and Coping across Development*. Hillsdale: Lawrence Erlbaum Associates, p. 47–68.

Glover, E. (1956). *On the Early Development of Mind*. London: Imago Publishing Co.

Golse, B. (1998). Du corporel au psychique. *Journal de la psychanalyse de l'enfant*, 23: 113–129.

Granjon, E. (1985). Travail psychanalytique et famille. *Revue de psychothérapie psychanalytique de groupe*, 1–2: 55–70.

Granjon, E. (1986). L'enveloppe familiale généalogique. In: Guérin, C., Thaon, M. (eds.), *Actes des journées d'études du COR: L'Œuvre ouverte, autour du concept de moi-peau et des travaux de Didier Anzieu*. Arles: Hôpital Joseph Imbert, p. 73–75.

Granjon, E. (1987a). Traces sans mémoire et liens généalogiques dans la constitution du groupe familial. *Dialogue*, 98: 10–16.

Granjon, E. (1987b). Des objets bruts aux objets de relation. In: Guérin, C. (ed.), *Actes des journées d'études du COR: Après Winnicott*, Arles, Hôpital Joseph Imbert, p. 23–29.

Granjon, E. (1989). Transmission psychique et transfert en thérapie familiale psychanalytique. *Gruppo*, 5: 47–58.

Green, A. (1975). The analyst, symbolization and absence in the analytic setting. *International Journal of Psychoanalysis*, 56: 1–22.

Green, A. (1977). L'hallucination négative. *L'Évolution psychiatrique*, 3(2): 645–646.

Green, A. (1982). La double limite. *Nouvelle Revue de psychanalyse*, 25: 267–283

Green, A. (1983). *Life Narcissism. Death Narcissism*, trans. Andrew Weller. London: Free Association Books, 2001.

Green, A. (1986a). Pulsion de mort, narcissisme négatif, fonction désobjectalisante. In: Widlöcher, D. (ed.), *La Pulsion de mort*. Paris: Presses Universitaires de France, p. 49–59.

Green, A. (1986b). Le travail du négatif. *Revue française de psychanalyse*, 50(1): 489–493.

Green, A. (1987). La capacité de rêverie et le mythe étiologique. *Revue française de psychanalyse*, 51(5): 1299–1315.

Green, A. (1988). La pulsion et l'objet. Preface in Brusset, B., *Psychanalyse du lien*. Paris: Le Centurion, p. i–xx.

Green, A. (1993). *The Work of the Negative*, trans. Andrew Weller. London: Free Association Books, 1999.

Green, A. (1995). *Propédeutique. La Métapsychologie revisitée*. Seyssel: Champ Vallon.

Green, A. (2000). La mort dans la vie. Quelques repères pour la pulsion de mort. In: Guillaumin, J. (ed.), *L'Invention de la pulsion de mort*. Paris: Dunod, p. 161–184.

Green, A. (2007). *Pourquoi les pulsions de destruction ou de mort?* Paris: Éditions du Panama.

Green, J. (1947). *If I Were You*, trans. J.H.F. McEwen. London: Eyre and Spottiswoode, 1950.

Grosskurth, P. (1986). *Melanie Klein, Her World and Her Work*. Cambridge, MA: Harvard University Press.

Grotstein, J.S. (1981). *Splitting and Projective Identification*. New York: Jason Aronson.

Grotstein, J.S. (2005). "Projective transidentification": an extension of the concept projective identification. *The International Journal of Psychoanalysis*, 86(4): 1051–1069.

Grunberger, B. (1975). *Le Narcissisme*. Paris: Payot.

Guignard, F. (1985). Limites et lieux de la psychose et de l'interprétation. Essai sur l'identification projective. *Topique*, 35–36: 173–184.

Guignard, F. (2015a). *Psychoanalytic Concepts and Technique in Development: Psychoanalysis, Neuroscience and Physics*, trans. Andrew Weller. London: Routledge, 2020.

Guignard, F. (2015b). *Quelle psychanalyse pour le XXIe siècle? Tome 1. Concepts psychanalytiques en mouvement*. Paris: Ithaque.

Guillaumin, J. (1987). La pulsion de mort et la négativité dans la pensée de Freud, dans les années vingt. In: *Entre blessure et cicatrice*. Seyssel: Champ Vallon, p. 189–219.

Guillaumin, J. (2000). L'invention de la pulsion de mort et le deuil du père dans l'économie créatrice de Freud. In: Guillaumin, J. (ed.), *L'Invention de la pulsion de mort*. Paris: Dunod, p. 7–53.

Guyotat, J. (1980). *Mort/Naissance et Filiation*. Paris: Masson.

Guyotat, J. (1982). Recherches psychopathologiques sur la coïncidence mort/naissance. *Psychanalyse à l'université*, 7(27): 463–476.

Guyotat, J. (1991). *Études cliniques d'anthropologie psychiatrique*. Paris: Masson.

Haag, G. (1983). Autisme, psychoses infantiles précoces et psychanalyse. *Neuropsychiatrie de l'enfance et de l'adolescence*, 31ème année, 5–6: 261–263.

Haag, G. (1984a). Autisme infantile précoce et phénomènes autistiques. Réflexions psychanalytiques. *La Psychiatrie de l'enfant*, 27(2): 293–354.

Haag, G. (1984b). Réflexions sur les premiers niveaux d'identification à partir de la confrontation de certaines données de l'observation directe des nourrissons et de la clinique des psychoses précoces. Discussions. In: Mannoni, M. (eds.), *Travail de la métaphore*. Paris: Denoël, p. 136–182.

Haag, G. (1985a). La mère et le bébé dans les deux moitiés du corps. *Neuropsychiatrie de l'enfance et de l'adolescence*, 33ᵉ année, 2–3: 107–114.

Haag, G. (1985b). De l'autisme à la schizophrénie chez l'enfant. *Topique*, 35–36: 47–66.

Haag, G. (1986). Adhésivité, identité adhésive, identification adhésive. *Gruppo*, 2: 110–116.

Haag, G. (1987a). Petits groupes analytiques d'enfants autistes et psychotiques avec ou sans troubles organiques. *Revue de psychothérapie psychanalytique de groupe*, 7–8: 73–88.

Haag, G. (1987b). Réflexions théoriques et techniques à partir de l'expérience clinique avec des enfants autistes et psychotiques. In: Vaneck, L. (ed.), *L'Enfant psychotique et son évolution*. Lyon: Césura Lyon Édition, p. 21–42.

Haag, G. (1988a). Réflexions sur quelques jonctions psychotoniques et psychomotrices dans la première année de la vie. *Neuropsychiatrie de l'enfance et de l'adolescence*, 36ᵉ année, 1: 1–8.

Haag G. (1988b). Aspects du transfert concernant l'introjection de l'enveloppe en situation analytique individuelle et groupale: duplication et dédoublement, introjection du double feuillet. *Gruppo*, 4: 71–84.

Haag, G. (1988c). La psychanalyse des enfants psychotiques. Quelques problèmes techniques et leurs rapports avec les données actuelles de l'investigation. *Journal de la psychanalyse de l'enfant*, 5: 185–202.

Haag, G. (1990a). Identifications intracorporelles et capacités de séparation. *Neuropsychiatrie de l'enfance et de l'adolescence*, 38ᵉ année, 4–5: 245–248.

Haag, G. (1990b). Le dessin préfiguratif de l'enfant, quel niveau de représentation? *Journal de la psychanalyse de l'enfant*, 8: 91–129.

Haag, G. (1991). Nature de quelques identifications dans l'image du corps. Hypothèses. *Journal de la psychanalyse de l'enfant*, 10: 73–92.

Haag, G. (1992). Imitation et identification chez les enfants autistes. In: Hochmann, J., Ferrari, P. (eds.), *Imitation, Identification chez l'enfant autiste*. Paris: Bayard, p. 107–126.

Haag, G. (1993). Hypothèse d'une structure radiaire de contenance et ses transformations. In: Anzieu, D. (ed.), *Les Contenants de pensée*. Paris: Dunod, p. 41–59.

Haag, G. (1994). Rencontres avec Frances Tustin. In: Monographie de la *Revue française de psychanalyse, Autismes de l'enfance*. Paris: Presses Universitaires de France, p. 69–90.

Haag, G. (1995). Comment l'esprit vient au corps. In: Lacroix, M.-B., Monmayrant M. (eds.), *Les Liens d'émerveillement. L'observation des nourrissons selon Esther Bick et ses applications*. Toulouse: Érès, p. 273–279.

Haag, G. (1997). Contribution à la compréhension des identifications en jeu dans le moi corporel. *Journal de la psychanalyse de l'enfant*, 20: 104–125.

Haag, G. (1998). Travail avec les représentants spatiaux et architecturaux dans les groupes de jeunes enfants autistes et psychotiques. *Revue de psychothérapie psychanalytique de groupe*, 30: 47–62.

Haag, G. (1999). Propositions pour la compréhension des différentes formes de violence chez le jeune enfant. In: Lacroix, M.-B., Monmayrant, M. (eds.), *Enfants terribles, Enfants féroces*. Toulouse: Érès, p. 177–190.

Haag, G. (2018). *Le Moi corporel. Autisme et développement*. Paris: Presses Universitaires de France.

Haag, G., Tordjman, S., Duprat, A., Clément, M., Cukierman, A., Druon, C., Jardin, F., Maufras du Chatellier, A., Tricaud, S., Urwand, S. (1995). Grille de repérage clinique des étapes évolutives de l'autisme infantile traité. *La Psychiatrie de l'enfant*, 38(2): 495–527

Haag, G., Urwand, S. (1989). Processus groupal et enveloppes psychiques au travers de psychanalyses groupales avec des enfants psychotiques et déficitaires. In: Privat, P. (ed.), *Les Psychothérapies de groupes d'enfants au regard de la psychanalyse*. Paris: Clancier-Guénaud, p. 71–93.

Haag, M. (1984). *À propos des premières applications françaises de l'observation régulière et prolongée d'un bébé dans sa famille selon la méthode de Mrs Esther Bick: des surprises profitables*, Vol. 1. Paris: Autoédition.

Haag, M. (2002). *À propos et à partir de l'œuvre et de la personne d'Esther Bick, Vol. 1, La méthode d'Esther Bick pour l'observation régulière et prolongée du tout-petit au sein de sa famille*. Paris: autoédition.

Hammes, G.J.W., Langdell, T. (1981). Precursors of symbol formation and childhood autism. *Journal of Autism and Developmental Disorders*, 1: 331–345.

Harlow, H.F. (1958). The nature of love. *The American Psychologist*, 13: 673–685.

Harris, M. (1970). Some notes on maternal containment in 'good-enough' mothering. In: Harris, M. (ed.), *Collected Papers of Martha Harris and Esther Bick*. Perthshire: The Clunie Press, p. 141–163.

Harris, M. (1976). Contribution of observation of mother-infant interaction and development to the equipment of a psycho-analyst or psychoanalytic psychotherapist. In: Harris, M. (ed.), *Collected Papers of Martha Harris and Esther Bick*. Perthshire: Clunie Press, p. 225–239.

Harris, M. (1977). The Tavistock training and philosophy. In: Harris, M. (ed.), *Collected Papers of Martha Harris and Esther Bick*. Perthshire: Clunie Press, p. 259–282.

Harris, M., Bick E. (1987). *Collected Papers of Martha Harris and Esther Bick*. Perthshire: Clunie Press.

Hartmann, H. (1964). *Essays on Ego Psychology: Selected Problems in Psycho-Analytic Theory*. New York: International Universities Press.

Heimann, P. (1952a). Certain functions of introjection and projection in early infancy In: Klein M., Heimann P., Isaacs, S., Rivière J. (eds.), *Developments in Psychoanalysis*. London: Hogarth, p. 122–168.

Heimann, P. (1952b). Notes on the theory of the life and death instincts. In: Klein M., Heimann P., Isaacs, S., Rivière J. (eds.), *Developments in Psychoanalysis*. London: Hogarth, p. 321–337.

Herbinet, É., Busnel, M.-C. (eds.) (1981). *L'Aube des sens*. Paris: Stock.

Héritier-Augé, F. (1987). Fait-on rire les enfants en Afrique? Approche anthropologique. In: Soulé, M. (ed.), *Bonjour gaîté: la genèse du rire et de la gaîté chez le jeune enfant*. Paris: ESF, p. 59–70.

Herman, N. (1987). *Why Psychotherapy?* London: Free Association Books.

Herman, N. (1988). *My Kleinian Home*. London: Free Association Books.

Hermann, I. (1945). *L'Instinct filial* (trad. fr.). Paris, Denoël, 1972.

Hobson, R.P. (1989). Beyond cognition: A theory of autism. In: Dawson, G. (ed.), *Autism: Nature, Diagnosis and Treatment*. New York: Guilford, p. 22–48.

Hobson, R.P. (1993). *Autism and the Development of Mind*. Hove: Lawrence Erlbaum Associates Publishers.

Hochmann, J. (2009). *Histoire de l'autisme*. Paris: Odile Jacob.

Hochmann, J., Ferrari, P. (eds.) (1992). *Imitation, Identification chez l'enfant autiste*. Paris: Bayard.

Hopkins, J. (1987). Failure of the holding relationship: Some effects of physical rejection on the child's attachment and on his inner experience. *Journal of Child Psychotherapy*, 13: 5–17.

Hopkins, J. (1990). The observed infant of attachment theory. *British Journal of Psychotherapy*, 6(4): 460–470.
Houzel, D. (1985a). Le monde tourbillonnaire de l'autisme. *Lieux de l'enfance*, 3: 169–184.
Houzel, D. (1985b). L'évolution du concept d'espace psychique dans l'œuvre de Mélanie Klein et de ses successeurs. In: Gammil, J. (ed.), *Mélanie Klein aujourd'hui*. Lyon: Césura Lyon Édition, p. 123–135.
Houzel, D. (1986). Interprétation: métaphore ou analogie. *Journal de la psychanalyse de l'enfant*, 1: 159–173.
Houzel, D. (1987). Le concept d'enveloppe psychique. In: Anzieu, D. (ed.), *Les Enveloppes psychiques*. Paris: Dunod, p. 23–45.
Houzel, D. (1988a). Les enclaves autistiques dans les psychanalyses d'enfants. *Journal de la psychanalyse de l'enfant*, 5: 71–97.
Houzel, D. (1988b). Autisme et conflit esthétique. *Journal de la psychanalyse de l'enfant*, 5: 98–115.
Houzel, D. (1991). Le traumatisme de la naissance. *Journal de la psychanalyse de l'enfant*, 9: 33–49.
Houzel, D. (1992a). Peut-on parler d'enveloppe institutionnelle? In: Bléandonu, G. (ed.), *Filiations et Affiliations*. Lyon: Césura Lyon Édition, p. 71–78.
Houzel, D. (1992b). Enveloppe institutionnelle et temporalité. In: Bléandonu G. (ed.), *Cadres thérapeutiques et Enveloppes psychiques*. Lyon: presses Universitaires de Lyon, p. 77–85.
Houzel, D. (1993). Aspects spécifiques du transfert dans les cures d'enfants autistes. In: *Hommage à Frances Tustin* (collective work). Saint-André de Cruzières: Audit Éditions, p. 77–92.
Houzel, D. (1994). Enveloppe familiale et fonction contenante. In: Anzieu, D. (ed.), *Émergences et Troubles de la pensée*. Paris: Dunod, 2000, p. 27–40.
Houzel, D., Catoire, G. (1989). Cadre et transfert en thérapie familiale psychanalytique. *Gruppo*, 5: 37–46.
Hoxter, S. (1975). The residual autistic condition and its effect on learning: Pfiffie. In: Meltzer, D., Bremner, J., Hoxter, S., Weddell, D., Wittenberg, I. (eds.), *Explorations in Autism: A Psychoanalytic Study*. Perthshire: Clunie Press, p. 169–199.
Isaacs, S. (1952). The nature and function of phantasy. In: Klein, M., Heimann, P., Isaacs, S., Rivière J. (eds.), *Developments in Psychoanalysis*. London: Routledge, p. 67–121.
Jaques, E. (1955). Social systems as a defence against persecutory and depressive anxiety. In: Klein, M. Heimann, P., Money-Kyrle, R. (eds.),

New Directions in Psycho-Analysis. London: Tavistock Publications, p. 478–498.

Jaques, E. (1972). Le concept kleinien de névrose infantile et son impact sur la théorie et la technique (trad. fr.). *La Psychiatrie de l'enfant*, 15(1) 5–19.

Jones, E. (1913). The phantasy of the reversal of generations. In: *Papers in Psychoanalysis*. London: Baillière, Tindall and Cox, 1918, p. 658–667.

Jones, E. (1929). Fear, guilt and hate. *The International Journal of Psychoanalysis*, 10: 383–397.

Jones, V., Prior, M. (1985). Motor imitation abilities and neurological signs in autistic children. *Journal of Autism and Developmental Disorders*, 15: 37–46.

Kaës, R. (1976a). Analyse intertransférentielle, fonction alpha et groupe conteneur. *L'Évolution psychiatrique*, 41(2): 239–247.

Kaës, R. (1976b). *L'Appareil psychique groupal. Construction du groupe*. Paris: Dunod.

Kaës, R. (1979). Introduction à l'analyse transitionnelle. In: Kaës, R. (ed.), *Crise, Rupture et Dépassement*. Paris: Dunod, p. 1–81.

Kaës, R. (1983). Identification multiple, personne-conglomérat, moi groupal. Aspects de la pensée freudienne sur les groupes internes. *Bulletin de psychologie*, 37(363): 113–120.

Kaës, R. (1984). La transmission psychique intergénérationnelle et intra-groupale. In: Guérin, C. (ed.), *Actes des Journées d'études du COR: Penser la famille*. Arles: Hôpital Joseph Imbert, p. 4–9.

Kaës, R. (1985). Filiation et affiliation. Quelques aspects de la réélaboration du roman familial dans les familles adoptives, les groupes et les institutions. *Gruppo*, 1: 23–46.

Kaës, R. (1987). Réalité psychique et souffrance dans les institutions. In: Kaës, R. (ed.), *L'Institution et les Institutions. Études psychanalytiques*. Paris: Dunod, p. 1–46.

Kaës, R. (1988a). La diffraction des groupes internes. *Revue de psychothérapie psychanalytique de groupe*, 11: 159–174.

Kaës, R. (1988b). Destins du négatif: une métapsychologie transsubjective. In: Gagnebin, M., Guillaumin, J. (eds.), *Pouvoirs du négatif dans la psychanalyse et la culture*. Seyssel: Champ Vallon, p. 40–48.

Kaës, R. (1989a). Le pacte dénégatif dans les ensembles transsubjectifs. In: Missenard, A. (ed.), *Le Négatif, figures et modalités*. Paris: Dunod, p. 101–136.

Kaës, R. (1989b). Alliances inconscientes et pactes dénégatifs dans les institutions. *Revue de psychothérapie psychanalytique de groupe*, 13: 27–38.

Kaës, R. (1992). Pactes dénégatifs et alliances inconscientes. *Gruppo*, 8: 117–132.

Kaës, R. (1993). *Le Groupe et le Sujet du groupe*. Paris: Dunod.

Kaës, R. (1994). *La Parole et le Lien. Processus associatifs dans les groupes*. Paris: Dunod.

Kaës, R. (2000). Travail de la mort et théorisation. In: Guillaumin, J. (ed.), *L'Invention de la pulsion de mort*. Paris: Dunod, p. 89–111.

Kaës, R. (2012). *Le Malêtre*. Paris: Dunod.

Kaës, R. (ed.). (1987). *L'Institution et les Institutions. Études psychanalytiques*. Paris: Dunod.

Kaës, R. (ed.). (1996). *Souffrance et Psychopathologie des liens institutionnels*. Paris: Dunod.

Kanner, L. (1943). Autistic disturbances of affective contact. *Nervous Child*, 2: 217–250.

Kanner, L. (1944). Early infantile autism. *Journal of Pediatrics*, 25: 211–217.

Kant, E. (1781). *Critique of Pure Reason*, ed. P. Guyer, A. Wood. Cambridge: Cambridge University Press.

Kernberg, O.F. (1975). *Borderline Conditions and Pathological Narcissism*. New York: Aronson.

Kernberg, O.F. (1987). Projection and projective identification: Developmental and clinical aspects. *Journal of the American Psychoanalytical Association*, 35(4): 795–819.

Klaus, M.H., Kennell, J.H. (1982). *Parent-Infant Bonding*. London: C.H. Mosby.

Klein, M. (1927). Criminal tendencies in normal children. In: *The Collected Works of Melanie Klein, Vol.1, Love, Guilt and Reparation and Other Works, 1921-1945*. London: Hogarth, 1975, p. 170–185.

Klein, M. (1928). Early stages of the Oedipus conflict. In: *The Collected Works of Melanie Klein, Vol.1, Love, Guilt and Reparation and Other Works, 1921-1945*. London: Hogarth, 1975, p. 186–198.

Klein, M. (1929). Infantile anxiety situations reflected in a work of art and in the creative impulse. In: *The Collected Works of Melanie Klein, Vol.1, Love, Guilt and Reparation and Other Works, 1921-1945*. London: Hogarth, 1975, p. 210–218.

Klein, M. (1930). The importance of symbol-formation in the development of the ego. In: *The Collected Works of Melanie Klein, Vol.1, Love, Guilt and Reparation and Other Works, 1921-1945*. London: Hogarth, 1975, p. 219–232.

Klein, M. (1931). A contribution to the theory of intellectual inhibition. In: *The Collected Works of Melanie Klein, Vol.1, Love, Guilt and Reparation and Other Works, 1921-1945.* London: Hogarth, 1975, p. 236–247.

Klein, M. (1932). *The Psychoanalysis of Children*, trans. A. Strachey. London: Hogarth and the Institute of Psychoanalysis, 1986.

Klein, M. (1935). A contribution to the study of the psychogenesis of manic-depressive states. In: *The Collected Works of Melanie Klein, Vol.1, Love, Guilt and Reparation and Other Works, 1921-1945.* London: Hogarth, 1975, p. 262–289.

Klein, M. (1940). Mourning and its relation to manic-depressive states. In: *The Collected Works of Melanie Klein, Vol.1, Love, Guilt and Reparation and Other Works, 1921-1945.* London: Hogarth, 1975, p. 344–369.

Klein, M. (1945). The Oedipus complex in the light of early anxieties. In: *The Collected Works of Melanie Klein, Vol.1, Love, Guilt and Reparation and Other Works, 1921-1945.* London: Hogarth, p. 370–419.

Klein, M. (1946). Notes on some schizoid mechanisms. In: *Envy and Gratitude and Other Papers, 1946–1963: The Writings of Melanie Klein, Vol. 3.* London: Hogarth, p. 1–25..

Klein, M. (1948a). On the theory of anxiety and guilt. In: Klein, M., Heimann, P., Isaacs, S., Rivière, J. (eds.), *Developments in Psychoanalysis.* London: Hogarth, 1952, p. 271–291.

Klein, M. (1948b). Preface to the 3rd edition. In: *The Psychoanalysis of Children*, trans. A. Strachey. London: Hogarth and the Institute of Psychoanalysis, 1949.

Klein, M. (1952a). Some theoretical conclusions regarding the emotional life of the infant. In: Klein M., Heimann P., Isaacs, S., Rivière J. (eds.), *Developments in Psychoanalysis.* London: Hogarth, p. 198–236.

Klein, M. (1952b). On observing the behaviour of young infants. In: Klein, M., Heimann, P., Isaacs, S., Rivière, J. (eds.), *Developments in Psychoanalysis.* London: Hogarth, p. 237–270.

Klein, M. (1955). On Identification. In: *Envy and Gratitude and Other Papers, 1946–1963: The Writings of Melanie Klein, Vol. 3.* London: Hogarth, p. 141–175.

Klein, M. (1957). Envy and gratitude. In: *Envy and Gratitude and Other Papers, 1946-1963: The Writings of Melanie Klein, Vol. 3.* London: Hogarth, p. 176–235.

Klein, M. (1958). On the development of mental functioning. In: *Envy and Gratitude and Other Papers, 1946-1963: The Writings of Melanie Klein, Vol. 3.* London: Hogarth, p. 236–246.

Klein, M. (1959). Our adult world and its roots in infancy. In: *Envy and Gratitude and Other Papers, 1946-1963: The Writings of Melanie Klein, Vol. 3.* London: Hogarth, p. 247–263.

Klein, M. (1960). A note on depression in the schizophrenic. In: *Envy and Gratitude and Other Papers, 1946–1963: The Writings of Melanie Klein, Vol. 3.* London: Hogarth, p. 264–267.

Klein, M. (1961). *Narrative of a Child Analysis.* London: Routledge and The International Psychoanalytical Library.

Klein, M. (1975). *Envy and Gratitude and Other Works, 1946–1963.* London: Hogarth.

Klein, M., Heimann, P., Isaacs, S., Rivière, J. (1952). *Developments in Psychoanalysis.* London: Hogarth.

Klein, S. (1980). Autistic phenomena in neurotic states. *The International Journal of Psycho-Analysis*, 61: 395–402.

Klinnert, M.D. (1985). The regulation of infant behaviour by maternal facial expression. *Infant Behaviour and Development*, 7: 447–465.

Kreisler, L., Cramer, B. (1981). Sur les bases cliniques de la psychiatrie du nourrisson. *La Psychiatrie de l'enfant*, 34(1): 223–263.

Lacroix, M.-B., Monmayrant, M. (eds.) (1995). *Les Liens d'émerveillement. L'observation des nourrissons selon Esther Bick et ses applications.* Toulouse: Érès.

Lamour, M. (1989). Les nourrissons de parents psychotiques. In: Lebovici, S., Weil-Halpern, F. (eds.), *Psychopathologie du nourrisson.* Paris: Presses Universitaires de France, p. 655–673.

Lamour, M., Barraco, M. (1988). Le nourrisson de mère psychotique: une singulière exposition. *Nouvelle Revue d'ethnopsychiatrie*, 12: 105–118.

Lamour, M., Barraco, M. (1995). Perturbations précoces des interactions parent–nourrisson et construction de la vie psychique. Le jeune enfant face à une mère psychotique. *La Psychiatrie de l'enfant*, 38(2): 529–554.

Laplanche, J., Pontalis, J.-B. (1964). Fantasy and the origins of sexuality. *International Journal of Psychoanalysis*, 49: 1–18.

Lebovici, S. (1961). La relation objectale chez l'enfant. *La Psychiatrie de l'enfant*, 3(1): 147–226.

Lecanuet, J.-P., Fifer, W.P., Krasnegor, N., Smotherman, W.P. (eds.). (1995). *Fetal Development: A Psychobiological Perspective.* Hillsdale: Erlbaum

Lecanuet, J.-P., Granier-Deferre, C., Busnel, M.-C. (1989). Sensorialité fœtale: ontogenèse des systèmes sensoriels, conséquences de leur fonctionnement fœtal. In: Relier, J.-P., Laugier, J., Salle, B.L. (eds.), *Médecine périnatale.* Paris: Flammarion, p. 201–225.

Lelord, G., Muh, J.-P., Sauvage, D., Petit, M. (1989). *Autisme et Troubles du développement global de l'enfant*. Paris: Expansion scientifique française.
Lelord, G., Sauvage, D., Masson, E. (1990). *L'Autisme de l'enfant*. Paris: Masson.
Leslie, A.M. (1987). Pretence and representation: The origins of "theory of mind". *Psychological Review*, 94: 412–426.
Lhopital, M. (1992). Les cruelles failles dans la peau psychique de Jean-Baptiste Grenouille. Libres associations à partir du roman *Le Parfum, Histoire d'un meurtrier* de Patrick Süskind. *Thérapie psychomotrice et Recherches*, 93: 26–37.
Lhopital, M. (1997). L'insoutenable capacité de panser-penser la séparation. *Cahiers de psychologie clinique*, 8: 113–135.
Luquet, P. (1962). Les identifications précoces dans la structuration et la restructuration du moi. *Revue française de psychanalyse*, special edition, 26: 117–247.
McDougall, J. (1974). Le psyché-soma et le psychanalyste. *Nouvelle Revue de psychanalyse*, 10: 131–149.
McDougall, J. (1986). Un corps pour deux. In: Gachelin, G., McDougall, J. (eds.), *Corps et Histoire*. Paris: Les Belles Lettres, p. 9–43.
McDougall, J. (1989). *Theatres of the Body: A Psychoanalytic Approach to Psychosomatic Illness*. New York: Norton & Co.
McFarlane, A. (1977). *The Psychology of Childbirth*. London: Fontana/Open Books.
Mahler, M. (1968). *On Human Symbiosis and the Vicissitudes of Individuation: Infantile Psychosis*. New York: International Universities Press.
Maiello, S. (1988). L'expérience de l'espace. Premiers pas d'un enfant autistique dans le monde humain (trad. fr.). *Journal de la psychanalyse de l'enfant*, 5: 146–162.
Maiello, S. (2000). Trames sonores rythmiques primordiales. Réminiscences auditives dans le travail psychanalytique. *Journal de la psychanalyse de l'enfant*, 26: 77–103.
Main, M., Solomon, J. (1986). Discovery of an insecure disorganized-disoriented attachment pattern. In: Brazelton T.B. (ed.), *Affective Development in Infancy*. New York: Abley, p. 95–124.
Main, M., Stadtman, J. (1981). Infant response to rejection of physical contact by the mother: aggression, avoidance and conflict. *Journal of Child Psychiatry*, 20: 292–307.
Manzano, J., Lalive J. (1983). Les jeunes mères psychotiques et leurs enfants. Expérience d'un programme de prévention primaire et secondaire. *L'Information psychiatrique*, 59(5): 671–685.

Manzano, J., Palacio-Espasa, F. (1978). Négativisme, dénégation et fonctionnement psychotique précoce. *Revue française de psychanalyse*, 50(5–6): 1105–1110.
Manzano, J., Palacio-Espasa, F. (1983). *Étude sur la psychose infantile*. Lyon-Villeurbanne: Simep.
Manzano, J., Palacio-Espasa, F., Knauer, D. (1984). Problèmes des interventions thérapeutiques en psychiatrie du nourrisson. *Neuropsychiatrie de l'enfance et de l'adolescence*, 32nd year, 9: 443–450.
Marcelli, D. (1981). Le rôle du clivage dans les prépsychoses. *La Psychiatrie de l'enfant*, 24(2): 301–335.
Marcelli, D. (1983). La position autistique. Hypothèses psychopathologiques et ontogénétiques. *La Psychiatrie de l'enfant*, 26(1): 5–55.
Marcelli, D. (1985). De l'hallucination d'une présence à la pensée d'une absence: à propos du rôle de l'absence dans les relations d'objet précoces. *La Psychiatrie de l'enfant*, 28 (2): 403–440.
Marcelli, D. (2006). *Les Yeux dans les yeux. L'énigme du regard*. Paris: Albin Michel.
Marty, P. (1968). La dépression essentielle. *Revue française de psychanalyse*, 32(3): 595–598.
Marty, P. (1976). *Les Mouvements individuels de vie et de mort*, tome I. Paris: Payot.
Maurer, D., Salapatek, P. (1976). Developmental changes in the scanning of faces by young infants. *Child Development*, 47: 523–527.
Mehler, J., Barriere, M., Jassik-Gerschenfeld, D. (1978). Infant recognition of mother's voice. *Perception*, 7: 491–497.
Mehler, J., Jusczyk, P., Lambertz ,G., Halsted, N., Bertoncini, J., Amiel-Tison, C. (1988). A precursor of language acquisition in young infants. *Cognition*, 29: 143–178.
Mellier, D. (2005). *Les Bénés en détresse. Intersubjectivité et travail de lien*. Paris: Presses Universitaires de France.
Meltzer, D. (1966). The relation of anal masturbation to projective identification. *The International Journal of Psychoanalysis*, 47(2–3): 335–342.
Meltzer, D. (1967). *The Psycho-Analytical Process*. London: Karnac.
Meltzer, D. (1972). *Sexual States of Mind*. London: Karnac.
Meltzer, D. (1975). Adhesive identification. *Contemporary Psychoanalysis*, 11: 289–310.
Meltzer, D. (1976). *Un modèle psychanalytique de l'enfant-dans-sa-famille-dans-la-communauté* (trad. fr.). Paris: Éditions du Collège, 2004.
Meltzer, D. (1978). *The Kleinian Development*. Strathclyde: Clunie Press.

Meltzer, D. (1984a). Les concepts d'"identification projective" (Klein) et de "contenant-contenu" (Bion) en relation avec la situation analytique (trad. fr.). *Revue française de psychanalyse*, 48(2): 541–550.

Meltzer, D. (1984b). L'objet esthétique (trad. fr.). In: Touzé, J. (ed.), *Donald Meltzer à Paris. Conférences et séminaires au GERPEN*. Larmor-Plage: Éditions du Hublot, 2013, p. 27–31.

Meltzer, D. (1984c). *Dream Life: A Reexamination of the Psychoanalytic Theory and Technique*. Strathclyde: Clunie Press.

Meltzer, D. (1985). Théâtre intérieur et développement du langage (trad. fr.). In: Touzé, J. (ed.), *Donald Meltzer à Paris. Conférences et séminaires au GERPEN*. Larmor-Plage: Éditions du Hublot, 2013, p. 47–58.

Meltzer, D. (1986). Aesthetic conflict: Its place in development. In: Meltzer, D., Harris Williams, M. (eds.), *The Apprehension of Beauty: the Role of Aesthetic Conflict in Development, Art and Violence*. Strathclyde: Clunie Press, 1988, p. 29–50.

Meltzer, D. (1987a). Présence de l'objet et séparation d'avec lui. Attaques envieuses et intolérance au conflit esthétique (trad. fr.). In: Touzé, J. (ed.), *Donald Meltzer à Paris. Conférences et séminaires au GERPEN*. Larmor-Plage: Éditions du Hublot, 2013, p. 85–93.

Meltzer, D. (1987b). Sadomasochisme et tyrannie-et-soumission: une différenciation essentielle (trad. fr.). In: Touzé, J. (ed.), *Donald Meltzer à Paris. Conférences et séminaires au GERPEN*. Larmor-Plage: Éditions du Hublot, 2013, p. 101–108.

Meltzer, D. (1988). À propos de l'identification projective (trad. fr.). In: Touzé, J. (ed.), *Donald Meltzer à Paris. Conférences et séminaires au GERPEN*. Larmor-Plage: Éditions du Hublot, 2013, p. 109–110.

Meltzer, D. (1989a). Réflexions sur l'identification projective (trad. fr.). *Le Bulletin du groupe d'études et de recherches psychanalytiques pour le développement de l'enfant et du nourrisson*, publication interne, 16: 3–15.

Meltzer, D. (1989b). Réflexions sur l'identification adhésive (trad. fr.). *Le Bulletin du groupe d'études et de recherches psychanalytiques pour le développement de l'enfant et du nourrisson*, publication interne, 16: 57–60.

Meltzer, D. (1992). *The Claustrum*. Strathclyde: Clunie Press;

Meltzer, D., Bremner, J., Hoxter, S., Weddell, D., Wittenberg, I. (1975). *Explorations in Autism: A Psycho-Analytical Study*. Perthshire: Clunie Press.

Meltzer, D., Harris, M. (1980). Les deux modèles du fonctionnement psychique selon M. Klein et selon W.R. Bion (trad. fr.). *Revue française de psychanalyse*. 44 (2): 355–367

Meltzer, D., Harris Williams, M. (1988). *The Apprehension of Beauty: The Role of Aesthetic Conflict in Development, Art and Violence*. Strathclyde: Clunie Press, 1988.

Meltzer, D., Milana, G., Maiello, S., Petrelli, D. (1982). The conceptual distinction between projective identification (Klein) and container-contained (Bion). *Journal of Child Psychotherapy*, 8(2): 185–202.

Meltzer, D., Sabatini Scolmati, A. (1985). La maladie psychotique dans la petite enfance (trad. fr.). *Lieux de l'enfance*, 3: 93–110.

Meltzoff, A.N. (2002). La théorie du *like me*, précurseur de la compréhension sociale chez le bébé (trad. fr.). In: Nadel, J. Decety, J. (eds.), *Imiter pour découvrir l'humain*. Paris: Presses Universitaires de France, p. 33–57.

Meltzoff, A.N., Moore, M.K. (1977). Imitation of facial and manual gestures by human neonates. *Science*, 198: 75–78.

Meltzoff, A.N., Moore, M.K. (1979). Intermodal matching by human neonates. *Nature*, 282: 403–404.

Meltzoff, A.N., Moore, M.K. (1983). Newborn infants imitate adult facial gestures. *Child development*, 54: 702–709.

Meltzoff, A.N., Moore, M.K. (1994). Imitation, memory and the representation of persons. *Infant Behaviour and Development*, 17: 83–99.

Miller, L. (ed.) (1989). *Closely Observed Infants*. London: Duckworth.

Milner, M. (1955). The role of illusion in symbol formation. In: Klein, M., Heimann, P., Money-Kyrle, R. (eds.), *New Directions in Psychoanalysis*. London: Tavistock, p. 82–108.

Misès, R., Grand, Ph. (1997). *Parents et Professionnels devant l'autisme*. Paris: CTNERHI.

Money-Kyrle, R. (1968). On cognitive development. *The International Journal of Psycho-analysis*, 9: 692–698.

Mundy, P., Sigman, M. (1989). The theoretical implications of joint-attention deficits in autism. *Developmental Psychopathology*, 1: 173–183.

Mundy, P., Sigman, M., Kasari, C. (1994). Joint attention, developmental level and symptom presentation in autism. *Developmental Psychopathology*, 6: 389–401.

Nadel, J. (1992). Imitation et communication. Un abord comparatif de l'enfant pré-langagier et de l'enfant autiste. In: Hochmann, J., Ferrari, P. (eds.), *Imitation, Identification chez l'enfant autiste*. Paris: Bayard, p. 79–104.

Nadel, J., Camaioni, L. (1993). *New Perspectives in Early Communicative Development*. London: Routledge.

Nathan, T. (1990). La transmission des contenants formels. In: Anzieu, D. (ed.), *L'Épiderme nomade et la Peau psychique*. Paris: Apsygée, p. 149–157.

Negri, R. (1995). Observation de la vie fœtale (trad. fr.). In: Lacroix, M.B., Monmayrant, M. (eds.), *Les Liens d'émerveillement. L'observation des nourrissons selon Esther Bick et ses applications*. Toulouse: Érès, p. 137–155.

Negri, R. (1997). Quelques processus sur la "personnalité" du fœtus (trad. fr.). In: Busnel, M.-C., Daffos, F., Dolto-Tolitch, C., Lecanuet, J.-P., Negri, R. (eds.), *Que savent les fœtus?* Toulouse: Érès, p. 79–102.

Negri, R. (ed.) (1990). Correlazione tra vita prenatale et formazione della personalità. *Quaderni di psicoterapia infantile*, 22: 148–165.

Ogden, T.H. (1982). *Projective Identification and Psychotherapeutic Technique*. New York and London: Jason Aronson.

Ogden, T.H. (1989). On the concept of an autistic-contiguous position. *The International Journal of Psycho-analysis*, 70(1): 127–140.

Ogden, T.H. (1994). *Subjects of Analysis*. London: Karnac.

Palacio-Espasa, F. (1977). Défenses mélancoliques *versus* défenses maniaques. *Revue française de psychanalyse*, 41(1–2): 217–226.

Palacio-Espasa, F. (1980). Les états psychotiques infantiles et les relations d'objet précoces. Une tentative de rapprochement des idées de M. Klein et de son école avec celle de M. Mahler dans la compréhension des psychoses de l'enfant. *La Psychiatrie de l'enfant*, 23(2): 349–382.

Pankow, G. (1983). *Structure familiale et Psychose*, new revised and enlarged edition. Paris: Aubier Montaigne.

Parat, C. (1995). *L'Affect partagé*. Paris: Presses Universitaires de France.

Parkes, C.M., Stevenson-Hinde, J. (eds.) (1982). *The Place of Attachment in Human Behaviour*. London: Tavistock.

Perez-Sanchez, M. (1981). *Baby Observation: Emotional Experiences in the First Year of Life*. Perthshire: Clunie Press.

Perez-Sanchez, M. (1987). Observation psychanalytique du nourrisson (trad. fr.). *Journal de la psychanalyse de l'enfant*, 3: 209–226.

Petot, J.-M. (1982). *Mélanie Klein, le moi et le bon objet, 1932–1960*. Paris: Dunod.

Piaget, J. (1935). *The Origins of Intelligence in Children*, trans. M. Cook. New York: W.W. Norton & Co.

Pichon-Rivière E. (1971). *El Proceso grupal*. Buenos-Aires: Nueva Vision.

Pinol-Douriez M. (1984). *Bébé agi-Bébé actif: l'émergence du symbole dans l'économie interactionnelle*. Paris: Presses Universitaires de France.

Piontelli, A. (1987). Infant observation from before birth. *International Journal of Psycho-Analysis*, 68: 453–463.

Piontelli, A. (1989). A study on twins before and after birth. *International Review of Psycho-Analysis*, 16(4), 413–426.

Piontelli, A. (1992a). L'observation du comportement humain à partir des stades les plus précoces (trad. fr.). *Journal de la psychanalyse de l'enfant*, 12: 154–172.

Piontelli, A. (1992b). *From Foetus to Child: An Observational and Psychoanalytic Study*. London: Routledge.

Pomey-Rey, D. (1979). Pour mourir guérie. *Cutis*, 3: 151–157.

Premack, D., Premack, A. (2003). *Original Intelligence: Unlocking the Mystery of Who We Are*. New York: McGraw-Hill.

Premack, D., Woodruff, G. (1978). Does the chimpanzee have a "theory of mind"? *Behavioral and Brain Science*, 4: 515–526.

Racamier, P.-C. (1953). Étude clinique des frustrations précoces. *Revue française de psychanalyse*, 17(3): 328–350.

Racamier, P.-C. (1954). La pathologie frustrationnelle. *Revue française de psychanalyse*, 18(4): 576–632.

Racamier, P.-C. (1978). À propos des psychoses de la maternalité. In: Soulé, M. (ed.), *Mère mortifère, Mère meurtrière, Mère mortifiée*. Paris: ESF, p. 41–50.

Racamier, P.-C. (1980a). *Les Schizophrènes*. Paris: Payot.

Racamier, P.-C. (1980b). De l'objet non-objet. *Nouvelle Revue de psychanalyse*, 21: 235–241.

Racamier, P.-C. (1986). Entre agonie psychique, déni psychotique et perversion narcissique. *Revue française de psychanalyse*, 50(5): 1299–1309.

Racamier, P.-C. (1987). De la perversion narcissique. *Gruppo*, 3: 11–23.

Racamier, P.-C. (1992). *Le Génie des origines*. Paris: Payot.

Racamier, P.-C. (1995). *L'Inceste et l'Incestuel*, 2nd edition, Paris: Dunod, 2010.

Racamier, P.-C. (ed.) (1961). La mère et l'enfant dans les psychoses du post-partum. *L'Évolution psychiatrique*, 26(4): 525–557.

Reich, W. (1927). *The Function of the Orgasm*. Ohio: Orgone Institute Press, 1942.

Reich, W. (1933). *Character Analysis*, trans. Vincent R. Carfagno. London: Farrar, Strass and Giroux, 1980.

Resnik, S. (1973). *Personne et Psychose*. Paris: Payot.

Resnik, S. (1985). La visibilité de l'inconscient. *Revue de psychothérapie psychanalytique de groupe*, 1–2: 47–54.

Resnik, S. (1986a). *L'Expérience psychotique*. Lyon: Césura Lyon Édition.

Resnik, S. (1986b). Espace et psychose. *Revue de psychothérapie psychanalytique de groupe*, 3–4: 9–16.

Resnik, S. (1986c). Bion, psychose et multiplicité. *Revue de psychothérapie psychanalytique de groupe*, 5–6: 57–66.

Resnik, S. (1989). Transfert entre multiplicité et groupalité. *Revue de psychothérapie psychanalytique de groupe*, 12: 9–12.

Resnik, S. (1994). *Mental Space*, trans. David Alcorn. London: Karnac, 1995.

Resnik, S. (1999). *Le Temps des glaciations. Voyage dans le monde de la folie.* Toulouse: Érès.

Resnik, S. (ed.) (1982). *Semiologia dell'incontro*. Rome: Il pensiero scientifico.

Rey, A.E., Exbrayat, C., Pierot-Blanc, A., Rousselon, V. (2016). Où en est-on dans l'accompagnement des enfants avec autisme ? État des lieux des théories et interventions en neuropsychologie. *Approche neuropsychologique des apprentissages chez l'enfant*, 141: 1–7.

Rogers, S.J., Pennington, B.F. (1991). A theoretical approach to the deficits in infantile autism. *Development and Psychopathology*, 3: 137–162.

Rolf, J., Masten, A.S. (eds.) (1990). *Risk and Protective Factors in the Development of Psychopathology*. Cambridge: Cambridge University Press.

Rosenberg, B. (1988). Pulsion de mort, négation et travail psychique: ou la pulsion de mort mise au service de la défense contre la pulsion de mort. In: Guillaumin, J. (ed.), *Pouvoirs du négatif dans la psychanalyse et la culture*. Seyssel: Champ Vallon, p. 65–73.

Rosenfeld, D. (1986). Identification and its vicissitudes in relation to the Nazi phenomenon. *The International Journal of Psycho-Analysis*, 67(1): 53–64.

Rosenfeld, D. (1997). Aspects autistiques dans la pharmacodépendance et dans les maladies psychosomatiques. *Journal de la psychanalyse de l'enfant*, 20: 168–188.

Rosenfeld, H. (1947). Analysis of a schizophrenic state with depersonalization. In: Rosenfeld, H. (ed.), *Psychotic States: A Psychoanalytical Approach*. New York: International Universities Press, 1965, p. 13–33.

Rosenfeld, H. (1949). Remarks on the relation of male homosexuality to paranoia, paranoid anxiety, and narcissism. In: Rosenfeld, H. (ed.), *Psychotic States: A Psychoanalytical Approach*. New York: International Universities Press, 1965, p. 34–51.

Rosenfeld, H. (1952a). Notes on the psycho-analysis of the superego conflict in an acute schizophrenic patient. In: Rosenfeld, H. (ed.), *Psychotic States: A Psychoanalytical Approach.* New York: International Universities Press, 1965, p. 63–103.

Rosenfeld, H. (1952b). Transference-phenomena and transference-analysis in an acute catatonic schizophrenic patient. In: Rosenfeld, H. (ed.),

Psychotic States: A Psychoanalytical Approach. New York: International Universities Press, 1965, p. 104–116.

Rosenfeld, H. (1960). On drug addiction. In: Rosenfeld, H. (ed.), *Psychotic States: A Psychoanalytical Approach*. New York: International Universities Press, 1965, p. 128–143.

Rosenfeld, H. (1963). Notes on the psychopathology and psycho-analytic treatment of schizophrenia. In: Rosenfeld, H. (ed.), *Psychotic States: A Psychoanalytical Approach*. New York: International Universities Press, 1965, p. 155–168.

Rosenfeld, H. (1964a). On the psychopathology of narcissism: A clinical approach. *The International Journal of Psychoanalysis*, 45(2–3): 332–337. Also in: Roseenfeld, H. (ed.), *Psychotic States: A Psychoanalytical Approach*. New York: International Universities Press, 1965, p. 169–179.

Rosenfeld, H. (1964b). The psychopathology of hypochondriasis. In: Rosenfeld, H. (ed.), *Psychotic States: A Psychoanalytical Approach*. New York: International Universities Press, 1965, p. 180–199.

Rosenfeld, H. (1964c). The psychopathology of drug addiction and alcoholism: A critical review of the psychoanalytic literature. In: Rosenfeld, H. (ed.), *Psychotic States: A Psychoanalytical Approach*. New York: International Universities Press, 1965, p. 217–242.

Rosenfeld, H. (1965). *Psychotic States: A Psychoanalytical Approach*. New York: International Universities Press.

Rosenfeld, H. (1970). On projective identification. *Scientific Bulletin of the British Psycho-analytical Society*, 41, internal publication.

Rosenfeld, H. (1971). A clinical approach to the psychoanalytical theory of the life and death instincts: An investigation into the aggressive aspects of narcissism. *International Journal of Psychoanalysis*, 52: 169–178.

Rosenfeld, H. (1987). *Impasse and interpretation: Therapeutic and Anti-Therapeutic Factors in the Psychoanalytic Treatment of Psychotic, Borderline and Neurotic Patients*. London: Routledge.

Rosolato, G. (1985). *Éléments de l'interprétation*. Paris: Gallimard.

Roussillon, R. (1977). L'institution-environnement: contribution à l'approche psychanalytique de l'institution. *Bulletin de psychologie clinique*, Université Lyon 2, 2: 3–33.

Roussillon, R. (1981). Paradoxe et continuité chez Winnicott: les défenses paradoxales. *Bulletin de psychologie*, 34(350): 503–509.

Roussillon, R. (1991). *Paradoxes et Situations limites de la psychanalyse*. Paris: Presses Universitaires de France.

Roussillon, R. (1995). La métapsychologie des processus et la transitionnalité. *Revue française de psychanalyse*, special edition, 59: 1349–1519.

Roussillon, R. (1999). *Agonie, Clivage et Symbolisation*. Paris: Presses Universitaires de France.

Roussillon, R. (2001). *Le Plaisir et la Répétition*. Paris: Dunod.

Roussillon, R. (2018). La réalité psychique de la subjectivité et son histoire (avec interventions d'A. Ciccone). In: Roussillon, R. (ed.), *Manuel de psychologie et de psychopathologie clinique générale* (3rd enlarged edition). Paris: Elsevier-Masson, p. 1–137.

Ruffiot, A. (1981a). Le groupe-famille en analyse. L'appareil psychique familial. In: Ruffiot, A., Eiguer, A., Litovsky, D. (eds.), *La Thérapie familiale psychanalytique*. Paris: Dunod, p. 1–98.

Ruffiot, A. (1981b). Appareil psychique familial et appareil psychique individuel, hypothèses pour une onto-éco-genèse. *Dialogue*, 79: 31–42.

Ruffiot, A. (1988). La théorie classique de la psychose et ses impasses, une perspective de compréhension groupale. *Gruppo*, 4: 87–110.

Rutter, M. (1981a). *Maternal Deprivation Reassessed*. Harmondsworth: Penguin Books.

Rutter, M. (1981b). Stress, coping and development: some issues and questions. *Journal of Child Psychology and Psychiatry*, 22: 323–356.

Rutter, M. (1983). Cognitive deficits in the pathogenesis of autism. *Journal of Child Psychology and Psychiatry*, 24: 513–531.

Rybas, D. (2004). *Controverses sur l'autisme et Témoignages*. Paris: Presses Universitaires de France.

Rybas, D. (2013). Autisme et psychanalyse. *Revue française de psychanalyse*, 77(1): 138–144.

Salapatek, P. (1975). Pattern perception in early infancy. In: Cohen, L.B., Salapatek, P. (eds.), *Infants Perception: From Sensation to Cognition, Vol. 1*. New York: Academic Press, p. 133–248.

Sameroff, A.J., Emde, R.N. (eds.) (1989). *Relationship Disturbances in Early Childhood: A Developmental Approach*. New York: Basic Books.

Sami-Ali, M. (1974). *L'Espace imaginaire*. Paris: Gallimard.

Sandler, J. (1960). The background of safety. *The International Journal of Psycho-Analysis*, 41: 352–356.

Sandri, R. (ed.) (1994). *L'Observation du nourrisson selon Esther Bick et ses applications*. Lyon: Césura Lyon Édition.

Sauvage, D. (ed.) (1988). *Autisme du nourrisson et du jeune enfant*. 2nd enlarged edition. Paris: Masson.

Scaife, M., Bruner, J.S. (1975). The capacity for joint attention in the infant. *Nature*, 253: 265–266.

Schmideberg, M. (1930). The role of psychotic mechanisms in cultural development. *The International Journal of Psycho-Analysis*, 11: 387–418.

Searles, H. (1959). The effort to drive the other person crazy: an element in the aetiology and psychotherapy of schizophrenia. In: *Collected Papers on Schizophrenia and Related Subjects*. London: Karnac, p. 254–283.

Searles, H. (1962). The differentiation between concrete and metaphorical thinking in the recovering schizophrenic. *Journal of the American Psychoanalytical Association*, 10: 22–49.

Searles, H. (1965). *Collected Papers on Schizophrenia and Related Subjects*. London: Karnac.

Searles, H. (1971). Pathological symbiosis and autism. In: Landis, B., Tauber, E. (eds.), *In the Name of life: Essays in Honor of Erik Fromm*. New York: Holt, Rinehart and Winston, p. 69–83.

Searles, H. (1979). *Countertransference and Related Subject: Selected Papers*. Madison, CT: International Universities Press.

Segal, H. (1950). Some aspects of the analysis of a schizophrenic. *The International Journal of Psycho-Analysis*, 3: 268–278.

Segal, H. (1956). Depression in the schizophrenic. *International Journal of Psycho-Analysis*, 37(4–5): 339–43.

Segal, H. (1957). Notes on symbol formation. *International Journal of Psycho-Analysis*, 38: 391–397.

Segal, H. (1964). *Introduction to the Work of Melanie Klein*. New York: Basic Books.

Segal, H. (1967). Melanie Klein's Technique. In: Wolman, B. (ed.), *Psychoanalytic Techniques*. New York: Basic Books, p. 168–190.

Segal, H. (1972). A delusional system as a defence against the re-emergence of a catastrophic situation. *International Journal of Psychoanalysis*, 53(3): 393–401.

Segal, H. (1975). A psycho-analytic approach to the treatment of psychoses. In: Segal, H. (ed.), *The Work of Hanna Segal: A Kleinian Approach to Clinical Practice*. Northvale, NJ: Jason Aronson, 1981, p. 131–136.

Segal, H. (1981). *The Work of Hanna Segal: A Kleinian Approach to Clinical Practice*. Northvale, NJ: Jason Aronson.

Segal, H. (1993). On the clinical usefulness of the death instinct. *International Journal of Psychoanalysis*, 74(1): 55–61

Sibton, H., Mazet, P. (1991). Harmonisation affective et transmodalité: mère et bébé en communion. *Devenir*, 3(2): 87–95.

Sigman, M., Mundy, P. (1987). Social and cognitive deficits in young autistic children. In: Grémy, F. (ed.), *Autisme infantile. Infantile Autisme*, *Vol. 146.* Paris: INSERM, p. 169–174.

Sigman, M., Ungerer, J.A. (1984). Attachment behaviors in autistic children. *Journal of Autism and Developmental Disorders*, 14: 231–244.

Sorce, J., Emde, R.N. (1981). Mother's presence is not enough: Effect of emotional availability on infant exploration. *Developmental psychology*, 17(6): 737–745.

Soulé, M. (1978). Essai de compréhension de la mère d'un enfant autistique par l'étude des mécanismes défensifs et des processus pathogènes, ou "l'enfant qui venait du froid". In: Soulé, M. (ed.), *Mére mortifère, Mère meurtrière, Mère mortifiée*. Paris: ESF, p. 79–109.

Spitz, R.A. (1957). *No and Yes: On the Genesis of Human Communication*. New York, NY: International Universities Press.

Spitz, R.A. (1965). *The First Year of Life. A Psychoanalytic Study of Normal and Deviant Development in Object Relations*. New York, NY: International Universities Press.

Stern, D.N. (1974). The goal and structure of mother–infant play. *Journal of American Academy of Child Psychiatry*, 13(3): 402–421.

Stern, D.N. (1985). *The Interpersonal World of the Infant: A View from Psychoanalysis and Developmental Psychology*. New York, NY: Basic Books

Stern D.N. (1993), L'"enveloppe prénarrative". Vers une unité fondamentale d'expérience permettant d'explorer la réalité psychique du bébé (trad. fr.). *Journal de la psychanalyse de l'enfant*, 14: 13–65.

Stern, D.N. (1997). Le processus de changement thérapeutique. Intérêt de l'observation du développement de l'enfant pour la psychothérapie de l'adulte (trad. fr.). In: Ciccone, A., Gauthier, Y., Golse, B., Stern, D.N. (eds.), *Naissance et Développement de la vie psychique*. Toulouse: Érès, p. 39–57.

Stern, D.N. (2003). *The Present Moment in Psychotherapy and Everyday Life*. New York: Norton Professional Books.

Stone, W.L., Lemanek, K.L, Fishel, P.T, Fernandez, M.C, Altemeier, W.A. (1990) Play and imitation skills in the diagnosis of autism in young children. *Pediatrics*, 86(2): 267–272.

Suarez-Labat, H. (2013). À la recherche de la dynamique du transfert chez l'enfant autiste. In: Passone, S.M., Suarez-Labat, H. (eds.), *Après l'autisme. Comment sortir de l'état autistique*. Paris: In Press, p. 35–64.

Süskind, P. (1985). *Perfume: The Story of a Murderer*, trans. John E. Woods. 1986. New York: Knopf.

Thom, R. (1972). *Stabilité structurelle et Morphogenèse. Essai d'une théorie génétique des modèles.* Paris: Édiscience.

Tisseron, S., Rand, N., Torok, M. (1995). *Le Psychisme à l'épreuve des générations. Clinique du fantôme.* Paris: Dunod.

Torok, M. (1968). The illness of mourning and the fantasy of the exquisite corpse. In: Rand, N. (ed.) *The Shell and the Kernel, Vol. 1,* trans. N. Rand. Chicago: Chicago University Press, 1994, p. 107–138.

Trevarthen, C. (1979). Communication and cooperation in early infancy: a description of primary intersubjectivity. In: Bullowa, M. (ed.), *Before Speech: The Beginning of Interpersonal Communication.* Cambridge: Cambridge University Press, p. 321–347.

Trevarthen, C. (1980). The foundations of intersubjectivity: development of interpersonal and cooperative understanding in infants. In: Olson, D. (ed.), *The Social Foundations of Language and Thought: Essays in Honor of J.S. Bruner.* New York: W.W. Norton, p. 314–342.

Trevarthen, C. (1989a). Les relations entre autisme et développement socio-culturel normal. Arguments en faveur d'un trouble primaire de la régulation du développement cognitif par les émotions (trad. fr.). In: Lelord, G., Muk, J., Petit, M. (eds.), *Autisme et Troubles du développement global de l'enfant.* Paris: Expansion Scientifique Française, p. 56–80.

Trevarthen, C. (1989b). Racines du langage avant la parole (trad. fr.). *Devenir,* 1997, 9(3): 73–93.

Trevarthen, C., Aitken, K.J. (1996). La fonction des émotions dans la compréhension des autres (trad. fr.). *Cahiers du Cerfee,* Université Montpellier 3, 13: 9–56.

Trevarthen, C., Aitken, K.J. (1997). Self/other organization in human psychological development. *Development and Psychopathology,* 9: 653–677

Tronick, E.Z., Als, H., Adamson, L., Wise, S., Brazelton T.B. (1978). The infant's response to entrapment between contradictory messages in face to face interaction. *Journal of the American Academy of Child Psychiatry,* 17: 1–13.

Tronick, E.Z., Cohn J.F. (1989). Infant-mother face-to-face interactions: Age and gender differences and the occurrence of miscoordination. *Child Development,* 60(1): 85–92.

Tronick, E.Z., Weinberg, M.K. (1997). Depressed mothers and infants: Failure to form dyadic states of consciousness. In: Murray, L., Cooper, P.J. (eds.), *Postpartum Depression and Child Development.* New York: Guilford Press, p. 54–81.

Turquet, P.-M. (1974). Threats to identity in the large group. In. Kreeger, L. (ed.), *The Large Group: Dynamics and Therapy*. London: Routledge, 1975, p. 87–144.

Tustin, F. (1972). *Autism and Child Psychosis*. London: Hogarth.

Tustin, F. (1980). Autistic objects. *International Review of Psycho-Analysis*, 7: 27–39.

Tustin, F. (1981a). Psychological birth and psychological catastrophe. In: Grotstein, J. (ed.), *Do I Dare Disturb the Universe?* Beverly Hills, CA: Caesura Press, p. 181–196.

Tustin, F. (1981b). *Autistic States in Children*. London: Routledge and Kegan Paul.

Tustin, F. (1981c). Conférences et discussions sur les états autistiques chez l'enfant. l'éducation des enfants autistes, l'autisme normal et l'autisme pathologique (trad. fr.). *Bulletin du centre régional pour l'enfance et l'adolescence inadaptée: rencontre avec Frances Tustin*. Toulouse:publication interne.

Tustin, F. (1984a). Autistic shapes. *International Review of Psychoanalysis*, 11: 279–290.

Tustin, F. (1984b). Développement de la compréhension. Itinéraire personnel. Interview (trad. fr.). *Patio*, 3: 109–133.

Tustin, F. (1985a). Améliorer les états autistiques, quelques considérations importantes (trad. fr.). *Lieux de l'enfance*, 3: 15–34.

Tustin, F. (1985b). Réflexions sur l'éducation des enfants autistes, discussions (trad. fr.). *Le Bulletin du groupe d'études et de recherches psychanalytiques pour le développement de l'enfant et du nourrisson*, publication interne, 3: 2–16.

Tustin, F. (1985c). Contours autistiques et pathologie adulte (trad. fr.) *Topique*, 35–36: 9–24.

Tustin, F. (1986). *Autistic Barriers in Neurotic Patients*. London: Karnac.

Tustin, F. (1987). What autism is and what autism is not. In: Szur, R., Miller, S. (eds.), *Extending Horizons*. London: Karnac, 1991.

Tustin, F. (1988). "To be or not to be" – a study of autism. *Winnicott Studies*, 3. London: Routledge and CRC Press, p. 43–55.

Tustin, F. (1990). *The Protective Shell in Children and Adults*. London: Karnac.

Tustin, F. (1991a). Revised understandings of psychogenetic autism. *International Journal of Psychoanalysis*, 72(4): 585–591.

Tustin, F. (1991b). On psychogenic autism. *Psychoanalytic Inquiry*, 13(1): 34–41.

Tustin, F. (1994a). The perpetuation of an error. *Journal of Child Psychotherapy*, 20(1): 3–23.

Tustin, F. (1994b). Autistic children who are assessed as not brain-damaged. *Journal of Child Psychotherapy*, 20(1): 103–131.

Ungerer, J.A., Sigman, M. (1981). Symbolic play and language comprehension in autistic children. *Journal of the American Academy of Child and Adolescent Psychiatry*, 20: 318–337.

Urwand, S., Haag, G. (1993). Premières identifications et enveloppes groupales, à partir de groupes analytiques d'enfants autistes et psychotiques. *Dialogue*, 120, p. 63–75.

Vauclair, J., Deputte, B. (2002). Se représenter et dire le monde. Développement de l'intelligence et du langage chez les primates. In: Picq, Y., Coppens, P. (eds.), *L'Origine de l'homme*. Paris: Fayard, p. 288–329.

Vurpillot, É. (1972). *Les Perceptions du nourrisson*. Paris: Presses Universitaires de France.

Waddell, M. (1998). *Inside Lives: Psychoanalysis and the Growth of Personality*. London: Karnac (revised edition), 2002.

Wallon, H. (1941). *L'Évolution psychologique de l'enfant*. Paris: Armand Colin, 1968.

Weiss, E. (1935). Todestrieb und masochismus. *Imago*, 21: 393–411.

Wenar, C., Ruttenburg, B., Kalish-Weiss, B., Wolf, E. (1986). The development of normal and autistic children: a comparative study. *Journal of Autism and Developmental Disorders*, 16: 317–333.

Wimmer, H., Perner, J. (1983). Beliefs about beliefs: representation and constraining function of wrong beliefs in young children's understanding of deception. *Cognition*, 13: 103–128.

Wing, L. (1976). *Early Childhood Autism*. London: Pergamon Press.

Winnicott, D.W. (1941). The observation of infants in the set situation. *International Journal of Psychoanalysis*, 22: 229–249.

Winnicott, D.W. (1947). The baby as a person. In: Caldwell, L., Robinson, H. (eds.), *Collected Works of D.W. Winnicott*, Vol. 3. Oxford: Oxford University Press, p. 285–288.

Winnicott, D.W. (1949). The mind and its relation to psyche-soma. In: Winnicott, D.W. (ed.), *Through Paediatrics to Psychoanalysis*. London: Tavistock, 1958, p. 243–256.

Winnicott, D.W. (1951). Transitional objects and transitional phenomena. In: Winnicott, D.W. (ed.), *Through Paediatrics to Psychoanalysis*. London: Tavistock, 1958, p. 229–242.

Winnicott, D.W. (1952a). Psychoses and child care. In: Winnicott, D.W. (ed.), *Through Paediatrics to Psychoanalysis*. London: Tavistock, 1958, p. 219–228.

Winnicott, D.W. (1952b). Anxiety associated with insecurity. In: Winnicott, D.W. (ed.), *Through Paediatrics to Psychoanalysis*. London: Tavistock, 1958, p. 97–100.

Winnicott, D.W. (1953). Transitional objects and transitional phenomena. In: Winnicott, D.W. (ed.), *Through Paediatrics to Psychoanalysis*. London: Tavistock, 1958, p. 229–242.

Winnicott, D.W. (1954). Metapsychological and clinical aspects of regression within the psychoanalytical set-up. In: Winnicott, D.W. (ed.), *Through Paediatrics to Psychoanalysis*. London: Tavistock, 1958, p. 278–294.

Winnicott, D.W. (1955). Clinical varieties of transference. In: Winnicott, D.W. (ed.), *Through Paediatrics to Psychoanalysis*. London: Tavistock, 1958, p. 295–299.

Winnicott, D.W. (1956a). Primary maternal preoccupation. In: Winnicott, D.W. (ed.), *Through Paediatrics to Psychoanalysis*. London: Tavistock, 1958, p. 300–305.

Winnicott, D.W. (1956b). The antisocial tendency. In: Winnicott, D.W. (ed.), *Through Paediatrics to Psychoanalysis*. London: Tavistock, 1958, p. 306–315.

Winnicott, D.W. (1957). On the contribution of direct child observation to psycho-analysis. In: Winnicott, D.W. (ed.), *The Maturational Processes and the Facilitating Environment*. London: Hogarth, 1965, p. 109–114.

Winnicott, D.W. (1958a). The first year of life. Modern views on the emotional development. In: Winnicott, D.W. (ed.), *The Maturational Processes and the Facilitating Environment*. London: Hogarth, 1965, p. 3–14.

Winnicott, D.W. (1958b). Psychoanalysis and the sense of guilt. In: Winnicott, D.W. (ed.), *The Maturational Processes and the Facilitating Environment*. London: Hogarth, 1965, p. 15–28.

Winnicott, D.W. (1959). Classification: Is there a psychoanalytic contribution to psychiatric classification? In: *The Maturational Processes and the Facilitating Environment*. London: Hogarth, 1965, p. 124–139.

Winnicott, D.W. (1960a). The theory of the parent-infant relationship. *International Journal of Psychoanalysis*, 41: 585–595.

Winnicott, D.W. (1960b). Ego-distortion in terms of true and false self. In: Winnicott, D.W. (ed.), *The Maturational Processes and the Facilitating Environment*. London: Hogarth, 1965, p. 140–152.

Winnicott, D.W. (1961). The effect of psychotic parents on the emotional development of the child. In: Winnicott, D.W. (ed.), *The Family and Individual Development*. London: Tavistock, 1965, p. 69–78.

Winnicott, D.W. (1962a). Ego integration in child development. In: Winnicott, D.W. (ed.), *The Maturational Processes and the Facilitating Environment*. London: Hogarth, 1965, p. 56–63.

Winnicott, D.W. (1962b). Providing for the child in health and crisis. In: Winnicott, D.W. (ed.), *The Maturational Processes and the Facilitating Environment*. London: Hogarth, 1965, p. 64–72.

Winnicott, D.W. (1963). Morals and education. In: Winnicott, D.W. (ed.), *The Maturational Processes and the Facilitating Environment*. London: Hogarth, 1965, p. 93–108.

Winnicott, D.W. (1967). Mirror role of mother and family in child development. In: Winnicott, D.W. (ed.), *Playing and Reality*, 1971, p. 149–159.

Winnicott, D.W. (1971). *Playing and Reality*. London: Tavistock.

Winnicott, D.W. (1974). Fear of breakdown. *International Review of Psycho-Analysis*, 1(1–2): 103–107.

Wittenberg, I. (1975). Primal depression in autism. In: Meltzer, D., Bremner, J., Hoxter, S., Weddell, D., Wittenberg, I. (eds.), *Explorations in Autism: A Psycho-Analytical Study*. Perthshire: Clunie Press, p. 57–98.

Zaltzman, N. (1986). Baiser la mort? Une sexualité mélancolique. *Topique*, 38: 103–119.

Zweig, S. (1942). *The Royal Game and Other Stories*. New York: EP Dutton, 1981.

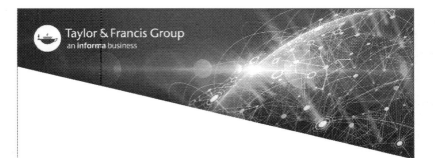

Taylor & Francis eBooks

www.taylorfrancis.com

A single destination for eBooks from Taylor & Francis with increased functionality and an improved user experience to meet the needs of our customers.

90,000+ eBooks of award-winning academic content in Humanities, Social Science, Science, Technology, Engineering, and Medical written by a global network of editors and authors.

TAYLOR & FRANCIS EBOOKS OFFERS:

- A streamlined experience for our library customers
- A single point of discovery for all of our eBook content
- Improved search and discovery of content at both book and chapter level

REQUEST A FREE TRIAL
support@taylorfrancis.com

Printed in the United States
by Baker & Taylor Publisher Services